# BASIC COOKERY
## *The Process Approach*

**Daniel R. Stevenson**

Head of
The Catering, Tourism and Hotel Operations Department,
Bournemouth & Poole College of Further Education

**Stanley Thornes (Publishers) Ltd**

First published in 1991 by:
Stanley Thornes (Publishers) Ltd
Old Station Drive
Leckhampton
CHELTENHAM GL53 0DN
England

The author would like to thank the following for their assistance:

Dr David Atkinson
Christine Briscoe
Jacques Gianino
David Simmons
Stuart Soames
David Walker

The author gratefully acknowledges the invaluable assistance provided by Dr Patricia M.G. Scobie, Caterer Dietitian, University of Surrey and thanks her for permission to use material and tables.

The author and the publishers are grateful to the following for permission to use material and tables, and to reproduce photographs:

G.F.E. Bartlett & Sons, page 83(L); Falcon Catering Equipment, pages 43(R), 83(R), 93(L), 134, 135(R), 174, 221; Fields & Pimblett Ltd, page 220; Lune Metal Spinning Co Ltd, pages 43(L), 70, 71, 93(R), 106(R), 147; The Meat and Livestock Commission; Merrychef, page 185(R); Morwood Vulcan Ltd, pages 106(L), 135(L); Philips Electronics, page 185(L); Stott Benham Ltd, page 124.

British Library Cataloguing in Publication Data

Stevenson, Daniel R.
1. Cookery
I. Title
641.5

ISBN 0-7487-0421-3

Typeset by Tech-Set, Gateshead, Tyne & Wear.
Printed and bound in Great Britain at The Bath Press, Avon.

Other books by the same author published by Stanley Thornes (Publishers) Ltd:

*Catering for Health*
*Professional Cookery: The Process Approach*

# CONTENTS


| | | |
|---|---|---|
| Introduction | | v |
| General organisation and preparation | | 1 |
| Basic preparations | | 23 |
| *Process 1:* | Boiling | 42 |
| *Process 2:* | Poaching | 70 |
| *Process 3:* | Steaming | 83 |
| *Process 4:* | Stewing | 93 |
| *Process 5:* | Braising | 106 |
| *Process 6:* | Roasting | 124 |
| *Process 7:* | Grilling | 134 |
| *Process 8:* | Shallow-frying | 146 |
| *Process 9:* | Deep-frying | 174 |
| *Process 10:* | Microwave cooking | 184 |
| *Process 11:* | Cold preparations | 194 |
| *Process 12:* | Baking | 220 |
| Glossary | | 256 |
| Index | | 259 |

This book is dedicated to
the memory of my mother and father.

# INTRODUCTION

## THE AIM OF THIS BOOK

This book is specifically written for *competence based* cookery courses and training programmes, e.g. National Vocational Qualifications and Caterbase programmes (Food Preparation and Cookery – Levels II and III); Master Chef – Level IV; City and Guilds 705, 706/1, 706/2 and 706/3. It is also designed to offer a thorough knowledge of food production for BTEC Certificate and Diploma courses, BTEC Higher Certificate, and Higher Diploma and undergraduate courses.

### *The process approach*

This approach concentrates on the techniques and skills that make up *methods* of cookery and which are common to all dishes whether regional or international. The intention is to highlight basic cookery skills and techniques and promote their transferability throughout different types of cookery.

Each chapter within the book is devoted to a method of cookery (e.g. poaching) and this is divided into culinary processes. Each process demonstrates a base method – such as shallow-poaching fish – and then gives a variety of further dishes using the same base method: such as fillets of sole florentine and supreme of halibut cubat. In this way, students are able to recognise the basic cooking principle behind dishes, and can then go on to improvise upon the base methods to create new dishes.

## HEALTHY EATING AND TRADITIONAL PRACTICES

### *Do the foods we eat affect our health?*

In recent years most health professionals have come to believe that there has been an increase in ill health which is directly related to our eating habits. A diet that is too high in fat, especially saturated fat, can contribute towards increasing the risk of coronary heart disease. High blood pressure is another contributory factor, and this is associated with high salt intake. There are many other ailments and illnesses associated with our diet. Cancer of the large bowel is thought to be linked with low intake of cereals and pulses, and high intake of fat, sugar and eggs. Eating an excess of sugar is the main cause of tooth decay. On the other hand, a diet high in fibre can help prevent constipation and diseases of the colon.

### *What is healthy eating?*

There have been several reports on the subject of food and health. The National Advisory Committee on Nutrition Education (NACNE) in 1983 published dietary goals for the 1980s and 1990s. This was followed by a Government report published in 1984 on coronary heart disease by the Committee on Medical Aspects of Food Policy (COMA): *Health and Social Subjects No. 28*, HMSO.

### *Current dietary advice*

The common message which is fundamental to these reports is to:

**Eat less fat** – cut down by 25 per cent
Not more than approximately one third of a person's total energy requirements is to be provided by fat. Energy supplied by saturated fat to be no more than 10 per cent of total energy (NACNE).

**Eat less sugar** – cut down by 50 per cent
The NACNE report proposes that sugar intake should be reduced to 20 kg per head per year. It is particularly important to reduce the amount eaten as snacks and in soft drinks, which should be less than 28 g/1 oz per day.

**Eat less salt** – The NACNE report recommends a reduction in salt by 3 g per day from the average intake of 8–12 g per day, i.e. down to 5 g per day per person.

**Eat more fibre** – increase by 50 per cent
The NACNE report recommends that fibre intake be increased to 30 g/1 oz per day.

Fibre in the diet is divided into two main groups:

1 *Insoluble fibre* This aids the prevention of bowel disorders such as constipation, cancer of the colon and diverticulitis. Insoluble fibre is provided by wheat, rice, pulses etc.
2 *Soluble fibre* This is believed to prevent coronary heart disease, by keeping cholesterol levels low in the blood. Soluble fibre is provided by gels in oatmeal and pulses, and by pectin in fruits.

It is important to remember that foods contain natural fats, sugar and salt and that the figures refer to total quantities and not amounts added when cooking.

A diet which can be considered as healthy, therefore, should:

a) contain an appropriate total energy content for the consumer (to maintain an ideal body weight)
b) obtain the correct proportion of that energy from fat, protein and carbohydrate.

In addition, the diet should contain sufficient vitamins, minerals and dietary fibre, and avoid an excess of any one nutrient.

In 1986 the British Medical Association in its document *Nutrition, Diet and Health* gave figures for the national average diet based on the long-term NACNE proposals and this included figures for fats, carbohydrates and salt. The table below is a summary of these proposals which will act as a guide, but will obviously need to be adapted for individual needs.

Sugar and salt have decreased by 50% and 25% respectively. Unrefined carbohydrates are now likely to provide 50% of energy, while protein provides 11%, fat 30% and saturated fatty acids 10%.

Practical guidance on how to follow healthy eating practices together with tables which state the quantity of fat, sugar, salt and fibre in basic commodities are given in the chapter on General Organisation and Preparation (pages 1–22). For further information, see D.R. Stevenson and Dr. P.M.G. Scobie, *Catering for Health,* (Stanley Thornes [Publishers] Ltd, 1985).

## HOW IS THIS BOOK DIFFERENT FROM OTHER BOOKS?

Rather than simply presenting traditional recipes which are often high in fat, sugar and salt, and low in fibre, many of the recipes have been constructed so that they are low in fat, sugar and salt and have increased fibre. However, the traditional methods of producing the recipes are also featured as tips in the page margins.

This format provides the reader with simple instructions on how to:

a) prepare dishes with reduced fat (especially saturated fat), salt and sugar
b) prepare dishes with increased fibre
c) cook the same dishes in the usual traditional manner
d) know when recipes are high in fat, salt or sugar
e) amend traditional recipes so that they have less fat, sugar and salt and more fibre.

In this text the following commodities are stated in recipes:

**margarine** – this refers to margarine low in saturated fatty acids (see page 6)

**oil** – this refers to oil low in saturated fatty acids (see page 6).

## HOW TO USE THIS BOOK

1 Look up the recipe title in the index (pages 259–266).
2 Follow the instructions given in the base method on how to produce the dish.

*Note*: when an instruction in the base method does not apply (e.g. one relating to an ingredient not used in the dish you are cooking) move on to the next instruction.

### *Vegetarian dishes*

Vegetarian recipes have been included in this book together with vegetarian alternatives to many popular dishes, e.g. mousses, jellies and bavarois.

### *Regional specialities*

Many regional specialities and classical dishes from different countries have also been featured in the book.

### *Portion yield*

Most of the recipes in this book are for 1–4 portions with some recipes producing greater quantities. The portion yield for each recipe is clearly stated.

# GENERAL ORGANISATION AND PREPARATION

This chapter begins with some basic points on work organisation, safety, hygiene and nutrition. These topics are also dealt with in relation to particular commodities later in this chapter and at the start of the process chapters.

## WORK ORGANISATION

### BEFORE YOU START

- If you know in advance what dishes you will be preparing, look them up in your textbook and pay attention to important points such as food quality, equipment required, cooking times and so on. Try to consult your lecturer or *chef de partie* in good time on any queries you may have about the production.

- Many dishes have to be ready for service by a certain time, so it is often wise to prepare a time plan (example opposite) which sets out your order of work. Working to a time plan often requires a sense of urgency (not panic but not a carefree attitude).

- When you enter the kitchen, check that you have all the food materials required for the production. Also collect any trays, bowls and small equipment you may need.

- Check fridges first thing for:

**a)** food to be used
**b)** food to be discarded
**c)** spillages and leaking containers.

*Remember the rule:* first in first out.
Also check the temperature of the fridge to ensure that it is working correctly.

- Check that any large equipment required is ready for use, e.g. ensure that stoves are switched on and oven thermostats set to the temperatures required. *Remember:* you must have been instructed on the use of equipment before you can use it.

- Be thoroughly aware of the safety regulations and any requirements laid down in your kitchen *Code of Conduct.* Remember that your safety and the safety of people you work with is in your hands. You are legally required to work in a safe manner without causing danger to yourself or others.

- Make sure that you know what to do in the event of an emergency: particularly

**a)** fire **b)** a gas leak **c)** an accident.

- Always keep your oven cloth (*rubber*) dry. Using a wet cloth to carry hot foods is dangerous.

*Preparing a*
### PRODUCTION TIME PLAN

This involves considering the following factors:

**a)** Dishes with long cooking times should be cooked first or started as early as possible. Those with short cooking times may be prepared early then kept chilled until required for use (e.g. small whole fish prepared ready for cooking, veal escalopes, chicken suprêmes and peeled vegetables).
**b)** Allow for some things taking longer to prepare and cook than expected, e.g. meat stews, braisings and complex garnishes.
**c)** Dishes or items with short cooking times should be cooked or finished last, especially if they deteriorate when held for service, e.g. portioned melon, deep-fried foods, hot vegetables. The rule here is to *cook the food in batches* so that it is stored for as short a time as possible during service.
**d)** Some items must be cooked for service or they deteriorate rapidly, e.g. omelettes and cuts of meat cooked to a specific degree of cooking, such as steaks ordered underdone.
**e)** Careful consideration must be given to dishes which must be served immediately when cooked, e.g. soufflés.
**f)** Do not leave too many items to be prepared at the last minute. Remember that some items have no set time at which they must be prepared and can be slotted in to suit other requirements. For example, mise en place items required for service such as grated cheese, chopped parsley, tomato concassées, mayonnaise or buttercream could be made at various times as long as they are ready when they are needed.

- Ensure that pot handles are not sticking out over the edge of the stove and likely to cause an accident.

- Wipe up any liquid which has been spilled immediately to avoid staff falling and being injured.

**WHILE WORKING**

● Work in an organised manner. Avoid making unnecessary journeys about the kitchen: this can increase the risk of cross-contamination. Remember also that your time and energy is precious. Organising your work on a preparation table or cutting board requires working to a set pattern, usually from your left to your right side (for right-handed people) e.g.

peeled vegetables (placed to your left) → slicing → sliced vegetables (placed to your right)

● Keep your working surface clean at all times. Clean as you go then you don't have to go and clean.

● Arrange food in containers, i.e. on trays or in bowls at all times, and keep your working surface clear to avoid cross contamination and to enable you to work efficiently.

● Keep any unwanted peelings, trimmings or rubbish in a bin specially reserved for the purpose; empty and clean it regularly.

# HYGIENE

● Be thoroughly aware of the hygiene regulations and any requirements laid down in your kitchen *Code of Conduct*. All food handlers should have basic training in hygiene.

● Always wash your hands before you start work in the kitchen. Also wash your hands regularly during food preparation; especially between handling different types of food, e.g. raw foods and cooked food, to avoid infection. Hands must *always* be washed after handling raw food. Cooked food should be free of food-poisoning bacteria, but handling should be avoided if possible: the use of gloves is recommended.

● Ensure you are dressed correctly i.e. are wearing clean chef whites or kitchen overalls. If possible, also wear well-fitting protective shoes for comfort and safety.

● Never use the same board for cutting raw and cooked foods. Use colour-coded cutting boards for different types of commodities. Knives may also be colour coded.

**A COMMON SYSTEM OF COLOUR CODING**

| | | |
|---|---|---|
| RED | – | RAW MEATS |
| YELLOW | – | COOKED MEATS |
| BLUE | – | RAW FISH |
| WHITE | – | DAIRY PRODUCTS |
| GREEN | – | FRUITS, SALAD VEGETABLES |
| BROWN | – | VEGETABLES (SOIL) |

● Store food correctly until required for use.

**a)** Keep different types of food separate to avoid food poisoning or tainting of flavours, e.g. keep unwashed fresh vegetables away from prepared food such as dried vegetables.

**b)** Keep all food clean and covered. Place food requiring cold storage in refrigerators as soon as possible, e.g. milk, cream, fish, butcher meats etc. Do not leave food out on the working surface. Always work cleanly and tidily.

● Ensure that you follow the Department of Health guidelines when preparing and storing food, especially when reheating cook-chill foods (see page 184).

● Always cool hot foods as quickly as possible and store chilled until required for use.

● Never mix hot and cold foods together, e.g. stocks, sauces, soups and stews. This can cause rapid souring and increase the risk of food poisoning.

● Ensure that foods which are likely to cause food poisoning are thoroughly cooked, e.g. chicken and pork.

● Always wash your work areas thoroughly after use with a bactericidal detergent, especially after handling high risk foods such as raw chicken, pork and offal.

● Always close a refrigerator door as soon as possible after opening it and never walk away leaving it open.

● Organise refrigerator storage so that different types of food (raw/cooked) are stored apart or *kept in a separate refrigerator* until required for use.

# NUTRITION AND CATERING FOR HEALTH

Nowadays many people are interested in healthy eating and the caterer should be able to respond to these changes. To prepare dishes which aim to meet the requirements of current dietary guidelines the following practices should be followed:

## REDUCE FAT

a) Cut down on the use of saturated fats: lard, butter, cream, eggs, cheese etc.
b) Use margarines and oils which are low in saturated fats, e.g. sunflower margarine and oil, and olive oil.
c) Use lower-fat commodities, e.g. skimmed milk, lower-fat cheeses, low-fat yoghurt, fromage frais, half-cream.
d) Trim off visible fat from meat, poultry and game.
e) Use methods of cooking which result in less fat being used, e.g. grill foods rather than fry them.
f) Skim fat from stock, sauces, soups and stews during cooking. Also drain surface fat from fried foods before serving.
g) Plan menus which keep dishes high in fat to a minimum, e.g. deep-fried foods and high fat pastries.

## REDUCE SALT

a) Cut down considerably on the salt you use when cooking. This also applies to stock cubes and bouillon mixes which are high in salt.
b) Use convenience foods which are low in salt; read the label to determine the salt content.
c) Where possible, use herbs and spices to flavour food instead of salt.
d) Do not season foods after cooking, even those traditionally salted such as boiled potatoes and freshly cooked vegetables; leave this to the customer.

## REDUCE SUGAR

a) Poach fruits in natural unsweetened fruit juice or low-sugar syrups.
b) Use convenience foods which have no added sugar, such as canned fruits and sauces, yoghurt and fruit purées. (Check the label which should state 'no added sugar'.) However, if a sweet fruit or fruit juice has been added to sweeten the product (e.g. apple) it may still be high in sugar.
c) Use reduced sugar recipes.

## INCREASE FIBRE

Use commodities which provide valuable fibre and do not use techniques which remove fibre.

a) Use wholemeal flour instead of white flour wherever possible, e.g. most brown sauces, stews and sautés of meat and poultry.
b) Mixtures of white and wholemeal flours can be used in many sauces, pastries and cakes.
c) Chick-pea flour (besan) or mixtures of plain and besan flours may be used when preparing white sauces, soups and stews.
d) Use wholemeal breadcrumbs for items which would traditionally have white breadcrumbs, e.g. stuffings.
e) Use wholemeal bread and pastas, and brown rices.
f) Extend vegetable garnishes to include high fibre items such as wholegrain cereals and pulses, e.g. oats, millet, lentils, red beans, mung beans.
g) Leave the skin on vegetables if possible, e.g. potatoes, tomatoes, cucumbers, courgettes. Do not peel every vegetable just because it is traditional practice.
h) Wherever possible, do not remove or strain out commodities which provide fibre, e.g. vegetables.

Remember that healthy eating does not mean more expense. Foods which are high in saturated fats such as butter, beef, eggs, cream and cheese are often the most expensive foods. Using less of these foods or replacing them can often reduce costs.

## CONSERVE VITAMINS AND MINERALS

Be aware that cooking food results in the loss of valuable vitamins and minerals, so always use cooking techniques which keep these losses to a minimum. Examples of this are as follows:

- Always keep cooking liquids to a minimum. This is one of the most important factors in retaining the valuable vitamins in foods. Apply this rule whether cooking stews, braised items, or different types of vegetables.

- Because many foods deteriorate during storage and especially hot storage, cook food in batches to ensure that storage is for as short a time as possible. This is particularly important when cooking vegetables which quickly loose valuable nutrients.

- Where possible avoid blanching, refreshing and reheating fresh and frozen vegetables.

- Start the cooking of vegetables in boiling liquid where possible (avoid the myth of starting the cooking of some vegetables in cold liquid just because they grow under the ground).

- Keep a constant eye on what is cooking and make sure that foods do not overcook or burn; even a short period of prolonged cooking can destroy valuable nutrients.

## FAT, SUGAR, SALT AND FIBRE LEVELS IN BASIC COMMODITIES

The following information can be used as a guide when purchasing food materials and menu planning.

### MEAT AND POULTRY

**The average fat content of common cuts of raw meat, poultry and game**

| *Fat class* | *Cuts of meat, poultry and game* |
|---|---|
| *Very low-fat meats* (fat content less than 5% of raw weight) | Duck (flesh only), chicken (flesh only), grouse (flesh only), rabbit, lambs' kidney, pigs' kidney, veal (lean), ox kidney, turkey (flesh only). |
| *Low-fat meats* (fat content 5–10% of raw weight) | Pheasant, ox liver, partridge, calves' liver, turkey (meat and skin), pigs' liver, venison, chicken liver, lambs' hearts. |
| *Moderate-fat meats* (fat content 11–20% of raw weight) | Leg of lamb, chicken (including skin), ox tongue, minced beef, rump steak (lean and fat), pigeon, topside of beef, stewing steak, lambs' liver. |
| *Moderately high-fat meats* (fat content 21–30% of raw weight) | Loin of pork, scrag and middle neck of lamb, shoulder of lamb, goose, fore rib of beef, sirloin steak (lean and fat), leg of pork. |
| *High-fat meats* (fat content 31–40% of raw weight) | Duck (including skin), streaky bacon, back bacon, best end of lamb, belly of pork, loin of lamb. |

**Meat**
The fat of meat is high in saturated fatty acids and it is important to choose carcases and cuts which have both a light fat covering and a low *lean muscle* fat content.

The proportion of fat in meat is very variable and depends on several factors.

*Animal type* Sheep have the highest levels, followed by pigs; while cows have the lowest levels.
*Breed* Some breeds are naturally leaner.
*Age* Younger animals have laid down less fat.
*Feed* Grass- and silage-fed cattle have less saturated fat than grain-fed cattle.

Caterers and butchers can buy leaner carcases if they specify their requirements. The Meat and Livestock Commission (MLC) operate a classification scheme which specifies fatness.

*Pork*
The Meat and Livestock Commission grade the fat content of pork according to a measurement taken on the long loin above the last rib bone. The depth of fat is measured in millimetres and is indicated on the carcase. The lower the measurement, the less fat on the carcase.

*Beef*
There are seven fat classes:

| *Very lean* | | | | | | *Very fat* |
|---|---|---|---|---|---|---|
| 1 | 2 | 3 | 4L* | 4H | 5L | 5H |

*Light = light; H = heavy.

Currently a typical beef carcase is in fat class 4L. A leaner carcase with a lower fat content can be achieved by specifying fat class 2 or 3.

*Lamb and mutton*
There are five fat classes ranging from 1 (very lean) to 5 (very fat). Fat class 3 may be divided into 3L and 3H and a typical sheep carcase is in this class.

**Meat products**

Meat products are often very high in fat. The content of sausages and meat products is controlled by Food Regulations (1967/68) which state a minimum meat content. The table below gives some examples.

**Fat and meat content of various meat products**

| *Product* | *Minimum meat content (%)* | *Average fat content (%)* |
|---|---|---|
| Meat with gravy | 75 | 13 |
| Faggots | 35 | 18 |
| Meat with jelly | 80 | 23 |
| Frankfurter | 75 | 25 |
| Pork pie | 25 | 27 |
| Luncheon meat | 80 | 27 |
| Pork sausage | 65 | 32 |
| Salami | 75 | 45 |

**Poultry and game**

*Chicken* and *turkey* meat are both lower in total fat and saturated fatty acids than red meat and as such make good menu alternatives that should be included at least twice in any 7-day main meal cycle. *Duck* is higher in fat than chicken and turkey, but the majority of this is associated with the skin. If the breast meat only is used it becomes similar to chicken in fat content. In contrast both the flesh and skin of *goose* are high in fat.

Game birds are wild rather than reared and therefore do not build up fat stores until older and tough, so it is best to choose young roasters and not casserole birds. The level of polyunsaturates in game birds is often high, with *grouse* – the first bird in season – also the first on the list for having the highest level.

## FISH

White fish contain very little fat and oily fish have moderate amounts, but these are mainly polyunsaturated and include the essential fatty acids. Recent research has indicated that the essential fatty acids in fish reduce the risk of suffering heart attacks and it is therefore recommended that both oily fish and white fish are regularly consumed in the diet (3–4 times a week).

**White fish**

There is very little fat in the flesh of this fish because most of the fat is stored in the fish liver. Examples: sole, plaice, whiting, cod, halibut.

**Oily fish**

The flesh of this type of fish is quite rich in fat. Examples: trout, salmon, herring, mackerel, pilchards.

## DAIRY FOODS

**Cheese**

**Fat content of various cheeses**

| *Cheese* | *Fat content (%)* | *Comments* |
|---|---|---|
| Quark | 1 | A skimmed-milk, soft cheese of German origin similar to fromage frais but thicker in consistency, which makes it an ideal ingredient when firmer mixtures are required (such as cheesecake). |
| Cottage cheese | 4 | Liquidise to produce a smooth alternative to cream cheese. |
| Fromage frais | 1–8 | A soft cheese of French origin used to make salad dressings, dips and sauces. Not acidic and goes well with fresh fruit. Blend with flour as thickening agent. Use in place of cream to lighten sauces and desserts. |
| Fromage blanc | 1–8 | As for fromage frais (above). |
| Bodyline (Express Catering Foods) | 14.5 | Low-fat hard cheese similar to cheddar and can be used as a substitute in most recipes but should not be subjected to prolonged heating. |
| Parmesan | 30 | Expensive and high in fat – use sparingly. |
| Cheddar | 33 | Mustard enhances the flavour and enables less cheese to be used. Use a low-fat hard cheese alternative. |
| Cream cheese | 47 | Use alternatives: cottage or quark. |

**Milk and cream**

The fat in all animal milk is high in saturated fatty acids therefore any product made with whole milk or milk fat will also contain a high proportion of saturated fatty acids.

**Fat content of cream**

| *Cream* | *Minimum fat content (%)* |
|---|---|
| Half cream | 12 |
| Single cream | 18 |
| Whipping cream | 35 |
| Double cream | 48 |
| Clotted cream | 55 |

**Fat content of milk**

| *Milk* | *Minimum fat content (%)* |
|---|---|
| Pasturised whole milk | 3.8 |
| Channel Islands whole milk | 4.8 |
| Skimmed | <0.3 |
| Semi-skimmed | 1.5–1.8 |
| Dried skimmed | As fresh |

*Note:* Dried skimmed milk powder with added vegetable fat has a variable saturated fatty acid content as many products are based on palm and coconut oil (see *salad oils*, below).

## FATS AND OILS

These contain a high proportion of fat (81–99.9% of their weight); water; and some fat-soluble vitamins. Wherever possible, use margarines and oils low in saturated fatty acids as given below.

*Spreading fats*

Avoid the use of butter, hard margarines and vegetable/animal oil-based soft margarines. Use instead: soft margarines with a vegetable oil base or sunflower margarine; both of which have a better fatty-acid profile.

*Salad oils*

Use oils low in saturated fatty acids such as groundnut, corn, sunflower, rape and safflower oils; these may also be used for brush-roasting and shallow-frying. Avoid using coconut or palm oils as these are high in saturated fatty acids. Olive oil may be used in combination with an oil low in saturated fatty acids to give flavour.

*Cooking fats*

Avoid the use of dripping, lard or pastry margarine: use oil or margarine low in saturated fatty acids in place of these. White margarine may be used instead of lard, but this contains some trans-fatty acids (similar in effect to saturated fatty acids).

*Frying oils*

Use high-life oils low in saturated fatty acids wherever possible. Both the solid-fat based and cheaper oil-based varieties have a higher uptake by foods during cooking and contain more saturated fatty acids: these should therefore be avoided.

## FRUITS, VEGETABLES AND CEREALS

**The fibre content *per portion* of some fruit and vegetables**

| *Fruit/vegetable* | *Fibre (g)* |
|---|---|
| Lettuce | <0.5 |
| Orange | 1.0 |
| Onions | 1.3 |
| Apple | 1.5 |
| Pear | 1.7 |
| Cauliflower | 2.6 |
| Potatoes (peeled) | 2.6 |
| Leeks | 3.1 |
| Blackberries | 3.1 |
| Carrots | 3.6 |
| Cabbage | 4.2 |
| Peas (frozen) | 4.7 |
| Potatoes (unpeeled) | 5.2 |
| Spinach | 6.0 |

**The fibre content of cereals**

| *Cereal* | *Rating as fibre source* |
|---|---|
| White bread | ** |
| Brown bread | *** |
| Granary bread | *** |
| Wholemeal bread | *** |
| Cornflour | * |
| Plain flour | ** |
| Besan flour | **** |
| Wholemeal flour | **** |
| White rice | ** |
| Brown rice | *** |
| Spaghetti | ** |
| Wholemeal pasta | **** |

**** *rich* ** *poor*
*** *moderate* * *negligible*

Follow the advice given at the start of each chapter. This gives important points on work organisation, safety, hygiene and nutrition for the processes and dishes in each chapter.

# BASIC PREPARATION OF VEGETABLES AND FRUITS

## WORK ORGANISATION, HYGIENE AND SAFETY

- Basic preparation of fruits and vegetables should be carried out as near to cooking time as possible, as vitamins (especially vitamin C) start to be destroyed as soon as cutting commences.

- Wash or scrub vegetables prior to preparation to avoid dirt (and hence bacteria), contaminating the work surfaces.

- Always keep unwashed vegetables and fruits apart. In most commercial kitchens these two commodities will be prepared in separate areas, i.e. vegetables in the kitchen and fruits in the pantry.

- Always thoroughly wash the skins of fruits if they are to be eaten.

- Work from left to right to maintain a good work flow. Items to be cut should be placed to the left of the cutting board in trays or bowls. After cutting, the items should be passed to the right and again placed into clean trays or bowls.

- Always use a hygienic type of chopping board (colour coded) when cutting vegetables. Wooden boards are unhygienic.

Always follow the safety guidelines in your kitchen *Code of Conduct* on the use of hand tools and motorised cutting equipment such as food processors and electric slicers.

## HANDLING KNIVES

When preparing vegetables and fruits by hand it is important to practise and become competent in good knife-cutting techniques. A well-trained chef works in a safe and efficient manner and this is an area in which it is often demonstrated. The following points are a guide to help you develop knife-handling skills when preparing vegetables and fruits.

- When slicing most vegetables, use a cutting motion where the blade moves downwards and forwards when cutting, then backwards and upwards prior to the next downward cutting stroke. Develop the technique of keeping the blade of the knife on the board (no. 5, p. 8). However, when slicing mushrooms, cucumbers and soft fruits the knife may be lifted clear of the board, above the vegetable.

- Always keep your knives sharp. *Remember:* a blunt knife is a dangerous knife.

- Never leave knives in a sink, especially in water where they cannot be seen.

- Always select the correct knife for the job in hand. Most of the basic techniques for preparing vegetables are done with the peeler and two sizes of cooks' knife: 200 mm/8 inch blade and 250 mm/10 inch blade.

- Avoid carrying knives about the kitchen. When a knife has to be carried, keep the point to the floor and the sharp edge of the blade to the back.

- Correct knife technique and finger movements should be practised until a smooth well co-ordinated cutting motion is achieved.

## CUTTING TECHNIQUES

**1 Holding a cook's knife**
Hold the knife between the thumb and forefinger with the remaining fingers curling under the handle.

**2 Holding the item to be cut**
Hold the item with the fingers turned parallel to the knife blade and the thumb tucked behind. Curl the nails inwards to avoid injury.

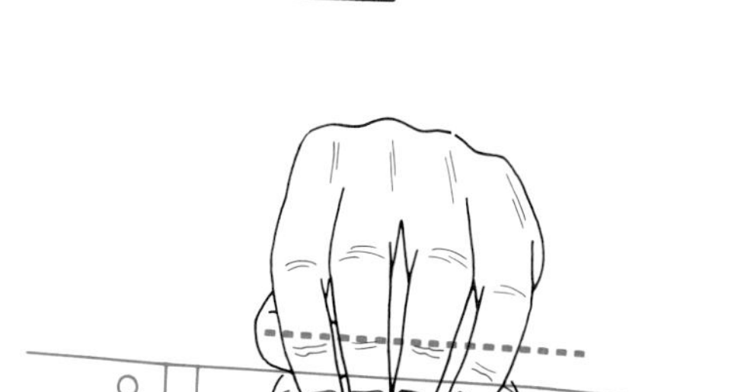

**3 Thin peeling technique**
This involves using a peeler to remove the skin. Use for peeling apples, carrots, cucumber, parsnips, pears, potatoes and small turnips.

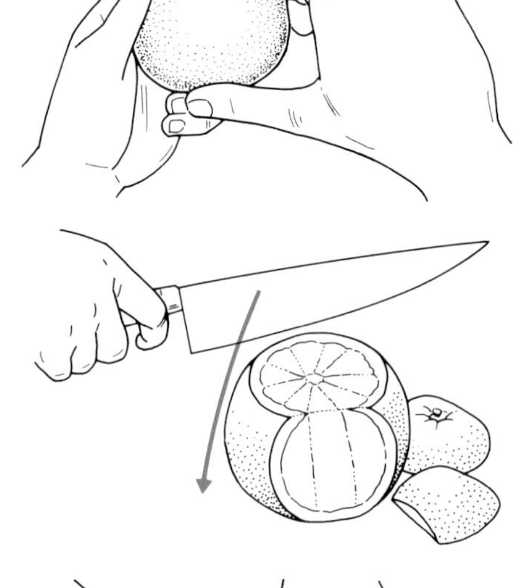

**4 Thick peeling technique**
This involves cutting the skin off the vegetable or fruit using a cook's knife. Use for peeling swedes and large turnips, oranges, lemons and grapefruit.

**5 Basic slicing technique** (most vegetables)
This involves using a knife to slice with a cutting action, moving downwards and forwards. Use a smooth circular motion keeping the knife blade on the board.

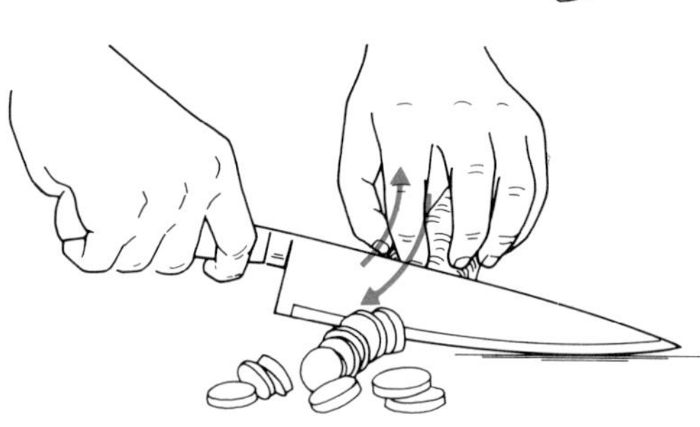

**Finely chopping or dicing an onion**

**a)** Peel the onion.
**b)** Cut in half from top to bottom.
**c)** Place down on the cutting board with the root end to the top.
**d)** Make a series of cuts through the onion but keep attached at the root end (**A**).
**e)** Also make a series of cuts across the onion (**B**).
**f)** Cut with a slicing action into fine pieces (**C**).

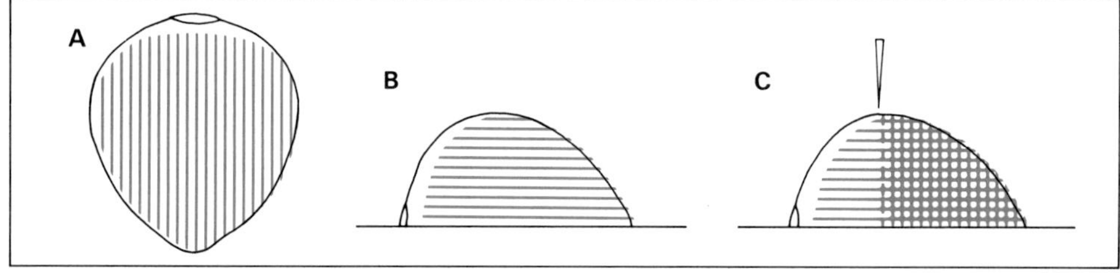


## BASIC CUTS OF VEGETABLES

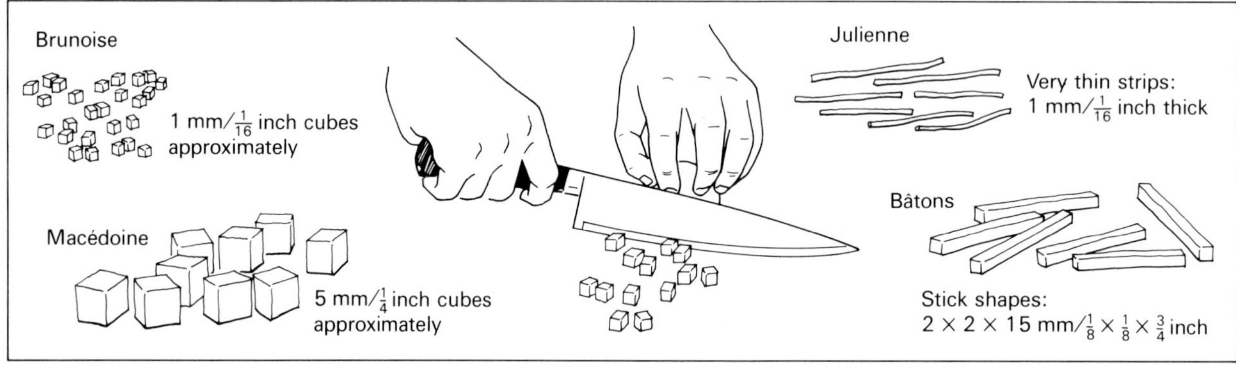

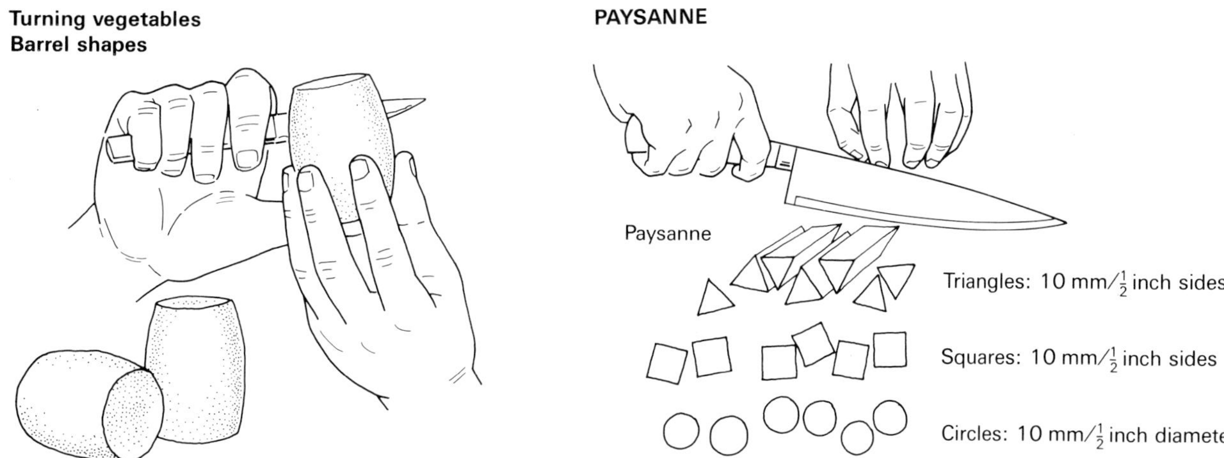


# BASIC PREPARATION OF BUTCHER MEATS, POULTRY AND GAME

The Meat and Livestock Commission (MLC) provides a comprehensive system of grading meat within the United Kingdom.

## BEEF *BOEUF*

Carcase weights: 115 kg/250 lb approximately.

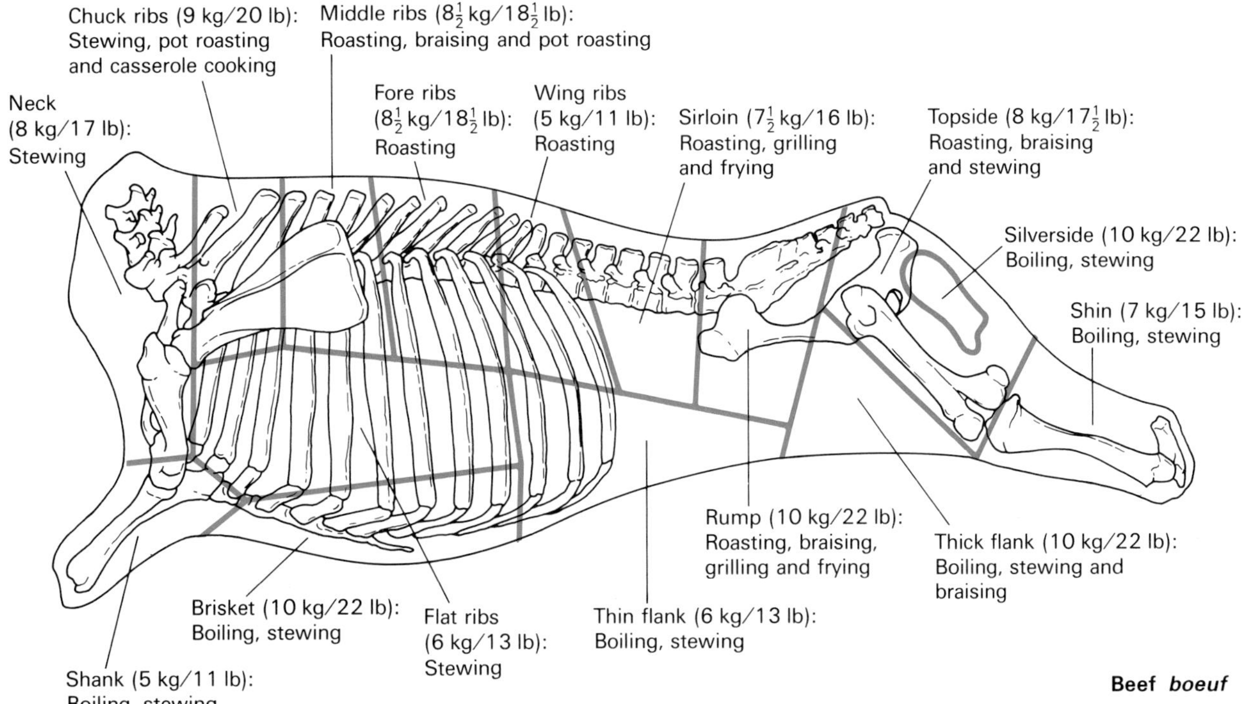


**Beef** ***boeuf***

## IMPORTANT FACTORS CONCERNING BEEF

*Fat content:* Fat should be creamy-white in colour with a brittle texture. MLC grades: 1–5: 1 being the least fatty and 5 the most fatty.

*Conformation:* A well-fleshed animal yielding a high meat content is best. MLC grades: E–P (EUROP): E is the best grade and P the poorest grade.

*Colour:* Flesh should be a good red colour.

*Smell:* Flesh should have a healthy smell with no unpleasant odours.

*Hanging and conditioning:* To ensure maximum flavour and tenderness, beef should be hung in a dry, well-ventilated atmosphere at a temperature of 2–3°C/35–37°F. Times: Sirloin 2–3 weeks, Rump 3–4 weeks.
Well-hung meat usually develops a dark-brown red colour, especially on the outer or cut surfaces.

## WORK ORGANISATION, HYGIENE AND SAFETY

- Store raw meat below 5 °C/40 °F.
- Keep raw and cooked foods apart, preferably in separate, marked refrigerators. If only one refrigerator can be used, store raw foods at the bottom of the unit.
- Keep different types of raw foods apart, such as beef and pork. Place raw meats on suitable trays to avoid dripping.
- Clean working surfaces and all equipment after preparing one type of raw meat and before working on another type.
- The boning knife is one of the most dangerous knives therefore you must be thoroughly trained in its use before working on raw meat. A protective apron should also be worn when boning meat.

## PREPARATION OF SIRLOIN

**Fillet**

1. Bone out the fillet by cutting down between the eye of the meat at **B** and along the flat top of the T-shaped bone.
2. Bone out the contrefilet by also cutting down between the eye of meat at **A** and along the flat top of the T-shaped bone.
3. Carefully trim the fillet by removing the outer covering of sinew and excess fat.

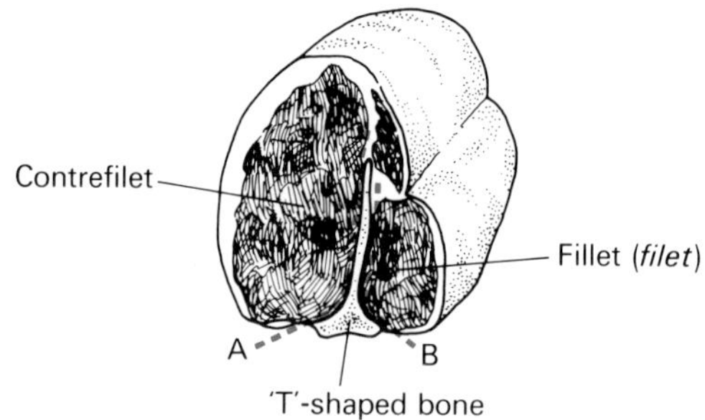


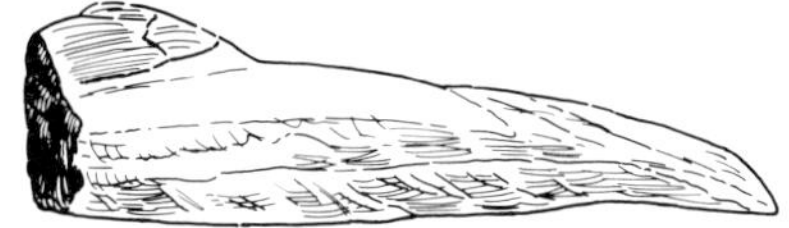

**Contrefilet**

1. Remove the sinew and nerve at the top layer of fat at **C**.
2. Trim off the bottom flap along the length of the contrefilet at **D**.
3. Trim off excess fat at **E** and any remaining sinew at **F**.

## WING AND FORE RIBS

1. Cut down between the eye of the meat and the flat piece of bone to the base of the backbone (**A**).
2. Remove the backbone along the base of the ribs (**B**) with a saw or cleaver.
3. Remove the thick part of sinew under the top layer of fat (**C**).
4. Tie the joint with the bones placed back into position.

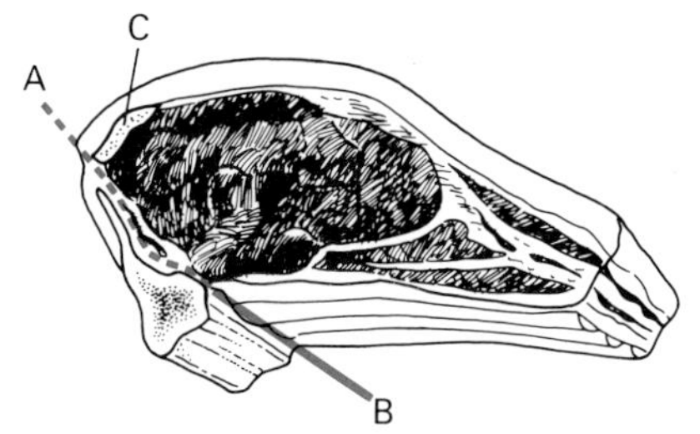

# LAMB AND MUTTON *AGNEAU ET MOUTON*

Carcase weights: 15–25 kg/32–55 lb.

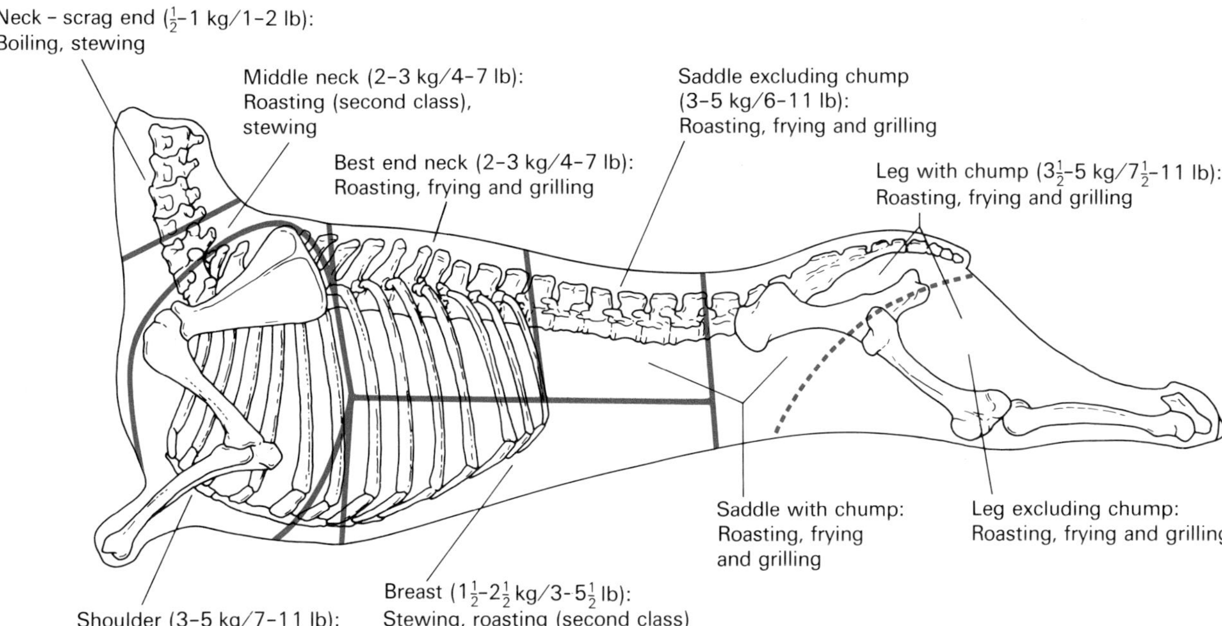


**Lamb and mutton** ***agneau et mouton***

## IMPORTANT FACTORS CONCERNING LAMB AND MUTTON

*Age of animal:* As a general rule, lamb is the term used to define an animal which is under twelve months old at the time of slaughter. After it is one year old the term mutton must be used.

*Fat content:* Fat should be firm and creamy-white in colour and evenly distributed across the carcase. MLC GRADES: 1–5: 1 being the least fatty and 5 the most fatty.

*Conformation:* A well-fleshed animal yielding a high meat content is best. MLC grades: E signifies very good conformation, C poor conformation and Z very poor conformation. Note that average conformation is not indicated by a symbol.

*Colour:* Lamb flesh should be a dull red colour and mutton flesh a dull brownish-red.

*Smell:* Lamb and mutton should have a pleasant smell with no undesirable odours.

*Hanging and conditioning:* The carcase should be hung for 2–7 days depending on temperature (7 days at 2 °C/35 °F).

## WORK ORGANISATION, HYGIENE AND SAFETY

As for beef (page 10).

## PREPARATION OF LAMB CUTS

### Leg *gigot*

Preparation of whole leg for roasting.

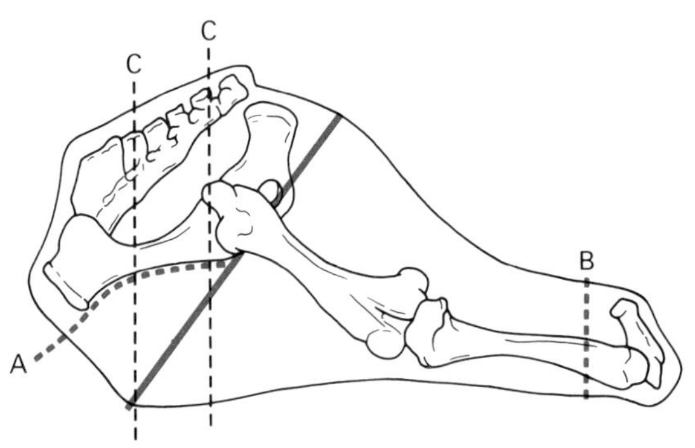


1 Cut down along the aitch bone and through the ball and socket joint (**A**).
2 Bone out the aitch bone.
3 Trim the bottom knuckle and bone (bottom 40 mm/$1\frac{1}{2}$ inch approximately) (**B**).
4 Saw off the knuckle.
5 Tie with string to draw the meat together (**C**).

**Saddle *selle*** (excluding chump)

Preparation for roasting.

1 Pull off the skin.
2 Remove the kidneys, excess fat and sinew.
3 Trim the flaps to fit the underside neatly.
4 Neatly score the top fat in a criss-cross fashion.
5 Tie with string across the saddle to retain shape.

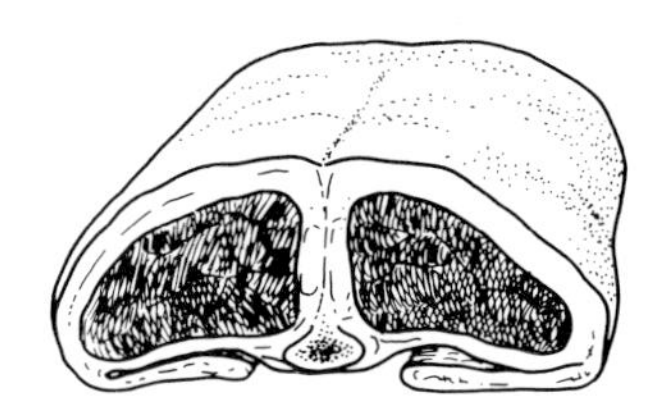

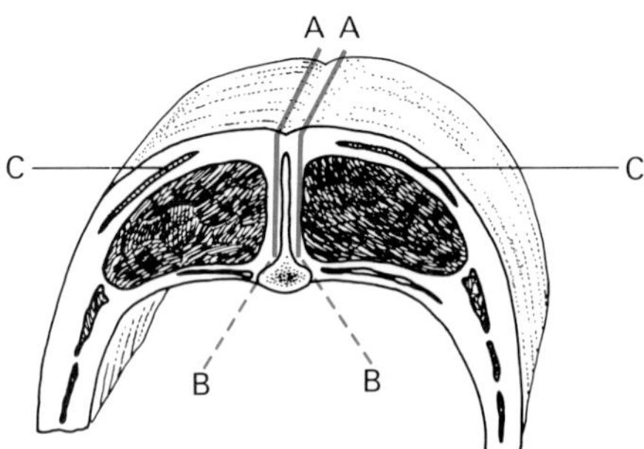


**Best end *carré***

Preparation for roasting and cutlets.

1 Cut down each side of the backbone along the length of the best end (**A**).
2 Cut at an angle through the chine bone (**B**), using a saw or cleaver, until joining cut **A**.
3 Remove the skin from each best end.
4 Remove the tip of the blade bone (**C**), if present, with a small knife.
5 Remove the tough yellow sinew which runs along the top inside of the fat (**D**).
6 Cut across the fat into the rib bones parallel to the eye of the meat (**E**). Cut off the fat.
7 Cut out the fat from between the ribs at **F**, then clean the rib bones.
8 Shorten the rib bones with a cleaver if necessary (**G**).

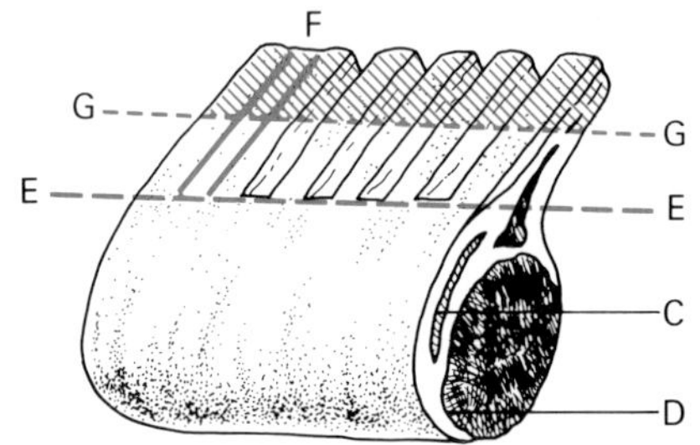


## VEAL *VEAU*

Carcase weights: 50 kg/110 lb approximately.

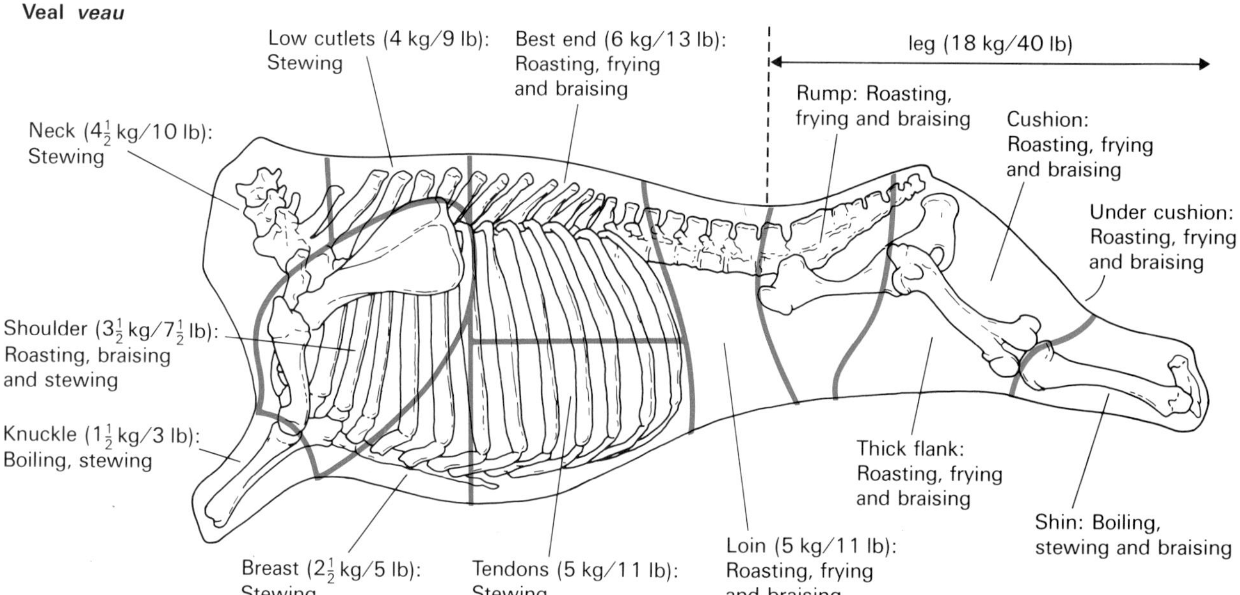

## IMPORTANT FACTORS CONCERNING VEAL

*Age of animal:* A milk-fed calf (known as fed veal) which is 2–3 months old is considered to be the best eating quality.

*Fat content:* There should be a thin covering of creamy-white fat.

*Conformation:* Joints should be well-fleshed with pinkish white bones.

*Colour:* The flesh should be a very pale pink colour.

*Texture:* The flesh should be firm in texture with a fine grain.

*Smell:* The smell should be pleasant with no undesirable odours.

*Hanging and conditioning:* Veal is usually only hung for a short period after slaughter (4–7 days). It should be hung in a dry, well-ventilated atmosphere at 2–3 °C/35–37 °F).

## WORK ORGANISATION, HYGIENE AND SAFETY

As for beef (page 10).

## BONING OUT A LEG OF VEAL

1 Remove the shin (**A**).
2 Remove the aitch bone (**B**).
3 Trim off the outer fat.
4 Bone out the joints following the seams between the joints.

# PORK *PORC*

Side of pork: $26\frac{1}{2}$ kg/58 lb approximately.

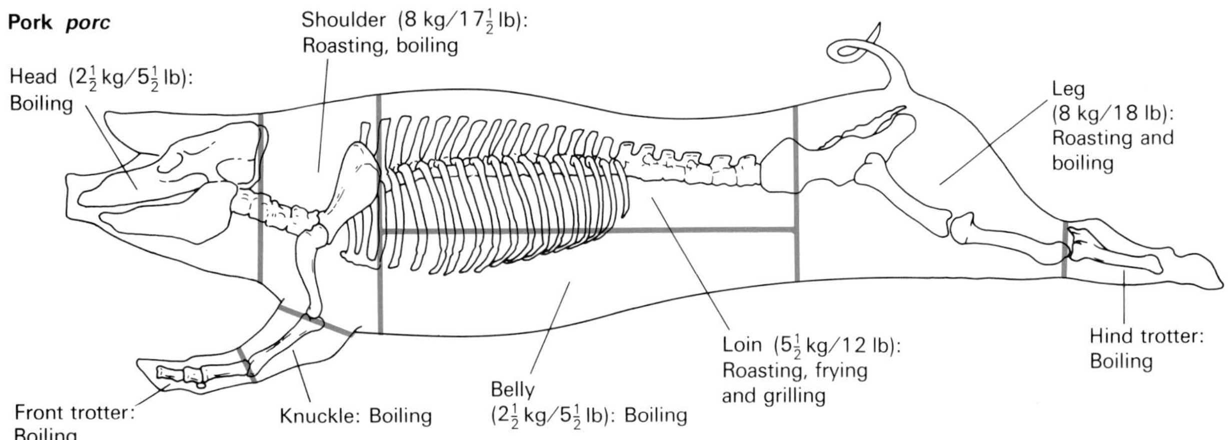


## IMPORTANT FACTORS CONCERNING PORK

*Fat:* Carcases low in fat should be selected, as excessive fat means a poor lean meat content. The fat should be reasonably firm and white in colour.

*Conformation:* Joints should be well-fleshed without excessive fat.

*Colour:* The flesh should be pale pink in colour.

*Texture:* The flesh should be firm with a fine texture. The skin should be smooth.

*Smell:* The smell should be pleasant with no undesirable odours.

*Hanging and conditioning:* Pork requires very little hanging. A period of 4–7 days in a dry, well-ventilated atmosphere at 2–3 °C/35–37 °F is sufficient to condition the meat.

## WORK ORGANISATION, HYGIENE AND SAFETY

Care must be taken when handling pork because of the risk of food poisoning (especially worm infection). All equipment which is used when preparing pork e.g. cutting boards, knives and trays, should be thoroughly cleaned after use. For other points see page 10.

## PREPARATION OF PORK CUTS

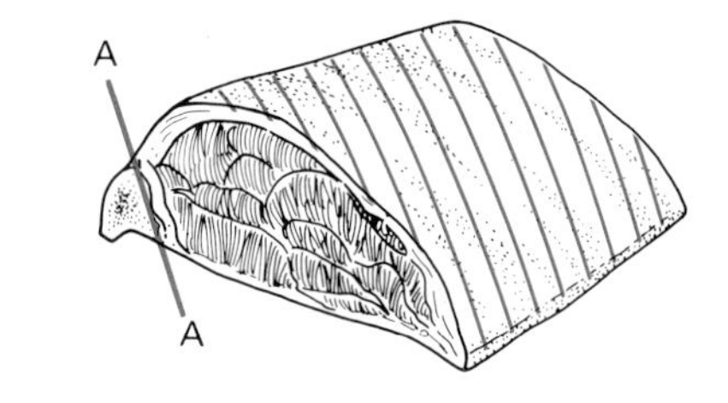


**Preparation of loin of pork for roasting** (rib end)

1 Saw off the bottom of the chine bone (**A**).

2 Score through the skin.

**Preparation of leg of pork for roasting**

Prepare as for *leg of lamb* on page 11.

**Pork escalopes**

1 Trim the fillet removing the fat and sinew.

2 Cut the fillet at an angle (**A**) into thick slices.

3 Place between polythene then flatten to a large thin slice using a cutlet bat.

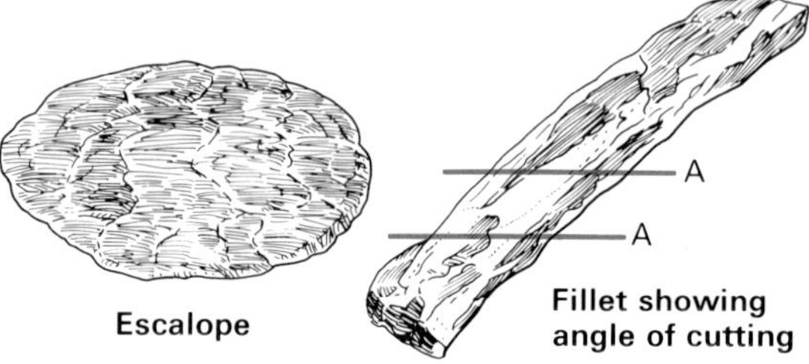


**Escalope** **Fillet showing angle of cutting**

## BACON AND HAM *LARD ET JAMBON*

Bacon is the name given to a side of pork from a *bacon pig* which has been cured by being salted in brine only, or salted in brine and then smoked. The term *green* is used to indicate unsmoked bacon.

Side of bacon: 27 kg/60 lb approximately.

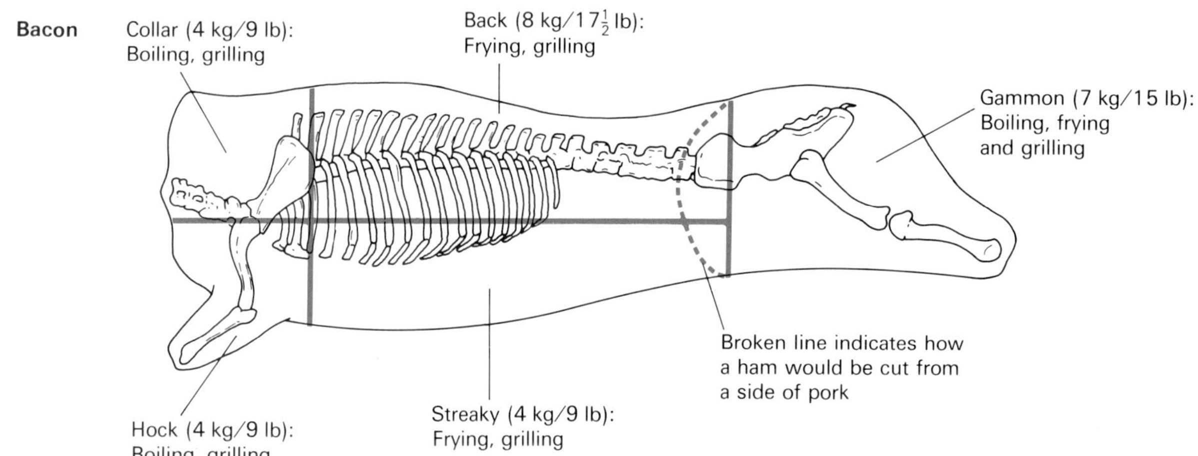


## IMPORTANT FACTORS CONCERNING BACON

*Fat content:* The fat should be firm and white with a slight tinge of pink. The covering of fat should not be excessive and the rind should be smooth, thin and flexible.

*Conformation:* Joints should have a good lean content without excessive fat.

*Texture:* The flesh should be firm and dry and there should be very little sign of mould on inside surfaces.

*Smell:* There should be no unpleasant smell, especially at bone joints or shoulder pockets.

*Storage:* Bacon and ham should be stored in a cool, dry, well-ventilated atmosphere (6–8 °C/43–46 °F).

## WORK ORGANISATION, HYGIENE AND SAFETY

Bacon is often sliced on a ham slicing machine but this should only be done by people trained to operate the machine. A ham slicing machine is a *prescribed dangerous machine*, therefore you should read the conditions for use and cleaning in your *Safety Code of Conduct.*

**Gammon**
This is a hind leg cut from a side of bacon. It is usually cut square across the aitch bone.

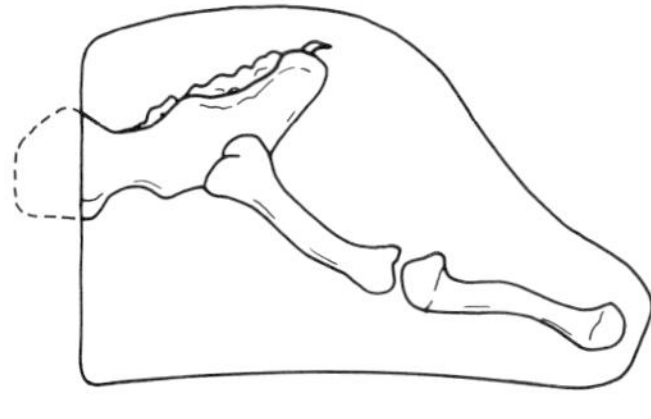

**Ham**
This is the hind leg cut from a side of pork. It is usually cut with a round end (around the aitch bone). It may be cured *dry* in salt and saltpetre or *wet* in brine. Some hams are also smoked.

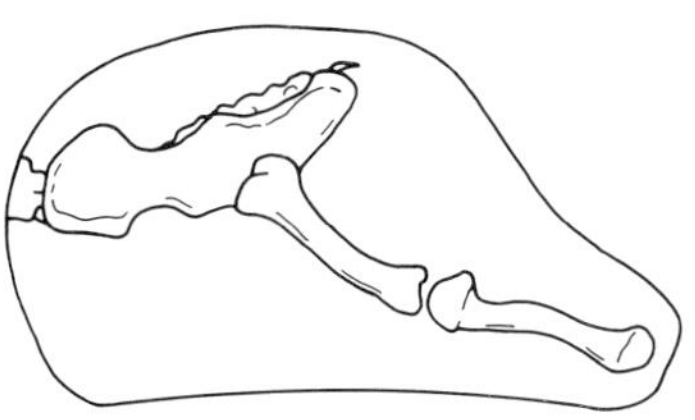

## COMMON CUTS FROM BEEF, VEAL, LAMB AND PORK

### BEEF

1 **Entrecôte steak (*entrecôte*)** 175–250 g/7–9 oz. Cut from the contrefilet.

2 **Minute steak (*entrecôte minute*)** 175–250 g/7–9 oz. A flattened entrecôte steak.

3 **Chateaubriand** 500 g +/1 lb +. A large fillet steak cut from the head of the fillet (page 10). Serves 2 people.

4 **Fillet steak (*filet*)** 150 g +/6 oz +. A general name for a steak cut from a fillet of beef.

5 **Tournedos** 150 g +/6 oz +. A neat round steak cut from the middle of the fillet (page 10). Each steak is usually tied with string.

6 **T-bone steak** 900 g +/2 lb +. A large steak cut through the whole sirloin and containing contrefilet and a large piece of fillet. Usually serves two people.

### VEAL

7 **Escalope** 75–125 g/3–5 oz. (Also obtained from veal, pork and venison.) A piece of flesh from a high quality muscle (veal cushion, under cushion or thick flank and pork fillet) which is flattened to a large thin slice.

8 **Médallion** 25–50 g/1–2 oz. (Also obtained from beef, veal, pork and venison.) Small, thinly cut slices of high quality muscle e.g. beef fillet, pork fillet and veal cuts as escalopes above.

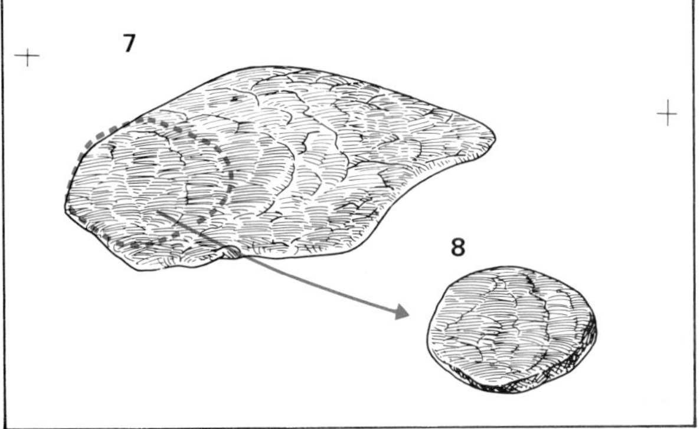

## LAMB AND PORK

9 **Loin chop** 100–175 g/4–7 oz. A chop cut across a single loin.

10 **Chump chop** 100–175 g/4–7 oz. A chop cut across the top of the leg at the aitch bone.

11 **Barnsley chop** (crown or butterfly chop) 200 g/8 oz. A chop cut across a whole saddle of lamb usually containing two pieces of kidney held in place with skewers.

12 **Cutlets** 75–125 g/3–5 oz. (Also obtained from veal, pork and venison.) The trimmed best end (page 12) divided into cutlets.

13 **Noisette** 75–100 g/3–4 oz. (Also obtained from veal, pork and venison.) A small pear-shaped cut of loin consisting of a well-trimmed eye of meat with a small triangular tail of fat.

14 **Rosette** 75–100 g/3–4 oz. (Also obtained from veal, pork and venison.) A small, round cut of loin consisting of a well-trimmed eye of meat and surrounding fat secured with string.

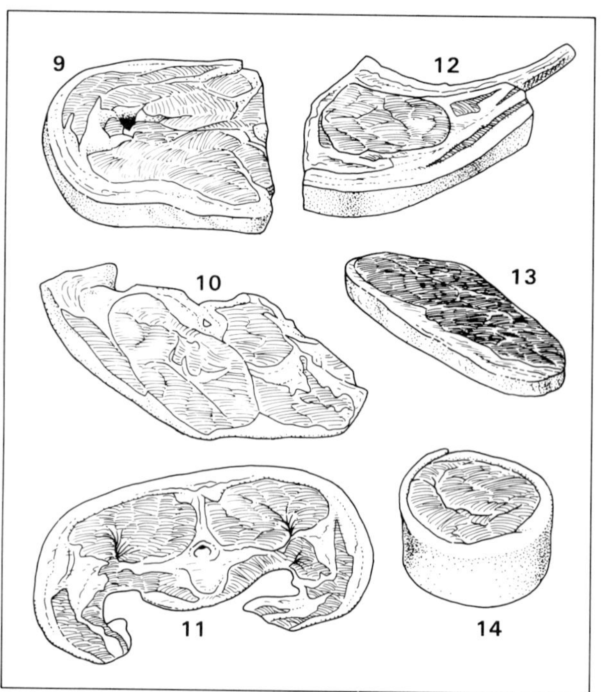


# BASIC PREPARATION OF POULTRY AND FEATHERED GAME

## WORK ORGANISATION, HYGIENE AND SAFETY

Care must be taken when handling poultry and feathered game because of the risk of food poisoning (especially salmonella). Most establishments now work with dressed poultry which has the claws, head and intestines removed, because fresh poultry which requires cleaning and drawing is becoming less available to the caterer (due to EEC guidelines). Many 'prepared' raw chickens have been shown to be contaminated with salmonella bacteria. Feathered game, however, is still frequently prepared by the caterer.

## SOME IMPORTANT POINTS

- Keep different types of raw poultry and feathered game apart, e.g. chicken, duckling, turkey and pheasant. This rule applies both to storage and preparation for cooking.
- Use different cutting surfaces for raw and cooked poultry (colour-coded equipment is desirable).
- Thoroughly clean all equipment that has been used for preparing poultry, i.e. cutting boards, knives and trays.
- Wash your hands each time you handle poultry and as necessary during preparation.

## CHICKEN *POULET*

Chicken is classified mainly by weight:

| | |
|---|---|
| Spring chicken *poussin* | 400 g/14 oz |
| Double spring chicken *poussin double* | 800 g/1$\frac{3}{4}$ lb |
| Small chicken *poulet de grain* | 1$\frac{1}{4}$ kg/2$\frac{3}{4}$ lb |
| Medium chicken *poulet à la reine* | 1$\frac{1}{2}$ kg/3$\frac{1}{4}$ lb |
| Large chicken *poularde* | 2 kg/4 lb |
| Capon *chapon* | 3$\frac{1}{2}$ kg/7 lb |

### IMPORTANT FACTORS

*Conformation:* The chicken should have firm, plump breasts and full, fleshy legs.
*Colour:* Skin should be creamy white and not dried out or torn.
*Smell:* There should be a sweet smell with no undesirable odours.
*Bones:* The lower tip of the breast bone should be pliable.

See **general preparation** below.

## DUCK AND DUCKLING *CANARD ET CANETON*

Weights vary depending on type of duck and duckling, falling between $1\frac{1}{2}$–$2\frac{1}{2}$ kg/3–5 lb.

### IMPORTANT FACTORS

*Season:* Available all year round, but best between March and August.
*Conformation:* The birds should be well fleshed without excessive fat under the skin.
*Smell:* The smell should be fresh and sweet.

See **general preparation** below.

## TURKEY *DINDE, DINDON, DINDONNEAU*

Sizes and weights vary considerably between 3–25 kg/6–50 lb.

### IMPORTANT FACTORS

*Conformation:* The turkey should have firm, plump breasts and full, fleshy legs.
*Colour:* Skin should be creamy white and not dried out or torn.
*Smell:* There should be a sweet smell with no undesirable odours.

See **general preparation** below.

## PHEASANT *FAISAN*

Carcase weights: 1–2 kg/2–4 lb.

### IMPORTANT FACTORS

*Season:* Fresh pheasant is available from October–February.
*Quality:* Young birds should have smooth legs and a flexible breast bone.
*Hanging time:* Store in a dry, well-ventilated atmosphere below 5 °C/40 °F.

See **general preparation** below.

### GENERAL PREPARATION OF POULTRY AND FEATHERED GAME

**Preparing a bird for grilling**

1. Remove the wish bone.
2. Cut off the claws (if necessary).
3. Split the bird through the back using a large knife.
4. Open out the bird and lightly flatten with a cutlet bat.
5. Remove the ribs using a small knife.

**Plucking** Pluck out the feathers by pulling in the opposite direction to which they lie using a wet thumb and forefinger.

**Singeing** (not always required with dressed poultry and game). Hold the bird at the head and claws and pass it over a small gas or spirit flame. Singe off the small feathers and hairs but do not burn or blacken the skin.

**Drawing and gutting**

1. Slit the skin along the back of the neck then cut off the head.
2. Remove the neck from the skin and pull out the crop bag and windpipe.
3. Cut off the neck close to the body.
4. Push the forefinger into the neck opening and loosen the intestines from the breast cavity.
5. Turn the bird round and cut a slit at the vent end.
6. Insert the forefinger and loosen the intestines.
7. Draw out the intestines. Take care not to burst the gall bladder (attached to the livers).
8. Ensure the lungs have been removed from the top (inside) of the carcase.
9. Thoroughly wash the bird in cold water then wipe dry with disposable towels.
10. Place on a tray and store at 2–3 °C/35–37 °F until required for use.
11. Thoroughly wash all working surfaces, boards and equipment.

**Trussing** (two-string method)

1. Remove the wish bone and wing tips (the winglets are removed in many establishments).
2. If the claws are present, cut off all the spurs and toes but leave the middle toes long (i.e. remove the nails).
3. Push the bird into shape: press down the legs and raise the breast.
4. Insert the needle through the bird at the middle of the leg (**A**).
5. Turn the bird over, and pass the needle through the wing bone. Then sew down the neck flap, coming out through the opposite wing bone (**B**).
6. Tie securely, producing a neat shape.
7. Draw the legs down into shape by inserting the needle through the base of the carcase and loop over the legs (**C**). Tie securely.

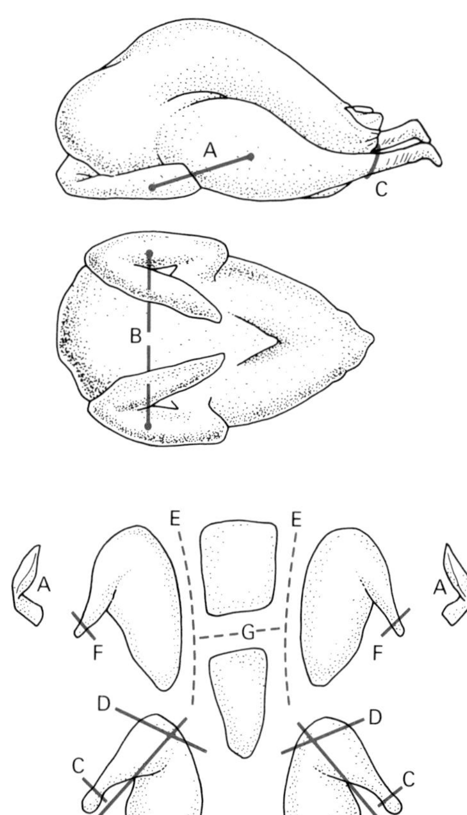


**Jointing a bird or cutting for sauté** (4 portions)

1. Remove the wish bone.
2. Cut off the winglets (**A**).
3. Remove the legs then cut in half at **B**.
4. Cut off the knuckle pieces at **C** and **D**.
5. Remove the wings by cutting parallel to the breast bone and down through the wing joints (**E**).
6. Trim the wing joints and chop off the bottom knuckle (**F**).
7. Remove the breast from the carcase using a large cook's knife.
8. Cut the breast into two equal sized portions (**G**).

**Preparing suprêmes**

1. Remove the wishbone, winglets and legs.
2. Remove the skin from the breast.
3. Cut along and down the breast bone then down through the wing joint (**A**).
4. Carefully remove the suprême using the top of the cook's knife in a filleting action.
5. Remove the other suprême in the same manner.
6. Trim the flesh from the wing bones and scrape the bones clean.
7. Chop off the bottom knuckles.
8. Trim off the small sinews from the fillets.
9. Lightly flatten and trim the fillet if required.

*Note:* The fillets are sometimes stuffed into a pocket which is formed by making a slit along the thick side of each suprême.

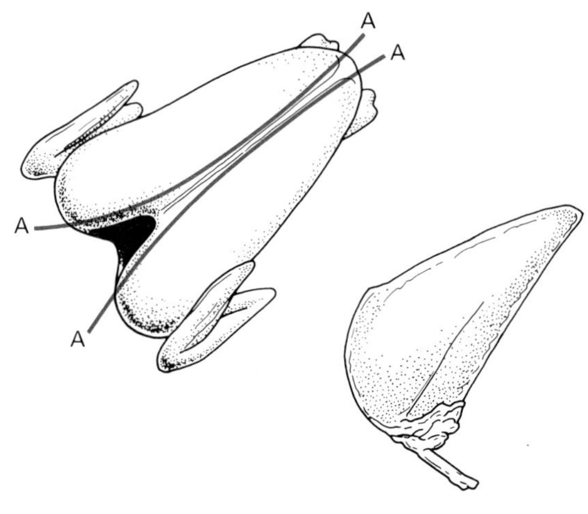

# BASIC PREPARATION OF FISH AND SHELLFISH

## WORK ORGANISATION, HYGIENE AND SAFETY

Fish odours can quickly taint other foods, so it is desirable wherever possible to separate fish from other foods in storage and work areas. Work areas for fish and shellfish usually require sufficient sink space (with plenty of cold running water) to wash and clean the fish.

## STORAGE AND HYGIENE

- Store fresh fish (or defrosted fish) at 0–2 °C/ 32–35 °F, preferably in a refrigerator specially designed for fish or in a suitable compartment or section of a larder refrigerator.
- Store fresh or defrosted fish for as short a time as possible before cooking, e.g. 1–3 days at the above temperature.
- Cook live shellfish as soon as possible after delivery.
- See storage of live shellfish on page 21.
- Store frozen fish or shellfish in a freezer at −18 °C/ 0 °F or below.
- When handling fish be careful of small bones, barbs or spines which may cause injury.
- Use different cutting surfaces and equipment for raw fish, cooked fish and shellfish (colour-coded equipment is desirable).
- All equipment which is used when preparing fish or shellfish, e.g. cutting boards, knives and trays, should be thoroughly cleaned after use.
- Wash your hands each time you handle fish, and as necessary during preparation.
- Always store raw fish apart from cooked fish to avoid cross-contamination.

# FISH

## IMPORTANT FACTORS FOR FISH

*Conformation:* The fish should be well fleshed.
*Texture:* The flesh should be firm with moist skin and scales.
*Smell:* There should be a pleasant fish smell.
*Appearance:* Eyes should have a moist, fresh appearance and the gills should be bright red.

## BASIC PREPARATION OF FISH

**Washing** Wash fish under cold running water at each stage of basic preparation i.e. removing scales, fins, gills and intestines.

**Removing scales** Hold the fish at the tail and scrape off the scales from tail to head with a knife held at a slight angle.

**Removing fins** Cut off the fins in the opposite direction to which they lie using fish scissors.

**Removing gills** Open the gill slits and cut out the gills using a small knife or scissors.

**Removing intestines**

*Flat fish:*

a) Cut a slit from the head and into the pocket which holds the intestines.
**b)** Remove the intestines, roe and blood.

*Round fish*

**a)** Cut a slit along the belly from the vent.
**b)** Remove the intestines with the back of a spoon or small ladle.
**c)** Scrape the bone to remove the blood tract.

*Note:* Be careful not to break the ligament between the bottom of the head and the belly.

## SKINNING FISH

**Flat fish** (lemon sole, plaice, flounder)
These are skinned from head to tail:

**a)** Cut around the top of the head and down along the side fins (**A**).
**b)** Cut from the gill slits and down along the opposite side fins (**B**).
**c)** Loosen the skin at the top of the head and across the body (**C**).
**d)** Hold the head with the palm of the hand and pull off the black skin.

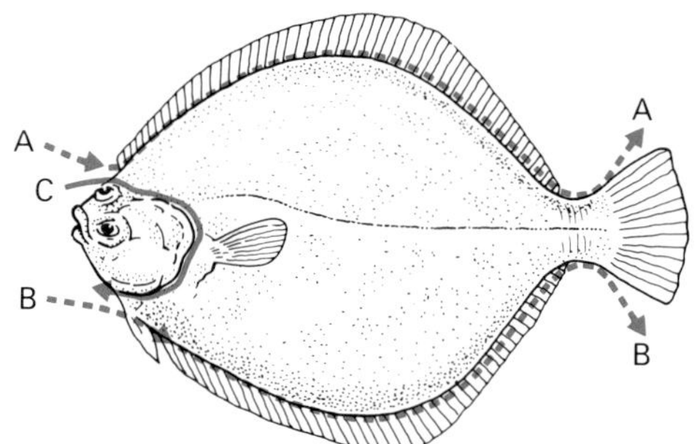

**Dover sole**
Dover soles are skinned from tail to head:

**a)** Cut across the tail through the skin.
**b)** Scrape to loosen enough skin to be gripped with the fingers (**A**).
**c)** Pull off the black skin.
**d)** If required, repeat the procedure to remove the white skin.

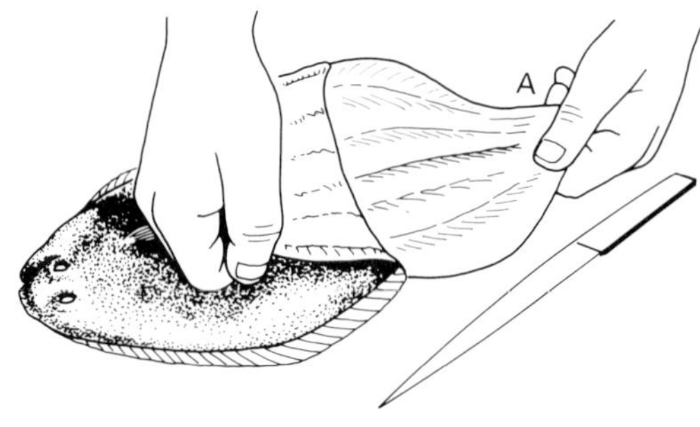


**Fish fillets**

**a)** Place the fillet with the skin down on the cutting board.
**b)** Hold the tail and cut through the flesh to the skin.
**c)** Hold the blade at an angle (45°) and move it forwards and backwards with a slight pushing action; at the same time lightly pull the skin from the tail end (**A**).

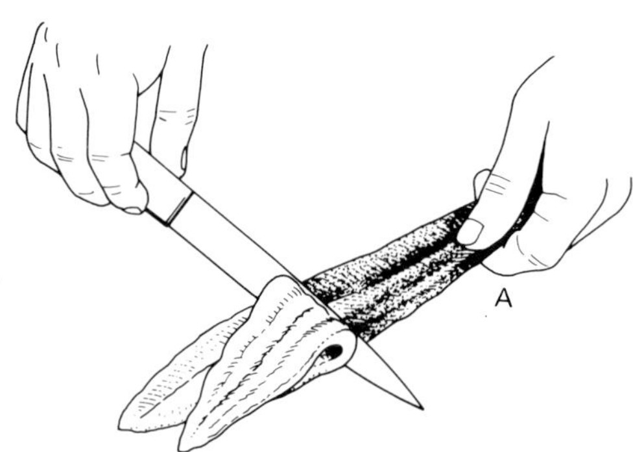


## FILLETING FISH

**Flat fish** (all common flat fish)

**a)** Cut down the centre of the fish to the tail (**A**).
**b)** Fillet off the flesh by drawing the knife down the backbone (**B**). The fillet is lifted back by the other hand during cutting.
**c)** Turn the fish round and remove the opposite fillet the same way.
**d)** Turn the fish over and repeat steps (a)–(c) above to remove the other fillets.

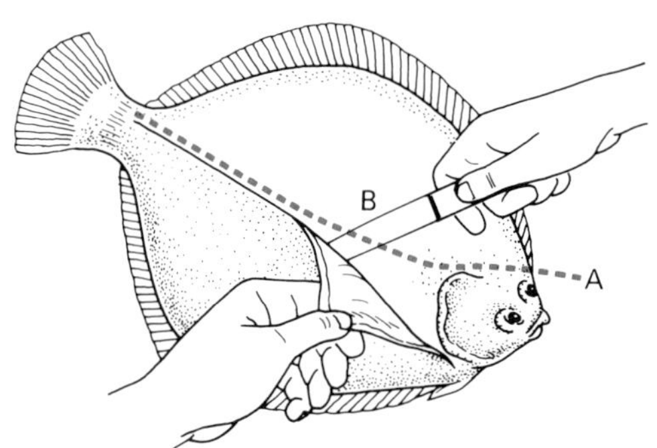


**Round fish**

**a)** Cut up behind the head to the backbone.
**b)** Turn the knife and cut down the centre of the fish following the backbone (**A**).
**c)** Turn the fish over and repeat the procedure to remove the second fillet. Alternatively cut under the bone without turning the fish.

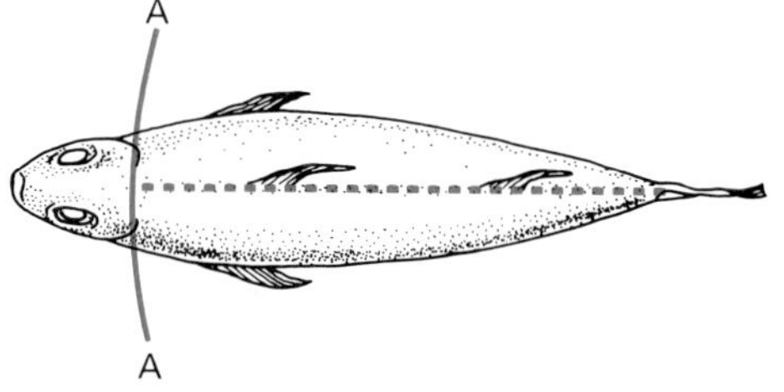

## PREPARING WHOLE FISH FOR POACHING, GRILLING AND SHALLOW-FRYING

(This applies to flat fish and round fish)

**a)** Carry out the basic preparation, i.e. remove scales, fins, black skin (on flat fish) and intestines.

**b)** Cut off the head (all fish: but see box right).

**c)** If the head is to be left on (e.g. Dover sole, trout, salmon and red mullet) then remove the gills and eyes.

> **Preparing whole salmon for poaching**
> Prepare the fish (see left) making as small a cut as possible to remove the intestines. The fish may be stuffed and wrapped in a cloth to help it keep its shape during cooking.

## CUTS OF FISH

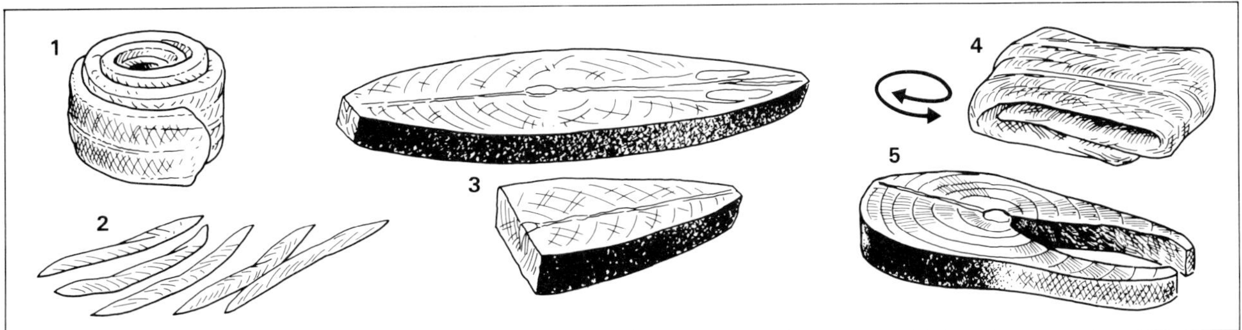


**1 PAUPIETTE** (most small fish fillets)
A rolled-up fillet usually stuffed with fish forcemeat.

**a)** Lightly flatten the fillet.

**b)** Spread with the fish forcemeat.

**c)** Roll up like a small Swiss roll.

**2 EN GOUJONS** (fillets of sole, plaice, flounder etc.)
Thin strips of fish fillet which are often breaded.

**a)** Remove both skins from the fillets.

**b)** Cut at an angle into thin strips 50 mm × 5 mm/ 2 × $\frac{1}{4}$ inch approximately.

**3 TRONÇON** (halibut, turbot, brill etc.)
A steak cut from a flat fish.
Cut the steak across the prepared fish or halve the prepared fish.

**4 DÉLICE** (sole, plaice, whiting, haddock, trout etc.)
A trimmed folded fillet from a flat fish.
Lightly flatten the fillet and fold together as indicated.

**5 DARNE** (cod, ling, salmon, pike)
A steak cut from a round fish.
Cut the steak across the prepared fish.

# SHELLFISH

## IMPORTANT FACTORS FOR PURCHASING LIVE SHELLFISH

**Molluscs** (cockles, mussels, oysters, scallops and clams)

**a)** The shells should be tightly closed indicating that the fish is alive.

**b)** Any shell which is slightly open should be tapped with the finger. If it remains open then the fish is dead and therefore should be discarded.

**Crustaceans** (shrimps, prawns, scampi, lobster, crayfish)
The shellfish should be alive and heavy in relation to size.

## STORAGE OF LIVE SHELLFISH

Store live crustaceans in specially aerated tanks. If this is not possible, store in a cool place covered with a wet cloth and cook as soon as possible. Store molluscs in the same manner but sprinkle with a little salt before covering with the wet cloth.

## PREPARATION OF SHELLFISH

**Preparing scallops for cooking**

**a)** Wash the scallops.
**b)** Hold the scallop with the flat shell downwards. *Important:* A stout cloth should be used to protect the hand during this procedure.
**c)** Insert a thin-bladed knife through the small opening between the shells in the right side of the hinge (**A**).
**d)** Cut along the flat shell to sever the muscle from the shell (**B**).
**e)** Remove the fish then trim off the fringe leaving only the white flesh and curved orange roe (**C**).
**f)** Wash and drain.

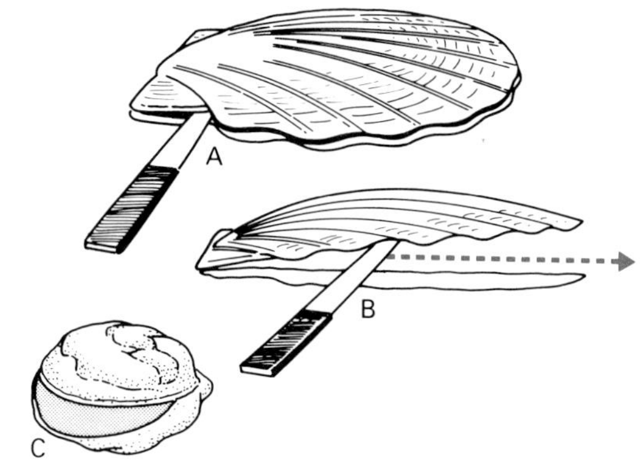


**Cutting a cooked lobster**

**a)** Remove the claws and legs.
**b)** Pull back the bottom pincer of each claw and break off: this should remove the blade bone from each claw (**A**).
**c)** Crack the claws with the back of a knife and remove the flesh.
**d)** Split the lobster in half lengthwise (**B**).
**e)** Remove the cooked flesh from the tail.
**f)** Remove and discard the intestines. The red coral may be kept and used as a decoration for shellfish dishes.
**g)** Wash and drain both half shells (*carapaces*).
**h)** If required, neatly slice the cooked flesh of the tail at an angle so that it retains its shape.

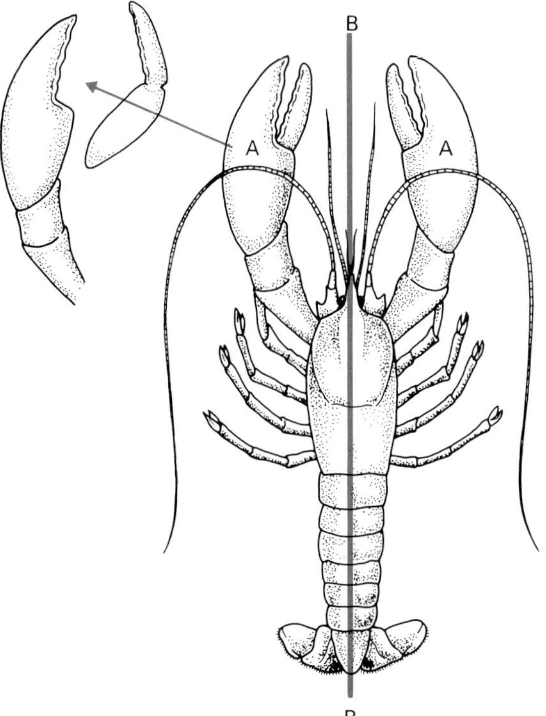

# BASIC PREPARATIONS

The following items are fundamental to many dishes therefore their preparation in advance of cooking (mise en place) is a common occurrence in many kitchens.
(*Note:* The most healthy approach to these preparations has been given here as standard. Where relevant, the more traditional alternative has also been given.)

## BASIC PREPARATIONS: SAVOURY

### ASPIC JELLIES

Yield: 1 litre/2 pt

**Poultry, beef and game aspics**

| | | |
|---|---|---|
| $1\frac{1}{2}$ litre | appropriate strong, cold stock (chicken, beef, veal, game: page 36) | 3 pt |
| 150 g | lean minced beef | 6 oz |
| 100 g | finely cut vegetables (onion, carrot, celery, leek) | 4 oz |
| 2 | egg whites (size 3) | 2 |
| 50 g | *leaf gelatine | 2 oz |
| 3–4 | peppercorns | 3–4 |
| 2–3 | parsley stalks | 2–3 |
| | sprig of thyme, $\frac{1}{2}$ bay leaf | |
| | small pinch salt | |

**Fish aspic**

| | | |
|---|---|---|
| $1\frac{1}{2}$ litre | strong, cold fish stock (page 36) | 3 pt |
| 150 g | minced white fish flesh (haddock, sole, whiting etc.) | 6 oz |
| 100 g | chopped onion | 4 oz |
| 2 | egg whites (size 3) | 2 |
| 50 g | *leaf gelatine | 2 oz |
| 3–4 | peppercorns | 3–4 |
| 2–3 | parsley stalks | 2–3 |
| | sprig of thyme, $\frac{1}{2}$ bay leaf | |
| | small pinch salt | |

**The exact quantity of gelatine required depends on the strength of the basic stock.*

1. Soak the gelatine in cold water and allow to soften.
2. Thoroughly mix together the minced flesh, vegetables and egg whites.
3. Place the mixture into a saucepan, add the stock and whisk together thoroughly.
4. Squeeze the surplus water from the gelatine then add to the saucepan.
5. Add the peppercorns.
6. Place onto the stove and slowly bring to the boil. Stir during the first stages of heating only. Do not stir when the mixture is hot (over 50 °C/122 °F).
7. Simmer slowly, allowing a crust to form on the top. Simmering time: *Chicken, beef, veal, game:* $1\frac{1}{2}$ hours. *Fish:* 15–20 minutes.
8. Strain carefully through a double-folded muslin into a clean bowl.
9. Remove any surface grease by floating a dishpaper on top of the aspic.
10. Check the seasoning, then test the setting property of the jelly: Drop a small quantity of the mixture onto a chilled plate and place into a refrigerator to set. If the aspic is too firm, add a little clear stock and retest.
11. Cool quickly and use as required.

### BATTERS

Frying batters are used for deep-fried fish, chicken, veal Orly, vegetables and sweet or savoury fritters.

**CRÊPE BATTER** See page 170.

#### POWDER-AERATED FRYING BATTER

Yield: 350 ml/$\frac{3}{4}$ pt approximately

| | | |
|---|---|---|
| 200 g | plain flour | 8 oz |
| 10 g | baking powder | $\frac{1}{2}$ oz |
| 250 ml | milk | $\frac{1}{2}$ pt |
| | small pinch salt | |

1. Sieve together the flour, baking powder and salt.
2. Add half the milk and whisk to a smooth thick paste.
3. Whisk in the remaining milk in stages until a smooth batter of coating consistency is obtained.

Use within 30 minutes of preparation.

#### TRADITIONAL FRYING BATTER

Yield: 350 ml/$\frac{3}{4}$ pt approximately

| | | |
|---|---|---|
| 200 g | plain flour | 8 oz |
| 250 ml | milk | $\frac{1}{2}$ pt |
| 10 ml | oil | $\frac{1}{2}$ fl oz |
| 2 | egg whites | 2 |
| | small pinch salt | |

1. Place the flour (which should be sieved if lumps are present) into a mixing bowl.
2. Add half the milk and the oil then whisk to a smooth thick paste.
3. Whisk in the remaining milk in stages until a smooth batter of coating consistency is obtained.
4. Whisk the egg whites to a stiff snow, adding the pinch of salt.
5. Fold the egg whites through the batter and use as soon as possible.

## YEAST FRYING BATTER

Yield: 350 ml/$\frac{3}{4}$ pt approximately

| | | |
|---|---|---|
| 200 g | strong flour | 8 oz |
| 5 g | caster sugar | $\frac{1}{4}$ oz |
| 10 g | yeast | $\frac{1}{2}$ oz |
| 250 ml | warm milk (40 °C/100 °F) | $\frac{1}{2}$ pt |
| | small pinch salt | |

1 Sieve together the flour, sugar and salt.
2 Break down the yeast in half the milk and add to the flour.
3 Whisk to a smooth thick paste.
4 Whisk in the remaining milk in stages until a smooth batter of coating consistency is obtained.
5 Leave in a warm place to ferment and double in volume: 40 minutes approximately.

Use as soon as possible.

# COURT-BOUILLONS

See pages 74 and 75.

# FLAVOURINGS

## BOUQUET GARNI

1 small faggot of herbs

| | | |
|---|---|---|
| 1 | bay leaf | 1 |
| | sprig of thyme | |
| 2–3 | parsley stalks | 2–3 |
| | leek leaf or muslin | |

Place the bay leaf, parsley stalks and thyme into the leek leaf or muslin and tie with string.

*Uses:* Adding flavour to stocks, sauces, soups and stews etc.

## MIREPOIX

Yield: 250 g/10 oz approximately

| | | |
|---|---|---|
| 100 g | onion | 4 oz |
| 100 g | carrot | 4 oz |
| 50 g | celery | 2 oz |
| 50 g | leek | 2 oz |
| | sprig of thyme, bay leaf and parsley stalks | |

Wash, peel and roughly chop the vegetables.

*Uses:* The fundamental vegetable flavouring in many soups, sauces, stews, braised dishes and marinades.

## WHITE MIREPOIX *MIREPOIX BLANC*

Yield: 250 g/10 oz

| | | |
|---|---|---|
| 150 g | onion | 6 oz |
| 50 g | celery | 2 oz |
| 50 g | white leek | 2 oz |
| | sprig of thyme, bay leaf | |

Wash, peel and roughly chop the vegetables.

*Uses:* A fundamental vegetable flavouring in certain white soups, sauces and stews.

## STUDDED ONION *OIGNON CLOUTÉ*

| | | |
|---|---|---|
| 1 | small onion | 1 |
| 1 | bay leaf | 1 |
| 2 | cloves | 2 |

Peel the onion, then attach the bay leaf by piercing through with the cloves.

*Uses:* Béchamel sauce, bread sauce, boiled meat dishes and certain soups.

# GARNISHES

## CROÛTONS (No added fat)

4 portions

| | | |
|---|---|---|
| 1 | slice wholemeal (or white) bread | 1 |

1 Remove the crusts from the bread.
2 Cut into 5 mm/$\frac{1}{4}$ inch cubes.
3 Spread out on a tray and toast under a grill until crisp and golden brown.

*Uses:* Accompaniment to certain soups, especially pulse soups.

**Croûtons (traditional)**

Prepare as above but shallow-fry the cubes in 10 g/$\frac{1}{2}$ oz margarine or butter until crisp and golden brown.

## DUXELLES

Yield: 100 g/4 oz

| | | |
|---|---|---|
| 100 g | mushrooms | 4 oz |
| 5 g | margarine (or 10 g/$\frac{1}{2}$ oz butter) | $\frac{1}{4}$ oz |
| 25 g | chopped shallot or onion | 1 oz |
| 10 g | *wholemeal breadcrumbs (or white breadcrumbs) | $\frac{1}{2}$ oz |
| | small pinch salt and pepper | |

**Optional*

1 Wash and drain the mushrooms then squeeze out excess liquid.
2 Finely chop them, then squeeze out any further liquid.
3 Melt the margarine in a sauteuse.
4 Add the shallot or onion and lightly cook without colouring.
5 Add the mushrooms and cook until a fairly dry mass is obtained. Add the breadcrumbs if required. Stir occasionally during cooking to avoid burning.
6 Lightly season and use as required.

*Uses:* Basic ingredient for stuffed tomatoes, onions and cucumbers. Also used in certain meat, poultry and game garnishes.

## GAME FARCE *FARCE À GRATIN*

This is used as a stuffing for roast feathered game. It is also spread on croutons which are used for the service of roast pheasant and grouse (see page 128).

4 portions

| | | |
|---|---|---|
| 5 g | margarine (or 25 g/1 oz butter) | $\frac{1}{4}$ oz |
| 25 g | chopped onion | 1 oz |
| 1 | small clove crushed garlic | 1 |
| | sprig of thyme, bay leaf | |
| 25 g | lean bacon (or 50 g/2 oz fat bacon) | 1 oz |
| 100 g | chicken livers | 4 oz |
| | pinch pepper | |

1 Melt the margarine then add the onion, garlic, bacon and herbs.
2 Slowly cook without developing colour for 4–5 minutes.
3 Add the livers and cook in the hot fat until firm.
4 Remove the bay leaf and thyme then pass the mixture through a coarse mincer.

## LARDONS

Yield: 50–75 g/3–4 oz

| | | |
|---|---|---|
| 50–75 g | lean bacon | 3–4 oz |

1 Remove any rind and trim off any excess fat.
2 Cut into dice (10 mm/$\frac{1}{2}$ inch) or stick shapes (20 × 5 × 5 mm/$\frac{3}{4}$ × $\frac{1}{4}$ × $\frac{1}{4}$ inch).
3 Place in a saucepan and cover with cold water.
4 Bring to the boil and simmer until cooked.
5 Refresh under cold water, then drain.

## TOMATO CONCASSÉES, RAW
### *TOMATES CONCASSÉES CRU*

Yield: 500 g/1 lb approximately

| | | |
|---|---|---|
| 750 g | firm tomatoes | 1 lb |

1 Fill a saucepan with water sufficient to cover the tomatoes and bring to the boil.
2 Remove the eyes from the tomatoes then place the tomatoes into a wire basket.
3 Submerge in the boiling water for 5–10 seconds.
4 Remove, then test to see if the skins can be removed. If not, immerse the tomatoes for a further 2–3 seconds. Avoid cooking the tomatoes.
5 Immediately plunge into cold water.
6 Drain, then peel off the skins.
7 Halve the tomatoes across the middle then remove the seeds.
8 Roughly chop the flesh into large pieces.

*Uses:* An ingredient for soups, sauces, entrées and vegetable dishes.

## TOMATO CONCASSÉES, COOKED
### *TOMATES CONCASSÉES CRU*

Yield: 500 g/1 lb approximately

| | | |
|---|---|---|
| 500 g | raw tomato concassées | 1 lb |
| 25 g | olive oil | 1 fl oz |
| 50 g | finely chopped shallot/onion | 2 oz |
| | small pinch salt and pepper | |

1 Heat the oil in a sauteuse.
2 Add the shallot or onion and lightly cook without colouring.
3 Add the raw concassées, lightly season, then toss them in the hot oil and shallots until heated. Avoid overcooking.

*Uses:* A garnish for omelettes, pasta dishes, potato and vegetable dishes.

# GLAZES

(Suitable for fish, meat, poultry and game)

Yield: 100–150 ml/4–6 fl oz

| | | |
|---|---|---|
| 5 litres | appropriate stock | 10 pt |

1 Boil down the stock in a saucepan.
2 Decant into a smaller saucepan and continue boiling.
3 When thick and concentrated, pour into jars, seal and quickly cool.
4 Store chilled for a short period until required for use.

*Uses:* Adding flavour or increasing the strength of flavour of stocks and certain sauces.

# MARINADES AND PICKLES

## INSTANT MARINADE

Yield: 125 ml/$\frac{1}{4}$ pt

| | | |
|---|---|---|
| 25 g | finely chopped shallot/ onion | 1 oz |
| | good pinch chopped parsley | |
| 50 ml | lemon juice (1 medium lemon) | 2 fl oz |
| 75 ml | oil | 3 fl oz |
| | small pinch salt and pepper | |

1 Place all the ingredients into a porcelain or stainless steel dish.
2 Add the fish, chicken or veal etc. and coat with the marinade.
3 Cover with a sheet of lightly oiled greaseproof paper.
4 Store in a cool place for a short period until required for cooking.

*Uses:* Marinading fish, meat and poultry cooked Orly style (page 177).

## PLAIN MARINADE

Yield: 250 ml/1 pt

| | | |
|---|---|---|
| 200 g | mirepoix (page 24) | $\frac{1}{2}$ lb |
| 6 | peppercorns | 6 |
| 200 ml | red or white wine | 8 fl oz |
| 50 ml | wine vinegar | 2 fl oz |

1 Place all the ingredients into a porcelain or stainless steel dish.
2 Add the meat or game and coat with the marinade.

3 Cover with a sheet of lightly oiled greaseproof paper.
4 Store in a cool place.
5 Turn the item/s occasionally during marinading and at the same time baste with the liquor.

*Uses:* Marinading joints or pieces of meat and game prior to roasting, braising or stewing (pages 109, 130).

# MOUSSE AND MOUSSELINE MIXTURES

These are savoury mixtures which are light in texture. They are usually lightly set with gelatine or vegetable gum and are often served as a buffet item or starter course to a meal.

## FISH MOUSSE AND MOUSSELINE MIXTURE

(sole, cod, trout, salmon etc.)
6–8 portions

| | | |
|---|---|---|
| 250 g | poached fish | 10 oz |
| 50 ml | fish stock | 2 fl oz |
| 10 g | leaf gelatine | $\frac{1}{2}$ oz |
| $\frac{1}{4}$ | lemon | $\frac{1}{4}$ |
| 100 ml | *fromage frais | 4 fl oz |
| 50 ml | *half-cream | 2 fl oz |

small pinch salt and cayenne pepper
pinch ground white pepper

**For a traditional recipe, replace the fromage frais and half-cream with double or whipping cream.*

Prepare as for ham and chicken mousse below.

## HAM AND CHICKEN MOUSSE AND MOUSSELINE MIXTURE

Ingredients as for fish mousse, but replace the fish with 250 g/10 oz cooked chicken or ham and use the appropriate stock.

1 Place the gelatine in a bowl of cold water and allow to soften.
2 Squeeze out excess liquid and place the gelatine into a small saucepan.
3 Add the stock and lemon juice, then heat until the gelatine dissolves.
4 Allow to become cold.
5 Remove any skin or bone from the fish, ham or chicken.
6 Cut into pieces and place into a liquidiser (or rub through a sieve).
7 Add the gelatine liquor, fromage frais and half-cream and lightly season.
8 Liquidise to a smooth paste then use as required.

*Note:* When using double cream or whipping cream, liquidise the fish and gelatine mixture then fold through the cream which should be whisked until heavy.

## VEGETABLE MOUSSE AND MOUSSELINE MIXTURE (vegetarian)

6–8 portions

| | | |
|---|---|---|
| 50 g | onion | 2 oz |
| 1 | clove crushed garlic | 1 |
| 50 g | carrot | 2 oz |
| 50 g | leek | 2 oz |
| 1 | medium red pepper | 1 |
| 25 g | mushrooms | 1 oz |
| 1 | medium avocado | 1 |
| 50 g | tofu | 2 oz |
| 100 ml | strong vegetable stock | 4 fl oz |
| 5 g | sodium alginate | $\frac{1}{4}$ oz |
| 100 ml | fromage frais | 4 fl oz |
| 75 ml | half-cream | 3 fl oz |

small pinch salt and cayenne pepper
pinch ground white pepper

1 Wash, peel and roughly chop the onion, carrot, leek and pepper.
2 Wash and slice the mushrooms.
3 Place all the vegetables except the avocado into a saucepan.
4 Add the stock and bring to the boil.
5 Whisk in the sodium alginate.
6 Cover with a lid and simmer until cooked.
7 Allow to cool then place into a liquidiser.
8 Meanwhile, peel the avocado and remove the stone.
9 Add the avocado, tofu and seasoning and liquidise to a smooth paste.
10 Mix through the fromage frais and half-cream and use or mould immediately.

*Note:* When using double cream or whipping cream, liquidise the mixture (step 9) then fold through the cream which should be whisked until heavy.

# PASTRY

## CHOUX PASTE

Yield: 250 g/10 oz approximately

| | | |
|---|---|---|
| 100 ml | water | 4 fl oz |
| 40 g | margarine (or butter) | $1\frac{3}{4}$ oz |
| 60 g | strong flour | $2\frac{1}{2}$ oz |
| $1\frac{1}{2}$–2 | eggs (size 3) | $1\frac{1}{2}$–2 |

1 Place the water and fat into a saucepan.
2 Bring to the boil, allowing the fat to melt.
3 Add all the flour at the one time and mix to form a stiff dough.
4 Cook over a low heat for 1 minute approximately, stirring continuously.
5 Allow to cool.
6 Beat the paste and add the eggs a little at a time. Scrape down the bowl occasionally.
7 Test for consistency – the paste should be a soft dropping consistency with the ability to hold its shape when piped.

## HOT WATER PASTRY

Yield: 350 g/14 oz pastry

**Lower-fat**

| | | |
|---|---|---|
| 200 g | plain flour | 8 oz |
| 50 g | margarine | 2 oz |
| 125 ml | water | $\frac{1}{4}$ pt |

**Traditional**

| | | |
|---|---|---|
| 200 g | plain flour | 8 oz |
| 100 g | lard | 4 oz |
| 60 ml | water | $2\frac{1}{2}$ fl oz |
| | small pinch salt | |

1 Sieve the flour to remove any lumps, and place into a mixing bowl.
2 Place the water and fat (and any salt) into a saucepan and bring to the boil.
3 Make a bay in the flour.
4 Pour in the boiling water and melted fat, stirring constantly to produce a smooth dough. Do not overmix.
5 Use the pastry while warm, i.e. knead, roll out and shape the pastry while warm.

## PUFF PASTRY

**Full puff pastry** (yield: 500 g/$1\frac{1}{4}$ lb)

| | | |
|---|---|---|
| 200 g | strong flour | 8 oz |
| 25 g | cake margarine | 1 oz |
| 125 ml | cold water | $\frac{1}{4}$ pt |
| 175 g | pastry margarine | 7 oz |
| | pinch cream of tartar | |
| | pinch salt | |

**Three-quarter puff pastry** (yield: 475 g/1 lb 3 oz)

| | | |
|---|---|---|
| 200 g | strong flour | 8 oz |
| 15 g | cake margarine | $\frac{1}{2}$ oz |
| 125 ml | cold water | $\frac{1}{4}$ pt |
| 135 g | pastry margarine | $5\frac{1}{2}$ oz |
| | pinch cream of tartar | |
| | pinch salt | |

**Half puff pastry** (yield: 425 g/1 lb 1 oz)

| | | |
|---|---|---|
| 200 g | strong flour | 8 oz |
| 15 g | cake margarine | $\frac{1}{2}$ oz |
| 125 ml | cold water | $\frac{1}{4}$ pt |
| 85 g | pastry margarine | $3\frac{1}{2}$ oz |
| | pinch cream of tartar | |
| | pinch salt | |

1 Sieve together the flour, cream of tartar and salt.
2 Place into a mixing bowl then rub in the cake margarine.
3 Add the water and mix to a smooth dough.
4 Cover and allow to rest for 20–30 minutes.
5 Meanwhile work the pastry margarine until it has the same pliability as the dough.
6 Roll out the dough into a rectangle which is 10 mm/$\frac{1}{2}$ inch in thickness.
7 Divide the prepared margarine into small pieces and place evenly across two-thirds the area of the dough.
8 Fold the uncovered piece of dough on to the top of the margarine, then fold again to completely enclose the margarine.
9 Roll out the dough (towards the open ends) into a rectangle.
10 Fold one end of the dough two-thirds of the way along the rectangle then brush off excess flour and fold the other end on top. This is known as *one single turn.*
11 Repeat the above operation and give one further single turn.
12 Cover and allow to rest for 1 hour approximately.
13 Roll out the dough giving two more single turns then cover and allow to rest for a further 1 hour approximately.
14 Finally give two more single turns (six in total).
15 Cover and allow to rest for 30 minutes before use.

## SHORT PASTRY: SAVOURY

**Lower-fat** (yield: 325 g/13 oz pastry)

| | | |
|---|---|---|
| 200 g | plain flour | 8 oz |
| $2\frac{1}{2}$ g | baking powder | $\frac{1}{2}$ tsp |
| 75 g | margarine | 3 oz |
| 50 ml | water | 2 fl oz |

**Traditional** (yield: 340 g/$12\frac{3}{4}$ oz pastry)

| | | |
|---|---|---|
| 200 g | plain flour | 8 oz |
| 100 g | margarine (or butter) | 4 oz |
| 40 ml | water | $1\frac{3}{4}$ fl oz |
| | small pinch salt | |

1 Sieve the flour with any baking powder.
2 Add the fat and rub in to obtain a sandy texture.
3 Mix together any salt and water.
4 Add to the fat and flour and mix until combined.

## SHORT PASTRY: SWEET

**Lower-fat** (yield: 350 g/14 oz pastry)

| | | |
|---|---|---|
| 200 g | plain flour | 8 oz |
| $2\frac{1}{2}$ g | baking powder | $\frac{1}{2}$ tsp |
| 75 g | margarine | 3 oz |
| 25 g | caster sugar | 1 oz |
| 50 ml | water | 2 fl oz |

**Traditional** (yield: 350 g/14 oz pastry)

| | | |
|---|---|---|
| 200 g | plain flour | 8 oz |
| 100 g | margarine (or butter) | 4 oz |
| 50 g | caster sugar | 2 oz |
| 20 ml | egg (size 3) | $\frac{1}{2}$ |
| | pinch grated lemon zest | |

1 Sieve the flour with any baking powder.
2 Add the fat and rub in, to obtain a sandy texture.
3 Mix together the sugar and egg or water.
4 Add to the fat and flour and mix until combined.

**Lining a flan ring**

8 portions

| | | |
|---|---|---|
| 1 × 200 mm | flan ring | 1 × 8 inch |
| 250 g | short pastry | 9 oz |

1 Lightly grease and flour a baking tray.

2 Lightly grease the flan ring if using the lower-fat pastry, and place onto the baking tray.
3 Mould the pastry into a ball.
4 Roll out the ball into a round shape which is 3–4 mm/$\frac{3}{16}$ inch in thickness and 30 mm/1$\frac{1}{4}$ inch larger than the flan ring.
5 Trim the pastry to the above size if necessary.
6 Carefully lift up the pastry by rolling it round the rolling pin; then unroll it loosely over the flan ring.
7 Shape the pastry into the flan ring ensuring the sides are lined.
8 Trim off excess pastry by rolling the pin across the top of the ring.
9 Lightly press up the top edge of the pastry with the fingers until even in thickness and just higher than the ring.
10 Decorate the top of the pastry by crimping with your fingers or some pastry tweezers.

**Baking empty flan cases (baking blind)**

1 Line the flan ring as described above.
2 Pierce the base with a fork or docker.
3 Line with a circle of greaseproof paper. Cover the base and sides with the paper.
4 Fill with dried beans or peas.
5 Bake at 200 °C/390 °F until three-quarters cooked, i.e. 20–25 minutes.
6 Remove the beans and paper.
7 Remove the flan ring and wipe clean with a dry cloth.
8 Return to the oven and allow to bake until cooked: a further 10 minutes approximately.

*Note:* The above procedure is time-consuming, especially when several flans are baked at the same time. The following practice is recommended in a professional situation.

1 Place the flan without any beans or paper into the oven.
2 During the initial stages of baking, regularly inspect the flan.
3 When any movement of the pastry has occurred, press back into shape with the hand (covered with a clean dry cloth).
4 Repeat the above procedure until the pastry dries out and maintains its shape.
5 Remove the flan ring and allow to bake until cooked.

## WHOLEMEAL PASTRY

**Lower-fat** (yield: 335 g/13$\frac{1}{2}$ oz pastry)

| | | |
|---|---|---|
| 200 g | wholemeal flour | 8 oz |
| 2$\frac{1}{2}$ g | baking powder | $\frac{1}{2}$ tsp |
| 75 g | margarine | 3 oz |
| 60 ml | water | 2$\frac{1}{2}$ fl oz |

**Traditional** (yield: 350 g/14 oz pastry)

| | | |
|---|---|---|
| 200 g | wholemeal flour | 8 oz |
| 100 g | margarine (or butter) | 4 oz |
| 50 ml | water | 2 fl oz |
| | small pinch salt | |

1 Thoroughly mix together the flour and any baking powder.
2 Add the fat and rub in, to obtain a sandy texture.
3 Mix together any salt with the water.
4 Add to the fat and flour and mix until combined.

# SALPICONS OR SAVOURY FILLINGS

These are savoury mixtures which consist of pieces of cooked fish, shellfish, meat, poultry, game or vegetables bound with a sauce. *Uses:* A savoury filling for bouchées, vol-au-vent, crepes etc.

## SALPICON OF CHICKEN

4 portions

| | | |
|---|---|---|
| 200 g | cooked chicken (boneless) | 8 oz |
| 125 ml | low-fat chicken velouté | $\frac{1}{4}$ pt |
| 25 ml | fromage frais (or cream) | 1 fl oz |

1 Skin the chicken then cut it into small cubes.
2 Place the sauce in a saucepan and bring to the boil.
3 Add the chicken and heat gently but thoroughly.
4 Add the fromage frais or cream.

## SALPICON OF CHICKEN AND MUSHROOM

Prepare as above but cook 50 g/2 oz diced mushrooms in the saucepan with a little skimmed milk before adding the sauce. *Note:* It is traditional practice to sweat the mushrooms in a little butter before adding the sauce.

## SALPICON OF GAME

4 portions

| | | |
|---|---|---|
| 200 g | cooked game (boneless) | 8 oz |
| 125 ml | low-fat brown sauce or jus lié | $\frac{1}{4}$ pt |
| 25 ml | port | 1 fl oz |
| 2 g | redcurrant jelly | 1 tsp |

1 Skin the game then cut it into small cubes.
2 Place the sauce or jus lié, port and redcurrant jelly into a saucepan and bring to the boil.
3 Add the game and heat gently but thoroughly.

## SALPICON OF SEAFOOD

This is made using a mixture of fish and shellfish. The fish should be firm-cooking types such as monkfish, brill or turbot, while the shellfish could be shelled prawns, shrimps, scampi, mussels or pieces of lobster.

4 portions

| | | |
|---|---|---|
| 100 g | fish | 4 oz |
| 100 g | cooked shellfish | 4 oz |
| 10 ml | fish stock | $\frac{1}{2}$ fl oz |
| 25 ml | white wine | 1 fl oz |
| 125 ml | low-fat fish velouté | $\frac{1}{4}$ pt |
| 25 ml | fromage frais (or cream) | 1 fl oz |

1 Cut the fish into pieces, then place into a saucepan.
2 Add the fish stock and wine, cover with a lid and lightly cook.

3 Add the shellfish and thoroughly reheat.
4 Add the sauce, heat through and finish with the fromage frais or cream.

### VEGETARIAN SALPICON

4 portions

| | | |
|---|---|---|
| 5 g | margarine | $\frac{1}{4}$ oz |
| 25 g | chopped onion | 1 oz |
| 1 | clove crushed garlic | 1 |
| 2 | medium tomatoes | 2 |
| 50 g | diced red and green pepper | 2 oz |
| 50 g | cooked mung beans | 2 oz |
| 50 g | lightly cooked lentils | 2 oz |
| 25 g | sweetcorn kernels | |
| | pinch ground cumin | |
| | small pinch cayenne pepper | |
| 3–4 | drops rich soy sauce | 3–4 |

1 Heat the margarine in a saucepan then add the onion and garlic.
2 Cover with a lid and lightly cook.
3 Add the cumin and cayenne pepper and cook for a short period without burning.
4 Cut the tomatoes into pieces and add to the saucepan.
5 Add the soy sauce and peppers and lightly cook.
6 Add the remaining ingredients and thoroughly reheat.

## SAVOURY SAUCES: HOT

### APPLE PULP/APPLE SAUCE
***SAUCE AUX POMMES***

Yield: 1 litre/2 pt

| | | |
|---|---|---|
| 2 kg | cooking apples | 4 lb |
| 75 g | sugar | 3 oz |
| | juice of 1 lemon | |
| 200 ml | water | 8 fl oz |
| (50 g) | (margarine or butter) | (2 oz) |

1 Peel, core and wash the apples.
2 Cut into slices or pieces and place into a suitable saucepan.
3 Add the sugar, lemon juice and water.
4 Cover with a lid and place over a low heat.
5 Allow to cook to a soft pulp stirring occasionally to prevent burning.
6 Leave as a pulp, liquidise or pass through a sieve.
7 If required, reheat in a clean pan and blend through any recipe butter.

### BOLONAISE SAUCE (lower-fat)

Yield: 1 litre/2 pt

| | | |
|---|---|---|
| 50 g | red lentils | 2 oz |
| 200 g | finely chopped onion | 8 oz |
| 15 g | crushed garlic | $\frac{3}{4}$ oz |
| 400 g | lean minced beef | 1 lb |
| 25 g | tomato purée | 1 oz |
| 500 ml | lower-fat brown sauce (page 30) | 1 pt |
| | small pinch salt and pepper | |

1 Place the lentils in a saucepan and cover with cold water.
2 Bring to the boil and simmer until soft.
3 Refresh under cold running water, then drain and place aside.
4 Place the minced beef, onion and garlic in a saucepan.
5 Dry-fry stirring occasionally to avoid sticking or lumps forming.
6 Add the tomato purée and brown sauce and bring to the boil.
7 Allow to simmer until almost cooked (20–30 minutes) stirring occasionally to avoid burning. Also skim off any surface fat during cooking.
8 Add the lentils and complete the cooking: a further 15 minutes approximately. *Note:* Add a little extra stock if the sauce becomes too thick during cooking.

### BOLONAISE SAUCE (traditional)

Yield: 1 litre/2 pt

| | | |
|---|---|---|
| 100 g | margarine (or butter) | 4 oz |
| 200 g | finely chopped onion | 8 oz |
| 15 g | crushed garlic | $\frac{3}{4}$ oz |
| 500 g | minced beef | 1 lb |
| 25 g | tomato purée | 1 oz |
| 500 ml | traditional brown sauce (page 30) | 1 pt |
| | small pinch salt and pepper | |

1 Heat the butter in a saucepan.
2 Add the onion and garlic and cook until lightly coloured.
3 Add the minced beef and also cook until lightly coloured.
4 Stir in the tomato purée then add the brown sauce.
5 Allow to simmer until cooked: 45 minutes approximately.
6 During cooking, stir occasionally to prevent burning and skim as required. Top up with a little extra stock during cooking if necessary.

**Bolonaise and vegetable sauce**

Reduce the minced beef in the main recipe by half and replace with vegetables (carrot, turnip, celery, pepper, courgette) which have been cut into small cubes. Also add a suitable variety of cooked small beans (e.g. mung beans) to the sauce to increase the fibre content.

### BREAD SAUCE ***SAUCE PAIN***

Yield: 1 litre/2 pt

| | | |
|---|---|---|
| 1 litre | skimmed milk (or whole milk) | 2 pt |
| 1 | small studded onion (page 24) | 1 |
| 125 g | white breadcrumbs | 5 oz |
| | small pinch salt and pepper | |
| (50 g) | (margarine or butter) | (2 oz) |

1 Place the milk and studded onion into a saucepan.
2 Cover with a lid and bring to the boil.
3 Remove from the boil and keep hot for 10–15 minutes to infuse the flavour from the studded onion.

4 Sprinkle in the breadcrumbs, stirring constantly to avoid forming lumps.
5 Slowly simmer for 2–3 minutes, stirring frequently.
6 Remove the studded onion.
7 Lightly season (and blend through any margarine or butter).

## BROWN SAUCE: LOWER-FAT ESPAGNOLE

Yield: 1 litre/2 pt

| | | |
|---|---|---|
| 15 ml | oil | $\frac{3}{4}$ fl oz |
| 100 g | onion | 4 oz |
| 100 g | carrot | 4 oz |
| 50 g | celery | 2 oz |
| 50 g | leek | 2 oz |
| 900 ml | brown stock | $1\frac{3}{4}$ pt |
| 50 g | tomato purée | 2 oz |
| | sprig of thyme, bay leaf and parsley stalks | |
| | *Thickening paste:* | |
| 75 g | wholemeal flour | 3 oz |
| 100 ml | cold brown stock | 4 fl oz |
| | blackjack | |

1 Wash, peel and roughly chop the vegetables.
2 Heat the oil in a suitable saucepan.
3 Add the vegetables and herbs and shallow-fry until golden brown.
4 Add the stock, then mix in the tomato purée.
5 Bring to the boil then simmer for 45 minutes approximately.
6 Prepare the thickening paste:
   **a)** Place the flour into a small bowl.
   **b)** Add two-thirds of the cold stock and whisk to a smooth thick mixture.
   **c)** Add the remaining stock and whisk.
7 Whisk the paste into the boiling stock and vegetables and bring back to the boil.
8 Allow to simmer for 20–30 minutes.
9 Check the colour and add a little blackjack if necessary.
10 Strain into a clean pan.

## BROWN SAUCE: TRADITIONAL ESPAGNOLE

Yield: 1 litre/2 pt

| | | |
|---|---|---|
| 75 g | lard or dripping | 3 oz |
| 125 g | flour | 5 oz |
| 50 g | tomato purée | 2 oz |
| $1\frac{1}{2}$–2 litre | brown stock | 3–4 pt |
| 15 g | lard or dripping | $\frac{3}{4}$ oz |
| 100 g | onion | 4 oz |
| 100 g | carrot | 4 oz |
| 50 g | celery | 2 oz |
| 50 g | leek | 2 oz |
| | sprig of thyme, bay leaf and parsley stalks | |

1 Wash, peel and roughly chop the vegetables.
2 Melt the fat in a suitable saucepan.
3 Stir in the flour.
4 Cook to a golden brown colour stirring frequently.
5 Allow to cool: taking care as the roux will be very hot.
6 Stir in the tomato purée.
7 Add three-quarters of the stock gradually, stirring until smooth with each addition of liquid.
8 Bring to the boil.
9 Meanwhile, shallow-fry the vegetables and herbs in the lard or dripping until golden brown.
10 Add the vegetables to the sauce and slowly simmer for 3–4 hours.
11 During cooking skim off surface fat and top up with the additional stock as required.
12 Strain into a clean pan.

**Demi-glace** (refined espagnole sauce)
Prepare espagnole sauce above and add extra rich brown stock in stages (1 litre/2 pt in total). Allow the sauce to simmer gently and reduce back to the desired consistency.

## BROWN SAUCE: JUS LIÉ (light consistency)

Yield: 1 litre/2 pt

| | | |
|---|---|---|
| 200 g | small veal bones | $\frac{1}{2}$ lb |
| 100 g | onion | 4 oz |
| 100 g | carrot | 4 oz |
| 50 g | celery | 2 oz |
| 50 g | leek | 2 oz |
| 1 litre | brown stock | 2 pt |
| 25 g | tomato purée | 1 oz |
| | sprig of thyme, bay leaf and parsley stalks | |
| | *Thickening:* | |
| 20 g | arrowroot | $\frac{3}{4}$ oz |
| 50 ml | cold water | 2 fl oz |

1 Place the bones into a roasting tray.
2 Cook in a hot oven until golden brown.
3 Wash, peel and roughly chop the vegetables.
4 Add the vegetables and herbs to the roasting tray and continue cooking until coloured.
5 Remove the bones and vegetables from the tray and place into a suitable saucepan leaving behind any fat.
6 Add the stock, then mix in the tomato purée.
7 Bring to the boil and simmer for 2–3 hours. Top up with additional stock as required.
8 Dilute the arrowroot in the cold water then stir into the boiling mixture.
9 Simmer for 2–3 minutes then strain into a clean pan.

### DERIVATIVES OF BROWN SAUCE AND JUS LIÉ

(1 litre/2 pt)

**Bordelaise sauce *sauce bordelaise***
**a)** Place 100 g/4 oz chopped onion, sprig of thyme, bay leaf and a good pinch mignonette pepper into a saucepan.
**b)** Add 250 ml/$\frac{1}{2}$ pt red wine and boil down quickly to reduce the excess liquid.
**c)** Add the brown sauce and simmer for 15–20 minutes.
**d)** Strain.

**Charcutière sauce** ***sauce charcutière***

a) Place 100 g/4 oz chopped onion and a pinch of mignonette pepper into a saucepan.
b) Add 100 ml/4 fl oz each of vinegar and white wine.
c) Boil down quickly to reduce the liquid, then add the brown sauce.
d) Add 2 tsp English mustard diluted in a little water and simmer for 15–20 minutes.
e) Strain, then garnish with 100 g/4 oz gherkins cut into thin strips.

**Devil sauce** ***sauce diable***

a) Place 100 g/4 oz chopped onion and good pinch each of mignonette and cayenne pepper into a saucepan.
b) Add 100 ml/4 fl oz each of vinegar and white wine.
c) Boil down quickly to reduce the liquid, then add the brown sauce.
d) Simmer for 15–20 minutes then strain.

**Honey mustard sauce** ***sauce au miel et moutarde***

a) Add 50–75 g/2–3 oz honey and the juice from half a lemon to the brown sauce after straining.
b) Allow to simmer for 2–3 minutes.
c) Add enough grainy mustard to produce a good flavour (50–75 g/2–3 oz approximately).

**Italian sauce** ***sauce Italienne***

a) Shallow-fry 100 g/4 oz finely chopped onion in 10 g/$\frac{1}{2}$ oz margarine (or butter) until soft.
b) Add 200 g/8 oz chopped mushrooms and cook for 4–5 minutes.
c) Add 200 g/8 oz tomato concassées (page 25), 100 g/4 oz chopped lean ham and the brown sauce.
d) Bring to the boil and simmer for 2–3 minutes.
e) Garnish with chopped fresh mixed herbs.

**Lyonnaise sauce** ***sauce Lyonnaise***

a) Shallow-fry 400 g/1 lb sliced onion in 25 g/1 oz margarine (or butter) until golden brown.
b) Add 100 ml/4 fl oz each of vinegar and white wine.
c) Boil down quickly to reduce by two-thirds then add the brown sauce.
d) Simmer for 3–4 minutes then strain.

**Madeira sauce** ***sauce Madère***

Place the brown sauce into a saucepan and add 125 ml/$\frac{1}{4}$ pt Madeira wine then reduce to a coating consistency.

**Piquante sauce** ***sauce piquante***

Prepare devil sauce (above) and garnish when strained with 150 g/6 oz chopped gherkins, 50 g/2 oz chopped capers and a good pinch of fresh mixed herbs.

**Reform sauce** ***sauce Reform***

a) Shallow-fry 250 g/10 oz mirepoix (page 24) in a saucepan with a little oil (10 ml/$\frac{1}{2}$ fl oz approximately).
b) Add 100 ml/4 fl oz vinegar and a good pinch of mignonette pepper.
c) Boil down quickly to reduce by two-thirds then add the brown sauce.
d) Simmer for 30 minutes approximately then strain.
e) Add 75 g/3 oz redcurrant jelly.
f) Garnish the sauce with 50 g/2 oz each of cooked egg white, mushrooms, beetroot, tongue and gherkins all cut into thin strips. *Traditionally:* Strips of truffle are also added.

## CRANBERRY PULP/CRANBERRY SAUCE
### *SAUCE AUX AIRELLES*

Yield: 1 litre/2 pt

| | | |
|---|---|---|
| 750 g | cranberries | 1 lb 14 oz |
| 200 g | sugar | 8 oz |
| 500 ml | water | 1 pt |

1 Remove any stalks or foreign bodies from the cranberries then wash and drain.
2 Place into a tin-lined or stainless steel saucepan.
3 Add the sugar and water and bring to the boil.
4 Allow to cook until tender (30–40 minutes), stirring occasionally to prevent burning.
5 Either leave as cooked, liquidise or pass through a sieve.

**Gooseberry pulp/Gooseberry sauce**
***sauce aux groseille à maquereau***

Yield: 1 litre/2 pt

Prepare as for cranberry sauce (above) using 750 g/1 lb 14 oz gooseberries, 125 g/5 oz sugar, the juice of 1 lemon and 250 ml/$\frac{1}{2}$ pt water.

## CURRY SAUCE *SAUCE KARI* (roux-thickened)

Yield: 1 litre/2 pt

| | | |
|---|---|---|
| 100 g | margarine (or butter) | 4 oz |
| 200 g | finely chopped onion | 8 oz |
| 1 | clove crushed garlic | 1 |
| 25 g | curry powder | 1 oz |
| 100 g | flour (preferably wholemeal | 4 oz |
| 25 g | tomato purée | 1 oz |
| 900 ml | brown stock | $1\frac{3}{4}$ pt |
| 25 g | dessicated coconut | 1 oz |
| 25 g | chopped sultanas | 1 oz |
| 25 g | mango chutney | 1 oz |
| 50 g | chopped cooking apple | 2 oz |

1 Melt the margarine (or butter) in a saucepan.
2 Add the onion and garlic and cook for 4–5 minutes.
3 Mix in the curry powder and cook over a low heat for 1–2 minutes. Do not burn the spice.
4 Stir through the flour and cook out over a low heat for 4 minutes approximately.
5 Mix in the tomato purée.
6 Add the stock gradually, stirring until smooth with each addition of liquid.
7 Bring to the boil, then add the coconut, sultanas, chutney and chopped cooking apples.
8 Simmer until cooked (45 minutes approximately). During cooking, skim off surface fat as necessary and stir occasionally to prevent burning.
9 Either leave plain, liquidise or pass through a strainer.

## CURRY SAUCE (vegetarian, low fat)

Yield: 1 litre/2 pt

| | | |
|---|---|---|
| 10 ml | oil | $\frac{1}{2}$ fl oz |
| 200 g | chopped onion | 8 oz |
| 6 | cloves garlic | 6 |
| 5 g | ground cumin | 1 tsp |
| 5 g | ground coriander | 1 tsp |
| 5 g | garam masala | 1 tsp |
| 10 g | paprika | 2 tsp |
| 1 | medium chopped chilli pepper | 1 |
| 10 g | chopped root ginger | $\frac{1}{2}$ oz |
| 75 g | peeled sliced potato | 3 oz |
| 75 g | peeled sliced turnip or swede | 3 oz |
| 100 g | sliced carrot | 4 oz |
| 2 | medium sliced tomatoes | 2 |
| 500 ml | vegetable stock | 1 pt |
| | good pinch fresh chopped coriander leaves | |

1 Lightly cook the onion and garlic in the oil.
2 Add the spices, chopped chilli pepper and root ginger and cook over a low heat without burning.
3 Add the potato, turnip or swede, carrot, tomatoes and stock then bring to the boil.
4 Allow to simmer for 45 minutes approximately.
5 Liquidise or purée the mixture to produce a thickened sauce.
6 Adjust consistency with additional stock if necessary.
7 Add the chopped coriander leaves.

## HARD BUTTER SAUCES (compound butters)

These are flavoured butters which are allowed to melt over hot food. They have a very high fat content and would not, therefore, be included in a health-conscious menu. *Uses:* Melted over grilled fish, meat and poultry dishes.

**Parsley butter *beurre maître-d'hôtel***

Yield: 100 g/4 oz

| | | |
|---|---|---|
| 100 g | butter | 4 oz |
| | squeeze lemon juice | |
| 5 g | chopped parsley | $\frac{1}{4}$ oz |
| | pinch ground pepper | |
| | small pinch cayenne pepper | |

Prepare using the base method below.

**Garlic butter *beurre d'ail***

Yield: 100 g/4 oz

| | | |
|---|---|---|
| 100 g | butter | 4 oz |
| 3–4 | medium cloves crushed garlic | 3–4 |

Prepare using the base method below.

**Base method for preparing compound butters:**

1 Lightly cream the butter.
2 Add the flavouring ingredients, e.g. crushed garlic, lemon juice, chopped parsley, spices etc.
3 Mix together until combined.
4 Place on to a small sheet of dampened greaseproof paper.
5 Roll up to form a neat cylinder: 20 mm/$\frac{3}{4}$ inch diameter.
6 Place in a refrigerator and allow to harden.
7 Remove the paper and cut into rondels: 5 mm/$\frac{1}{4}$ inch thick.
8 Place on top of the hot food when serving or serve separately in a sauceboat of ice water.

## HOLLANDAISE SAUCE

Hollandaise sauce and all its derivatives have a very high fat content and would not, therefore, be included on a health-conscious menu. There is also a risk of food poisoning if the sauce is cooked incorrectly.

Yield: 500 ml/1 pt

| | | |
|---|---|---|
| 500 g | butter | 1 lb |
| 50 ml | vinegar | 2 fl oz |
| 8 | crushed peppercorns | 8 |
| 4 | egg yolks (size 3) | 4 |
| 50 ml | cold water | 2 fl oz |
| | small pinch cayenne pepper | |
| | squeeze lemon juice | |

1 Place the butter in a small pot and sit it in a bain-marie.
2 Allow to melt and become clear.
3 Place the vinegar and crushed peppercorns into a sauteuse.
4 Bring to the boil and reduce until almost completely evaporated. Allow to cool slightly.
5 Prepare a sabayon:
   **a)** Add the cold water and egg yolks into the sauteuse and whisk together.
   **b)** Place the sauteuse in the bain-marie and whisk continuously until the egg mixture becomes very light and thick in consistency (ribbon stage).
6 Remove the sabayon from the heat and continue whisking.
7 Slowly add the warm clear butter in stages while whisking continuously.
8 Lightly season with the cayenne pepper then whisk through the lemon juice.
9 Pass through muslin into a clean bowl and keep warm.

*Note:* To avoid the procedure of passing the sauce through muslin:

**a)** Reduce the vinegar and crushed peppercorns by two-thirds.
**b)** Remove from the heat and add the cold water.
**c)** Strain the liquid into the sauteuse.
**d)** Add the egg yolks and proceed as stated (from step 5).

**DERIVATIVES OF HOLLANDAISE SAUCE:**

**Béarnaise sauce *sauce béarnaise***

Prepare as for hollandaise sauce but:

a) Use tarragon vinegar.
b) Add 25 g/1 oz finely chopped shallots and 10 g/$\frac{1}{2}$ oz chopped tarragon stalks to the vinegar and peppercorns at step 3.
c) After straining the sauce, add chopped fresh tarragon and chervil.

**Mousseline sauce *sauce mousseline***

Prepare as for hollandaise sauce and fold whipped cream (50 ml/2 fl oz) through the strained sauce when serving. Alternatively, place a quenelle of whipped cream on top of hollandaise sauce served in a sauceboat (to be folded through the sauce at table).

**Paloise sauce *sauce paloise***

Prepare as for bearnaise sauce but use plain vinegar and replace the tarragon with mint. Finish with chopped mint.

## TOMATO SAUCE (lower-fat)

Yield: 1 litre/2 pt

| | | |
|---|---|---|
| 10 g | margarine | $\frac{1}{2}$ oz |
| 1 | clove crushed garlic | 1 |
| 100 g | onion | 4 oz |
| 100 g | carrot | 4 oz |
| 50 g | celery | 2 oz |
| 50 g | leek | 2 oz |
| 100 g | tomato purée | 4 oz |
| 750 ml | ham or vegetable stock | $1\frac{3}{4}$ pt |
| | sprig of thyme, bay leaf and parsley stalks | |
| | *Thickening paste:* | |
| 100 g | *flour | 4 oz |
| 125 ml | cold chicken or vegetable stock | $\frac{1}{4}$ pt |

**Preferably wholemeal.*

1 Wash, peel and roughly chop the vegetables.
2 Heat the margarine in a suitable saucepan.
3 Add the vegetables and herbs and shallow-fry until golden brown.
4 Add the stock, then mix in the tomato purée.
5 Bring to the boil then allow to simmer for 45 minutes approximately. Skim during cooking.
6 Prepare the thickening paste:
   a) Place the flour into a small bowl.
   b) Add two-thirds of the cold stock and whisk to a smooth thick mixture.
   c) Add the remaining cold stock and whisk together.
7 Whisk the paste into the boiling stock and vegetables and bring back to the boil.
8 Allow to simmer for 20–30 minutes.
9 Remove the thyme and bay leaf, then liquidise or strain into a clean pan.

## TOMATO SAUCE (traditional, roux-thickened)

Yield: 1 litre/2 pt

| | | |
|---|---|---|
| 100 g | margarine (or butter) | 4 oz |
| 100 g | flour | 4 oz |
| 1 | clove crushed garlic | 1 |
| 100 g | onion | 4 oz |
| 100 g | carrot | 4 oz |
| 50 g | celery | 2 oz |
| 50 g | leek | 2 oz |
| 100 g | tomato purée | 4 oz |
| 1 litre | ham or vegetable stock | 2 pt |
| | sprig of thyme, bay leaf and parsley stalks | |

1 Wash, peel and roughly chop the vegetables.
2 Melt the margarine (or butter) in a saucepan.
3 Add the vegetables and herbs and cook for 4–5 minutes.
4 Mix in the flour and cook over a low heat for 4–5 minutes.
5 Mix in the tomato purée.
6 Slowly blend in the hot stock adding a little at a time.
7 Bring to the boil and slowly simmer until the vegetables are cooked (45 minutes approximately).
8 During cooking, skim off any surface fat and impurities.
9 Remove the thyme and bay leaf.
10 Pass the sauce through a soup machine or liquidiser.
11. Place into a clean pan and reboil.

## WHITE SAUCE: LOWER-FAT BÉCHAMEL

Yield: 1 litre/2 pt

| | | |
|---|---|---|
| 900 ml | skimmed milk | $1\frac{3}{4}$ pt |
| 40 g | margarine | $1\frac{3}{4}$ oz |
| 1 | small studded onion (page 24) | 1 |
| | small pinch salt and white pepper | |
| | *Thickening paste:* | |
| 75 g | plain flour | 3 oz |
| 25 ml | cold skimmed milk | $\frac{1}{4}$ pt |

1 Place the milk, margarine and studded onion into a saucepan and bring to the boil.
2 Prepare the thickening paste:
   a) Place the flour into a small bowl.
   b) Add two-thirds of the cold milk and whisk to a smooth thick mixture.
   c) Add the remaining milk and whisk together.
3 Whisk the paste into the boiling milk and bring back to the boil.
4 Allow to simmer for 6–8 minutes then lightly season.
5 Strain into a clean pan if required.

## WHITE SAUCE: TRADITIONAL BÉCHAMEL

Yield: 1 litre/2 pt

| | | |
|---|---|---|
| 1 litre | milk | 2 pt |
| 1 | studded onion (page 24) | 1 |
| 75 g | margarine (or butter) | 3 oz |
| 75 g | plain flour | 3 oz |
| | small pinch salt and white pepper | |

1 Place the milk and studded onion into a saucepan and bring to the boil.
2 Melt the margarine or butter in a saucepan.
3 Mix in the flour then cook over a low heat for 4–5 minutes. Do not allow to colour.
4 Add the milk gradually, stirring until smooth at each addition of liquid.
5 Bring to the boil then add the studded onion.
6 Slowly simmer for 6–8 minutes then season lightly.
7 Strain into a clean pan if required.

## WHITE SAUCE: VELOUTÉ

These are white sauces made with white stocks e.g. chicken, fish, mutton, veal or vegetable stocks.

**Preparing velouté sauces:**
Prepare as for lower-fat or traditional béchamel sauce but replace the milk with the appropriate stock and omit the studded onion.

### DERIVATIVES OF BÉCHAMEL SAUCE (1 litre/2 pt)

**Anchovy sauce** ***sauce aux anchois***
Add enough anchovy essence to produce the flavour required.

**Cheese sauce** (see also Mornay sauce)
Add 50 g/2 oz grated mature cheddar cheese (or 100 g/4 oz cheese) into the hot béchamel and stir until melted.

**Cream sauce** ***sauce crème***
Add 100 ml/4 fl oz half cream (or 200 ml/8 fl oz cream) into the hot sauce.

**Egg sauce** ***sauce aux oeufs***
Add a small dice of 2 hard-boiled eggs (or 4 hard-boiled eggs) into the sauce.

**Mornay sauce** ***sauce Mornay***
Prepare cheese sauce (above) but use equal quantities of parmesan and gruyère cheese in place of cheddar.

**Mustard sauce** ***sauce moutarde***
Add enough diluted English mustard to produce the flavour required.

**Onion sauce** ***sauce aux oignons***
Cook 200 g/8 oz diced onion under cover in a little milk, then add to the finished sauce.

**Parsley sauce** ***sauce persil***
Add chopped parsley to garnish the sauce.

**Soubise sauce** ***sauce Soubise***
Prepare as for onion sauce but strain out the onions after developing the flavour.

### DERIVATIVES OF VELOUTÉ SAUCES (1 litre/2 pt)

**Aurore sauce** ***sauce aurore***
Prepare suprême sauce (next column) but add 50 g/2 oz tomato purée to the sauce when cooking.

**Caper sauce** ***sauce aux câpres***
Add a garnish of 75 g/3 oz whole capers to mutton velouté after straining.

**Hungarian sauce** ***sauce Hongroise***
1 Place 200 ml/8 fl oz white wine into a saucepan.
2 Add 200 g/8 oz finely chopped onion and 25 g/1 oz paprika.
3 Quickly boil down to remove excess liquid then add chicken velouté.
4 Simmer for 2–3 minutes.

**Suprême sauce** ***sauce suprême***
Add white mushroom trimmings (50–75 g/2–3 oz) and the juice of half a lemon to a chicken velouté when cooking. Strain and add 50 ml/2 fl oz half-cream.

# SAVOURY SAUCES: COLD

## CUCUMBER RAITA

Yield: 1 litre/2 pt approximately

| | | |
|---|---|---|
| 1 | large cucumber | 1 |
| 3–4 | peeled cloves garlic | 3–4 |
| 1 | small chilli pepper (seeds removed) | 1 |
| 5 g | grated lemon zest | 1 tsp |
| 10 ml | lemon juice | $\frac{1}{2}$ fl oz |
| 350 ml | low-fat natural yogurt | 14 fl oz |
| | pinch ground black pepper | |
| | chopped fresh coriander leaves and/or chopped fresh mint leaves | |

1 Cut the cucumber into pieces and place into a liquidiser.
2 Add the garlic, chilli pepper, lemon zest and juice and one-quarter of the yogurt.
3 Liquidise the ingredients then pour into a bowl.
4 Add the remaining yogurt and blend together.
5 Lightly season with the black pepper then mix through the chopped coriander and/or mint leaves.

(*Uses:* salad dressing and tandoori dishes)

## FROMAGE FRAIS DRESSING: AVOCADO

Yield: 1 litre/2 pt approximately

| | | |
|---|---|---|
| 4 | ripe avocados | 4 |
| 125 g | cooked peas | 5 oz |
| 25 g | peeled sliced onion | 1 oz |
| 5 g | chopped parsley | 1 tsp |
| 25 ml | lemon juice | 1 fl oz |
| 350 ml | fromage frais | 14 fl oz |
| | small pinch pepper and cayenne pepper | |

1 Peel the avocados and remove the stones.
2 Place all the ingredients into a liquidiser.
3 Liquidise to a thick purée.
4 Adjust consistency with fromage frais if required.

**Lemon or lime dressing/dip**
Add a squeeze of lemon or lime juice to low-fat fromage frais.

## MAYONNAISE SAUCE
### *SAUCE MAYONNAISE*

Mayonnaise has a very high fat content and therefore should be replaced by a lower-fat dressing wherever possible.

Yield: 1$\frac{1}{4}$ litre/2$\frac{1}{4}$ pt

| | | |
|---|---|---|
| 125 ml | *pasteurised egg yolks | $\frac{1}{4}$ pt |
| $\frac{1}{2}$ tsp | dry mustard | $\frac{1}{2}$ tsp |
| 75 ml | vinegar | 3 fl oz |
| 1 litre | olive oil | 2 pt |
| | squeeze lemon juice | |
| | small pinch salt and white pepper | |

**The alternative use of shell (fresh) eggs to prepare mayonnaise may result in salmonella food poisoning.*

1 Place the liquid yolk into a mixing bowl.
2 Add the mustard, salt and pepper and three-quarters of the vinegar then whisk together.
3 Slowly add the oil in stages while whisking continuously. If the sauce becomes too thick, adjust the consistency with the remaining vinegar. The sauce should be thick enough to hold its shape when placed on a serving spoon.
4 Add the lemon juice and use as soon as possible.

**Important points:**

- Using different types of oil and mustards will produce a variety of flavours.
- Store mayonnaise at a temperature between 5–8 °C/40–45 °F.
- Curdled mayonnaise may be corrected by whisking it slowly into a small quantity of pasteurised egg yolk or boiling water.
- Reasons for curdled mayonnaise:
  **a)** Oil too cold.
  **b)** Oil cloudy.
  **c)** Oil added too quickly.
  **d)** Insufficient whisking when adding the oil.

## LOWER-FAT DRESSING

Blend together equal quantities of mayonnaise and thick-set low-fat yogurt. This may produce a sauce with a thin consistency.

### DERIVATIVES OF MAYONNAISE AND LOWER-FAT DRESSING

Yield: 1 litre/2 pt

**Andalouse sauce** ***sauce andalouse***

Add 125 ml/$\frac{1}{4}$ pt tomato ketchup to 900 ml/1$\frac{3}{4}$ pt lower-fat dressing or mayonnaise. Garnish with 100 g/4 oz diced red pimento.

**Herb sauce/dip**

Add a selection of fresh, chopped herbs e.g. chopped chives, chervil, tarragon and parsley to the lower-fat dressing or mayonnaise then season with ground black pepper.

**Marie-Rose sauce** ***sauce Marie-Rose***

Add the following ingredients to 900 ml/1$\frac{3}{4}$ pt lower-fat dressing or basic mayonnaise and mix together:

**a)** 4–5 drops Worcester sauce.
**b)** 125 ml/$\frac{1}{4}$ pt tomato ketchup.
**c)** Good pinch chopped parsley.
**d)** Optional: whipped cream (100 ml/4 fl oz) and/or 25 g/1 oz finely chopped shallot.

**Remoulade sauce** ***sauce rémoulade***

Add the following ingredients to 750 ml/1$\frac{1}{2}$ pt lower-fat dressing or basic mayonnaise and mix together:

**a)** 1–2 dessert spoons French mustard.
**b)** 4–5 drops anchovy essence.
**c)** 200 g/8 oz chopped gherkins.
**d)** 100 g/4 oz chopped capers.
**e)** Good pinch chopped chervil and tarragon.

**Tartare sauce** ***sauce tartare***

Add the following ingredients to 750 ml/1$\frac{1}{2}$ pt lower-fat dressing or basic mayonnaise and mix together:

**a)** 200 g/8 oz chopped gherkins.
**b)** 100 g/4 oz chopped capers.
**c)** Good pinch chopped parsley.

## MINT SAUCE

Yield: 500 ml/1 pt

| | | |
|---|---|---|
| 100 g | fresh mint leaves | 4 oz |
| 25 g | caster sugar | 1 oz |
| 450 ml | vinegar | 18 fl oz |

1 Pick and wash the leaves, then dry them with a cloth.
2 Chop the leaves together with the sugar then place into a bowl.
3 Add the vinegar and allow to stand for 30–40 minutes.

*Uses:* Accompaniment to roast lamb.

## VINAIGRETTE
## (basic salad dressing: lower-fat recipe)

A lower-fat vinaigrette may be made by reversing the traditional formula (below). Use 3 parts lemon juice or vinegar to 1 part oil.

Yield: 400 ml/16 fl oz

| | | |
|---|---|---|
| 300 ml | lemon juice or vinegar | 12 fl oz |
| 100 ml | oil | 4 fl oz |
| 1 dsp | French mustard | 1 dsp |
| | small pinch salt and pepper | |

Place all the ingredients in a mixing bowl and thoroughly whisk together. Also whisk before service.

## VINAIGRETTE
## (basic salad dressing: traditional recipe)

Use 3 parts oil to 1 part lemon juice/vinegar.

Yield: 400 ml/16 fl oz

| | | |
|---|---|---|
| 300 ml | oil | 12 fl oz |
| 100 ml | lemon juice or vinegar | 4 fl oz |
| 1 dsp | French mustard | 1 dsp |
| | small pinch salt and pepper | |

Place all the ingredients in a mixing bowl and thoroughly whisk together. Also whisk before service.

**DERIVATIVES OF LOWER-FAT OR TRADITIONAL VINAIGRETTE**
Yield: 400 ml/16 fl oz

**Garlic dressing**
Add 10 g/$\frac{1}{2}$ oz crushed garlic to the vinaigrette and season with ground black pepper. *Note:* This dressing can also be made with lower-fat dressing or mayonnaise (page 35).

**Lemon salad dressing**
Prepare the basic lower-fat vinaigrette using lemon juice and 3–4 drops of tabasco sauce instead of French mustard.

**Mustard and dill sauce/dressing**

| | | |
|---|---|---|
| 2$\frac{1}{2}$–5 g | English mustard | 1–2 tsp |
| 10 g | caster sugar | $\frac{1}{2}$ oz |
| 100 ml | red wine vinegar | 4 fl oz |
| 300 ml | oil | 12 fl oz |
| 50 g | finely chopped dill leaves | 2 oz |
| | small pinch salt and white pepper | |

Place all the ingredients in a mixing bowl and thoroughly whisk together.

**Spiced salad dressing**

| | | |
|---|---|---|
| 300 ml | lemon juice | 12 fl oz |
| 100 ml | oil | 4 fl oz |
| 2–3 tsp | ground cumin | 2–3 tsp |
| 3 | cloves crushed garlic | 3 |
| | pinch cayenne pepper | |
| | chopped parsley | |

Place all the ingredients in a mixing bowl and thoroughly whisk together.

**Wine vinegar dressing**

| | | |
|---|---|---|
| 200 ml | wine vinegar | 8 fl oz |
| 200 ml | olive oil | 8 fl oz |
| | ground black pepper (to taste) | |
| | chopped parsley | |

Place all the ingredients in a mixing bowl and thoroughly whisk together.

# STOCKS

## MEAT, POULTRY AND GAME STOCKS (white and brown stocks)

Yield: 5 litres/10 pt

| | | |
|---|---|---|
| 2 kg | raw bones (see step 2) | 4$\frac{1}{2}$ lb |
| 200 g | peeled onion | $\frac{1}{2}$ lb |
| 200 g | peeled carrot | $\frac{1}{2}$ lb |
| 100 g | washed, trimmed celery | 4 oz |
| 100 g | washed, trimmed leeks | 4 oz |
| 2 | bay leaves | 2 |
| | large sprig thyme | |
| 6–8 | parsley stalks | 6–8 |
| 5 litres | cold water | 10 pt |

1 Break up the bones and remove all the fat and marrow.
2 Place the bones on a roasting tray and cook in an oven to melt off and remove any fat.
*White stocks:* Do not allow the bones to develop any colour.
*Brown stocks:* Allow the bones to develop colour then add the onion, carrot, celery and leek. Continue cooking allowing the vegetables to develop colour.
3 Place the bones in a saucepan or stockpot.
4 Add the vegetables and herbs then cover with the cold water.
5 Bring to the boil and skim off any surface fat and impurities.
6 Slowly simmer until cooked:
*Beef, veal, ham, lamb, mutton, venison:* 6–8 hours
*Chicken, feathered game:* 3 hours.
7 During cooking, skim off any fat or impurities and top up with water as necessary.
8 Strain into a clean container and use as required.

**White beef stock *fonds blanc***
**Brown beef stock *fonds brun***
Use beef bones in the base recipe.

**White veal stock *fonds de veau***
**Brown veal stock *fonds brun de veau***
Use veal bones in the base recipe.

**White mutton stock *fonds de mouton***
**Brown mutton stock *fonds brun de mouton***
Use mutton bones in the base recipe.

**White chicken stock *fonds de volaille***
**Brown chicken stock *fonds brun de volaille***
Use chicken bones, trimmings or giblets in the base recipe.

**Ham stock *fumet de jambon***
Use ham bones in the base recipe. *Note:* Before using the bones, soak them in several changes of cold water to reduce the salt content.

**Brown game stock *fonds brun de gibier***
Use game bones and trimmings (venison, hare, grouse, pheasant) in the base recipe.

## FISH STOCK *FUMET DE POISSON*

Yield: 5 litres/10 pt

| | | |
|---|---|---|
| 2 kg | white fish bones | 4$\frac{1}{2}$ lb |
| | (sole, turbot, haddock or whiting) | |
| 250 g | peeled, sliced onion | 10 oz |
| 2 | bay leaves | 2 |
| 6–8 | parsley stalks | 6–8 |
| 50 ml | lemon juice (1 lemon) | 2 fl oz |
| 5 litres | cold water | 10 pt |
| 5 | peppercorns | 5 |

1 Remove any roe or blood, then wash and drain the bones.
2 Place the bones in a saucepan, then add the remaining ingredients.
3 Bring to the boil and skim off impurities.
4 Slowly simmer for 20 minutes skimming as required.
5 Strain into a clean container.

**Traditional practice:** Sweat the fish bones, onion and herbs in 50 g/2 oz butter for 6–8 minutes before adding the lemon juice, water and peppercorns.

## VEGETABLE STOCK

Many different vegetables may be used to prepare vegetable stock. Simply add vegetables to taste but avoid vegetables high in starch (e.g. potatoes, Jerusalem artichokes etc.) which deteriorate and cloud the stock. Also avoid the seeds and pulp of vegetables such as peppers which may produce a bitter taste.

Yield: 5 litres/10 pt

| | | |
|---|---|---|
| 1 kg | peeled onions | 2 lb |
| 600 g | peeled carrots | $1\frac{1}{2}$ lb |
| 400 g | washed, trimmed leeks | 1 lb |
| 300 g | washed, trimmed celery | $\frac{3}{4}$ lb |
| 5 g | peeled garlic | $\frac{1}{4}$ oz |
| 300 g | tomato trimmings | $\frac{3}{4}$ lb |
| 50 g | mushroom trimmings | 2 oz |
| 100 g | *peeled swede or turnip | 4 oz |
| 50 g | *sliced cabbage | 2 oz |
| 25 g | watercress stalks | 1 oz |
| 2 | bay leaves | 2 |
| | large sprig thyme | |
| | large sprig marjoram | |
| 1 | bunch parsley stalks | 1 |
| 5 litres | cold water | 10 pt |

**These vegetables produce strong flavours and are also likely to develop off-flavours with prolonged cooking periods.*

1. Cut all the whole vegetables into small pieces.
2. Place the water into a saucepan or stockpot and bring to the boil.
3. Add all the vegetables and bring back to the boil.
4. Slowly simmer until all the vegetables are cooked: 20–30 minutes.
5. Strain into a clean container.

# STUFFINGS: RAW

These are used for stuffing a joint or bird prior to roasting. They may also be rolled in oiled greaseproof paper, steamed until cooked then portioned.

Using wholemeal breadcrumbs will increase the fibre content.

## CHESTNUT STUFFING

Yield: 500 g/1 lb approximately

| | | |
|---|---|---|
| 50 g | chopped onion | 2 oz |
| 1 tsp | dried mixed herbs | 1 tsp |
| 75 g | fresh breadcrumbs | 3 oz |
| 200 g | peeled, lightly boiled chestnuts | 8 oz |
| 150 g | lower-fat pork sausagemeat | 6 oz |
| 1 | small egg | 1 |
| | small pinch salt and pepper | |

Place all the ingredients in a bowl and thoroughly mix together.

## ENGLISH STUFFING

Yield: 500 g/1 lb

| | | |
|---|---|---|
| 150 g | chopped onion | 6 oz |
| 1 tbsp | chopped parsley | 1 tbsp |
| 1 tsp | dried thyme | 1 tsp |
| | grated zest from 1 lemon | |
| 150 g | fresh breadcrumbs | 6 oz |
| 150 g | lower-fat pork sausagemeat | 6 oz |
| 1 | small egg | 1 |
| | small pinch salt and pepper | |

Place all the ingredients in a bowl and thoroughly mix together.

## SAGE AND ONION STUFFING

Prepare as for English stuffing but increase the onion to 200 g/8 oz and replace the thyme with 2 tsp sage. Also omit the lemon zest.

# STUFFINGS: COOKED

These are served with roast meat, game and poultry and are usually quite high in fat. They are prepared separately from the roast and served as an accompaniment.

## SAGE AND ONION STUFFING

The lard/dripping content of this dish gives it a very high fat content.

Yield: 500 g/$1\frac{1}{4}$ lb

| | | |
|---|---|---|
| 100 g | *lard or dripping | 4 oz |
| 200 g | chopped onion | 8 oz |
| 2 tsp | dried sage | 2 tsp |
| 1 tbsp | chopped parsley | 1 tbsp |
| 200 g | fresh wholemeal breadcrumbs | 8 oz |
| | small pinch salt and pepper | |

**This is often taken from the roasting tray.*

1. Lightly cook the onion in the fat without colouring.
2. Add the sage and cook slowly without burning for 1–2 minutes.
3. Add the breadcrumbs, chopped parsley and seasoning.
4. Combine the ingredients and heat through.

**Herb and lemon stuffing**

Prepare as for sage and onion stuffing (above) but replace the sage with dried mixed herbs and add the grated zest of 2 lemons.

# THICKENINGS

## BEURRE MANIÉ

Yield: 30 g/1 oz

| | | |
|---|---|---|
| 15 g | butter | $\frac{3}{4}$ oz |
| 10 g | flour | $\frac{1}{2}$ oz |

1. Place the butter and flour in a bowl.
2. Cream together until light.

3 Blend through the mixture to be thickened (usually while shaking the pan) until the right consistency is reached.

*Uses:* Thickening French-style peas and certain fish sauces.

### LIAISON

Yield: 75 ml/3 fl oz approximately (This is sufficient for thickening ½ litre/1 pt sauce or soup)

| | | |
|---|---|---|
| 2 | egg yolks | 2 |
| 50 ml | cream | 2 fl oz |

1 Place the yolks into a small bowl.
2 Add the cream and whisk.
3 Whisk the liaison into the soups or sauce.
4 Cook for a short period but *do not* reboil.

*Uses:* Thickening and enrichening blanquettes, fricasées, certain soups and fish dishes.

### LOW-FAT THICKENING PASTE

Yield: 75 ml/3 fl oz

| | | |
|---|---|---|
| 125 ml | fromage frais | ¼ pt |
| 50 oz | flour | 2 oz |

1 Mix together the ingredients.
2 Whisk the paste into the boiling soup, sauce or stew.
3 Bring back to the boil.
4 Reduce heat and simmer slowly until cooking is complete.

# BASIC PREPARATIONS: SWEET

## BUTTERCREAM

A simple buttercream is made by creaming together an equal quantity of sieved icing sugar and fresh butter and adding appropriate flavouring or colouring. Its high fat and sugar content would preclude it from any health-conscious menu. Buttercream is used as a filling for various gateaux and cakes.

### CHOCOLATE BUTTERCREAM

Yield: 500 g/1¼ lb

| | | |
|---|---|---|
| 200 g | butter | 8 oz |
| 200 g | sieved icing sugar | 8 oz |
| 100 g | melted chocolate | 4 oz |

See the base method below.

### COFFEE BUTTERCREAM

Yield: 500 g/1¼ lb

| | | |
|---|---|---|
| 250 g | butter | 10 oz |
| 250 g | sieved icing sugar | 10 oz |
| | coffee essence (to taste) | |

See the base method below.

### VANILLA BUTTERCREAM

Yield: 500 g/1¼ lb

| | | |
|---|---|---|
| 250 g | butter | 10 oz |
| 250 g | sieved icing sugar | 10 oz |
| | vanilla essence (to taste) | |

See the base method below.

**Base method for preparing buttercream:**

1 Place the butter (softened) and icing sugar into a mixing bowl.
2 Mix together then beat until light and aerated. Scrape down the bowl with a plastic scraper as required during beating.
3 Add the flavouring: e.g. melted chocolate, coffee essence or vanilla essence, and thoroughly mix together.

## CRÊPE BATTER

See page 170.

## GLAZES

These are used to coat: fruit in fruit flans, fruit slices, savarins and babas.

### APRICOT GLAZE

Yield: 500 ml/1 pt

| | | |
|---|---|---|
| 400 g | apricot jam | 1 lb |
| 100 ml | water | 4 fl oz |

1 Place the jam and water into a saucepan.
2 Bring to the boil occasionally whisking.
3 Strain and use hot.

**Red glaze**

Prepare as for apricot glaze, using redcurrant jelly in place of apricot jam.

### PLAIN FRUIT GLAZE (arrowroot type)

Yield: 500 ml/1 pt

| | | |
|---|---|---|
| 500 ml | fruit juice | 1 pt |
| 25 g | arrowroot | 1 oz |
| | squeeze lemon juice | |

1 Place the fruit juice and lemon juice into a saucepan and bring to the boil.
2 Dilute the arrowroot in a little cold water.
3 Whisk the diluted arrowroot into the boiling fruit juice and bring back to the boil.
4 Simmer for 2–3 minutes until clear.
5 Use hot.

## PASTRY CREAM

Pastry cream is used as a filling for flans, certain gateaux and Danish pastries. It is quite high in fat and sugar.

Yield: 500 ml/1 pt approximately

| | | |
|---|---|---|
| 500 ml | milk | 1 pt |
| 3 | egg yolks | 3 |
| 100 g | caster sugar | 4 oz |
| 4–5 drops | vanilla essence | 4–5 drops |
| 50 g | flour | 2 oz |

1 Place the milk into a saucepan and bring to the boil.
2 Place the yolks, sugar and vanilla essence into a bowl and cream together.
3 Mix in the flour.
4 Whisk the milk on to the yolks, sugar and flour.
5 Return to a clean saucepan and bring to the boil, stirring continuously.
6 Cook for 2 minutes stirring continuously to avoid burning.
7 Pour into a bowl, cover with lightly oiled greaseproof paper and cool quickly.
8 Remove the paper and stir thoroughly before use.

*Note:* A little cream may be added to correct the consistency before use.

## SAUCES: HOT

### ARROWROOT-THICKENED SAUCES

Yield: 1 litre/2 pt approximately

#### JAM AND SYRUP SAUCES

**Apricot sauce**

| | | |
|---|---|---|
| 800 g | apricot jam | 2 lb |
| 400 ml | water | $\frac{3}{4}$ pt |
| 50 g | arrowroot | 2 oz |
| 25 ml | kirsch (optional) | 1 fl oz |

See the base method below.

**Jam sauce (raspberry or strawberry)**

| | | |
|---|---|---|
| 800 g | jam | 2 lb |
| 400 ml | water | $\frac{3}{4}$ pt |
| 50 g | arrowroot | 2 oz |

See the base method below.

**Syrup sauce**

| | | |
|---|---|---|
| 600 g | golden syrup | $1\frac{1}{2}$ lb |
| 800 ml | water | $1\frac{1}{2}$ pt |
| 50 g | arrowroot | 2 oz |
| | squeeze lemon juice | |

See the base method below.

**Base method for jam/syrup sauces thickened with arrowroot:**

1 Place the jam or syrup and water into a saucepan and bring to the boil.
2 Dilute the arrowroot in a little cold water.
3 Whisk the diluted arrowroot into the boiling liquid.
4 Simmer for 2–3 minutes, stirring occasionally to avoid burning.

#### CITRUS SAUCES

**Lemon sauce**

| | | |
|---|---|---|
| 8 | lemons | 8 |
| 200 g | sugar | 8 oz |
| 50 g | arrowroot | 2 oz |
| 900 ml | water | $1\frac{3}{4}$ pt |

See the base method below.

**Orange sauce**

| | | |
|---|---|---|
| 4 | large oranges | 4 |
| 100 g | sugar | 4 oz |
| 50 g | arrowroot | 2 oz |
| 900 ml | water | $1\frac{3}{4}$ pt |
| | squeeze lemon juice | |

See the base method below.

**Base method for citrus sauces thickened with arrowroot:**

1 Thinly peel off the zest from the fruit and cut into thin strips.
2 Squeeze the juice from the fruit.
3 Place the zest, sugar and water into a saucepan and bring to the boil.
4 Dilute the arrowroot in a little cold water.
5 Whisk the diluted arrowroot into the boiling liquid and simmer for 2–3 minutes, stirring occasionally to avoid burning.
6 Add the fruit juice.

### CHOCOLATE SAUCE

This recipe has a high fat and sugar content. The alternative cornflour-thickened chocolate sauce (page 40) contains much less fat.

Yield: 1 litre/2 pt approximately

| | | |
|---|---|---|
| 600 g | plain chocolate | $1\frac{1}{2}$ lb |
| 600 ml | water | $1\frac{1}{4}$ pt |
| 100 g | sugar | 4 oz |
| 100 ml | cream (optional) | 4 fl oz |

1 Break up the chocolate into pieces.
2 Place the water, chocolate and sugar into saucepan and bring to the boil.
3 Slowly simmer for 10–15 minutes stirring occasionally.
4 Whisk in the cream then strain.

### CORNFLOUR-THICKENED SAUCES

Whole milk may be used in place of skimmed milk in these recipes but this would increase the fat content.

Yield: 1 litre/2 pt

**Custard sauce**

| | | |
|---|---|---|
| 1 litre | skimmed milk | 2 pt |
| 50 g | custard powder | 2 oz |
| 100 g | sugar | 4 oz |

See the base method below.

**Almond sauce**

| | | |
|---|---|---|
| 1 litre | skimmed milk | 2 pt |
| 50 g | cornflour | 2 oz |
| 100 g | sugar | 4 oz |
| 6–8 drops | almond essence | 6–8 drops |

See the base method below.

**Brandy sauce**
Prepare as for almond sauce, substituting 150 ml/6 fl oz brandy in place of the almond essence.

**Base method for preparing cornflour-thickened sauces:**

1 Place the custard powder or cornflour into a suitable bowl or jug.
2 Add a little of the cold milk and mix to a smooth paste.
3 Place the remaining milk into a saucepan and bring to the boil.
4 Whisk the diluted custard powder or cornflour into the boiling milk.
5 Simmer for 2–3 minutes, stirring occasionally to avoid burning.
6 Add the sugar and any essence or brandy.

**Chocolate sauce** (made with cornflour)

*With cocoa powder:* Prepare as for custard sauce using cornflour in place of custard powder. Add 50 g/2 oz cocoa powder to the cold milk with the cornflour and blend together.

*With chocolate:* Prepare as above without the cocoa powder, but add 200 g/8 oz block chocolate to the milk when heating.

## EGG CUSTARD SAUCE (FRESH)
### *SAUCE ANGLAISE*

This recipe is quite high in sugar and high in fat. It would not be included on a health-conscious menu.

Yield: 1 litre/2 pt approximately

| | | |
|---|---|---|
| 8 | egg yolks | 8 |
| 100 g | caster sugar | 4 oz |
| 6–8 drops | vanilla essence | 6–8 drops |
| 1 litre | milk | $1\frac{3}{4}$ pt |

1 Place the milk in a saucepan and bring almost to the boil.
2 Place the yolks, sugar and essence into a bowl and whisk together.
3 Whisk in the hot milk.
4 Return to a clean saucepan and place over a low heat or in a bain-marie.
5 Stir constantly until the sauce thickens then remove from the heat. Do not allow to boil as the sauce will curdle.

# SAUCES: COLD

## BRANDY CREAM

This recipe is high in fat.

Yield: 1 litre/2 pt approximately

| | | |
|---|---|---|
| 750 ml | whipping cream | $1\frac{1}{2}$ pt |
| 25 g | caster sugar | 1 oz |
| 100 ml | brandy | 4 fl oz |

1 Place the cream and sugar into a mixing bowl.
2 Whisk until heavy (or fairly stiff).
3 Mix in the brandy.

**Liqueur cream** (Cointreau, Curacao, Kirsch etc.)
Prepare as brandy cream above using the appropriate liqueur.

## CHANTILLY CREAM *CRÈME CHANTILLY*

This recipe is high in fat.

Yield: 1 litre/2 pt approximately

| | | |
|---|---|---|
| 750 ml | whipping cream | $1\frac{1}{2}$ pt |
| 25 g | caster sugar | 1 oz |
| 4–5 drops | vanilla essence | 4–5 drops |

1 Place the cream, sugar and essence into a mixing bowl.
2 Whisk until heavy (or fairly stiff).

## MELBA SAUCE (using fresh raspberries)

For melba sauce made with jam, see *jam sauce* below.

Yield: 1 litre/2 pt approximately

| | | |
|---|---|---|
| $1\frac{1}{4}$ kg | raspberries | $2\frac{1}{2}$ lb |
| 500 g | caster sugar | 1 lb |
| 125 ml | water | $\frac{1}{4}$ pt |

1 Place the raspberries, sugar and water into a saucepan.
2 Bring to the boil and allow to simmer for 4–5 minutes.
3 Pass through a strainer to remove the seeds, and cool quickly.

## JAM SAUCE (strawberry, raspberry, cherry etc.)

Yield: 1 litre/2 pt

| | | |
|---|---|---|
| 900 g | jam | $1\frac{3}{4}$ lb |
| 200 ml | water | 8 fl oz |

1 Place the water and jam into a saucepan and bring to the boil.
2 Stir until thoroughly combined.
3 Strain if required and cool quickly.

**Melba sauce (jam variety)** Prepare as above, using raspberry jam.

# SELF-RAISING FLOUR

This is a mixture of plain flour and baking powder added in the ratio of 50 g/2 oz baking powder per 1 kg/2 lb plain flour. Sieve together the flour and baking powder three times to ensure thorough mixing.

*Uses:* To provide aeration (chemical) in many bakery products, e.g. cakes, scones and Scotch pancakes.

**Baking powder**
This is a mixture of cream of tartar/phosphoric acid derivative and bicarbonate of soda.

Yield: 300 g/12 oz

| | | |
|---|---|---|
| 200 g | cream of tartar | 8 oz |
| 100 g | bicarbonate of soda | 4 oz |

Sieve together three times to ensure that the powders are thoroughly mixed together and store in an airtight container.

## STOCK SYRUP

Yield: 1 litre/2 pt

| | | |
|---|---|---|
| 1 litre | water | 2 pt |
| 400 g | sugar | 1 lb |
| | juice from 2 lemons | |

Place the water, sugar and lemon juice into a pan and bring to the boil.

*Uses:* For poaching fruits.

## SYRUP FOR BABAS AND SAVARINS

See page 255.

# Process 1 BOILING

**DEFINITION** Boiling is a moist method of cooking where prepared food is cooked in a liquid which contains water (water, aromatic cooking liquor, stock, milk). The boiling action may be quick and rapid (when cooking green leaf vegetables); or slow, with a gentle surface movement known as simmering (used when boiling most foods).

## REASONS FOR BOILING FOODS

1 To make foods tender: by breaking down and softening starch, cellulose, protein and fibrous material.
2 To make foods more palatable and digestible.
3 To make foods safer to eat: by destroying bacteria which can cause food poisoning.
4 To produce a particular quality in food, of colour, flavour and texture (e.g. boiled cabbage).

## METHODS OF BOILING FOODS

These are divided into two groups:

1 **Food is placed into cold liquid,** brought to the boil and cooked.
Reasons for this procedure:
   - **a)** Assisting clarity; clear liquids are more likely to be produced by this procedure. Scum and impurities rise to the surface as the liquid comes to the boil. This is important when preparing stocks and clarified liquids such as consommés and jellies.
   - **b)** Safety; it is safe and easy to cover food with cold liquid then bring to the boil.

   (See also *cookery myths* below.)

2 **Food is placed into boiling liquid** and cooked.
Reasons for this procedure:
   - **a)** To keep cooking times as short as possible.
   - **b)** To retain as much nutritional value and colour as possible, by keeping the cooking time as short as possible, e.g. when cooking vegetables.
   - **c)** To reduce vitamin loss when cooking vegetables by destroying oxidative enzymes.
   - **d)** To reduce the risk of burning cereals and starch mixtures such as rice and pastas.

**COOKERY MYTHS** It is often stated that placing food into very hot or boiling liquid seals in the juices and therefore retains goodness and reduces weight loss. This is a myth which should be ignored.

## COMMODITIES SUITABLE FOR BOILING

A wide range of foods can be boiled:

1 **Meat and poultry.** Boiling is used for the tougher joints and birds, e.g. silverside of beef, rolled brisket and hens. It is a suitable method for producing plain dishes, e.g. boiled gammon with cabbage and parsley sauce (page 58).
2 **Fish and shellfish.** Although it is more desirable to poach most fish, there are some classic dishes which are boiled. Lobsters are usually cooked by boiling. Lobsters are usually cooked by boiling.
3 **Eggs and pastas.** Examples are boiled eggs and fresh and dried pastas, e.g. noodles, spaghetti and macaroni.
4 **Fresh and frozen vegetables.** Examples are cabbage, cauliflower, turnips, peas, green beans and potatoes.
5 **Dried cereals and pulses.** Examples are rice, barley, oats, marrowfat peas, lentils and various dried beans.

**EQUIPMENT USED WHEN BOILING FOODS** Types of equipment include saucepans, stockpots, fast boiling pans, bratt pans and boilers.

Boiling pots

Electric boiling pan

## KEY POINTS

- Many boiled dishes have long cooking times (e.g. stocks, boiled meats and pulses); therefore ensure you allow for this in your time plan.
- Arrange saucepans of boiling food on the stove so that the correct cooking speed is maintained, i.e. rapid boiling or simmering. Also check saucepans regularly to ensure the correct speed of cooking and to determine degree of cooking.
- Be careful when draining foods with boiling liquid. Stand back from the saucepan, avoiding splashes of hot liquid.
- To avoid food poisoning, cool liquids and foods quickly then store chilled until required for use. Never leave boiled foods and liquor sitting in a warm kitchen.
- Store boiled foods at temperatures below 5 °C/40 °F, for as short a time as possible.
- Thoroughly cook dried beans as under-cooked beans contain a poison which can cause sickness. Dried beans should therefore be boiled rapidly for a minimum of 10 minutes and then simmered for the remaining cooking time.
- Always keep liquid content to a minimum when boiling food to ensure that valuable nutrients are not lost. Also serve the cooking liquor with the food whenever possible.
- Avoid soaking or storing vegetables in water (except pulses). Also start the cooking of vegetables in boiling liquid whenever possible.
- Cook vegetables in batches and as near to service as possible. Avoid cooking and reheating vegetables.
- Remove fat from the surface of stocks and sauces as it forms.
- Soak out as much salt as possible from salted joints prior to cooking, e.g. hams and gammons.

## 1.1 BROTHS

**CHEF'S TIP**

*Serving broths is a good way of providing a low-fat, high fibre dish. Accompanying the soup with slices of wholemeal bread adds extra fibre.*

Yield: 1 litre/2 pt

### BASE INGREDIENTS

| | | |
|---|---|---|
| 1 litre | stock | 2 pt |
| 25 g | pulse or cereal (see below) | 1 oz |
| 50 g | onion | 2 oz |
| 50 g | carrot | 2 oz |
| 50 g | turnip or swede | 2 oz |
| 25 g | leek | 1 oz |
| 25 g | celery | 1 oz |
| | small pinch salt and pepper | |
| | roughly chopped parsley | |

### BASE METHOD

1. Soak any barley, lentils, dried peas or dried beans in cold water for several hours.
2. Wash and peel the vegetables. Cut into small dice: 2–3 mm/$\frac{1}{8}$ inch.
3. Place the stock into a saucepan and bring to the boil.
4. Add the cereal (except rice) or pulse and simmer for 1 hour.
5. Skim as required and top up with additional stock if necessary.
6. Add the onion, carrot, turnip or swede, celery and rice and simmer for 15 minutes approximately.
7. Skim off any surface fat or impurities during cooking.
8. Add the leeks then simmer until cooked.
9. Check seasoning and adjust consistency with additional stock if necessary.
10. Serve sprinkled with the roughly chopped parsley.

**TRADITIONAL PRACTICE**

*Pieces of flesh, e.g. mutton, beef or chicken may be cooked and served in the broth. Add the flesh at step 3 then bring to the boil. When cooked, the flesh is removed, cut into small dice, then added back to the soup.*

**CHICKEN BROTH** Prepare as for the base recipe above using chicken stock, and rice as the cereal.

**SCOTCH BROTH** Prepare as for the base recipe above using mutton stock, and barley as the cereal.

**VEGETABLE BROTH (vegetarian)** Prepare as for the base recipe using vegetable stock. An assortment of pulses and cereals may be used to garnish the broth, e.g. mung beans, aduki beans, lentils, chick peas, corn kernels, brown rice. Further vegetables may be added provided their quantities are reduced to avoid the broth being too thick.

# 1.2 UNPASSED VEGETABLE SOUPS

**TRADITIONAL PRACTICE**

*Sweat the vegetables in 25 g/1 oz butter instead of margarine. This increases the saturated fat content.*

## BASE METHOD

1. Melt the margarine in a saucepan.
2. Add any onion, garlic, carrot, turnip, celery or leek.
3. Cover with a lid and slowly cook for 10–15 minutes. Stir occasionally to ensure even cooking and prevent burning.
4. Add the stock and simmer gently for 10 minutes.
5. Add any rice, spaghetti, potato, cabbage, tomato purée, fresh peas or French beans and allow to simmer until cooked i.e. 10–15 minutes.
6. Skim off any impurities or fat and top up with additional stock if necessary.
7. Add any tomato concassées just prior to service.
8. Check consistency and seasoning.
9. Sprinkle with parsley and serve with any accompaniments stated in the individual recipe.

**CHEF'S TIP**

*Thinly cut potatoes should be added near the end of the cooking period to avoid them breaking up.*

## POTAGE PAYSANNE

Yield: 1 litre/2 pt

| | | |
|---|---|---|
| 5 g | margarine | $\frac{1}{4}$ oz |
| 250 g | mixed vegetables (onion, carrot, turnip, celery, leek) | 10 oz |
| 50 g | potato | 2 oz |
| 1 litre | white stock | 2 pt |
| 25 g | peas | 1 oz |
| 25 g | French beans | 1 oz |
| | small pinch salt and pepper | |
| | roughly chopped parsley | |

Cut the onion, carrot, turnip, celery and leek into paysanne, and prepare as for the base recipe above.

**TRADITIONAL PRACTICE**

*Omit the garlic and add* pork fat pellets *to the soup at step 5. Recipe: 50 g/2 oz fat pork or bacon, 1–2 cloves garlic and a few parsley sprigs finely chopped together then rolled into small pellets. This increases the fat content of the soup.*

## MINESTRONE

Yield: 1 litre/2 pt

| | | |
|---|---|---|
| 5 g | margarine | $\frac{1}{4}$ oz |
| 2 | cloves crushed garlic | 2 |
| 150 g | mixed vegetables (onion, turnip, leek, carrot, celery) | $7\frac{1}{2}$ oz |
| 25 g | potato | 1 oz |
| 1 litre | ham stock | 2 pt |
| 10 g | long grain rice | $\frac{1}{2}$ oz |
| 20 g | spaghetti | $\frac{3}{4}$ oz |
| 20 g | tomato purée | $\frac{3}{4}$ oz |
| 20 g | peas | $\frac{3}{4}$ oz |
| 20 g | French beans | $\frac{3}{4}$ oz |
| 50 g | raw tomato concassées | 2 oz |
| | roughly chopped parsley | |

Break the spaghetti into short lengths. Cut the onion, carrot, turnip, celery, leek and potato into paysanne, and the French beans into diamonds. Prepare as for the base recipe. Serve accompanied with toasted bread flutes and a little grated Parmesan.

## 1.3 PURÉE SOUPS MADE WITH PULSE VEGETABLES

**CHEF'S TIP**

*Serving purée soups made with pulses is a good way of providing a low-fat, high fibre dish. Accompanying the soup with slices of wholemeal bread adds extra fibre.*

Yield: 1 litre/2 pt

### BASE INGREDIENTS

| | | |
|---|---|---|
| 200 g | pulse vegetable (see below) | 8 oz |
| $1\frac{1}{2}$ litres | ham stock | 3 pt |
| 50 g | onion | 2 oz |
| 50 g | carrot | 2 oz |
| 25 g | leek | 1 oz |
| 25 g | celery | 1 oz |
| | sprig of thyme, $\frac{1}{2}$ bay leaf, parsley stalks | |
| | small pinch pepper | |

### BASE METHOD

1. Soak the pulse vegetable in cold water for 12 hours approximately.
2. Wash, peel and roughly chop the vegetables. Note: Leave the carrot whole when preparing green split pea soup.
3. Place two-thirds of the stock in a saucepan.
4. Drain the water from the pulse. Discard the water.
5. Add the pulse to the saucepan.
6. Bring to the boil, stirring occasionally to prevent burning.
7. Skim off scum as it forms and remove any dried scum from the sides of the pan.
8. Add the vegetables and allow to simmer slowly.
9. Skim and top up with additional stock as necessary.
10. Allow to simmer until cooked ($1\frac{1}{2}$–2 hours).
11. Remove the carrot if preparing green split pea soup.
12. Pass the soup through a soup machine or liquidiser.
13. Place into a clean pan and reboil.
14. Check seasoning and consistency.
15. Serve accompanied with any garnish e.g. croûtons or sippets.

**CHEF'S TIP**

*Purée soups may be garnished with additional vegetables, e.g. corn kernels, cooked brown rice, small cooked beans etc. to supply added fibre.*

**LENTIL SOUP** Prepare as for the base recipe above, using lentils as the pulse vegetable.

**SPLIT PEA SOUP** Prepare as for the base recipe, using green split peas as the pulse vegetable.

**YELLOW SPLIT PEA SOUP** *PURÉE ÉGYPTIENNE* Prepare as for the base recipe, using yellow split peas as the pulse vegetable.

**RED BEAN SOUP** *PURÉE CONDÉ* Prepare as for the base recipe above, using red beans as the pulse vegetable. Also add 200 ml/8 fl oz red wine to the soup during cooking (step 10).

**HARICOT BEAN SOUP** *PURÉE SOISSONAISE* Prepare as for the base recipe above, using haricot beans as the pulse vegetable.

# 1.4 PURÉE SOUPS MADE WITH FRESH VEGETABLES

**TRADITIONAL PRACTICE**

*Sweat the vegetables in 25 g/1 oz butter instead of margarine. Also accompany the soups with croûtons (page 24). This increases fat content.*

## BASE METHOD

1. Wash, peel and slice the vegetables.
2. Heat the margarine in a saucepan.
3. Add any onion, garlic, leek, carrot, celery, cucumber and herbs.
4. Cover with a lid and cook slowly for 10–15 minutes. Stir occasionally to ensure even cooking and prevent burning.
5. Add the stock and bring to the boil.
6. Add any potato, rice, peas or lettuce and simmer until cooked: 20–30 minutes.
7. During cooking, skim off any impurities or fat and top up with stock if necessary.
8. When cooked, remove any bay leaf or parsley stalks, then pass through a soup machine or liquidiser.
9. Place into a clean pan and reboil.
10. Add any cream.
11. Check seasoning and consistency.
12. Add any garnish or parsley.

## POTATO SOUP *PURÉE PARMENTIER*

Yield: 1 litre/2 pt

| | | |
|---|---|---|
| 5 g | margarine | ¼ oz |
| 75 g | onion | 3 oz |
| 25 g | celery | 1 oz |
| 25 g | leek | 1 oz |
| 1 litre | chicken or vegetable stock | 2 pt |
| 400 g | potato | 1 lb |
| | small pinch salt and pepper | |
| | sprig of thyme, ½ bay leaf | |
| | roughly chopped parsley | |

Proceed as stated in the base method above.

## CRÉCY SOUP *PURÉE CRÉCY*

Prepare as for potato soup, adding 400 g/1 lb carrot to the vegetables and substituting 50 g/2 oz short grain rice for potato. Garnish with 25 g/1 oz boiled long grain rice.

## SUMMER VEGETABLE SOUP

Yield: 1 litre/2 pt

| | | |
|---|---|---|
| 5 g | margarine | ¼ oz |
| 75 g | onion | 3 oz |
| 100 g | leek | 4 oz |
| 250 g | cucumber | 10 oz |
| 1 litre | vegetable stock | 2 pt |
| 200 g | fresh or frozen peas | 8 oz |
| 1 | lettuce | 1 |
| | small pinch salt and pepper | |
| | sprig of chervil, mint, parsley stalks | |
| 25 ml | single cream | 1 fl oz |

Proceed as stated in the base method above, adding a garnish of 25 g/1 oz cooked peas.

**TRADITIONAL PRACTICE**

*Finish the soup with 50 ml/2 fl oz cream instead of the single cream. This increases fat content.*

## 1.5 WHITE VEGETABLE SOUPS AND CREAM SOUPS: TRADITIONAL

**HEALTH TIP**

*Using besan flour instead of plain flour will significantly increase the fibre.*

**CHEF'S TIP**

*Using vegetable stock will make the soup suitable for most vegetarians.*

**CHEF'S TIP**

*If the main vegetable is unavailable fresh then the frozen alternative may be used to make the soup. Add the frozen vegetable to the soup after step 7.*

Yield: 1 litre/2 pt

### BASE INGREDIENTS

| | | |
|---|---|---|
| 50 g | margarine | 2 oz |
| 75 g | onion | 3 oz |
| 25 g | celery | 1 oz |
| 25 g | white leek | 1 oz |
| 50 g | flour | 2 oz |
| 1 litre | chicken/vegetable stock | 2 pt |
| | small pinch salt and pepper | |
| | sprig of thyme, $\frac{1}{2}$ bay leaf | |
| 50 ml | cream (for cream soups) | 2 fl oz |

### BASE METHOD

1. Wash, peel and roughly chop the vegetables.
2. Melt the margarine or butter in a saucepan.
3. Add the vegetables.
4. Cover with a lid and cook slowly for 10–15 minutes. Stir occasionally to ensure even cooking without colouring.
5. Mix in the flour and cook over a low heat for 4–5 minutes. Do not allow to colour.
6. Slowly blend in the hot stock adding a little at a time.
7. Bring to the boil and simmer slowly.
8. During cooking, skim off any surface fat and impurities.
9. Simmer until the vegetables are cooked: 45 minutes approximately.
10. Remove the thyme and bay leaf.
11. Pass the soup through a soup machine or liquidiser.
12. Place into a clean pan and reboil.
13. Check seasoning and consistency.
14. Add the vegetable garnish if required.
15. If preparing a cream soup, blend through the cream and serve.

**ASPARAGUS SOUP/CREAM OF ASPARAGUS** ***CRÈME D'ASPERGES*** Add 400 g/1 lb asparagus trimmings to the base recipe. The finished soup may be garnished with pieces of cooked asparagus.

**CAULIFLOWER SOUP/CREAM OF CAULIFLOWER** ***CRÈME DU BARRY*** Add 200 g/$\frac{1}{2}$ lb cauliflower pieces to the base recipe. The finished soup may be garnished with small florets of cooked cauliflower.

**CELERY SOUP/CREAM OF CELERY** ***CRÈME DE CÉLERI*** Increase the celery in the base recipe to 200 g/8 oz. The finished soup may be garnished with a small dice of cooked celery.

**MUSHROOM SOUP/CREAM OF MUSHROOM** ***CRÈME DE CHAMPIGNONS*** Add 100 g/4 oz sliced white mushrooms to the base recipe. The finished soup may be garnished with sliced cooked mushrooms.

# 1.6 WHITE VEGETABLE SOUPS AND CREAM SOUPS: LOW FAT

**HEALTH TIP**

*Using besan flour instead of plain flour will significantly increase the fibre.*

**CHEF'S TIP**

*Using vegetable stock will make the soup suitable for most vegetarians.*

**CHEF'S TIP**

*If the main vegetable is unavailable fresh then the frozen alternative may be used to make the soup. Add the frozen vegetable to the soup after step 8.*

Yield: 1 litre/2 pt

### BASE INGREDIENTS

| | | |
|---|---|---|
| 10 g | margarine | $\frac{1}{2}$ oz |
| 75 g | onion | 3 oz |
| 25 g | celery | 1 oz |
| 25 g | white leek | 1 oz |
| 750 ml | chicken/vegetable stock | $\frac{3}{4}$ pt |
| | sprig of thyme, $\frac{1}{2}$ bay leaf | |
| | small pinch salt and pepper | |
| | *Thickening paste:* | |
| 50 g | flour | 2 oz |
| 250 ml | cold chicken/vegetable stock | $\frac{1}{4}$ pt |
| 50 ml | half cream (for cream soups) | 2 fl oz |

### BASE METHOD

1. Wash, peel and roughly chop the vegetables.
2. Melt the margarine in a saucepan.
3. Add the vegetables.
4. Cover with a lid and slowly cook for 10–15 minutes. Stir occasionally to ensure even cooking without colouring.
5. Add the hot stock and bring to the boil.
6. Whisk together the cold stock and flour to form a smooth paste.
7. Whisk the paste into the boiling stock and vegetables and return to the boil.
8. Simmer slowly until the vegetables are cooked: 45 minutes approximately.
9. During cooking, skim off any surface fat and impurities.
10. Remove the thyme and bay leaf.
11. Pass the soup through a soup machine or liquidiser.
12. Place into a clean pan and reboil.
13. Check seasoning and consistency.
14. Add the vegetable garnish if required.
15. If preparing a cream soup, blend through the half cream and serve.

**ASPARAGUS SOUP/CREAM OF ASPARAGUS** ***CRÈME D'ASPERGES*** Add 400 g/1 lb asparagus trimmings to the base recipe. The finished soup may be garnished with pieces of cooked asparagus.

**CAULIFLOWER SOUP/CREAM OF CAULIFLOWER** ***CRÈME DU BARRY*** Add 200 g/$\frac{1}{2}$ lb cauliflower pieces to the base recipe. The finished soup may be garnished with small florets of cooked cauliflower.

**CELERY SOUP/CREAM OF CELERY** ***CRÈME DE CÉLERI***
Increase the celery in the base recipe to 200 g/8 oz.
The finished soup may be garnished with a small dice of cooked celery.

**MUSHROOM SOUP/CREAM OF MUSHROOM** ***CRÈME DE CHAMPIGNONS*** Add 100 g/4 oz sliced white mushrooms to the base recipe. The finished soup may be garnished with sliced cooked mushrooms.

## 1.7 TOMATO SOUP: TRADITIONAL

> **HEALTH TIP**
>
> *Using besan flour instead of plain flour will significantly increase the fibre.*

> **CHEF'S TIP**
>
> *By leaving out the bacon scraps and using vegetable stock, this soup will become suitable for most vegetarians.*

Yield: 1 litre/2 pt

### BASE INGREDIENTS

| | | |
|---|---|---|
| 50 g | margarine | 2 oz |
| 1 | clove crushed garlic | 1 |
| 100 g | carrot | 4 oz |
| 100 g | onion | 4 oz |
| 50 g | celery | 2 oz |
| 50 g | leek | 2 oz |
| 50 g | bacon scraps | 2 oz |
| 50 g | flour | 2 oz |
| 100 g | tomato purée | 4 oz |
| 1 litre | white stock/vegetable stock | 2 pt |
| | sprig of thyme, ½ bay leaf, parsley stalks | |
| | small pinch salt and white pepper | |

### BASE METHOD

1. Wash, peel and roughly chop the vegetables.
2. Cut the bacon scraps into small pieces.
3. Melt the margarine in a saucepan.
4. Add the bacon and lightly cook.
5. Add the vegetables and continue cooking for 4–5 minutes.
6. Mix in the flour and cook over a low heat for 4–5 minutes.
7. Mix in the tomato purée.
8. Slowly blend in the hot stock adding a little at a time.
9. Bring to the boil and simmer slowly until the vegetables are cooked: 45 minutes approximately.
10. During cooking, skim off any surface fat and impurities.
11. Remove the thyme and bay leaf.
12. Pass the soup through a soup machine or liquidiser.
13. Place into a clean pan and reboil.
14. Check seasoning and consistency.

## 1.8 TOMATO SOUP: LOW-FAT

> **CHEF'S TIP**
>
> *By leaving out the bacon scraps and using vegetable stock, this soup will become suitable for most vegetarians.*

Yield: 1 litre/2 pt

| | | |
|---|---|---|
| 10 g | margarine | ½ oz |
| 1 | clove crushed garlic | 1 |
| 100 g | carrot | 4 oz |
| 50 g | leek | 2 oz |
| 100 g | onion | 4 oz |
| 50 g | celery | 2 oz |
| 50 g | flour | 2 oz |
| 100 g | tomato purée | 4 oz |
| 750 ml | ham/vegetable stock | 1½ pt |
| | sprig of thyme, ½ bay leaf, parsley stalks | |
| | *Thickening paste:* | |
| 50 g | flour | 2 oz |
| 250 ml | cold chicken/vegetable stock | ½ pt |
| | small pinch salt and pepper | |

Follow the base method for making lower-fat vegetable soups on page 49, adding the tomato purée after sweating the vegetables (step 4).

# 1.9 MEAT, POULTRY AND GAME CONSOMMÉS

**CHEF'S TIP**

*Strong stock must be used to make the consommé or the finished consommé will be weak in flavour.*

**CHEF'S TIP**

*Large volumes of consommé should be cooked in a pot or boiler with a tap at the bottom, allowing for ease of straining into a clean container.*

Yield: 1 litre/2 pt

## BASE INGREDIENTS

| | | |
|---|---|---|
| $1\frac{1}{2}$ litres | cold brown stock | 3 pt |
| 150 g | lean minced beef | 6 oz |
| 100 g | onion | 4 oz |
| 100 g | carrot | 4 oz |
| 100 g | celery | 4 oz |
| 100 g | leek | 4 oz |
| 40 ml | egg whites | $1\frac{1}{2}$ fl oz |
| 10 g | tomato purée (optional) | $\frac{1}{2}$ oz |
| 4 | peppercorns | 4 |
| | small pinch salt | |
| | sprig of thyme, $\frac{1}{2}$ bay leaf, parsley stalks | |

## BASE METHOD

1. Wash and peel the vegetables.
2. Cut the vegetables into small pieces, or mince them.
3. Place the minced beef, vegetables, herbs, egg whites, tomato purée and peppercorns into a bowl and thoroughly mix together.
4. Place the clarification into a saucepan.
5. Add the cold stock and thoroughly whisk all the ingredients together.
6. Place on a low heat and slowly bring to the boil. Stir only on initial heating. *Do not stir when the mixture is hot.*
7. Simmer slowly for $1\frac{1}{2}$ hours leaving the crust of the clarification undisturbed.
8. Check seasoning. If necessary, add a little salt through an opening in the crust.
9. Carefully strain the consommé through a double folded muslin into a clean pan or bowl.
10. Remove any surface grease with a dishpaper.
11. Check the colour, adding a little blackjack if necessary.

**BEEF CONSOMMÉ** Prepare as for the base recipe above, using brown beef stock.

**CHICKEN CONSOMMÉ** Prepare as for the base recipe above, using brown chicken stock. Adding pieces of chicken carcase and giblets to the clarification will also strengthen flavour.

**GAME CONSOMMÉ** Prepare as for the base recipe above, using brown game stock. Adding pieces of game, e.g. lean trimmings or small bones to the clarification will also strengthen flavour.

## 1.10 BOILING EGGS (HARD BOILED)

**CHEF'S TIP**

*Cook the eggs for the time stated, avoiding overcooking, and cool as quickly as possible when cooked. Overcooking and slow cooling result in a dark green deposit (ferrous sulphide) on the surface of the egg yolk.*

### BASE METHOD

1 Place a saucepan of water on the stove and bring to the boil.
2 Carefully place the eggs into a wire basket and submerge into the boiling water.
3 Bring back to the boil as quickly as possible.
4 Allow to simmer for 8 minutes (size 3 eggs).
5 Cool the eggs quickly under cold running water.
6 Shell the eggs and place into cold water.
7 Keep chilled until required for use.

*For hot service:* Submerge the eggs in very hot water (almost boiling) for 3–4 minutes.

**TRADITIONAL PRACTICE**

*Use traditional curry sauce in place of lower-fat sauce. This increases the fat content.*

### CURRIED EGGS

4 small portions

| | | |
|---|---|---|
| 4 | hard-boiled eggs (size 3) | 4 |
| 75 g | long grain rice | 3 oz |
| 200 ml | lower-fat curry sauce (page 31) | 8 fl oz |

1 Boil the rice (see Process 1.11 on page 53).
2 Reheat the boiled eggs.
3 Arrange the rice on a serving dish.
4 Halve the hot eggs and dress them on top of the rice.
5 Coat with the sauce and serve.

### TRIPE EGGS *OEUFS À LA TRIPE*

4 small portions

| | | |
|---|---|---|
| 4 | hard-boiled eggs (size 3) | 4 |
| 5 g | margarine | $\frac{1}{4}$ oz |
| 200 ml | soubise sauce (page 34) | 8 fl oz |
| | pinch chopped parsley | |

**HEALTH TIP**

*Brown rice provides more fibre than white rice.*

1 Reheat the boiled eggs.
2 Lightly grease a suitable serving dish.
3 Slice the eggs and arrange neatly on the dish.
4 Coat the eggs with the sauce.
5 Sprinkle with chopped parsley and serve.

### SCOTCH EGGS

1 portion

| | | |
|---|---|---|
| 1 | hard-boiled egg (size 3) | 1 |
| 100 g | sausagemeat | 4 oz |
| | flour | |
| | eggwash | |
| | breadcrumbs | |

1 Lightly flour the boiled egg.
2 Cover the egg with the sausagemeat.
3 Pass it through the flour, eggwash and breadcrumbs.
4 Deep-fry (see page 179).

# 1.11 BOILING RICE

**HEALTH TIP**

*Brown rice provides more fibre than white rice.*

**CHEF'S TIP**

*Brown rice may take slightly longer to cook, depending on the variety used.*

**CHEF'S TIP**

*When serving freshly cooked hot rice, drain the rice in a colander after cooking. If the rice is sticky, rinse with very hot water then drain thoroughly.*

## RIZ INDIENNE/RIZ NATURE

4 portions

### BASE INGREDIENTS

| | | |
|---|---|---|
| 200 g | long grain rice (brown or white) | 8 oz |
| 2 litres | water | 4 pt |
| | small pinch salt | |

### BASE METHOD

1 Place the water and salt into a saucepan.
2 Bring to the boil.
3 Sprinkle the rice into the water.
4 Stir frequently until the water reboils.
5 Simmer until the rice is cooked (12–16 minutes). During cooking, stir occasionally to keep the grains separate and to avoid burning.
6 When cooked, place the saucepan containing the rice under cold running water.
7 Refresh under the cold running water until the water is clear.
8 Store in a chill in cold water until required for use.
9 When required for service, drain the rice then thoroughly reheat in water which is almost boiling, for 1 minute approximately.
10 Drain the rice thoroughly then place on a tray or colander.
11 Cover with a clean cloth then place in a cool oven or on a hotplate and allow to dry out.

## RICE AND CRISP VEGETABLES WITH CHICK PEAS

4 portions

| | | |
|---|---|---|
| 200 g | long grain rice | 8 oz |
| 50 g | diced carrot | 2 oz |
| 50 g | diced red and green pepper | 2 oz |
| 50 g | diced celery | 2 oz |
| 50 g | sweetcorn kernels | 2 oz |
| 100 g | cooked chick peas | 4 oz |
| | pinch ground black pepper | |
| | small pinch salt | |

1 Cook, refresh and reheat the rice as stated in the base method.
2 Lightly boil the vegetables and reheat the chick peas.
3 Mix all the ingredients together.
4 Check seasoning.
5 Place into a suitable dish and serve.

## 1.12 BOILING FRESH PASTA

**HEALTH TIP**

*A very low-fat pasta may be made by leaving out the egg and oil and increasing the water to 125 ml/$\frac{1}{4}$ pt. To prevent the pasta from breaking up during cooking, partially dry it out after shaping and cook gently.*

### BASE INGREDIENTS

**PLAIN PASTA**
Yield: 300 g/12 oz approximately

| | | |
|---|---|---|
| 200 g | strong flour | 8 oz |
| 1 | egg (size 3) | 1 |
| 25 ml | olive oil | 1 fl oz |
| 50 ml | water | 2 fl oz |
| | small pinch salt | |

**GREEN PASTA**
Yield: 300 g/12 oz approximately

Ingredients as for plain pasta, adding 75 g/3 oz spinach purée (well drained).

**WHOLEMEAL PASTA**
Yield: 300 g/12 oz approximately

Ingredients as for plain pasta, substituting wholemeal flour for strong flour.

### BASE METHOD FOR PREPARING FRESH PASTA

1 Place the flour in a mixing bowl.
2 Make a bay in the centre then add the egg, oil, salt, any spinach purée and most of the water.
3 Thoroughly mix together to produce a smooth elastic dough. Add additional water if the dough is too stiff.
4 Cover and allow to rest for 1–2 hours, then use as required.

**CHEF'S TIP**

*Adding a small quantity of oil to the water prior to cooking helps to keep the pasta shapes separate.*

### BASE METHOD FOR COOKING FRESH PASTA

1 Place a good quantity of water into a saucepan and bring to the boil.
2 Add the pasta and stir lightly to keep separate.
3 Allow to simmer until cooked (6–8 minutes), stirring occasionally to keep separate and prevent burning.
4 Drain in a colander.
5 If the pasta is sticky, rinse with very hot water then drain thoroughly.

### REHEATING COOKED PASTA

1 After cooking the pasta (step 3), refresh it under cold running water until the water is clear.
2 Store in a chill in cold water until required for use.
3 When required for service, drain the pasta then reheat it in very hot, lightly salted water.
4 Drain thoroughly then use as required.

## NOODLES ITALIAN STYLE *NOUILLES ITALIENNE*

4 portions (use half quantities for a starter course)

| | | |
|---|---|---|
| 300 g | plain or wholemeal pasta | 12 oz |
| 25 ml | olive oil | 1 fl oz |
| 25 g | grated Parmesan | 1 oz |
| | pinch mill pepper | |

1 Roll out the pasta to form one or two very thin rectangles: take to a thickness of 1 mm/$\frac{1}{16}$ inch and a breadth of 250 mm/10 inches approximately.
2 Cut into 5 mm/$\frac{1}{4}$ inch strips i.e. 250 mm × 5 mm × 1 mm/10 × $\frac{1}{4}$ × $\frac{1}{16}$ inch.
3 Dust lightly with flour to avoid the noodles sticking together.
4 Boil the noodles and drain as stated.
5 Heat the oil in a sauteuse then add the hot noodles and Parmesan and mix together.
6 Lightly season with the mill pepper and serve.

**TRADITIONAL PRACTICE**

*Use 50 ml/2 fl oz olive oil or butter and double the quantity of Parmesan. Also accompany with a sauceboat of Parmesan. This increases the fat content.*

## LASAGNE VERDI AL FORNO

4 portions

| | | |
|---|---|---|
| 300 g | green pasta | 12 oz |
| 250 ml | low-fat bolonaise sauce (page 29) | $\frac{1}{2}$ pt |
| 150 ml | cream sauce flavoured with nutmeg (page 34) | 6 fl oz |
| 25 g | grated Parmesan | 1 oz |
| | pinch mill pepper | |

1 Roll out the pasta into one or two very thin rectangles – take to a thickness of 1 mm/$\frac{1}{16}$ inch and a breadth of 250 mm/10 inches approximately.
2 Cut into rectangular shaped pieces similar to postcard shapes i.e. 150 mm × 75 mm × 1 mm/6 × 3 × $\frac{1}{16}$ inch.
3 Place the lasagne on a floured cloth until ready for cooking.
4 Boil the lasagne as stated opposite then refresh and drain.
5 Place the lasagne on a clean towel to dry its surfaces.
6 Lightly grease an earthenware dish with olive oil.
7 Line the dish with a layer of lasagne.
8 Season with the mill pepper.
9 Coat with a layer of bolonaise sauce.
10 Place a second layer of lasagne on top.
11 Coat with a layer of cream sauce and sprinkle over the surface with Parmesan.
12 Repeat steps 7–11 until the dish has been filled; finish with a layer of lasagne topped with cream sauce and Parmesan.
13 Place into a moderate oven (200 °C/390 °F) and bake until golden brown and thoroughly reheated (30–40 minutes).

**TRADITIONAL PRACTICE**

*Use traditional bolonaise sauce instead of low-fat sauce and double the quantity of Parmesan. This increases fat and reduces fibre.*

## 1.13 BOILING DRIED PASTA

### BASE INGREDIENTS

Dried spaghetti, lasagne, macaroni, nouilles, tuchetti, rigatoni

Allow 50 g/2 oz dried pasta per portion (main course)

### BASE METHOD

1 Place a good quantity of water into a saucepan and bring to the boil.
2 Add the pasta and stir lightly to keep separate.
3 Allow to boil gently until cooked (12–15 minutes), stirring occasionally to keep pasta separate and prevent burning.
4 Drain in a colander.
5 If the pasta is sticky, rinse with very hot water then thoroughly drain.

**CHEF'S TIP**

*Add a small quantity of oil to the water if preparing lasagne. This helps to keep the pasta shapes separate.*

### REHEATING COOKED PASTA

1 After cooking the pasta (step 3 above), refresh it under cold running water until the water is clear.
2 Store in a chill in cold water until required for use.
3 When required for service, drain the pasta then reheat it in very hot, lightly-salted water.
4 Drain thoroughly then use as required.

### SPAGHETTI ITALIAN STYLE *SPAGHETTI ITALIENNE*

Prepare as for noodles Italian style on page 55, using 200 g/½ lb spaghetti in place of noodles.

### SPAGHETTI NAPLES STYLE *SPAGHETTI NAPOLITAINE*

4 portions (8 portions as a starter course)

| | | |
|---|---|---|
| 200 g | spaghetti | ½ lb |
| 200 g | raw tomato concassées | ½ lb |
| 400 ml | lower-fat tomato sauce (page 33) | ¾ pt |
| 15 g | grated Parmesan | ¾ oz |
| | mill pepper | |

1 Cook the spaghetti following the base method.
2 Place into a clean pan or sauteuse and lightly season with the mill pepper.
3 Add the tomato concassées and sauce and gently mix together.
4 Check seasoning and temperature.
5 Place into a serving dish.

**TRADITIONAL PRACTICE**

*After boiling and draining the spaghetti, toss it in 25 ml/1 fl oz hot olive oil or butter before adding the concassées. Also use traditional tomato sauce in place of lower-fat sauce. This increases the fat content. Also serve Parmesan separately.*

### SPAGHETTI MILAN STYLE *SPAGHETTI MILANAISE*

Prepare as for spaghetti Naples style above adding a julienne of ham, tongue and cooked mushrooms (50 g/2 oz each) at step 3. Traditionally, a small quantity of truffle cut into julienne would also be added.

## SPAGHETTI BOLONAISE

4 portions (8 portions as a starter course)

| | | |
|---|---|---|
| 200 g | spaghetti | $\frac{1}{2}$ lb |
| 500 ml | low-fat bolonaise sauce (page 29) | 1 pt |
| 15 g | grated Parmesan | $\frac{3}{4}$ oz |
| | mill pepper | |

1 Cook the spaghetti following the base method.
2 Lightly season with the mill pepper then place into a serving dish.
3 Serve the hot spaghetti accompanied with the bolonaise sauce and cheese separately. Alternatively, place the sauce into the middle of the spaghetti and sprinkle with cheese.

**TRADITIONAL PRACTICE**

*After boiling and draining the spaghetti, toss it in 25 ml/1 fl oz hot olive oil or butter before placing in the serving dish. Also use traditional bolonaise sauce in place of the low fat version. This increases the fat content. Also increase the Parmesan to 50 g/2 oz.*

## MACARONI AND MEAT PIE *PASTITSIO*

4 large portions (12 portions as a starter course)

| | | |
|---|---|---|
| 300 g | macaroni (plain or wholemeal) | 12 oz |
| 40 ml | olive oil | $1\frac{3}{4}$ fl oz |
| 250 g | minced meat | 10 oz |
| 100 g | chopped onion | 4 oz |
| 200 g | tomatoes (cut into small pieces) | 8 oz |
| 200 ml | brown stock | 8 fl oz |
| 25 g | grated Kefalotyri or Parmesan | 1 oz |
| 500 ml | low-fat béchamel sauce flavoured with nutmeg (page 34) | 1 pt |
| 2 | eggs (size 3) | 2 |
| | 1 bay leaf, pinch basil | |
| | small pinch salt and pepper | |

1 Heat 15 ml/$\frac{3}{4}$ fl oz oil in a saucepan.
2 Add the onion and shallow-fry until light brown.
3 Add the minced meat and cook until lightly coloured.
4 Add the tomatoes, bay leaf and basil.
5 Add the stock and lightly season.
6 Simmer slowly until cooked.
7 Prepare the béchamel, allow it to cool slightly then add the cheese. Also add the egg and whisk through the sauce.
8 Meanwhile cook and drain the macaroni leaving slightly underdone.
9 Heat 25 ml/1 fl oz oil then mix it through the drained macaroni.
10 Place a layer of macaroni in an earthenware dish then sprinkle some grated cheese over the surface.
11 Cover with the hot minced meat mixture.
12 Spread the remaining macaroni on top and sprinkle with grated cheese.
13 Cover with the béchamel and sprinkle with cheese.
14 Bake at 220 °C/425 °F until golden brown (15–20 minutes).

**TRADITIONAL PRACTICE**

*Increase both quantities of Kefalotyri or Parmesan to 75 g/3 oz cheese and double the amount of olive oil used at step 9. Also use traditional béchamel sauce instead of the low-fat sauce. This increases the fat content.*

## 1.14 BOILING PICKLED MEATS

### BASE METHOD

1 Soak the meat in cold water for 24 hours. Change the water several times if the meat is very salty.
2 Discard the soaking water.
3 Place the meat in a suitably sized saucepan, cover with cold water and bring to the boil.
4 Wipe the sides of the pan to remove any scum, and skim to remove any surface fat or impurities.
5 Add any herbs, bouquet garni or peppercorns.
6 Allow to simmer until three-quarters cooked: 1–2 hours. Skim as required during cooking.
7 Meanwhile, wash, peel and prepare the vegetables:
   a) leave small vegetables whole and cut large vegetables into neat, even-sized pieces
   b) tie any celery, leek or cabbage with string.
8 Also prepare any dumplings if appropriate.
9 Add the vegetables to the saucepan and continue cooking.
10 Add any dumplings to the saucepan and allow to *poach* until cooked.
11 When cooked, remove the joint and allow to cool slightly.
12 Remove any string, rind or fat from the meat then cut into neat slices across the grain. Also remove any string from the vegetables.
13 Arrange the slices of meat on a serving dish.
14 Neatly garnish with the vegetables and/or dumplings.
15 Coat with some hot cooking liquor.
16 Serve accompanied with the cooking liquor or sauce.

**CHEF'S TIP**

*Although an approximate cooking time is stated for the meats, the cooking times vary considerably.*

**CHEF'S TIP**

*To serve all the vegetables correctly cooked, add the vegetables to the saucepan according to their cooking time.*

### BOILED BEEF AND DUMPLINGS

4 portions

| | | |
|---|---|---|
| 400 g | lean pickled silverside | 1 lb |
| 4 | small onions | 4 |
| 8 | small carrots | 8 |
| 100 g | lower-fat pudding paste (page 86) | 4 oz |
| | small bunch parsley stalks, sage, thyme | |
| 4 | black peppercorns | 4 |

Prepare following the base method above. Mould the pudding paste into 8 small dumplings and add to the beef at the end of the cooking period as stated.

**TRADITIONAL PRACTICE**

*Increase the quantity of beef to 500–600 g/1¼–1½ lb. Also use suet pastry (page 86) instead of lower-fat pudding paste. This increases the fat content.*

### BOILED GAMMON WITH CABBAGE AND PARSLEY SAUCE

4 portions

| | | |
|---|---|---|
| 400 g | piece of lean boned gammon | 1 lb |
| 400 g | cabbage | 1 lb |
| 125 ml | parsley sauce (page 34) | ¼ pt |
| | 1 bouquet garni, 4 peppercorns | |

Proceed as stated in the base method above.

**TRADITIONAL PRACTICE**

*Increase the quantity of gammon to 500–600 g/1¼–1½ lb. This increases the fat content.*

## 1.15 BOILING FRESH MEATS OR POULTRY

### BASE METHOD

1 Place the meat or fowl into a saucepan.
2 Cover with cold water and bring to the boil.
3 Wipe the sides of the pan to remove any scum, and skim to remove any surface fat or impurities.
4 Add any herbs, bouquet garni or peppercorns.
5 Allow to simmer until three-quarters cooked: $1\frac{1}{2}$ hours approximately. Skim as required during cooking.
6 Meanwhile, wash, peel and prepare the vegetables:
   a) leave small vegetables whole and cut large vegetables into neat even-sized pieces
   b) tie any celery, leek or cabbage with string.
7 Add the vegetables by order of cooking times required:
   a) add any celery and continue cooking for 40 minutes approximately
   b) add any carrots and potatoes and simmer for 10 minutes
   c) add any turnip, cabbage and leeks and simmer for 10 minutes
   d) add any beans and simmer until all the vegetables and the meat or poultry are cooked.
8 Prepare any velouté sauce made from the cooking liquor.
9 When cooked, remove the joint or fowl and allow to cool slightly.
10 Remove the string and portion the meat or poultry:
   *Meat:* remove any excess fat then cut into neat slices across the grain.
   *Poultry:* remove the skin then cut into joints.
11 Arrange the meat or poultry on a serving dish.
12 Garnish with the vegetables and coat with a little hot cooking liquor.
13 Serve accompanied with the cooking liquor or sauce and any other stated accompaniments.

**CHEF'S TIP**

*Although an approximate cooking time is stated for the beef and fowl, the cooking times vary considerably.*

**CHEF'S TIP**

*Small green beans are cooked whole, but large beans are usually cut into thin strips.*

### BOILED BEEF FRENCH STYLE *BOEUF BOUILLI À LA FRANÇAISE*

4 portions

| | | |
|---|---|---|
| 400 g | piece lean silverside | 1 lb |
| 4 | small onions | 4 |
| 4 | small potatoes | 4 |
| 8 | small carrots | 8 |
| 100 g | turnip | 4 oz |
| 100 g | leek | 4 oz |
| 100 g | cabbage | 4 oz |
| | chopped parsley (optional) | |
| | 1 bouquet garni, 4 peppercorns | |

Prepare as stated in the base method above. Accompany with pickled gherkins and the cooking liquor.

**TRADITIONAL PRACTICE**

*Increase the quantity of beef to 500–600 g/$1\frac{1}{4}$–$1\frac{1}{2}$ lb and accompany with coarse salt when serving. This increases fat and salt.*

### BOILED FOWL WITH ONION SAUCE

4 portions

| | | |
|---|---|---|
| $1\frac{1}{2}$ kg | cleaned, trussed boiling fowl | 3 lb |
| 8 | small carrots | 8 |
| 100 g | green beans | 4 oz |
| 4 | small onions | 4 |
| 100 g | turnip | 4 oz |
| 125 ml | onion sauce (using cooking liquor: page 34) | $\frac{1}{4}$ pt |
| | 1 bouquet garni, 4 peppercorns | |

Proceed as stated in the base method above.

# 1.16 BOILING GREEN-LEAF AND LEGUMINOUS VEGETABLES

**CHEF'S TIP**

*To retain flavour and nutritive value, use only enough water to cook the vegetables without boiling dry.*

## BASE METHOD

1 Place a small quantity of water in a saucepan.
2 Bring to the boil and add a pinch of salt.
3 Add the prepared vegetables and cover with a lid.
4 Boil quickly. During cooking remove the lid occasionally and toss or turn over the vegetables. At short intervals check to see if the vegetables are cooked and inspect the water content: do not allow to boil dry.
5 When cooked, drain the vegetables in a colander.
6 Serve when cooked or finish as required.

**Cooking frozen vegetables:** Follow the same base method, but note that the cooking time is much less than that required for fresh vegetables.

**TRADITIONAL PRACTICE**

*Use enough water to cover the vegetables and do not use a lid. This results in a greater loss of soluble nutrients, especially vitamins.*

## CABBAGE *CHOU*

4 portions

| 500 g | fresh cabbage | 1 lb |
|---|---|---|

1 Wash the cabbage, then cut off the bottom stalk.
2 Remove any wilted leaves.
3 Quarter the cabbage and cut out the centre stalk.
4 Remove any large ribs from the leaves.
5 Finely shred the leaves then wash and drain.
6 Cook as stated in the base method above.

## BRUSSELS SPROUTS *CHOUX DE BRUXELLES*

4 portions

| 500 g | fresh Brussels sprouts | 1 lb |
|---|---|---|

1 Trim off any discoloured leaves with a turning knife.
2 Cut a small cross in the base of the stem: 1 mm/$\frac{1}{16}$ inch approximately.
3 Wash and drain.
4 Cook as stated in the base method above.

**CHEF'S TIP**

*Spinach usually contains excess water after cooking, and should therefore be squeezed gently when draining.*

## SPINACH *ÉPINARDS*

4 portions

| 1 kg | fresh spinach | 2 lb |
|---|---|---|

1 Remove the stems from the leaves.
2 Wash and drain.
3 Cook as stated in the base method above.

## PEAS *PETITS POIS*

4 portions

| 1 kg | fresh peas | 2 lb |
|---|---|---|

1 Remove the peas from their pods.
2 Wash and drain.
3 Cook as stated in the base method above.

## FRENCH BEANS *HARICOTS VERTS*

4 portions

| 500 g | fresh French beans | 1 lb |
|---|---|---|

1 Top and tail the beans.
2 Wash and drain.
3 Cook as stated in the base method opposite.

**TRADITIONAL PRACTICE**

*The skins are often removed from broad beans after cooking. This reduces the fibre content.*

## BROAD BEANS *FÈVES*

4 portions

| 1 kg | fresh broad beans | 2 lb |
|---|---|---|

1 Remove the beans from their pods.
2 Wash and drain.
3 Cook as stated in the base method opposite.

# STYLES OF SERVING BOILED VEGETABLES

**HEALTH TIP**

*Buttered vegetables are high in fat.*

## BUTTERED VEGETABLES (all vegetables)

1 Cook and drain the vegetables as stated.
2 Toss in foaming butter (25 g/1 oz). Alternatively, brush the vegetables with the butter.

## ENGLISH STYLE CABBAGE

1 Prepare the cabbage as stated, but also cook a few whole cabbage leaves.
2 After draining, line a large plate with half the leaves.
3 Place the cooked, shredded cabbage on top.
4 Cover with the remaining leaves and place a second plate on top.
5 Squeeze to compress and shape the cabbage.
6 Check temperature, cut into wedge-shaped portions and serve.

**TRADITIONAL PRACTICE**

*Use the traditional Mornay sauce instead of the low-fat type. This increases the fat content.*

## BRUSSELS SPROUTS MORNAY *CHOUX DE BRUXELLES MORNAY*

1 Cook and drain the sprouts as stated.
2 Place in a serving dish and coat with lower-fat Mornay sauce.
3 Sprinkle a little grated Parmesan over the top.
4 Place under a hot salamander and gratinate until brown.

## SPINACH PURÉE *ÉPINARDS EN PURÉE*

1 Cook and thoroughly drain the spinach as stated.
2 Finely chop or pass through a sieve.
3 Reheat in a little foaming margarine.
4 Check seasoning, then add a little mill pepper.
5 Place the hot purée in a serving dish then spread and mark with a palette knife dipped in hot water.

## MINTED PEAS *PETITS POIS À LA MENTHE*

1 Cook and drain as stated but add a few mint stalks to the water when cooking.
2 Place in a serving dish and garnish with blanched fresh mint leaves.

## 1.17 BOILING FLOWER, STEM AND FRUIT VEGETABLES

**CHEF'S TIP**

*To retain flavour and nutritive value, the quantity of water should only be enough to submerge the vegetable.*

**CHEF'S TIP**

*Cooking frozen vegetables: Cook in the same way as fresh vegetables but note that the cooking time is much less than that required for fresh vegetables.*

**CHEF'S TIP**

*With large asparagus it may be necessary to remove the tips of the leaves using the back of a small knife.*

### BASE METHOD

1 Place enough water into a saucepan to cook the vegetables.
2 Bring to the boil and add a pinch of salt.
3 Submerge the prepared vegetables in the boiling water.
4 Slowly simmer until cooked. Test for cooking regularly throughout the cooking period.
5 Carefully drain the vegetables in a colander.
6 Cut large whole vegetables such as cauliflower into portions if required. Remove the strings when cooking bundles of asparagus.
7 Serve when cooked or finish as required.

### ASPARAGUS *ASPERGES*

4 portions

| 4 bundles | asparagus (6–8 medium stalks each) | 4 bundles |
|---|---|---|

1 Lightly scrape each stem, from just under the flower downwards to the root using a peeler or small knife.
2 Wash, then tie into bundles with the heads level.
3 Cut the bundles evenly across at the root end.
4 Cook as stated in the base method above. Cooking time: 5–10 minutes.

### CAULIFLOWER *CHOU-FLEUR*

4–6 portions

| 1 | medium cauliflower | 1 |
|---|---|---|

1 Cut off the stalk at the base of the cauliflower just below the flower head.
2 Remove the outer leaves.
3 Hollow out a small hole in the base of the stem.
4 Wash in salted water ensuring that any dirt or insects have been removed.
5 Cook as stated in the base method above. Approximate cooking time: 15 minutes.

### BROCCOLI *BROCOLI*

4 portions

| 400 g | broccoli (without excessive stalk) | 1 lb |
|---|---|---|

1 Trim the stalks and wash the broccoli.
2 Cook as stated in the base method above. Cooking time: 8–10 minutes.

### CORN ON THE COB *MAÏS NATURE*

Allow 1 medium cob per portion.

1 Remove any outer fibrous leaves.
2 Trim the stem then wash the cob.
3 Cook as stated in the base method above. Approximate cooking time: 6 minutes.

## MARROW

4 portions

| 400 g | marrow | 1 lb |
|---|---|---|

1 Wash then peel the marrow.
2 Cut in half lengthways and remove the seeds.
3 Cut into pieces 40 mm/$1\frac{1}{2}$ inches approximately.
4 Cook as stated in the base method opposite. Cooking time: 8–10 minutes.

# STYLES OF SERVING BOILED VEGETABLES

## BUTTERED VEGETABLES (all vegetables)

1 Cook and drain the vegetables as stated.
2 Brush the vegetables with 20 g/$\frac{3}{4}$ oz melted butter.

## WITH CREAM *À LA CRÈME*

1 Cook and drain the vegetables as stated.
2 Coat with lower-fat cream sauce (150 ml/6 fl oz approximately: page 34), or serve the sauce separately.

## WITH FRESH HERBS *AUX FINES HERBES*

1 Cook and drain the vegetables as stated.
2 Sprinkle with freshly chopped herbs (parsley, chives and chervil etc.).

**HEALTH TIP**

*Vegetables with butter, hollandaise or cream, or cooked Milanaise style are high in fat.*

## HOLLANDAISE

1 Cook and drain the vegetables as stated.
2 Serve accompanied with hollandaise sauce (page 32).

**TRADITIONAL PRACTICE**

*Use a traditional Mornay sauce or cream sauce instead of the lower-fat sauces. This increases the fat content.*

## MORNAY

1 Cook and drain the vegetables as stated.
2 Place in a serving dish and coat with lower-fat Mornay sauce (page 34).
3 Sprinkle with a little grated Parmesan.
4 Place under a hot salamander and gratinate to a good brown colour.

## CORN ON THE COB WITH BUTTER

1 Cook and drain the corn cob as stated.
2 Insert corn skewers into the stem at each end of the cob.
3 Place on a serving dish and coat with melted butter. Alternatively, serve on a napkin with the melted butter in a sauceboat.

## MILANAISE

1 Cook and drain the vegetables as stated.
2 Sprinkle with a little grated Parmesan.
3 Place under a hot salamander and gratinate to a good brown colour.
4 Coat with a little nut-brown butter when serving.

## 1.18 BOILING ROOT VEGETABLES

**CHEF'S TIP**

*To retain flavour and nutritive value, the quantity of water should only be enough to submerge the vegetable. Also start the cooking of root vegetables in boiling water unless it is dangerous or impossible to do so.*

### BASE METHOD

1 Place enough water into a saucepan to cook the vegetables.
2 Bring to the boil and add a pinch of salt.
3 Submerge the prepared vegetables in the boiling water.
4 Simmer slowly until cooked. Test for cooking regularly throughout the cooking period.
5 When cooked, carefully drain the vegetables.
(Cooking beetroot: allow to cool then peel.)
6 Serve when cooked or finish as required.

**TRADITIONAL PRACTICE**

*Root vegetables are placed into cold water and brought to the boil. This increases the loss of nutrients by extending the cooking time.*

### CARROTS *CAROTTES*

4 portions

| 500 g | carrots | $1\frac{1}{4}$ lb |
|---|---|---|

1 Wash then top and tail the carrots i.e. cut off the top and bottom ends.
2 Peel with a peeler.
3 Leave small carrots whole. Cut large carrots into even-sized pieces.
4 Cook as stated in the base method above.

**CHEF'S TIP**

*Cooking frozen vegetables: Cook in the same way as fresh vegetables but note that the cooking time is much less than that required for fresh vegetables.*

### SMALL TURNIPS *NAVETS*

4 portions

| 500 g | small turnips | $1\frac{1}{4}$ lb |
|---|---|---|

1 Wash and peel the turnips (using a peeler).
2 Leave whole or cut into even-sized pieces.
3 Cook as stated in the base method above.

### SWEDES AND LARGE TURNIPS *RUTABAGAS ET NAVETS*

4 portions

| 500 g | swedes or large turnips | $1\frac{1}{4}$ lb |
|---|---|---|

1 Wash the swedes or turnips, then top and tail them with a cook's knife.
2 Cut off the skin around the sides. The thickness of the skin can be seen after the first piece of skin is cut from the vegetable.
3 Cut into even-sized pieces e.g. cubes, barrel shapes, stick shapes.
4 Cook as stated in the base method above.

### PARSNIPS *PANAIS*

4 portions

| 500 g | parsnips | $1\frac{1}{4}$ lb |
|---|---|---|

1 Wash the parsnips then top and tail them with a cook's knife.
2 Peel with a peeler.
3 Cut into even-sized pieces e.g. cubes, barrel shapes, stick shapes.
4 Cook as stated in the base method above.

## BEETROOT *BETTERAVE*

4 portions

| | | |
|---|---|---|
| 500 g | beetroot | 1 lb |

1 Wash and scrub the beetroot but do not damage the skin.
2 Leave whole and unpeeled.
3 Cook as stated in the base method opposite.

**CHEF'S TIP**

*Once the skin can be removed easily, the beetroot are cooked.*

## JERUSALEM ARTICHOKES *TOPINAMBOURS*

4 portions

| | | |
|---|---|---|
| 500 g | Jerusalem artichokes | 1 lb |

1 Wash the artichokes then peel with a peeler.
2 Leave whole or cut into even-sized pieces e.g. barrel shapes, stick shapes, thick slices.
3 Store in water with a squeeze of lemon juice until required for cooking.
4 Cook as stated in the base method opposite.

# STYLES OF SERVING BOILED ROOT VEGETABLES

## BUTTERED VEGETABLES (all vegetables)

1 Cook and drain the vegetables as stated.
2 Brush the vegetables with 20 g/$\frac{3}{4}$ oz melted butter.

**CHEF'S TIP**

*Buttered vegetables are high in fat.*

## MASHED TURNIPS *PURÉE DE NAVETS*

1 Cook and drain the vegetables as stated.
2 Pass through a sieve or ricer.
3 Leave plain or add 10 g/$\frac{1}{2}$ oz of margarine.
4 Thoroughly mix together and check seasoning and temperature.
5 Place the hot purée into a serving dish then spread and mark with a palette knife dipped in hot water.

**TRADITIONAL PRACTICE**

*Use 25 g/1 oz butter instead of margarine. This increases the saturated fat content.*

## MIXED VEGETABLES *MACÉDOINE DE LÉGUMES*

4 portions

| | | |
|---|---|---|
| 200 g | carrots | 8 oz |
| 200 g | turnips | 8 oz |
| 50 g | peas | 2 oz |
| 50 g | French beans | 2 oz |

1 Wash and peel the vegetables.
2 Cut the carrots and turnips into 5 mm/$\frac{1}{4}$ inch dice.
3 Cut the beans into diamonds.
4 Separately cook and drain each vegetable as stated.
5 Carefully mix the hot vegetables together.

**TRADITIONAL PRACTICE**

*Toss the cooked vegetables in hot margarine or butter (25 g/1 oz approximately) at step 5. This increases the fat content.*

## 1.19 COOKING GLAZED VEGETABLES

### BASE METHOD

1 Place the prepared vegetables into a small saucepan.
2 Add the margarine, sugar and seasoning.
3 Cover with water and bring to the boil.
4 Boil steadily, allowing the water to evaporate.
5 During cooking toss the vegetables frequently.
6 Continue cooking until all the water has evaporated and the vegetables are cooked and glazed.

**HEALTH TIP**

*All glazed vegetables are high in fat.*

**TRADITIONAL PRACTICE**

*Use butter in place of margarine. This increases the saturated fat content.*

### GLAZED CARROTS *CAROTTES GLACÉES*

4 portions

| | | |
|---|---|---|
| 500 g | carrots | 1 lb |
| 15 g | margarine | $\frac{3}{4}$ oz |
| 15 g | caster sugar | $\frac{3}{4}$ oz |
| | small pinch salt and white pepper | |

1 Wash then top and tail the carrots.
2 Peel with a peeler.
3 Cut into 10 mm/$\frac{3}{8}$ inch cubes (or any other suitable shapes e.g. barrel shapes or bâtons).
4 Cook as stated in the base method above.

**GLAZED TURNIPS, SWEDES OR PARSNIPS** Prepare as for glazed carrots using turnips, swedes or parsnips as the vegetable.

## 1.20 COOKING FRENCH STYLE PEAS

**HEALTH TIP**

*French style peas are high in fat.*

4 portions

### BASE INGREDIENTS

| | | |
|---|---|---|
| 1 kg | fresh peas | 2 lb |
| 10 g | butter | $\frac{1}{2}$ oz |
| 12 | button onions | 12 |
| 1 | medium lettuce | 1 |
| | small pinch salt and pepper | |
| | pinch caster sugar | |
| | *Thickening butter (beurre manié):* | |
| 20 g | butter | $\frac{3}{4}$ oz |
| 10 g | flour | $\frac{1}{2}$ oz |

### BASE METHOD

1 Remove the peas from their shells and wash.
2 Peel and wash the button onions.
3 Wash, drain and finely shred the lettuce.
4 Place the peas, butter, onions, lettuce, seasoning and sugar into a sauteuse or saucepan.
5 Barely cover with water.
6 Cover with a lid and bring to the boil.
7 Allow to cook until all the ingredients are tender.
8 Meanwhile prepare the thickening paste, i.e. cream together the butter and flour.
9 Slowly blend the thickening paste through the mixture while shaking the pan until it thickens.
10 Check seasoning and serve.

## 1.21 BOILING PULSE VEGETABLES

**HEALTH TIP**

*Serving pulse vegetables is an ideal way of providing vegetable dishes which are low in fat and high in fibre.*

**CHEF'S TIP**

*When preparing the vegetables for a vegetarian dish, use water or vegetable stock in place of ham stock.*

**HEALTH TIP**

*Dried beans contain a toxin which can cause sickness. However, thorough cooking (see steps 4–9), eliminates the danger.*

4 portions

### BASE INGREDIENTS

| | | |
|---|---|---|
| 100 g | pulse vegetable | 4 oz |
| 750 ml | ham stock or water | $1\frac{1}{2}$ pt |
| 50 g | whole onion | 2 oz |
| 50 g | whole carrot | 2 oz |
| 25 g | piece of celery | 1 oz |
| 25 g | piece of leek | 1 oz |
| | sprig of thyme, bay leaf, parsley stalks | |
| | chopped parsley (optional) | |

### BASE METHOD

1. Soak the pulse vegetable in cold water for 12 hours approximately.
2. After soaking, drain the water from the pulse vegetable.
3. Place the pulse vegetable into a saucepan and cover with the ham stock or fresh water.
4. Bring to the boil and boil quickly for 10 minutes. Stir occasionally to prevent burning.
5. Skim off scum as it forms and remove any dried scum from the sides of the pan.
6. Meanwhile, wash, peel and prepare the vegetables.
7. Add the vegetables and simmer slowly.
8. Skim and top up with additional stock as necessary.
9. Allow to simmer until the pulse vegetable is tender (45 minutes – 2 hours depending on the pulse used).
10. When cooked, remove the onion, carrot, celery, leek and herbs.
11. Serve the pulse vegetable with a little of the cooking liquor.
12. Sprinkle with chopped parsley.

**BUTTER BEANS** Follow the base recipe above using butter beans as the pulse vegetable.

**HARICOT BEANS** ***HARICOTS BLANCS*** Follow the base recipe above using haricot beans as the pulse vegetable.

**FLAGEOLET BEANS** ***HARICOTS FLAGEOLETS*** Follow the base recipe above using flageolet beans as the pulse vegetable.

**RED BEANS** ***HARICOTS ROUGES*** Follow the base recipe above using red beans as the pulse vegetable.

**MARROWFAT PEAS** Follow the base recipe above using marrowfat peas as the pulse vegetable.

**PULSE PURÉES/PEASE PUDDING (lentils, yellow split peas)**
Prepare as stated in the base recipe above using the appropriate pulse vegetable. Allow the pulse vegetable to dry out during cooking, then pass through a sieve after removing the fresh vegetables and herbs.

## 1.22 BOILING POTATOES

4 portions

### BASE INGREDIENTS

| 500 g | potatoes | 1 lb |
|---|---|---|

### BASE METHOD

1 Wash, scrub and peel the potatoes.
2 Cut into even-sized pieces or turn into barrel shapes.
3 Place in cold water until ready for cooking.
4 Place enough water into a saucepan to cook the potatoes.
5 Bring to the boil.
6 Submerge the potatoes in the boiling water.
7 Simmer slowly until cooked (15–20 minutes).
8 Carefully drain.
9 Serve plain in a vegetable dish.

**CHEF'S TIP**

*To retain flavour and nutritive value, the quantity of water should be only enough to submerge the potatoes. Also start the cooking of the potatoes in boiling water unless it is dangerous or impossible to do so. Starting them in cold water increases the loss of nutrients, by increasing the cooking time.*

**NEW BOILED POTATOES** *POMMES NOUVELLES* Prepare as for the base recipe above but use new potatoes and do not peel.

**TRADITIONAL PRACTICE**

*Brush the potatoes with melted butter before sprinkling with the parsley. This increases the fat content.*

**PARSLEY POTATOES** *POMMES PERSILLÉES* Prepare as for the base recipe above and sprinkle with chopped parsley when serving.

**BOILED SWEET POTATOES** Prepare as for the base recipe above.

**TRADITIONAL PRACTICE**

*Add and mix through 10 g/½ oz margarine or butter to the hot potatoes after sieving and use whole milk instead of skimmed milk. This increases the fat content.*

**MASHED POTATOES** *POMMES EN PURÉE* Prepare as for boiled potatoes, but after draining pass through a sieve or ricer into a clean pan. Stir in 25–50 ml/1–2 fl oz hot skimmed milk to produce a soft creamy texture and place into a vegetable dish. Smooth down with a palette knife and neatly mark with the knife or a spoon dipped in hot water.

**TRADITIONAL PRACTICE**

*Brush over the mashed potatoes with melted butter before sprinkling with a generous quantity of cheese. This increases the fat content.*

**MASHED POTATOES WITH CHEESE** *POMMES AU GRATIN* Prepare as for mashed potatoes above. After dressing the potatoes in a vegetable dish, sprinkle them with a little grated cheese. Place under a hot salamander and grill until golden brown.

**CREAMED POTATOES** *POMMES EN PURÉE À LA CRÈME* Prepare as for mashed potatoes above, but coat with a little warm cream prior to service.

## 1.23 DUCHESSE POTATO MIXTURE

4 portions

### BASE INGREDIENTS

| | | |
|---|---|---|
| 500 g | potatoes | 1 lb |
| 1 | egg yolk (size 2) | 1 |
| | small pinch salt, white pepper and nutmeg | |

### BASE METHOD

1 Wash, scrub and peel the potatoes.
2 Cut into even-sized pieces.
3 Boil until cooked.
4 Carefully drain the potatoes and leave in the saucepan at the side of the stove with the lid on to dry.
5 Pass through a sieve or ricer into a clean pan.
6 Lightly season and add the egg yolk.
7 Thoroughly mix through the egg yolk to produce a fine, pliable mass.

**TRADITIONAL PRACTICE**

*Add 10 g/$\frac{1}{2}$ oz margarine or butter to the potatoes at step 4. This increases the fat content.*

### DUCHESSE POTATOES *POMMES DUCHESSE*

1 Prepare the duchesse mixture as stated.
2 Pipe the mixture onto a greased tray in the shape of a solid spiral (40 mm × 40 mm/1 × 1 inch).
3 Place in a hot oven to heat through.
4 Remove, brush with eggwash then place back in the oven to develop colour (or brown under a salamander).

**MARQUIS POTATOES** *POMMES MARQUISE* Prepare as for duchesse above but pipe into nest shapes and fill with hot tomato concassées (page 25) after browning. Sprinkle with chopped parsley when serving.

**HEALTH TIP**

*Croquette and dauphine potatoes are high in fat.*

### CROQUETTE POTATOES *POMMES CROQUETTES*

1 Prepare the duchesse mixture as stated.
2 Roll out the mixture on a floured board into a long cylinder: 20 mm/$\frac{3}{4}$ inch thickness.
3 Cut into lengths: 40 mm/1 inch allowing three pieces per portion.
4 Pass each portion through flour, eggwash and breadcrumbs.
5 Place into a frying basket and deep-fry in hot fat (185 °C/365 °F) until thoroughly reheated and golden brown (see deep-fried potatoes on page 182).

### DAUPHINE POTATOES *POMMES DAUPHINE*

1 Thoroughly mix together the duchesse mixture and 125 g/5 oz choux paste (page 26).
2 Shape the mixture in the same way as for croquettes (above) then place onto pieces of lightly oiled greaseproof paper. Alternatively, shape with two spoons dipped in hot water.
3 Carefully slip the potatoes from the oiled paper into hot fat (185 °C/365 °F) and deep-fry until thoroughly reheated and a crisp golden brown (see deep-fried potatoes on page 182).

# Process 2 POACHING

**DEFINITION** Poaching is a moist method of cooking where prepared food is cooked in a liquid containing water (water, milk, stock, wine or court-bouillon). The food is cooked at temperatures below boiling point (75–93 °C/167–200 °F) with little or no liquid movement.

## REASONS FOR POACHING FOODS

1 To make foods tender: by breaking down starch, cellulose and protein.
2 To set or coagulate protein when poaching eggs.
3 To make foods more palatable and digestible.
4 To make foods safer: by destroying bacteria which can cause food poisoning.
5 To produce a particular quality in food: of colour, flavour and texture.
6 Poaching is a gentle method of cooking which is used to cook commodities which would break up or loose shape if boiled, e.g. poached eggs, poached fish, delicate fruits.

## METHODS OF POACHING FOODS

Methods of poaching are divided into two groups:

1 **Deep-poaching.** Food is covered with the minimum quantity of liquid then gently cooked. In most cases the food is placed into very hot liquid. Large whole fish are an exception: e.g. salmon, which is covered with cold liquid then brought to poaching temperature (to reduce the distortion of the fish when applying heat). Deep-poaching is a plain method of cooking, e.g. poached fruits.
2 **Shallow-poaching.** Food is partly covered with the poaching liquor (two-thirds the height of the commodity approximately) and then cooked gently under cover in an oven. This is a more complex method of cooking as the cooking liquor is reduced down and forms the base of the accompanying sauce. Many classic fish dishes are produced in this way (see examples on pages 77 and 78).

## COMMODITIES SUITABLE FOR POACHING

**Deep-poaching:** whole fish, portioned fish, shellfish, whole chickens, eggs, fresh and dried fruits. **Shallow-poaching:** small whole fish, e.g. trout, sole, plaice; cuts of fish, e.g. fillets and fish steaks; chicken suprêmes.

## EQUIPMENT USED WHEN POACHING FOODS

1 When deep-poaching: saucepans, shallow-sided pots, fish kettles.
2 When shallow-poaching: use plat à sauters and shallow-sided cooking dishes. For fish, oval fish-cooking dishes can also be used.

**Fish kettle**

**Shallow-sided saucepan**

## KEY POINTS

- Allow sufficient time to prepare poached foods which are to be cooked and then served cold. For example, a whole salmon for a cold buffet has to be cooked then thoroughly cooled before it can be moved from its poaching liquor. After this it must be skinned, decorated and garnished.
- Fish may be prepared 1–2 hours prior to cooking. For example, fish for fillets of sole bonne-femme may be kept raw in a chill, trayed up and covered with the cooking paper without any recipe liquid. This reduces the preparation time required for the dish especially during service time.
- Poached eggs are often cooked and kept chilled in ice water. When required for service, the eggs are reheated and then finished as required.
- Check regularly to see that the food is being poached and not boiled – this is important to maintain good quality.
- Always keep liquid content to a minimum when deep-poaching food to ensure that valuable nutrients are not lost.
- Remove any fat from the surface of food as it forms.
- Use reduced sugar syrups when poaching fruits.

## 2.1 POACHING EGGS *OEUFS POCHÉS*

### BASE INGREDIENTS

| 1 portion | | |
|---|---|---|
| 1 | egg | 1 |
| | water | |
| | vinegar | |

### BASE METHOD

1 Select a shallow-sided pan.
2 Add enough water to the pan to poach the eggs: a depth of 65 mm/ $2\frac{1}{2}$ inches is sufficient.
3 Add the vinegar and bring to the boil.
4 Reduce the heat allowing the water to leave the boil.
5 Carefully break the egg into the water with the white enveloping the yolk.
6 Cook until the white is set but the yolk still liquid (3–4 minutes depending on temperature). Do not allow to boil.
7 Carefully remove the egg with a perforated spoon then place into a bowl of ice water. Trim the egg if necessary.
8 When required for service, reheat the egg in very hot salted water for 1 minute approximately.
9 Drain on a cloth then use as required.

**CHEF'S TIP**

*Fresh eggs require very little vinegar. Use 1 part vinegar to 20 parts water approximately.*

**HEALTH TIP**

*Important: Serving undercooked eggs may cause food poisoning.*

### POACHED EGG MORNAY *OEUF POCHÉ MORNAY*

| | | |
|---|---|---|
| 1 | poached egg (hot) | 1 |
| 75 ml | lower-fat Mornay sauce (page 34) | 3 fl oz |
| 5 g | Parmesan cheese | $\frac{1}{4}$ oz |

1 Coat the base of a suitable dish with a little of the sauce then place the hot drained poached egg on top.
2 Coat with the remaining sauce, then sprinkle Parmesan over the surface.
3 Gratinate under a salamander until golden brown.

**TRADITIONAL PRACTICE**

*Use traditional Mornay sauce instead of the low-fat sauce. This increases the fat content.*

### POACHED EGG FLORENTINE *OEUF POCHÉ FLORENTINE*

Prepare as for egg Mornay but place a little hot cooked spinach (25 g/1 oz approximately) on the dish before adding the egg.

### EGGS BENEDICTINE *OEUF POCHÉ BÉNÉDICTINE*

Place the hot, drained egg on a circle of buttered toast lined with a slice of hot tongue. Coat with hollandaise sauce (page 32) then decorate with a slice of truffle.

**HEALTH TIP**

*This dish is high in fat.*

### POACHED EGG BOMBAY *OEUF POCHE BOMBAY*

| 1 small portion | | |
|---|---|---|
| 1 | poached egg (hot) | 1 |
| 25–50 g | cooked long grain rice (hot) | 1–2 oz |
| 50 ml | low-fat curry sauce (page 32) | 2 oz |

1 Dress the hot, drained rice in a suitable serving dish.
2 Place the drained poached egg on top.
3 Coat with the sauce and serve.

**TRADITIONAL PRACTICE**

*Use a traditional curry sauce instead of the low-fat sauce. This increases the fat content.*

## 2.2 CHOUX PASTE GNOCCHI *GNOCCHI PARISIENNE*

**TRADITIONAL PRACTICE**

*Use traditional cheese sauce instead of low-fat sauce and increase the Parmesan to 10 g/$\frac{1}{2}$ oz. This increases the fat content.*

4 portions

### BASE INGREDIENTS

| | | |
|---|---|---|
| 200 g | choux paste (page 26) | 8 oz |
| 250 ml | lower-fat cheese sauce (page 34) | $\frac{1}{2}$ pt |
| 5 g | grated Parmesan | $\frac{1}{4}$ oz |

### BASE METHOD

1. Place a saucepan of lightly salted water over the heat and bring to the boil.
2. Reduce the heat, bringing the water off the boil.
3. Place the choux paste into a piping bag with a small plain tube (5–8 mm/ $\frac{1}{4}$–$\frac{3}{8}$ inch diameter).
4. Pipe out the mixture into the water, cutting it into short lengths (15 mm/ $\frac{1}{2}$ inch). Use a small knife (occasionally dipping it into the water) to cut the gnocchi.
5. Allow to poach until cooked (8–10 minutes). Do not allow to boil.
6. When cooked, remove the gnocchi with a perforated spoon and drain.
7. Lightly bind the gnocchi with the cheese sauce.
8. Place into a serving dish and sprinkle with Parmesan cheese.
9. Gratinate until golden brown under a hot salamander.

## 2.3 POTATO GNOCCHI *GNOCCHI ITALIENNE*

**TRADITIONAL PRACTICE**

*Use 15 g/$\frac{3}{4}$ oz butter in place of margarine, and use traditional tomato sauce instead of the lower-fat sauce. This increases the fat content.*

4 portions

### BASE INGREDIENTS

| | | |
|---|---|---|
| 200 g | washed potatoes | 8 oz |
| 1 | egg yolk | 1 |
| 5 g | margarine | $\frac{1}{4}$ oz |
| 50 g | flour | 2 oz |
| 250 ml | lower-fat tomato sauce (page 33) | $\frac{1}{2}$ pt |
| 20 g | grated Parmesan | $\frac{3}{4}$ oz |
| | salt, pepper and nutmeg (to taste) | |

### BASE METHOD

1. Boil or bake the potatoes, then remove the skins.
2. Mash the potatoes and place into a bowl.
3. Mix through the flour, egg yolk, margarine and seasoning.
4. Mould the mixture into small balls then flatten slightly with a fork.
5. Place the gnocchi into simmering, salted water and poach until cooked (5–8 minutes).
6. Remove the gnocchi and drain.
7. Carefully mix together the gnocchi and tomato sauce, then place in a serving dish.
8. Sprinkle with Parmesan cheese and gratinate until golden brown under a hot salamander.

## 2.4 DEEP-POACHING CUTS OF FISH

### POACHED HALIBUT STEAK
***TRONÇON DE FLÉTAN POCHÉ***

1 portion

**BASE INGREDIENTS**

| | | |
|---|---|---|
| 1 × 200 g | halibut steak | 1 × 8 oz |
| 1 | piece lemon | 1 |
| 1 | small (or turned) plain boiled potato | 1 |
| | branch parsley | |
| | *White court-bouillon ($\frac{1}{4}$ litre/$\frac{1}{2}$ pt):* | |
| 25 g | peeled sliced onion | 1 oz |
| 2 | peppercorns | 2 |
| $\frac{1}{4}$ litre | water | $\frac{1}{2}$ pt |
| | sprig of thyme, $\frac{1}{2}$ bay leaf, parsley stalk | |
| | large squeeze lemon juice | |
| | small pinch salt | |

**CHEF'S TIP**

*Cuts of fish are placed into very hot liquor then cooked but whole fish are started in cold court-bouillon. (See Process 2.5 opposite.)*

**CHEF'S TIP**

*Fish required for cold service should be cooled quickly in the court-bouillon. The fish should also be stored chilled in the court-bouillon.*

**BASE METHOD**

1 Prepare the fish steak ready for cooking (page 21).
2 Place the ingredients for the court-bouillon into the fish-poaching pan and bring to the boil.
3 Allow to simmer for 2–3 minutes (strain if required).
4 Add the fish steak and allow to cook at a temperature just short of boiling point (5–6 minutes approximately), skimming during cooking if necessary.
5 Carefully remove the fish when cooked.
6 Remove the skin and place the fish on the serving dish.
7 Carefully remove the centre bone using the point of a turning knife.
8 Coat the fish with some of the cooking liquor and neatly decorate with the lemon, boiled potato and parsley.

**POACHED COD STEAK WITH JERUSALEM ARTICHOKES AND LIME** Poach a cod steak as stated in the base recipe above, and garnish with 2–3 boiled Jerusalem artichokes and one branch parsley. Accompany with a lime fromage frais (page 34).

**HEALTH TIP**

*Hollandaise sauce is high in fat.*

**POACHED SALMON STEAK WITH HOLLANDAISE SAUCE**
***DARNE DE SAUMON POCHÉE, SAUCE HOLLANDAISE***
Poach a salmon steak as stated in the base recipe above, but use a vinegar court-bouillon (opposite) when cooking and accompany with a sauceboat of hollandaise sauce (page 32).

## 2.5 DEEP-POACHING WHOLE FISH

### POACHED TROUT *TRUITE POCHÉE*

1 portion

**BASE INGREDIENTS**

| | | |
|---|---|---|
| 1 × 200 g | trout | 1 × $\frac{1}{2}$ lb |
| 1 | piece lemon | 1 |
| 1 | small (or turned) plain boiled potatoes | 1 |
| | branch parsley | |
| | *Vinegar court-bouillon ($\frac{1}{2}$ litre/1 pt):* | |
| 50 g | peeled sliced onion | 2 oz |
| 50 g | peeled sliced carrot | 2 oz |
| 25 g | sliced celery | 1 oz |
| 25 g | sliced leek | 1 oz |
| 4 | peppercorns | 4 |
| 50 ml | white vinegar | 2 fl oz |
| $\frac{1}{2}$ litre | water | 1 pt |
| | small pinch salt | |
| | sprig of thyme, 1 bay leaf, parsley stalks | |

**BASE METHOD**

1 Prepare the fish ready for cooking (page 21).
2 Place the ingredients for the court-bouillon into the fish-poaching pan and bring to the boil.
3 Allow to simmer for 15 minutes (strain if required).
4 Allow to cool.
5 Add the fish and allow to cook at a temperature just short of boiling point (8–10 minutes approximately), skimming during cooking if necessary.
6 Carefully remove the fish when cooked.
7 Remove the skin and place the fish on the serving dish.
8 Coat the fish with some of the cooking liquor and neatly decorate with the lemon, boiled potato and parsley.

**POACHED TROUT COURT-BOUILLON STYLE** ***TRUITE POCHÉE AU COURT-BOUILLON*** Prepare as in the base recipe above, but prepare the court-bouillon with the vegetables cut into neat shapes, e.g. paysanne. Serve with the court-bouillon, vegetables and garnish and accompany with a suitable sauce such as hollandaise or mousseline.

**POACHED HADDOCK WITH PARSLEY SAUCE** Prepare and skin the haddock ready for cooking. Poach in a suitable quantity of white court-bouillon which has been flavoured with freshly chopped fennel leaves or fennel seeds. Serve the fish accompanied with parsley sauce (page 34).

## 2.6 POACHING SHELLFISH

### BASE METHOD

1 Place the ingredients for the court-bouillon into a suitable saucepan and bring to the boil.
2 Allow to simmer: 15 minutes for vinegar court-bouillon; 2–3 minutes for wine court-bouillon.
3 Strain if required.
4 Add the shellfish and allow to cook at a temperature just short of boiling point.
5 Skim during cooking if necessary.
6 When cooked, cool quickly and store chilled until required for service.

**Two types of court-bouillon may be used:**

### VINEGAR COURT-BOUILLON

This is the usual cooking liquor. See page 75.

### WHITE WINE COURT-BOUILLON

This is used when the cooking liquor is required for sauces to accompany fish or shellfish.

Yield: 1 litre/2 pt

| | | |
|---|---|---|
| 750 ml | fish stock | $1\frac{1}{2}$ pt |
| 250 ml | white wine | $\frac{1}{2}$ pt |
| 50 g | sliced onion | 2 oz |
| 5 | peppercorns | 5 |
| | sprig of thyme, 1 bay leaf, parsley stalks | |
| | small pinch salt | |
| | good squeeze lemon juice | |

**SCALLOPS** *COQUILLES SAINT-JACQUES* Prepare the scallops ready for cooking (page 22), allowing 2–3 scallops per portion. Follow the instructions in the base method above, cooking for 4–5 minutes.

**SCAMPI/DUBLIN BAY PRAWNS** *LANGOUSTINES* Allow 125 g–150 g/5–6 oz scampi tails per portion. Cook the tails as stated in the base method above, cooking for 5–6 minutes.

**PRAWNS** *CREVETTES ROSÉS* Allow 150 g/6 oz whole prawns per portion. Cook the prawns as stated in the base method above, cooking them for 3 minutes approximately.

**SHRIMPS** *CREVETTES* Allow 150 g/6 oz whole shrimps per portion. Cook the shrimps as stated in the base method above, cooking them for 2–3 minutes.

## 2.7 SHALLOW-POACHING FISH FILLETS AND CUTS OF FISH

**TRADITIONAL PRACTICE**

*Add 50 ml/2 fl oz cream to the recipes and increase the cheese to 50 g/2 oz. Also use traditional béchamel sauce in place of the low-fat sauce. This increases the fat content.*

### FILLETS OF PLAICE MORNAY
### *FILETS DE PLIE MORNAY*

4 portions

**BASE INGREDIENTS**

| | | |
|---|---|---|
| 8 × 75 g | plaice fillets (trimmed and skinned) | 8 × 3 oz |
| 25 g | finely chopped onion or shallot | 1 oz |
| 50 ml | white wine | 2 fl oz |
| 150 ml | fish stock | 6 fl oz |
| 300 ml | low-fat béchamel sauce (page 33) | 12 fl oz |
| 25 g | grated Parmesan | 1 oz |
| 8 | fleurons (puff pastry crescents) | 8 |
| | squeeze lemon juice | |

**BASE METHOD**

1. Lightly grease the base of a fish-cooking dish.
2. Add the onion or shallot.
3. Neatly fold the fillets and place into the pan.
4. Add the lemon juice, wine and stock up to two-thirds the height of the fish.
5. Cover with a piece of buttered paper and lid.
6. Place on top of the stove and bring *almost* to the boil.
7. Place in an oven and cook at 175 °C/350 °F approximately. Cook for 8–10 minutes.
8. When cooked, remove the fillets and keep in a hot place covered with the cooking paper.
9. Reduce the cooking liquor by two-thirds.
10. Add any cream and also reduce by two-thirds.
11. Add the sauce and bring to the boil.
12. Mix in most of the cheese.
13. Check seasoning and consistency.
14. Coat the base of a suitable serving dish with a little sauce.
15. Place the fish fillets onto the sauce base and coat with the remaining sauce.
16. Sprinkle with the remaining cheese and gratinate under a hot salamander.
17. Garnish with the fleurons and serve.

**FILLETS OF SOLE FLORENTINE** ***FILETS DE SOLE FLORENTINE*** Prepare as for the base recipe, using sole fillets. Place a bed of cooked spinach (200 g/8 oz) on the serving dish and arrange the fish on top. Finish as stated.

**SUPRÊME OF HALIBUT CUBAT** ***SUPRÊME DE FLÉTAN CUBAT*** Prepare as for the base recipe, using halibut fillet cut into suprêmes (neat slices cut at an angle). Place a bed of duxelles (page 24) on the serving dish and arrange the fish on top. Finish as stated.

## 2.8 SHALLOW-POACHING WHOLE FISH

### TRADITIONAL PRACTICE

*Add 25 ml/1 fl oz cream to the recipes. Also use traditional velouté sauce in place of the low-fat sauce. This increases the fat content.*

### SABAYON

Yield: *100 ml/4 fl oz approximately.*
Ingredients: *2 egg yolks, 50 ml/2 fl oz water or fish stock. Place the egg yolk and water into a sauteuse and whisk together. Place the sauteuse into a bain-marie and whisk continuously until the egg mixture becomes very light and thick in consistency (ribbon stage).*

### LEMON SOLE BERCY *LIMANDE BERCY*

1 portion

#### BASE INGREDIENTS

| | | |
|---|---|---|
| 1 × 400 g | trimmed lemon sole | 1 × lb |
| 5 g | finely chopped onion or shallot | $\frac{1}{4}$ oz |
| 25 ml | white wine | 1 fl oz |
| 75 ml | fish stock | 3 fl oz |
| 100 ml | low-fat fish velouté (page 34) | 4 fl oz |
| 1 tbsp | sabayon | 1 tbsp |
| 2 | fleurons (puff pastry crescents) | 2 |
| | good pinch parsley | |
| | squeeze lemon juice | |

#### BASE METHOD

1. Lightly grease the base of a fish-cooking dish.
2. Add the onion or shallot.
3. Place the fish into the pan and sprinkle with parsley.
4. Add the lemon juice, wine and stock up to two-thirds the height of the fish.
5. Cover with a piece of buttered paper and lid.
6. Place on top of the stove and bring *almost* to the boil.
7. Place in an oven and cook at 175 °C/350 °F approximately. Cook for 8–10 minutes.
8. When cooked, remove the fish and lightly scrape off the skin with a palette knife.
9. Cover with the cooking paper and store in a hot place.
10. Reduce the cooking liquor by two-thirds approximately.
11. Add any cream and also reduce by two-thirds.
12. Add the fish velouté and bring to the boil.
13. Remove from the heat and fold through the sabayon.
14. Check seasoning and consistency.
15. Coat the base of a suitable serving dish with a little sauce.
16. Place the fish onto the sauce base and coat with the remaining sauce.
17. Glaze under a hot salamander, garnish with the fleurons and serve.

### DOVER SOLE BONNE-FEMME *SOLE BONNE-FEMME*

Prepare as for the base recipe above, using a trimmed and skinned Dover sole. Add 50 g/2 oz sliced button mushrooms to the cooking pan with the shallots and replace the fleurons with slices of boiled potato.

### TROUT MONTROSE

Prepare as for the base recipe above, but:

1. Use a trimmed trout and omit the parsley and sabayon.
2. Use whisky in place of white wine.
3. Add 50 g/2 oz tomato concassées with the shallot.
4. Garnish the cooked, skinned trout with 25 g/1 oz prawns heated in a little fish stock.
5. Coat with the sauce and serve.

# 2.9 POACHING PORTIONS OF POULTRY

**TRADITIONAL PRACTICE**

*Use traditional sauce (velouté) instead of low-fat sauce.*

**TRADITIONAL PRACTICE**

*Lightly shallow-fry the suprême in butter first (15 g/½ oz) but keep underdone and do not develop any colour. Also add 15 ml/½ fl oz cream where stated.*

## POACHED SUPREME OF CHICKEN WITH MUSHROOMS *SUPRÊME DE VOLAILLE POCHÉ AUX CHAMPIGNONS*

1 portion

### BASE INGREDIENTS

| | | |
|---|---|---|
| 1 × 175 g | chicken suprême | 1 × 7 oz |
| 5 g | finely chopped onion or shallot | ¼ oz |
| 25 g | sliced button mushrooms | 1 oz |
| 25 ml | white wine | 1 fl oz |
| 75 ml | white chicken stock | 3 fl oz |
| 100 ml | low-fat chicken velouté (page 34) | 4 fl oz |
| | small pinch salt and white pepper | |
| | squeeze lemon juice | |

### BASE METHOD

1. Lightly grease the bottom of a small sauteuse or plat à sauter with margarine.
2. Sprinkle the shallot or onion over the base of the sauteuse and add the mushrooms.
3. Place the suprême into the pan and add the lemon juice and white wine.
4. Add the chicken stock until barely covering the suprême.
5. Cover with a piece of lightly greased paper and a lid.
6. Heat on the stove and bring *almost* to the boil.
7. Poach over a low heat or place the pan into an oven at 175 °C/350 °F and allow to cook for 10–15 minutes.
8. When cooked, remove the suprême and keep hot, covered with the cooking paper.
9. Reduce the cooking liquor by two-thirds approximately.
10. Add any cream and also reduce by two-thirds.
11. Add the velouté and bring to the boil.
12. Check seasoning and consistency.
13. Coat the base of a suitable serving dish with a little sauce.
14. Place the suprême into the dish and coat with the remaining sauce.

**POACHED SUPRÊME OF CHICKEN WITH MELON AND PRAWNS** Prepare as for the base recipe, omitting the mushrooms and adding a small measure of brandy with the wine. When finishing the sauce (step 11) add 4–6 small melon balls, 4–6 shelled prawn tails and then thoroughly reheat.

**POACHED SUPRÊME OF CHICKEN TSARINA** Prepare as for the base recipe, but replace the mushrooms with a julienne of fennel. When dishing the chicken, garnish with small pieces of turned cucumber cooked in a little sour cream.

## 2.10 POACHING WHOLE POULTRY

### POACHED CHICKEN WITH BRAISED RICE AND SUPRÊME SAUCE *POULET POCHÉ AU RIZ, SAUCE SUPRÊME*

4 portions

**BASE INGREDIENTS**

| | | |
|---|---|---|
| 1 × $1\frac{1}{2}$ kg | chicken | 1 × $3\frac{1}{4}$ lb |
| | *Cooking liquor (2 litre/4 pt):* | |
| 2 litres | water or chicken stock | 4 pt |
| 100 g | whole peeled onion | 4 oz |
| 100 g | whole peeled carrot | 4 oz |
| 50 g | piece of celery | 2 oz |
| 50 g | piece of leek | 2 oz |
| 8–10 | peppercorns | 8–10 |
| | sprig of thyme, 1 bay leaf, parsley stalks | |
| | small pinch salt | |
| | *Braised rice (low-fat):* | |
| 5 g | margarine | $\frac{1}{4}$ oz |
| 50 g | finely chopped onion | 2 oz |
| 100 g | long grain rice | 4 oz |
| 175 ml | cooking liquor | 7 fl oz |
| | small pinch salt and white pepper | |
| | *Suprême sauce (low fat):* | |
| 500 ml | cooking liquor | 1 pt |
| 10 g | margarine | $\frac{1}{2}$ oz |
| 20 g | besan flour | $\frac{3}{4}$ oz |
| 20 g | plain flour | $\frac{3}{4}$ oz |

**TRADITIONAL PRACTICE**

*Use traditional sauce instead of lower-fat sauce and 50 g/2 oz butter instead of margarine when preparing the rice. This increases the fat content.*

**BASE METHOD**

1 Prepare the chicken ready for poaching (page 17).
2 Place all the ingredients for the cooking liquor into a saucepan of a suitable size and bring to the boil.
3 Allow to simmer for 20 minutes approximately.
4 Add the chicken and allow to simmer slowly until cooked: 45 minutes approximately.
5 Prepare the suprême sauce as stated on page 34.
6 Prepare the braised rice as stated on page 121.
7 Remove the chicken from the saucepan and allow to cool slightly.
8 Remove the skin and cut into joints.
9 Dress the braised rice in a service dish.
10 Arrange the chicken joints neatly on top and coat with the sauce.

**ENGLISH STYLE POACHED CHICKEN** *POULET POCHÉ À L'ANGLAISE* Prepare as for the base recipe, but:

1 Omit the braised rice.
2 Double the quantity of vegetables for the cooking liquor.
3 Add 100 g/4 oz turnip to the cooking liquor.
4 Add 100 g/4 oz shelled peas during cooking.
5 Heat 4 slices of ox tongue in the cooking liquor.
6 Place the chicken pieces in a service dish, coat with the sauce and neatly garnish with the vegetables and tongue.

## 2.11 POACHING FRESH FRUITS

**CHEF'S TIP**

*A lid or plate may also be required to keep the fruit covered with syrup during cooking.*

### BASE METHOD

1 Place the water, sugar and lemon juice into a suitable saucepan and bring to the boil.
2 Add the prepared fruit and bring back to the boil.
3 Cover with greaseproof paper.
4 Reduce the heat, allowing the fruit to cook slowly.
5 When almost cooked, remove from the heat and allow the fruit to cool in the syrup and cook tender.
6 Store chilled in the poaching syrup until required for use.

### POACHED WHOLE PEARS

4 portions

| | | |
|---|---|---|
| 4 | medium pears | 4 |
| | *Poaching syrup ($\frac{1}{2}$ litre/1 pt):* | |
| 500 ml | water | 1 pt |
| 50 g | granulated sugar | 2 oz |
| | juice of 1 lemon | |

1 Peel the pears, leaving on the stalks.
2 Remove the eyes with a small knife.
3 Neatly trim the base of each pear so that it will stand upright.
4 Place the pears into water and lemon juice to avoid discolouration prior to cooking.
5 Cook as stated in the base recipe.

**TRADITIONAL PRACTICE**

*Increase the sugar to 200 g/ 8 oz. This increases the preservative qualities of the fruit and decreases the likelihood of discolouration, but increases the sugar content.*

**OTHER SUITABLE FRUITS** include the following: **apples**, **blackcurrants and redcurrants**, **cherries, plums and peaches** and **gooseberries**.

## 2.12 POACHING VERY SOFT FRUITS

### RASPBERRIES AND STRAWBERRIES

8 portions

#### BASE INGREDIENTS

| | | |
|---|---|---|
| 600 g | raspberries or strawberries | $1\frac{1}{2}$ lb |
| | poaching syrup (process 2.11 above) | |

#### BASE METHOD

1 Remove the husks and any foreign matter.
2 Wash and drain, then place into a bowl.
3 Place the water, sugar and lemon juice into a suitable saucepan and bring to the boil.
4 Pour the hot syrup over the fruit.
5 Cool quickly and store in the cooking syrup.

## 2.13 POACHING RHUBARB

### BASE INGREDIENTS

| | | |
|---|---|---|
| 600 g | rhubarb | $1\frac{1}{2}$ lb |
| | poaching syrup (process 2.11 opposite) | |
| | red food colour (optional) | |

### BASE METHOD

1. Cut off the leaves and trim the stalks.
2. Wash and drain.
3. Cut the rhubarb stalks into suitable lengths: 40 mm/$1\frac{1}{2}$ inches approximately.
4. Place the rhubarb into a casserole or any other suitable dish.
5. Pour the hot syrup over the rhubarb, then cover with greaseproof paper.
6. Place into a cool oven (165 °C/330 °F) and allow to cook until tender.
7. Cool quickly and store in the poaching syrup.

## 2.14 POACHING DRIED FRUITS

**TRADITIONAL PRACTICE**

*Increase the sugar to 200 g/8 oz. This increases the preservative qualities of the fruit and decreases the likelihood of discolouration, but increases the sugar content.*

### APRICOTS, FIGS AND PRUNES

8 portions

### BASE INGREDIENTS

| | | |
|---|---|---|
| 600 g | dried fruit | $1\frac{1}{2}$ lb |
| | *Spiced poaching syrup:* | |
| 500 ml | water | 1 pt |
| 50 g | granulated sugar | 2 oz |
| $\frac{1}{2}$ | cinnamon stick | $\frac{1}{2}$ |
| 2–3 | slices peeled root ginger | 2–3 |
| 4–6 | coriander seeds | 4–6 |
| 3–4 | cloves | 3–4 |
| | juice of 1 lemon | |

### BASE METHOD

1. Wash the fruit and remove any foreign matter.
2. Soak the fruit *either* by placing the fruit in a saucepan, covering with hot water, and soaking at 80 °C/175 °F for two hours *or* by placing the fruit in a bowl, covering with cold water and soaking overnight.
3. Place the ingredients for the poaching syrup into a saucepan, bring to the boil and simmer for 15 minutes.
4. Add the soaked fruit and cover with a piece of greaseproof paper.
5. Bring to the boil, then reduce the heat and allow to cook slowly.
6. When tender, cool quickly and store in the cooking syrup.

# Process 3 STEAMING

**DEFINITION** Steaming is a moist method of cooking where prepared food is cooked in steam (water vapour) at varying degrees of pressure.

## REASONS FOR STEAMING FOODS

1 To make foods tender: by breaking down and softening starch, cellulose and protein.
2 To make foods more palatable and digestible.
3 To make foods safer to eat: by destroying bacteria which can cause food poisoning.
4 To produce a particular quality of colour, flavour and texture (e.g. steamed sponge pudding).
5 To keep the loss of soluble nutrients to a minimum, e.g. in vegetables.

## METHODS OF STEAMING FOODS

Methods of steaming are divided into two groups:

1 **Atmospheric or low-pressure steaming.** Food is cooked at atmospheric pressure or under low-pressure moist steam, usually between 0–17 kN $m^{-2}$/0–2 lb $in^{-2}$. This is the traditional method of steaming food: eggs, root vegetables, shellfish and steamed puddings are examples of commodities cooked by low-pressure steaming.
2 **High-pressure steaming.** Food is cooked at high pressures usually between 70–105 kN $m^{-2}$/10–15 lb $in^{-2}$. High-pressure steaming is fast and ideally suitable for most food except steamed puddings and sponge puddings. This type of steaming is a good method of cooking vegetables because there is very little water and air in the cooking chamber and this helps to retain valuable nutrients.

## COMMODITIES SUITABLE FOR STEAMING

1 Eggs.
2 Fish and shellfish.
3 Vegetables including potatoes.
4 Savoury and sweet puddings (low-pressure steaming only).

## EQUIPMENT USED WHEN STEAMING FOODS

Steaming oven

Types of equipment include atmospheric and low-pressure steamers; high-pressure steamers and jet steamers.

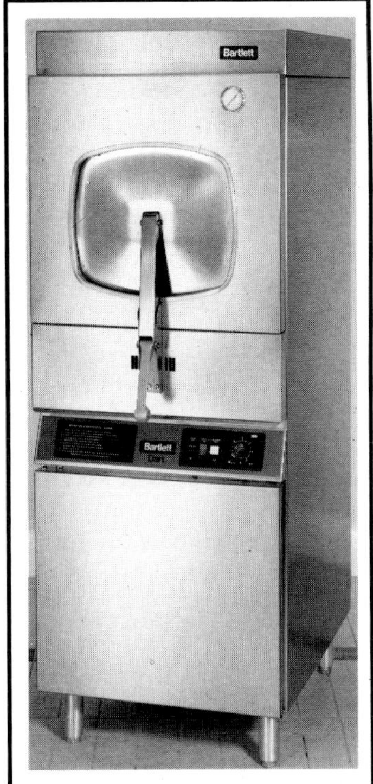


Dual pressure cooker

## KEY POINTS

- Switch on the machine in good time if preheating is required.
- Always turn off the steam before opening the door unless using a low-pressure steaming cabinet (which is not switched off during cooking).
- Always be careful when opening the door after use. Stand behind the door and use it as a shield against escaping steam. Cook vegetables as near to service time as required. A high-speed steamer is ideally designed for this purpose.
- Avoid overcooking food, especially with high-speed steaming where even short periods of overcooking will destroy nutrients.

## 3.1 STEAMING EGGS AND FISH (LOW PRESSURE)

### BASE METHOD

1 Ensure the steamer is preheated and ready for cooking.
2 Carefully open the steamer door using the door as a shield to prevent scalding.
3 Place the tray into the steamer then ensure the steamer door is closed correctly.
4 Set the timer (if appropriate) to the time required for cooking.
5 Steam the food at low pressure until cooked.
6 Turn off the steam (if appropriate) then allow any excess pressure to drop.
7 Carefully open the steamer door using the door as a shield.
8 Remove the cooking tray and finish as required.

**CHEF'S TIP**

*When the egg is to be used cold, cool immediately in cold running water to prevent discolouration.*

**STEAMED EGGS** Place the eggs (size 3) in a perforated steamer tray. Follow the instructions in the base method above, cooking the egg for 8 minutes.

### STEAMED FISH

1 portion

*Use one of the following:*

| | | |
|---|---|---|
| 350 g | flat fish (lemon sole, plaice) | 14 oz |
| 200 g | round fish (trout, haddock) | $\frac{1}{2}$ lb |
| 175 g | fish steaks (salmon, turbot) | 7 oz |
| 150 g | fish fillet (sole, haddock) | 6 oz |
| | *and:* | |
| 50 ml | fish stock or milk | 2 fl oz |
| | squeeze lemon juice | |
| | piece of lemon | |
| | sprig of parsley | |
| | small pinch salt and pepper | |

1 Prepare the fish for steaming (pages 19–21).
2 Lightly grease the base of a non-perforated tray with margarine.
3 Place the fish (prepared whole, steak or folded fillet) onto the tray and lightly season.
4 Sprinkle with lemon juice and add the fish stock or milk.
5 Cover with a lid then cook as stated in the base method above. Cook for 10–15 minutes depending on size.
6 Place the fish on a serving dish, coat with the cooking liquor and neatly garnish with the lemon and parsley.

**STEAMED FISH WITH LEMON AND ARTICHOKES** Prepare as for steamed fish above, but use a good squeeze of lime juice instead of lemon juice. A little grated lime zest may also be sprinkled over the fish. After cooking, place the fish on a serving dish and garnish with lime wedges and hot (boiled) Jerusalem artichokes. Coat with a little cooking liquor and serve.

## 3.2 STEAMING ROOT VEGETABLES (LOW PRESSURE)

### BASE METHOD

1 Ensure the steamer is preheated and ready for cooking.
2 Carefully open the steamer door using the door as a shield to prevent scalding.
3 Place the tray into the steamer then ensure the steamer door is closed correctly.
4 Set the timer (if appropriate) to the time required for cooking.
5 Steam the food until cooked. Check for cooking at regular intervals.
6 Turn off the steam (if appropriate) then allow any excess pressure to drop.
7 Carefully open the steamer door using the door as a shield.
8 Remove the cooking tray from the steamer.
9 Place the vegetables into a service dish.

### STEAMED TURNIPS

4 portions

| 500 g | turnips | $1\frac{1}{4}$ lb |
|---|---|---|

1 Wash and peel the turnips.
2 Cut the turnips into 10 mm/$\frac{1}{2}$ inch cubes.
3 Place into a perforated steamer tray and lightly season if required.
4 Follow the instructions in the base method above, cooking the turnips for 30–40 minutes.

**CHEF'S TIP**

*Small turnips may be left whole.*

### STEAMED BEETROOT

4 portions

| 400 g | beetroot | 1 lb |
|---|---|---|

1 Wash the beetroot then place unpeeled into a perforated steamer tray.
2 Follow the instructions in the base method above, cooking the beetroot for 2 hours approximately (depending on size).
3 Peel the beetroot when cooked.

**CHEF'S TIP**

*Small beetroot may be served whole, but large beetroot is normally sliced before serving.*

### STEAMED NEW POTATOES *POMMES NOUVELLES VAPEUR*

4 portions

| 400 g | potatoes | 1 lb |
|---|---|---|

1 Wash, scrub and remove any spots or mould.
2 Cut the potatoes into even-sized pieces if they are different sizes.
3 Place into a perforated steamer tray and lightly season if required.
4 Follow the instructions in the base method above, cooking the potatoes for 15–20 minutes.

## 3.3 STEAMING MEAT PUDDINGS (LOW PRESSURE)

**TRADITIONAL PRACTICE**

*Use 100 g/4 oz chopped suet in place of oil (added after step 1 and mixed through the flour). This increases the fat content, especially saturated fat.*

4 portions

### BASE INGREDIENTS

| | | |
|---|---|---|
| | meat filling (see below) | |
| 200 g | plain flour | $\frac{1}{2}$ lb |
| 10 g | baking powder | $\frac{1}{2}$ oz |
| 50 ml | oil | 2 fl oz |
| 125 ml | cold water | $\frac{1}{4}$ pt |
| | small pinch salt | |

### BASE METHOD

1. Sieve together the flour, baking powder and salt.
2. Whisk the oil and water together.
3. Add to the flour and lightly mix to form a fairly stiff paste.
4. Lightly grease a pudding basin (800 ml/28 fl oz).
5. Line the basin with three-quarters of the pastry.
6. Add the meat filling to the lined basin leaving a 10 mm/$\frac{1}{2}$ inch gap between the filling and the top of the basin.
7. Dampen around the edges of the paste with water.
8. Roll out the remaining paste to form the lid: cover the top of the pudding.
9. Seal around the edges then neatly trim if required.
10. Cover with a circle of lightly greased greaseproof paper. If possible, also wrap with a pudding cloth, tying both ends together and securing with string.
11. Place onto a perforated steamer tray and place into the steamer.
12. Allow to steam (at low pressure) for $3\frac{1}{2}$ hours.
13. When cooked, remove the cloth and paper and clean the sides of the basin.
14. When serving in the bowl, place onto a salver lined with a dishpaper then surround the basin with a folded napkin.

### STEAK AND KIDNEY PUDDING

| | | |
|---|---|---|
| 400 g | diced lean stewing steak (20 mm/$\frac{3}{4}$ inch) | 1 lb |
| 100 g | diced ox kidney (10 mm/$\frac{3}{8}$ inch) | $\frac{1}{4}$ lb |
| 75 g | chopped onion | 3 oz |
| 10 g | flour | $\frac{1}{2}$ oz |
| 5 ml | Worcester sauce | 1 tsp |
| 200 ml | cold brown stock | 8 fl oz |
| | good pinch chopped parsley | |
| | small pinch salt and pepper | |

Mix together the meat, kidney, onion, parsley, and flour and season lightly. Add the Worcester sauce, then mix in the cold stock. Store under cover in a chill until required for use. Cook following the base recipe above.

**STEAK, KIDNEY AND MUSHROOM PUDDING** Prepare as for steak and kidney pudding, adding 100 g/4 oz washed, quartered mushrooms to the pudding filling.

# 3.4 STEAMING SWEET SUET PUDDINGS (LOW PRESSURE)

**TRADITIONAL PRACTICE**

*Use 100 g/4 oz chopped suet in place of oil (added with the breadcrumbs at step 2). This increases the fat content, especially saturated fat. It also makes the pudding unsuitable for vegetarians.*

4–6 portions

## BASE INGREDIENTS

| | | |
|---|---|---|
| 100 g | plain flour | 4 oz |
| 5 g | baking powder | $\frac{1}{4}$ oz |
| 75 g | caster sugar | 3 oz |
| 100 g | white breadcrumbs | 4 oz |
| 50 ml | oil | 2 fl oz |
| $\frac{1}{2}$ | egg (size 3) | $\frac{1}{2}$ |
| 125–150 ml | milk | 5–6 fl oz |

## BASE METHOD

1. Sieve together the flour, baking powder and sugar.
2. Mix through the breadcrumbs.
3. Whisk the oil, egg and milk together.
4. Add to the flour and breadcrumbs then lightly mix together until a fairly stiff paste is formed.
5. Place the mixture into a greased pudding basin. Cover the basin with a circle of lightly greased greaseproof paper and a pudding cloth secured with string. Alternatively, place the mixture into a lightly greased pudding sleeve and secure the lid.
6. Place onto a perforated steamer tray and transfer to the steamer.
7. Allow to steam (at low pressure) for 2 hours.
8. When cooked, remove the cloth and paper and carefully turn out the pudding onto a suitable serving dish (or remove from pudding sleeve onto the dish). Serve with custard, jam or vanilla sauce.

**STEAMED RAISIN PUDDING** Prepare as for the base recipe, adding 75 g/3 oz raisins (washed and thoroughly dried) at the same time as the breadcrumbs then complete as stated.

**STEAMED DATE PUDDING** Prepare as for the base recipe, adding 75 g/3 oz cut dates (washed and thoroughly dried) at the same time as the breadcrumbs then complete as stated.

**STEAMED CHERRY PUDDING** Prepare as for the base recipe, adding 75 g/3 oz washed (and thoroughly dried) glace cherries. Cut the cherries into pieces and add at step 2 with the breadcrumbs. Complete as stated.

**STEAMED SULTANA PUDDING** Prepare as for the base recipe, adding 75 g/3 oz sultanas (washed and thoroughly dried) with the breadcrumbs at step 2. Complete as stated.

**STEAMED CURRANT PUDDING** Prepare as for the base recipe, adding 75 g/3 oz currants (washed and thoroughly dried) with the breadcrumbs at step 2. Complete as stated.

## 3.5 STEAMING SUET ROLLS (LOW PRESSURE)

**TRADITIONAL PRACTICE**

*Use 100 g/4 oz chopped suet in place of oil (added after step 1 and mixed through the flour). This increases the fat content, especially saturated fat. It also makes the pudding unsuitable for vegetarians.*

4–6 portions

### BASE INGREDIENTS

| | | |
|---|---|---|
| 200 g | plain flour | 8 oz |
| 10 g | baking powder | $\frac{1}{2}$ oz |
| 50 g | caster sugar | 2 oz |
| 50 ml | oil | 2 fl oz |
| 75 g | clean dried fruit (see below) | 3 oz |
| 125–150 ml | milk | 5–6 fl oz |

### BASE METHOD

1. Sieve together the flour, baking powder and sugar.
2. Whisk the oil and milk together.
3. Add to the flour and lightly mix together until a fairly stiff paste is formed.
4. Place the mixture into a lightly greased pudding sleeve and secure the lid. Alternatively, place the mixture into lightly greased greaseproof paper then carefully shape into a roll. Cover with a pudding cloth then tie both ends.
5. Place onto a perforated steamer tray and transfer to the steamer.
6. Allow to steam (at low pressure) for 2 hours.
7. When cooked, remove from the pudding sleeve or cloth and paper.
8. Cut into slices and place onto a serving dish.
9. Serve with custard, jam or vanilla sauce.

**STEAMED CURRANT ROLL** Prepare the basic steamed pudding above, adding currants as the dried fruit.

**STEAMED SULTANA ROLL** Prepare the basic steamed pudding above, adding sultanas as the dried fruit.

**STEAMED FRUIT ROLL** Prepare the basic steamed pudding above, adding a mixture of currants, raisins and sultanas as the dried fruit.

**STEAMED RAISIN ROLL** Prepare the basic steamed pudding above, adding raisins as the dried fruit.

**STEAMED DATE ROLL** Prepare the basic steamed pudding above, adding cut dates as the dried fruit.

**STEAMED CHERRY ROLL** Prepare the basic steamed pudding above, adding pieces of glacé cherries as the dried fruit.

# 3.6 CHRISTMAS PUDDING (Vegetarian)

### CHEF'S TIP

*Traditionally this pudding is prepared 2–3 months in advance and stored in a clean, dry atmosphere. To reduce the risk of mould forming on the cooking cloth during storage, the cloth is loosened and allowed to dry during cooling. The cloth is retied after cooling or (preferably) replaced with a clean cloth.*

### TRADITIONAL PRACTICE

*Use 100 g/4 oz chopped suet in place of oil (added with the dry ingredients at step 1) and white breadcrumbs instead of wholemeal breadcrumbs. This makes the pudding unsuitable for vegetarians and higher in fat.*

12 portions

## BASE INGREDIENTS

| | | |
|---|---|---|
| 100 g | wholemeal flour | 4 oz |
| 5 g | mixed spice | $\frac{1}{4}$ oz |
| 1 g | ground ginger | $\frac{1}{2}$ tsp |
| 1 g | ground cinnamon | $\frac{1}{2}$ tsp |
| $\frac{1}{2}$ g | ground nutmeg | $\frac{1}{4}$ tsp |
| 100 g | soft brown sugar | 4 oz |
| 100 g | wholemeal breadcrumbs | 4 oz |
| 25 g | ground almonds | 1 oz |
| 75 ml | oil | 3 fl oz |
| 125 g | currants | 5 oz |
| 100 g | raisins | 4 oz |
| 75 g | sultanas | 3 oz |
| 50 g | mixed peel | 2 oz |
| 25 g | grated carrot | 1 oz |
| $\frac{1}{2}$ | orange (zest and juice) | $\frac{1}{2}$ |
| $\frac{1}{2}$ | lemon (zest and juice) | $\frac{1}{2}$ |
| 25 ml | brandy | 1 fl oz |
| 25 ml | sherry | 1 fl oz |
| 50 ml | stout | 2 fl oz |
| 2 | eggs (size 3) | 2 |

## BASE METHOD

1. Place all the dry ingredients into a large bowl, i.e. flour, spices, sugar, breadcrumbs, almonds, dried fruit, peel and carrot.
2. Thoroughly mix together.
3. Make a bay and add the juice, zest, brandy, sherry, stout, eggs and oil.
4. Mix together until combined.
5. Cover and leave in a cool place for 24 hours (optional).
6. Lightly grease a large pudding basin then fill with the mixture. It is important to fill the basin to the top with the mixture.
7. *Lidded basins:* Cover with the snap-on lid. *Traditional basins:* Cover the mixture with a circle of lightly greased greaseproof paper and a pudding cloth, tying the ends of the cloth together and securing with string.
8. Place onto a perforated steamer tray and place into the steamer.
9. Allow to steam (at low pressure) for 6 hours approximately.
10. When cooked, cool quickly and store until required for service.
11. For service, steam the puddings for $2\frac{1}{2}$ hours.
12. Remove the lid (or cloth and paper) and carefully turn out onto the service dish.
13. Garnish the top of the pudding with a sprig of holly and dust the top with icing sugar. If required, flame with brandy.
14. Accompany with brandy sauce (page 40) or brandy cream (page 40).

## 3.7 STEAMING SPONGE PUDDINGS (LOW PRESSURE)

**HEALTH TIP**

*A low-fat sponge (page 246) can be used for these puddings.*

4 portions

### BASE INGREDIENTS

| | | |
|---|---|---|
| 60 g | margarine | $2\frac{1}{2}$ oz |
| 60 g | caster sugar | $2\frac{1}{2}$ oz |
| 1 | egg (size 3) | 1 |
| 100 g | plain flour | 4 oz |
| 5 g | baking powder | $\frac{1}{4}$ oz |
| 25 ml | milk | 1 fl oz |
| 250 ml | custard sauce (page 39) | $\frac{1}{2}$ pt |

### BASE METHOD

1 Assemble the ingredients for the mixture which should be at room temperature, i.e. 21 °C/70 °F.
2 Sieve together the flour and baking powder.
3 Place the fat and sugar into a mixing bowl and beat together until light and creamy.
4 Add the egg a little at a time while beating the mixture.
5 Occasionally scrape down the bowl to ensure that the mixture is evenly beaten.
6 Add the flour and carefully mix into the creamed fat, sugar and egg.
7 Lightly mix the milk through the cake batter.
8 Lightly grease the steam pudding moulds.
9 Place the mixture into the greased moulds.
10 Cover the moulds with lightly greased greaseproof paper.
11 Place onto a perforated steamer tray and place into the steamer.
12 Steam at low pressure for 1–$1\frac{1}{2}$ hours.
13 When cooked, turn out onto a serving dish and serve with the custard sauce.

**VANILLA SPONGE PUDDING** Prepare the basic sponge pudding above, adding 3–4 drops of vanilla essence to the fat and sugar at step 3.

**STEAMED SULTANA PUDDING** Prepare the basic sponge pudding above. After adding the milk (step 7), gently fold 50 g/2 oz sultanas (washed and thoroughly dried) into the cake mixture and complete as stated.

**CHOCOLATE SPONGE PUDDING** Prepare the basic sponge pudding above, but replace 20 g/$\frac{3}{4}$ oz of the flour with cocoa powder, i.e. use 80 g/$3\frac{1}{4}$ oz plain flour and 20 g/$\frac{3}{4}$ oz cocoa powder.

## 3.8 STEAMING ROOT VEGETABLES (HIGH PRESSURE)

**CHEF'S TIP**

*Cooking time depends on the size of the vegetables and the pressure at which the machine operates. The higher the pressure, the shorter the cooking time. Suggested cooking times are for a cooking pressure of 100 kN $m^{-2}$/14 lb $in^{-2}$.*

### BASE METHOD

1 Ensure the steamer is preheated (if appropriate) and ready for cooking.
2 Place the tray into the steamer then ensure the steamer door is closed correctly.
3 Set the timer to the time required for cooking.
4 Steam the food until cooked.
5 Allow the pressure to drop, then carefully open the steamer door.
6 Remove the cooking tray from the steamer.
7 Place the vegetables into a service dish.

**CHEF'S TIP**

*Small turnips may be left whole.*

### STEAMED TURNIPS

4 portions

| 500 g | turnips | $1\frac{1}{4}$ lb |
|---|---|---|

1 Wash and peel the turnips.
2 Cut the turnips into cubes: 10 mm/$\frac{1}{2}$ inch.
3 Place into a perforated steamer tray and lightly season if required.
4 Follow the instructions in the base method above, cooking the turnips for 4–5 minutes.

**CHEF'S TIP**

*Small beetroot may be served whole, but large beetroot is normally sliced before serving.*

### STEAMED BEETROOT

4 portions

| 400 g | whole, young beetroot | 1 lb |
|---|---|---|

1 Wash the beetroot, then place (unpeeled) into a perforated steamer tray.
2 Follow the instructions in the base method above cooking the beetroot for 8–10 minutes approximately (depending on size).
3 Peel the beetroot when cooked.

### STEAMED NEW POTATOES *POMMES NOUVELLES VAPEUR*

4 portions

| 400 g | potatoes | 1 lb |
|---|---|---|

1 Wash, scrub and remove any spots or mould.
2 Cut the potatoes into even-sized pieces if they are different sizes.
3 Place into a perforated steamer tray and lightly season if required.
4 Follow the instructions in the base method above, cooking the potatoes for 5–6 minutes.

## 3.9 GREEN-LEAF AND LEGUMINOUS VEGETABLES (HIGH PRESSURE)

**CHEF'S TIP**

*Frozen vegetables should be cooked from a frozen state.*

### BASE METHOD

1 Ensure the steamer is preheated (if appropriate) and ready for cooking.
2 Place the vegetables into a perforated steamer tray. Lightly season if required.
3 Place the tray into the steamer and ensure the steamer door is closed correctly.
4 Set the timer to the time required for cooking.
5 Steam the food until cooked.
6 Allow the pressure to drop, then carefully open the steamer door.
7 Remove the cooking tray from the steamer.
8 Place the vegetables into a service dish.

### STEAMED CABBAGE

4 portions

| | | |
|---|---|---|
| 500 g | fresh cabbage | $1\frac{1}{4}$ lb |
| | *or* | |
| 300 g | frozen cabbage | 12 oz |

1 Wash the cabbage, cut through the bottom stalk and remove any wilted leaves.
2 Cut into quarters, then remove the centre stalk. Also remove any large ribs in the leaves.
3 Shred the cabbage.
4 Cook as stated in the base method above, cooking the cabbage for $1-1\frac{1}{2}$ minutes (fresh and frozen).

### STEAMED FRENCH BEANS

4 portions

| | | |
|---|---|---|
| 400 g | fresh French beans | 1 lb |
| | *or* | |
| 300 g | frozen French beans | 12 oz |

1 Top and tail the beans, wash in cold water then drain.
2 Cook as stated in the base method above, cooking the beans for $1\frac{1}{2}-2$ minutes (fresh and frozen).

### STEAMED BRUSSELS SPROUTS

4 portions

| | | |
|---|---|---|
| 500 g | fresh Brussels sprouts | $1\frac{1}{4}$ lb |
| | *or* | |
| 300 g | frozen Brussels sprouts | 12 oz |

1 Trim off any discoloured leaves.
2 Cut a small cross in the base of the stem of each sprout (unless frozen).
3 Wash in cold water then drain.
4 Cook as stated in the base method above, cooking the sprouts for $2\frac{1}{2}-3$ minutes (fresh and frozen).

# Process 4 STEWING

**DEFINITION** Stewing is a moist method of cooking where prepared food (cut into pieces) is cooked in a minimum quantity of liquid. Both the food and the liquid form the stew therefore they are served together. Stewing is an ideal method of cooking for the tougher cuts of meat, poultry and game; and cooking and serving them in their cooking juices also saves valuable nutrients. Stewing is also a term used when slowly cooking fruits to a pulp (e.g. stewed apples).

## REASONS FOR STEWING FOODS

1 To make foods tender: by breaking down and softening starch, cellulose, protein and fibrous material.
2 To make foods more palatable and digestible.
3 To make foods safer to eat: by destroying bacteria which can cause food poisoning.
4 To produce a particular quality in food, of colour, flavour and texture (e.g. stewed beef).

## METHODS OF STEWING FOODS

Methods of stewing are grouped according to the following factors:

1 **Type of commodity** e.g. fish, meat, vegetable stews.
2 **Colour of stew** e.g. white and brown stews.
3 **Method of preparation:**
   **a)** stews cooked in a prepared sauce (e.g. fricassée)
   **b)** stews where the liquid is thickened at the end of the cooking process (e.g. blanquettes).

## COMMODITIES SUITABLE FOR STEWING

1 **Fish and shellfish.**
2 **Red and white meats.** Examples are beef, mutton, lamb, veal and pork. The tougher cuts of meat are used for stewing (see Chapter 1 for individual commodities).
3 **Poultry and feathered game.** Examples are chicken, duckling, partridge and pheasant.
4 **Vegetables.** Several vegetables are usually cooked together to form the stew, e.g. onions, garlic, courgettes, aubergines and tomatoes in a ratatouille.
5 **Fruits.** The cooking of apples, pears and rhubarb to form a coarse pulp.

## EQUIPMENT USED WHEN STEWING FOODS

Types of equipment include saucepans, boilers and bratt pans.

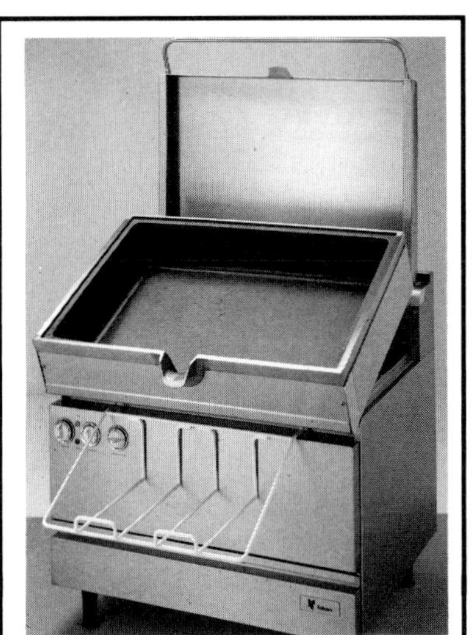

**Bratt pan**

**Saucepan**

## BASIC TECHNIQUES OF STEWING

**BLANCHING** This is done to remove impurities from meat when preparing blanquettes (page 102). It is done as follows:

1 Cover the prepared meat with cold water and bring it to the boil.
2 Remove from the stove and place under cold running water to rinse off all the scum which has formed.
3 Drain, and prepare the stew.

**LIAISING** This is a method of finishing a white stew, using a mixture of egg yolks and cream (a liaison) – see page 101. This increases fat content.

**SEARING** This is the initial shallow-frying of flesh when preparing brown stews (opposite). It is carried out to develop colour and flavour. It is often stated that this procedure *seals* in the juices and therefore retains goodness and reduces weight loss. This is a myth which should be ignored.

**SETTING** This is the method of lightly cooking or *stiffening* flesh in fat without developing colour. It is used when preparing fricassées – see page 101.

## KEY POINTS

- Most stews have long cooking times, therefore ensure you allow for this in your time plan. For example, beef stew made with shoulder steak may require 2–3 hours cooking before the meat is tender.
- Arrange saucepans on the stove so that the food is only simmering. Stir the stew regularly to prevent burning, and skim off surface fat and impurities.
- Check liquid content of stews during cooking and top up with additional stock as required.
- Remember that stews may be cooked in the oven under cover and this can provide much needed stove space for other items.
- Pay special attention to portion control. Estimating the number of portions from a large quantity of stew is difficult. Use ladles or spoons of standard sizes which will provide the correct portion size and number of portions expected.
- Avoid reheating stews but if they must be reheated, cool quickly and store in a chill below 5 °C/40 °F for as short a time as possible. When reheating stews, bring to the boil and simmer for 15–20 minutes to avoid food poisoning.
- Trim off as much visible fat from meat, poultry and game as possible before cooking. Also skim the stew regularly during cooking to remove surface fat.
- Where possible reduce the red meat content of stews and increase the quantity of foods which provide fibre, e.g. use vegetable garnishes of beans, brown rice, sweetcorn kernels and low-fat dumplings made with wholemeal flour.

# 4.1 BROWN STEWS

### TRADITIONAL PRACTICE

*Use 450–570 g/1$\frac{1}{4}$–1$\frac{1}{2}$ lb meat. Also replace the oil with 25 g/1 oz lard or dripping and use plain white flour. This increases the fat content and has less fibre.*

### HEALTH TIP

*Cut the carrot, onion and celery into neat pieces and do not strain out of the stew after cooking. Also add a selection of prepared vegetables during cooking, e.g. diced turnips, peppers, sweetcorn kernels and peas. This provides additional fibre. Serve with brown rice to increase the fibre content.*

### CHEF'S TIP

*Use a frying pan to colour the meat and fry the vegetables (steps 4 and 5) if the saucepan is unsuitable. When this has been done, transfer the meat and vegetables to the saucepan and continue as stated.*

## BASE INGREDIENTS

| | | |
|---|---|---|
| | stewing meat (see opposite) | |
| 10 ml | oil | $\frac{1}{2}$ oz |
| 50 g | onion | 2 oz |
| 50 g | carrot | 2 oz |
| 25 g | leek | 1 oz |
| 25 g | celery | 1 oz |
| $\frac{1}{2}$ litre | brown stock | 1 pt |
| 25 g | wholemeal flour | 1 oz |
| 25 g | tomato purée | 1 oz |
| | small pinch salt and pepper | |
| | sprig of thyme, $\frac{1}{2}$ bay leaf, parsley stalks | |

## BASE METHOD

1. Trim off any sinew and fat from the meat then cut into 20 mm/$\frac{3}{4}$ inch pieces. Cut any oxtails into sections through the joints and trim off all fat.
2. Wash, peel and roughly chop the vegetables.
3. Place the oil in a saucepan and heat until very hot.
4. Add the meat and fry quickly until brown on all sides.
5. Add the vegetables and continue cooking for 6–8 minutes.
6. Stir in the flour to coat the meat and vegetables.
7. Cook over a low heat for 4–5 minutes stirring frequently.
8. Mix in the tomato purée.
9. Mix in the hot stock a little at a time. Stir until smooth each time the stock is added.
10. Bring to the boil and simmer slowly. Beef, veal, lamb and mutton stews will need to simmer for 1$\frac{1}{2}$–2 hours, while oxtails will take 2–3 hours.
11. Skim off any surface fat and top up with stock if required during cooking.
12. When cooked, remove the meat and place into a clean saucepan.
13. Strain the sauce over the meat.
14. Check temperature, consistency and seasoning.
15. Dress in an entrée or service dish, and garnish (page 100) if appropriate.

### CHEF'S TIP

*The stew can be cooked under cover in a moderate oven with minimum risk of burning.*

**BROWN BEEF STEW** ***RAGOÛT DE BOEUF*** For 4 portions, use 400 g/1 lb lean stewing beef, and prepare following the base recipe above.

**BROWN VEAL STEW** ***RAGOÛT DE VEAU*** For 4 portions, use 400 g/1 lb lean stewing veal, and prepare following the base recipe above.

**BROWN LAMB OR MUTTON STEW** ***NAVARIN D'AGNEAU/ DE MOUTON*** For 4 portions, use 400 g/1 lb lean stewing mutton, and prepare following the base recipe above.

**STEWED OXTAILS** ***RAGOÛT DE QUEUE DE BOEUF*** For 4 portions, use 1 kg/2$\frac{1}{2}$ lb oxtails (lean as possible), and prepare following the base recipe above.

## 4.2 SPICED STEWS: BEEF GOULASH *GOULASH DE BOEUF*

### TRADITIONAL PRACTICE

*Use 450–570 g/$1\frac{1}{4}$–$1\frac{1}{2}$lb meat. Also replace the oil with 25 g/1 oz lard or dripping and use plain white flour. This increases the fat content and has less fibre.*

4 portions

### BASE INGREDIENTS

| | | |
|---|---|---|
| 400 g | beef (lean) | 1 lb |
| 25 g | wholemeal flour | 1 oz |
| 1 | small clove garlic | 1 |
| 10 g | tomato purée | $\frac{1}{2}$ oz |
| 10 ml | oil | $\frac{1}{2}$ fl oz |
| 100 g | onion | 4 oz |
| 25 g | paprika | 1 oz |
| $\frac{1}{2}$ litre | brown stock | 1 pt |
| | small pinch salt and pepper | |
| | *Garnish:* | |
| 200 g | diced or cubed potatoes | $\frac{1}{2}$ lb |
| 50 g | choux paste gnocchi (below) | 2 oz |

### BASE METHOD

1 Trim off any sinew and fat from the meat, then cut into 20 mm/$\frac{3}{4}$ inch pieces.
2 Finely chop the onion and crush the garlic.
3 Place the oil in a saucepan and heat until very hot.
4 Add the meat and fry quickly until brown on all sides.
5 Add the onion and garlic and continue cooking for 6–8 minutes.
6 Add the paprika and cook over a low heat for 2–3 minutes.
7 Mix in the flour and continue cooking over a low heat for 4–5 minutes stirring frequently.
8 Mix in the tomato purée.
9 Mix in the hot stock a little at a time. Stir until smooth each time the stock is added.
10 Bring to the boil and simmer slowly for $1\frac{1}{2}$–2 hours.
11 Skim off any surface fat and top up with stock if required during cooking.
12 When almost cooked, add the potatoes and complete the cooking. Also add any additional garnish when just cooked.
13 Check consistency and temperature.
14 Dress in an entrée or service dish then sprinkle with hot choux paste gnocchi.

### CHEF'S TIP

*The goulash can be cooked under cover in a moderate oven to minimise the risk of burning.*

### HEALTH TIP

*Adding prepared vegetables to the goulash during cooking will increase the fibre content, e.g. diced green and red peppers, celery and cooked kidney beans. Serve with brown rice to provide extra fibre.*

### CHOUX PASTE GNOCCHI

1 Prepare the choux paste as stated on page 26.
2 Place into a piping bag with a plain tube: 5 mm/$\frac{1}{4}$ inch diameter.
3 Pipe the mixture into a pan of very hot water; when piping cut the mixture into short or long lengths (according to taste) with a turning knife dipped in hot water.
4 Allow to cook in the very hot water for 8–10 minutes.

# 4.3 EUROPEAN SPICED STEWS: BEEF CURRY *KARI DE BOEUF*

### TRADITIONAL PRACTICE

*Use 450–570 g/1¼–1½ lb meat. Replace the oil with 25 g/1 oz lard or dripping and use plain white flour. This increases the fat content and has less fibre. Also increase the mango chutney to 50 g/2 oz and add 25 g/1 oz dessicated coconut at step 11.*

### TRADITIONAL PRACTICE

*Use white long grain rice instead of brown rice as the accompaniment.*

### CHEF'S TIP

*The hot, spicy taste of a curry can be intensified by adding a little tabasco sauce or extra cayenne pepper.*

### CHEF'S TIP

*Curries are often served with poppadoms, Bombay duck, chapatis and diced or chopped fruits and vegetables.*

4 portions

## BASE INGREDIENTS

| | | |
|---|---|---|
| 400 g | stewing beef | 1 lb |
| 150 g | onion | 6 oz |
| 25 g | wholemeal flour | 1 oz |
| 10 g | tomato purée | ½ oz |
| 50 g | cooking apples | 2 oz |
| 25 g | mango chutney | 1 oz |
| 10 ml | oil | ½ fl oz |
| 1 | clove garlic | 1 |
| 15 g | curry powder | ¾ oz |
| ½ litre | brown stock | 1 pt |
| 10 g | sultanas | ½ oz |
| | *Accompaniment:* | |
| 200 g | brown rice | 8 oz |

## BASE METHOD

1. Trim off any sinew and fat from the meat then cut into 20 mm/¾ inch pieces.
2. Finely chop the onion and crush the garlic.
3. Place the oil in a saucepan and heat until very hot.
4. Add the meat and fry quickly until brown on all sides.
5. Add the onion and garlic and continue cooking for 6–8 minutes.
6. Add the curry powder and cook over a low heat for 2–3 minutes.
7. Mix in the flour and continue cooking over a low heat for 4–5 minutes stirring frequently.
8. Mix in the tomato purée.
9. Mix in the hot stock a little at a time. Stir until smooth each time the stock is added.
10. Bring to the boil and simmer slowly.
11. Chop together the apple, sultanas and mango chutney.
12. Add to the curry during cooking: after 20 minutes cooking approximately.
13. Skim off any surface fat and top up with stock if required during cooking.
14. Check consistency and temperature.
15. Meanwhile boil the rice ready for service (page 53).
16. Dress in an entrée or service dish and serve with the rice and any accompaniments.

## 4.4 INDIAN SPICED STEWS: CHICKEN CURRY *MURGH KARI*

4 portions

### BASE INGREDIENTS

| | | |
|---|---|---|
| $1\frac{1}{2}$ kg | chicken | $3\frac{1}{2}$ lb |
| 15 ml | oil | $\frac{3}{4}$ oz |
| 175 g | onion | 7 oz |
| 100 g | diced tomatoes | 4 oz |
| 125 ml | chicken stock | $\frac{1}{4}$ pt |
| 125 ml | plain yoghurt | $\frac{1}{4}$ pt |
| | small pinch salt | |
| 10 g | chopped coriander leaves | $\frac{1}{2}$ oz |
| 10 ml | lemon juice | $\frac{1}{2}$ fl oz |
| | *Masala paste:* | |
| 10 g | peeled garlic | $\frac{1}{2}$ oz |
| 10 g | peeled root ginger | $\frac{1}{2}$ oz |
| 5 g | ground coriander | $\frac{1}{4}$ oz |
| | pinch cayenne pepper | |
| 5 g | ground cumin | $\frac{1}{4}$ oz |
| 5 g | garam masala | $\frac{1}{4}$ oz |
| 5 g | lemon zest | $\frac{1}{4}$ oz |
| | pinch ground fennel | |
| 25 ml | water | 1 fl oz |
| | *Accompaniment:* | |
| 200 g | brown rice | $\frac{1}{2}$ lb |

### BASE METHOD

1. Cut the chicken into joints then remove the skin (page 18).
2. Peel and finely chop the onion.
3. Prepare the masala paste by pounding the ingredients together in a mortar and pestle.
4. Place the oil in a saucepan and heat until very hot.
5. Add the pieces of chicken and fry quickly until brown on all sides.
6. Remove the chicken from the pan.
7. Add the chopped onion to the pan and fry until lightly coloured.
8. Add the masala paste and allow to sweat for 4–5 minutes occasionally stirring the mixture. Avoid burning the spices.
9. Add the tomatoes, coriander, stock, yoghurt and chicken and bring to the boil.
10. Simmer until cooked, allowing the sauce to thicken and coat the chicken pieces. Also skim off any surface fat which forms during cooking.
11. Stir in the lemon juice.
12. Check consistency and temperature.
13. Meanwhile boil the rice ready for service (page 53).
14. Dress in an entrée or service dish and serve with the rice.

**TRADITIONAL PRACTICE**

*Use white long grain rice instead of brown rice as the accompaniment. This has less fibre.*

**TRADITIONAL PRACTICE**

*Increase the oil to 50 ml/ 2 fl oz when frying the chicken and also add a little oil to the masala paste at step 4. This produces a curry with a rich taste but increases fat content.*

**CHEF'S TIP**

*Take care to cook the spice paste slowly, and add a little water to prevent burning if the temperature is too high.*

## 4.5 SPICED STEWS: CHILLI CON CARNE

**TRADITIONAL PRACTICE**

*Use 400 g/1 lb minced beef. Also replace the oil with 25 g/1 oz lard or dripping and use plain white flour. This increases the fat content and has less fibre.*

4 portions

### BASE INGREDIENTS

| | | |
|---|---|---|
| 350 g | lean minced beef | 14 oz |
| 10 ml | oil | $\frac{1}{2}$ fl oz |
| 75 g | onion | 3 oz |
| 2 | cloves garlic | 2 |
| $2\frac{1}{2}$ g | chilli powder | 1 tsp |
| 5 g | paprika | $\frac{1}{4}$ oz |
| $2\frac{1}{2}$ g | ground cumin | 1 tsp |
| 25 g | wholemeal flour | 1 oz |
| 10 g | tomato purée | $\frac{1}{2}$ oz |
| 125 g | tinned tomatoes | 5 oz |
| 100 g | red kidney beans (dried) | 4 oz |
| 250 ml | bean cooking liquor | $\frac{1}{4}$ pt |

### BASE METHOD

1. Soak the beans for 6–12 hours in cold water.
2. Cover the beans with brown stock and bring to the boil.
3. Boil rapidly for 10 minutes, then simmer until cooked.
4. Peel and chop the onion and crush the garlic.
5. Heat the oil in a saucepan then shallow-fry the onion and garlic until soft.
6. Add the minced beef and continue frying until lightly coloured.
7. Mix in the spices and continue cooking for 2–3 minutes.
8. Add the flour and allow to cook for 4–5 minutes.
9. Stir in the tomato purée and tinned tomatoes.
10. Mix in the hot bean cooking liquor and bring to the boil.
11. Simmer slowly until cooked: 30–40 minutes.
12. Add the beans and continue cooking for a further 4–5 minutes. Also add any garnish at this stage (the vegetables should remain crisp).
13. Check consistency and temperature.
14. Serve in an entrée dish.

**HEALTH TIP**

*Dried beans must always be boiled rapidly for a minimum of 10 minutes before simmering, to destroy a toxin which causes sickness.*

**CHEF'S TIP**

*For an interesting chilli with added fibre you can produce a dish with a crunchy texture. Add 200 g/8 oz prepared raw vegetables to the chilli and cook lightly, e.g. diced onions, peppers, sweetcorn kernels, celery and peas.*

**CHEF'S TIP**

*Accompany the chilli with a bowl of raw onion rings and hot tomato concassées.*

## 4.6 SALMIS OF GAME (feathered game only)

### PHEASANT SALMIS *SALMIS DE FAISAN*

4 portions

#### BASE INGREDIENTS

| | | |
|---|---|---|
| 1 | large pheasant | 1 |
| 5 ml | oil | $\frac{1}{4}$ oz |
| 50 g | onion | 2 oz |
| 50 g | carrot | 2 oz |
| 25 g | celery | 1 oz |
| 25 g | leek | 1 oz |
| 25 ml | brandy | 1 fl oz |
| 50 ml | red wine | 2 fl oz |
| $\frac{1}{2}$ litre | low-fat demi-glace (page 30) | 1 pt |
| | sprig of thyme, $\frac{1}{2}$ bay leaf, 2 parsley stalks | |
| | *Garnish:* | |
| 100 g | button mushrooms | 4 oz |
| | pinch chopped parsley | |

#### BASE METHOD

1. Prepare the pheasant ready for roasting (pages 17–18).
2. Wash, peel and slice the vegetables.
3. Roast the pheasant keeping it underdone (page 128).
4. Remove the pheasant from the tray, sit vent up and allow to cool slightly.
5. Cut the pheasant into portions then remove the skin.
6. Place the skinned pieces into a sauteuse or plat à sauter.
7. Add the brandy and a little demi-glace then cover with a lid and keep warm.
8. Chop up the carcase.
9. Add the vegetables and pieces of carcase to the roasting tray and fry until lightly coloured.
10. Decant off all the fat.
11. Swill with the red wine then reduce down by two-thirds.
12. Add the demi-glace, bring to the boil and simmer for 20 minutes approximately. Skim off any surface fat during cooking.
13. Lightly cook the mushrooms in a little oil then add to the pheasant.
14. Strain over the sauce and complete the cooking.
15. Serve in an entrée dish sprinkled with a little chopped parsley.

**TRADITIONAL PRACTICE**

*Use 25 g/1 oz lard or dripping in place of the oil when roasting the pheasant. Use traditional demi-glace and leave the skin on the pheasant pieces after portioning. Also fry the mushroom garnish in butter instead of oil at step 13. This increases the fat content.*

**TRADITIONAL PRACTICE**

*The chopped vegetables and carcase pieces are sometimes fried separately in butter rather than in the roasting tray (step 9). These changes substantially increase the fat content.*

**CHEF'S TIP**

*Avoid over-cooking at steps 12 and 14. Younger birds will cook quite quickly, but older birds may need further cooking. Proceed to step 13, but do not add the mushrooms. Strain the sauce over the pheasant and simmer slowly until cooked, then garnish with the mushrooms.*

**CHEF'S TIP**

*A salmis is sometimes served as a reheated dish using cooked game.*

#### GARNISHES FOR BROWN STEWS

**Jardinière** Garnish the stew with 50 g/2 oz each of bâtons of carrots and turnips (which have been plain boiled or cooked glazed – page 66) and 25 g/1 oz each of cooked peas and diamonds of French beans.

**With rice** Serve the stew on a bed of boiled brown or white long grain rice (100 g/4 oz rice approximately).

**With vegetables** Cut the base vegetables neatly and do not strain out of the stew. In addition, garnish the stew with an assortment of vegetables, e.g. 100 g/4 oz mixture of diced red and green peppers, cooked red beans, butter beans, diamonds of French beans, peas and sweetcorn kernels.

## 4.7 WHITE STEWS: FRICASSÉES

### CHICKEN FRICASSÉE *FRICASÉE DE VOLAILLE* (lower-fat)

4 portions

**BASE INGREDIENTS**

| | | |
|---|---|---|
| $1\frac{1}{2}$ kg | chicken | $3\frac{1}{2}$ lb |
| $\frac{1}{2}$ litre | chicken stock | 1 pt |
| 10 ml | oil | $\frac{1}{2}$ fl oz |
| 25 ml | half-cream cream | 1 fl oz |
| | small pinch salt and white pepper | |
| | *Thickening paste:* | |
| 125 ml | fromage frais | $\frac{1}{4}$ pt |
| 50 g | flour | 2 oz |

**BASE METHOD**

1 Cut the chicken into portions (page 18) and remove the skin.
2 Lightly heat the oil in a sauteuse or plat à sauter and add the chicken pieces.
3 Cover with a lid and cook lightly on all sides without colouring.
4 Add just enough stock to cover the chicken then bring to the boil.
5 Mix together the fromage frais and flour to a smooth paste, then whisk into the chicken mixture and reboil.
6 Simmer slowly until cooked, skimming off any surface fat as required.
7 Remove the chicken pieces and place into a clean pan.
8 Strain the sauce over the chicken.
9 Bring back to the boil and check consistency and seasoning.
10 Blend in the cream.
11 Dress the pieces in an entrée dish, sprinkle with chopped parsley and serve.

**CHEF'S TIP**

*Replace the plain flour with besan flour (chick pea flour) to increase fibre. Serving the dish with boiled brown or white rice will increase fibre still further.*

**CHICKEN FRICASSÉE ANCIENT STYLE** ***FRICASÉE DE VOLAILLE À L'ANCIENNE*** Add washed, peeled button onions and mushrooms (100 g/4 oz each) to the fricassée. Add the onions at the start of cooking (step 6) and the mushrooms 10 minutes later.

**HEALTH TIP**

*The traditional fricassée is high in fat.*

**TRADITIONAL FRICASSÉE** Prepare as for the base recipe, but with the following alterations:
1 Use 50 g/2 oz butter in place of the oil.
2 Add 40 g/$1\frac{3}{4}$ oz flour and stir through the chicken pieces after frying lightly (step 2). Gently cook for 2–3 minutes without colouring.
3 Blend in the stock, and simmer until cooked. Do not use the thickening paste.
4 Finish the stew with a liaison (page 38) at step 10 and do not reboil.

## 4.8 WHITE STEWS: BLANQUETTES

### CHEF'S TIP

*Replace the plain flour with besan flour (chick pea flour) to increase fibre. Also serve the dish with vegetables which provide valuable fibre, e.g. butterbeans, sweetcorn, or braised brown or white rice.*

### BLANQUETTE DE VEAU

4 portions

#### BASE INGREDIENTS

| | | |
|---|---|---|
| 400 g | lean stewing veal | 1 lb |
| 1 | whole peeled carrot | 1 |
| 1 | studded onion | 1 |
| ½ litre | white veal stock | 1 pt |
| | squeeze lemon juice | |
| 25 ml | half-cream cream | 1 fl oz |
| 1 | bouquet garni | 1 |
| | small pinch salt and white pepper | |
| | *Thickening paste:* | |
| 100 g | fromage frais | 4 oz |
| 30 g | flour | 1½ oz |

#### BASE METHOD

1 Trim off any fat from the veal then cut into 20 mm/¾ inch cubes.
2 Place into a saucepan and cover with cold water.
3 Bring to the boil, refresh under cold running water to remove the scum, then drain.
4 Place into a clean saucepan with the carrot, onion and bouquet garni.
5 Cover with the stock and bring to the boil.
6 Simmer until almost cooked: 45 minutes approximately.
7 Skim off any surface fat and top up with additional stock if required during cooking.
8 Remove the carrot, onion and bouquet garni.
9 Mix together the fromage frais and flour to form a paste.
10 Whisk in the thickening paste and reboil to thicken.
11 Simmer until cooked.
12 Add the lemon juice and cream.
13 Check temperature and consistency.
14 Dress in an entrée dish and sprinkle with a little chopped parsley.

### HEALTH TIP

*The traditional blanquette is high in fat.*

**TRADITIONAL BLANQUETTE** Prepare as above, but:

1 Increase the quantity of veal to 500 g/1 lb.
2 Thicken the stew with a roux, i.e. replace steps 9 and 10 with the following:
   a) melt 25 g/1 oz butter in a saucepan
   b) add 25 g/1 oz flour and cook over a low heat without colour
   c) mix in the hot cooking liquor from the veal (after step 8). Bring to the boil.
3 Strain the sauce over the veal and simmer slowly until cooked.
4 Finish the stew with a liaison (page 38) at step 12 and do not reboil.

## 4.9 IRISH STEW

**TRADITIONAL PRACTICE**

*Use 800 g/1¾ lb neck cutlets of lamb instead of the lean stewing lamb. This increases the fat content.*

**CHEF'S TIP**

*This stew can be transformed into a range of different dishes by adding further ingredients. For example, for* Irish stew with fennel and butterbeans *simply add 100 g/4 oz diced root fennel at step 10 and 75 g/3 oz cooked butterbeans when almost cooked (this increases fibre).*

4 portions

### BASE INGREDIENTS

| | | |
|---|---|---|
| 400 g | lean stewing lamb | 1 lb |
| 500 g | potato | 1¼ lb |
| 100 g | celery | 4 oz |
| 100 g | onion | 4 oz |
| 100 g | white leek | 4 oz |
| 100 g | button onions | 4 oz |
| 100 g | white cabbage | 4 oz |
| ½ litre | white stock | 1 pt |
| | small pinch salt and pepper | |
| | bouquet garni | |
| | chopped parsley | |

*Accompaniment:*
pickled red cabbage

### BASE METHOD

1. Trim any fat from the lamb and cut into cubes 25 mm/1 inch approximately.
2. Place into a saucepan and cover with cold water.
3. Bring to the boil, refresh under cold running water to remove any scum then drain.
4. Place into a clean saucepan and cover with the stock or water.
5. Bring to the boil and skim, removing any surface fat.
6. Wash and peel the vegetables.
7. Turn the potatoes into small barrel shapes (25 mm/1 inch long) and place aside.
8. Cut the potato trimmings, larger onions, celery, leeks and cabbage into small pieces.
9. Add the vegetables to the meat.
10. Simmer until the meat is almost cooked: 1 hour approximately, depending on the quality of the meat. Skim and top up with stock as required.
11. Add the button onions and simmer for 10 minutes approximately.
12. Add the turned potatoes and simmer until cooked.
13. Check seasoning and consistency.
14. Dress in an entrée dish and sprinkle with chopped parsley.
15. Serve accompanied with a dish of pickled red cabbage.

### IRISH STEW WITH ROOT FENNEL AND BUTTER BEANS

Prepare as for the base recipe, but add 50 g/2 oz cooked butter beans and 50 g/2 oz boiled root fennel to the stew when serving.

## 4.10 RATATOUILLE

**TRADITIONAL PRACTICE**

*Increase the olive oil to 50 ml/2 fl oz and use 200 g/8 oz raw tomato concassées in place of chopped tomatoes. Also peel the courgettes and aubergine. This increases fat and reduces fibre.*

4-6 portions

### BASE INGREDIENTS

| | | |
|---|---|---|
| 10 ml | olive oil | $\frac{1}{2}$ fl oz |
| 1 | clove garlic | 1 |
| 200 g | courgette | 8 oz |
| 200 g | chopped tomato | 8 oz |
| 100 g | onion | 4 oz |
| 50 g | pimento | 2 oz |
| 150 g | aubergine | 6 oz |
| | pinch chopped parsley | |
| | small pinch salt and pepper | |

### BASE METHOD

1 Wash and prepare the vegetables:
   a) Slice the onion and crush the garlic.
   b) Remove the seeds from the pepper and cut it into dice.
   c) Cut the aubergine into slices (5 mm/$\frac{1}{4}$ inch thick).
   d) Cut the courgette into slices (10 mm/$\frac{1}{2}$ inch thick).
2 Heat the oil in a sauteuse or saucepan, then add the onion and garlic.
3 Cook without colouring for 2–3 minutes.
4 Add the diced pepper and continue cooking for 2–3 minutes without colouring.
5 Add the aubergine and courgette and sweat for a further 6–8 minutes. Stir or toss the vegetables occasionally to maintain even cooking and avoid colouring or burning.
6 Add the tomatoes and simmer slowly until cooked.
7 Check seasoning and place in a vegetable dish.
8 Sprinkle with chopped parsley and serve.

## INDIAN VEGETABLE STEW *BRINJAL BARTHA*

**TRADITIONAL PRACTICE**

*Use ghee instead of oil and increase the quantity to 50 g/2 oz. This increases the fat content.*

4–6 portions

| | | |
|---|---|---|
| 10 ml | oil | $\frac{1}{2}$ fl oz |
| 150 g | roughly chopped onion | 6 oz |
| 5 g | grated root ginger | $\frac{1}{4}$ oz |
| 5 g | garam masala | $\frac{1}{4}$ oz |
| $2\frac{1}{2}$ g | red chilli powder | $\frac{1}{2}$ tsp |
| 5 g | turmeric | $\frac{1}{4}$ oz |
| 2 | small aubergines (sliced) | 2 |
| 100 g | chopped tomatoes | 4 oz |
| | small pinch salt and pepper | |

1 Heat the oil in a saucepan.
2 Add the onion and garlic. Cook lightly for 1–2 minutes.
3 Add the spices and cook gently for 1 minute. Avoid burning the spices.
4 Add the aubergine slices and sweat them for a further 6–8 minutes. Stir or toss the vegetables to maintain even cooking and to avoid colouring or burning.
5 Add the tomatoes. Simmer slowly until cooked.
6 Check seasoning and serve.

# 4.11 STEWING FRUITS

**CHEF'S TIP**

*If stewing cranberries, use a tin-lined or stainless steel pan. Do not use an aluminium or iron pan as the cranberries will discolour.*

**BASE METHOD**

1 Place the fruit in a saucepan.
2 Add the sugar, lemon juice and water.
3 Place on the heat and cook, stirring frequently to avoid burning.
4 Cook to a soft pulp. Avoid overcooking.
5 Check taste and consistency.

**TRADITIONAL PRACTICE**

*Increase the sugar to 25–50 g/1–2 oz.*

## STEWED APPLES (apple pulp)

Yield: 300 g/12 oz pulp

| | | |
|---|---|---|
| 300 g | cooking apples | 12 oz |
| | juice of $\frac{1}{4}$ lemon | |
| 10 g | sugar | $\frac{1}{2}$ oz |
| 25 ml | water | 1 fl oz |

Peel, core and wash the apples. Cut into pieces or slices and place in lemon water to avoid discolouration. Cook as stated in the base method.

**TRADITIONAL PRACTICE**

*Increase the sugar to 50–75 g/2–3 oz.*

## STEWED GOOSEBERRIES (gooseberry pulp)

Yield: 300 g/12 oz pulp

| | | |
|---|---|---|
| 300 g | gooseberries | 12 oz |
| | juice of $\frac{1}{4}$ lemon | |
| 25 g | sugar | 1 oz |
| 100 ml | water | 4 oz |

Top and tail the gooseberries. Lightly scrape over the surfaces with a small knife to remove any hairs, then wash and drain. Cook as stated in the base method.

**TRADITIONAL PRACTICE**

*Increase the sugar to 100 g/4 oz.*

## STEWED CRANBERRIES (cranberry pulp)

Yield: 300 g/12 oz pulp

| | | |
|---|---|---|
| 300 g | cranberries | 12 oz |
| 75 g | sugar | 3 oz |
| 100 ml | water | 4 fl oz |

Remove any stalks or foreign bodies from the cranberries then wash and drain. Cook as stated in the base method.

**TRADITIONAL PRACTICE**

*Increase the sugar to 75 g/3 oz.*

## STEWED RHUBARB (rhubarb pulp)

Yield: 300 g/12 oz pulp

| | | |
|---|---|---|
| 300 g | rhubarb | 12 oz |
| 50 g | sugar | 2 oz |
| 75 ml | water | 3 fl oz |

Cut off the rhubarb leaves and trim the stalk. Wash and drain, then cut into suitable lengths: 25 mm/1 inch approximately. Cook as stated in the base method.

# Process 5 BRAISING

**DEFINITION** Braising is a moist method of cooking, where prepared food is cooked in a covered container with a quantity of stock or sauce, under cover, in an oven. The food to be braised is usually placed on a vegetable base (mirepoix) and the liquid or sauce added to approximately two-thirds the height of the commodity. This rule does not apply when braising small cuts of meat and offal such as chops, rump steaks and sliced ox liver, where the food is covered with the cooking liquor or sauce to maintain even cooking. When the food is cooked it is portioned and served with the finished sauce or cooking liquor.

## REASONS FOR BRAISING FOODS

1 To make foods tender: by breaking down and softening starch, cellulose, protein and fibrous material.
2 To make foods more palatable and digestible.
3 To cook and serve foods in their own juices, thus conserving valuable nutrients.
4 To make foods safer to eat: by destroying bacteria which can cause food poisoning.
5 To produce a particular quality in food, of colour, flavour and texture (e.g. braised celery).

**METHODS OF BRAISING FOODS** Methods of braising are grouped according to the colour of the finished dish and the foods to be braised:

1 brown braising of meat, poultry, game, offal and vegetables
2 white braising of sweetbreads
3 braising rice.

## COMMODITIES SUITABLE FOR BRAISING

1 **Fresh butcher meats:** including beef, veal and venison.
2 **Fresh offal:** including ox liver and sweetbreads.
3 **Pickled meats and offal:** including ham and pickled tongue.
4 **Poultry and feathered game:** including duck, duckling, pheasant and partridge.
5 **Vegetables:** including cabbage, celery, leek and onion.
6 **Rice.**

## EQUIPMENT USED WHEN BRAISING FOODS

Types of equipment include braising pans, casseroles, lidded cooking vessels, plat à sauters with lids and bratt pans.

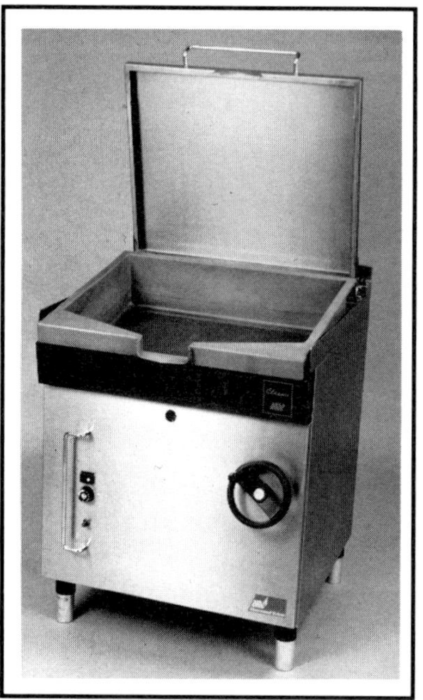

Bratt pan

Braising pan

## BASIC TECHNIQUES OF BRAISING

**BASTING** This is the process of coating the cooking item with the cooking liquor or sauce during cooking. This is done to assist even cooking and keep the surface of the item moist during cooking. A glazed shiny appearance on the surface of meat, poultry or game can also be produced by basting occasionally near the end of the cooking period while uncovered.

**BLANCHING** This applies to braising pickled meats, ox liver, sweetbreads and vegetables and means something different in each case.

1. *Blanching pickled meats (ham or tongue):* Cover with cold water, bring to the boil and simmer for 20 minutes approximately. This is done to remove excess salt from the pickled meat.
2. *Blanching ox liver:* Cover with cold water, bring to the boil, then refresh under cold water. This removes impurities and scum from the liver which would otherwise be present in the sauce.
3. *Blanching sweetbreads:* Cover with cold water, bring to the boil and simmer for 10–15 minutes. After this the sweetbreads are refreshed under cold running water then drained. When blanched, the tough membranes and tissue which surround the sweetbreads are trimmed off with a small knife (steps **1–5** on page 113).
4. *Blanching vegetables:* Place the prepared vegetable into boiling water, simmer for a specified period of time then refresh under cold running water (page 118). Vegetables are blanched for the following reasons:
   - **a)** crisp vegetables become limp and easy to shape
   - **b)** the process helps to retain colour in vegetables
   - **c)** bitterness is reduced in certain vegetables (e.g. mature celery)
   - **d)** the process reduces cooking time.

**LARDING** This process consists of inserting strips of bacon or pork fat through flesh with special needles. This is to produce a moist, rich eating quality but increases fat content.

**MARINADING** This process consists of soaking meat, poultry or game in wine with herbs and vegetables. The reason for marinading is to add flavour and increase tenderness. However, increasing tenderness by marinading may be less effective than was previously thought. Marinading times vary depending on type of flesh, size of joint and taste; varying between 2–18 hours.

**SEARING** This is the initial shallow-frying of flesh when preparing brown braisings (page 108). It is carried out to develop colour and flavour. It is often stated that this procedure *seals* in the juices and therefore retains goodness and reduces weight loss. This is a myth which should be ignored.

## KEY POINTS

- Special care is required when removing braising pans from the oven, especially when they contain large joints. The pan should be lifted carefully (with correct body posture and movement) using a thick, dry, folded oven cloth on each handle, remembering that the joint may move about as the pan is lifted.
- See also the key points for stewing on page 94.

## 5.1 BRAISING RED MEATS AND VENISON

**TRADITIONAL PRACTICE**

*Use 25 g/1 oz lard or dripping in the base recipe instead of oil to sear the meat. Also use traditional brown sauce in place of low-fat brown sauce. This increases fat content.*

### BASE INGREDIENTS

| | meat or venison (see opposite) | |
|---|---|---|
| 10 ml | oil | $\frac{1}{2}$ fl oz |
| 50 g | onion | 2 oz |
| 50 g | carrot | 2 oz |
| 25 g | leek | 1 oz |
| 25 g | celery | 1 oz |
| 200 ml | brown stock | 8 fl oz |
| 250 ml | low-fat brown sauce (page 29) | $\frac{1}{2}$ pt |
| $\frac{1}{2}$ | clove garlic | $\frac{1}{2}$ |
| | sprig of thyme, $\frac{1}{2}$ bay leaf, 2 stalks parsley | |
| | small pinch salt and pepper | |

### BASE METHOD

1. Set the oven thermostat to 175 °C/350 °F.
2. Assemble the recipe ingredients and carry out the basic preparation.
3. Wash, peel and roughly chop the vegetables, i.e. carrot, onion, celery and leek.
4. Peel and crush the garlic.
5. Heat the oil in the braising pan.
6. Add the prepared meat and fry quickly on all sides to develop colour.
7. Add the vegetables and continue cooking for 8–10 minutes.
8. Carefully decant off the excess fat.
9. *Joints:* Add the brown sauce and stock up to two-thirds the height of the meat.
   *Steaks and beef olives:* Barely cover with sauce and stock.
10. Bring to the boil and skim off any surface fat.
11. Cover with a lid and place into the oven. Joints will cook in 2–3 hours, while steaks and beef olives need only 2 hours approximately. Test for cooking.
12. When cooked, remove the meat, then strain the sauce into a clean pan.
13. Skim off surface fat and check consistency and temperature.
14. Remove the string from joints and cut into neat slices across the grain. Also remove any string or skewers from beef olives.
15. Dress the meat in an entrée dish then coat with some of the sauce.
16. Serve the remaining sauce in a sauceboat.

**CHEF'S TIP**

*Test for cooking: no resistance should be felt when piercing the meat with a thin needle or cocktail stick.*

### GARNISHES FOR BRAISED RED MEATS AND VENISON:

**Fleuriste** Garnish the dished meat with 4 scooped-out tomatoes filled with *jardinière* (page 100) and 4 large roast potatoes.

**Nemours** Garnish the dished meat with 50 g/2 oz each of cooked peas and carrots (or glazed carrots: page 66) and 4 duchesse potatoes.

**With succotash** Garnish the dished meat with a mixture of 75 g/3 oz cooked sweetcorn kernels and 50 g/2 oz cooked lima beans. Toss the hot cooked beans together (in 10 g/$\frac{1}{2}$ oz butter if required) and season lightly.

**CHEF'S TIP**

*Serve the braised meat or paupiettes with boiled or braised brown rice (pages 53, 121). This is an ideal accompaniment and increases the fibre content.*

**TRADITIONAL PRACTICE**

*Increase the quantity of meat to 600 g/1½ lb. This provides a larger portion of meat and therefore increases the fat content.*

## BRAISED BEEF *BOEUF BRAISÉ*

For 4 portions, use 400 g/1 lb lean piece of topside or rump beef. Trim the fat from the joint then tie with string. Cook as stated in the base recipe opposite.

## BRAISED STEAKS

For 4 portions, use 4 × 100 g/4 oz lean slices of topside or rump beef. Trim off any fat from the steaks, then complete as stated in the base recipe opposite.

## BRAISED VENISON *VENAISON BRAISÉE*

For 4 portions, use 400 g/1 lb lean piece of topside or rump venison. Trim the fat from the joint then tie with string. Complete as stated in the base recipe opposite.

## BEEF OLIVES *PAUPIETTES DE BOEUF*

| | *Stuffing:* | |
|---|---|---|
| 50 g | chopped onion | 2 oz |
| 50 g | diced carrot | 2 oz |
| 25 g | diced green pepper | 1 oz |
| 25 g | tomato purée | 1 oz |
| 1 | clove garlic (crushed) | 1 |
| 50 g | diced red pepper | 2 oz |
| 50 g | wholemeal breadcrumbs | 2 oz |
| | good pinch chopped parsley | |
| | good pinch mixed herbs | |

1 Mix together all the ingredients for the stuffing.
2 Trim off any fat from a 400 g/12 oz lean piece of topside or rump beef (4 portions).
3 Divide into 4 even-sized slices; cutting across the grain of the meat.
4 Flatten out with a cutlet bat.
5 Place quarter of the stuffing down the centre of each slice.
6 Neatly roll up and secure with string or small skewers.
7 Complete as stated in the base recipe opposite.

**TRADITIONAL PRACTICE**

*Replace the vegetable stuffing with a sausagemeat stuffing (page 37) in the beef olives. This increases fat content and provides less fibre.*

**CHEF'S TIP**

*The flattened slices may be neatly trimmed to 150 × 100 mm/ 6 × 4 inches. Finely chop or mince the trimmings and add them to the stuffing.*

## BRAISED BEEF OR VENISON IN RED WINE SAUCE

Prepare as for braised beef or venison, but marinade the meat with the recipe vegetables and 150 ml/6 fl oz red wine for 6 hours. Cook as stated in the base method, adding the vegetables (drained from the marinade) at step 7. Also add the wine from the marinade with the sauce at step 9.

## 5.2 BRAISING PICKLED MEATS AND OFFAL

**TRADITIONAL PRACTICE**

*Increase the quantity of ham to 600 g/1½ lb meat. Also use traditional brown sauce in place of jus lié or low-fat brown sauce. This increases the fat content.*

### BRAISED HAM *JAMBON BRAISÉ*

4 portions

**BASE INGREDIENTS**

| | | |
|---|---|---|
| 400 g | lean piece of boneless ham | 1 lb |
| 50 g | carrot | 2 oz |
| 50 g | onion | 2 oz |
| 25 g | celery | 1 oz |
| 25 g | leek | 1 oz |
| 250 ml | jus lié (page 30) *or* low-fat brown sauce (page 30) | ½ pt |
| 400 ml | brown stock | ¾ pt |
| | sprig of thyme, ½ bay leaf, 2 parsley stalks | |

**BASE METHOD**

1. Soak the ham in cold water for 6 hours to remove excess salt, then discard the soaking water.
2. Place the ham into a saucepan and cover with cold water.
3. Bring to the boil and simmer for 20 minutes approximately.
4. Allow to cool slightly then remove any rind and surface fat. Stud the top with 3 cloves.
5. Set the oven thermostat to 175 °C/375 °F.
6. Wash, peel and roughly chop the vegetables.
7. Place the vegetables into the braising pan then sit the ham on top.
8. Add the brown stock until at two-thirds the height of the ham.
9. Cover with a lid and bring to the boil on top of the stove.
10. Place into the oven and allow to cook for 2 hours approximately.
11. During cooking, frequently baste the joint with the cooking liquor and skim off any surface fat. Test for cooking.
12. Remove the joint when cooked and keep hot.
13. Boil down the cooking liquor until concentrated then add the jus lié.
14. Simmer for 2–3 minutes, then strain into a clean pan.
15. Skim off any fat from the surface of the sauce and check consistency.
16. Remove the string, trim off any remaining fat, then cut into slices across the grain.
17. Dress the slices in an entrée dish and coat with some of the sauce.
18. Serve the remaining sauce in a sauceboat.

**CHEF'S TIP**

*Taste the cooking liquor for saltiness after reducing at step 13. If the reduced liquor is salty, use only enough of it to add flavour to the sauce.*

**BRAISED TONGUE** Braise tongues following the base method for braised ham, but remove the skin after cooking. Note that fresh tongues are braised following Process 5.1 (page 108): *Braising red meats and venison.*

## 5.3 BRAISING POULTRY AND FEATHERED GAME

### TRADITIONAL PRACTICE

*Replace the low-fat brown sauce with traditional espagnole or demi-glace. This increases the fat content of the dish.*

### TRADITIONAL PRACTICE

*Place the chopped vegetables onto the roasting tray, sit the duckling on top then coat with 50 g/2 oz melted fat prior to roasting in the oven. This increases the fat content.*

### HEALTH TIP

*Serving the duckling without skin will considerably reduce the fat content.*

### BRAISED DUCKLING/DUCK
***CANETON/CANARD BRAISÉ***

4 portions

#### BASE INGREDIENTS

| | | |
|---|---|---|
| 2 kg | duckling/duck | 4 lb |
| 50 g | onion | 2 oz |
| 50 g | carrot | 2 oz |
| 25 g | celery | 1 oz |
| 25 g | leek | 1 oz |
| ½ | clove garlic (optional) | ½ |
| 500 ml | low-fat brown sauce (page 30) | 1 pt |
| 400 ml | brown stock | ¾ pt |
| | sprig of thyme, ½ bay leaf, 2 parsley stalks | |
| | small pinch salt and pepper | |

#### BASE METHOD

1. Clean and truss the bird ready for braising (pages 17–18).
2. Place on a roasting tray and transfer to a hot oven (220 °/430 °F).
3. Cook to remove excess fat and allow a good colour to develop.
4. Remove from the tray and drain well.
5. Meanwhile, wash, peel and roughly chop the vegetables.
6. Peel and crush the garlic.
7. Arrange the vegetables in the bottom of a braising pan or casserole and sit the bird on top: breast upwards.
8. Add the brown sauce and stock up to two-thirds the height of the bird.
9. Bring to the boil, then cover with a lid and place into an oven at 175 °C/350 °F.
10. Allow to cook until tender: 1 hour approximately (depending on the quality of the bird). During cooking, baste with the sauce and skim off surface fat.
11. Remove the bird and keep hot.
12. Strain the sauce into a clean pan.
13. Skim off surface fat and check consistency and seasoning.
14. Remove the string from the bird and cut into portions or leave whole.
15. Dress on an entrée dish and coat with some of the sauce.
16. Serve the remaining sauce in a sauceboat.

## 5.4 BRAISING WHITE MEATS

**TRADITIONAL PRACTICE**

*Increase the quantity of veal to 600 g/1½ lb meat. This provides a larger portion of meat and therefore increases the fat content. Also use 25 g/1 oz lard or dripping in place of oil to sear the meat, and use traditional brown sauce instead of jus lié or low-fat brown sauce.*

**CHEF'S TIP**

*To test for cooking: pierce the centre of the joint with a thin needle or cocktail stick, then withdraw it, allowing the juices to escape. There should be no trace of blood. The internal temperature should be 75 °C/180 °F.*

### BRAISED CUSHION OF VEAL *NOIX DE VEAU BRAISÉE*

4 portions

#### BASE INGREDIENTS

| | | |
|---|---|---|
| 400 g | piece nut of veal | 1 lb |
| 50 g | carrot | 2 oz |
| 50 g | onion | 2 oz |
| 25 g | celery | 1 oz |
| 10 ml | oil | ½ fl oz |
| 25 g | leek | 1 oz |
| 400 ml | brown stock | ¾ pt |
| 250 ml | jus lié or low-fat brown sauce (page 30) | ½ pt |
| | sprig of thyme, ½ bay leaf, 2 parsley stalks | |
| | small pinch salt | |

#### BASE METHOD

1. Set the oven thermostat to 175 °C/375 °F.
2. Trim the fat from the joint then tie with string.
3. Wash, peel and roughly chop the vegetables.
4. Heat the oil in a small braising pan or casserole, add the joint and fry quickly on all sides to develop colour.
5. Decant off the excess fat.
6. Place the vegetables in the braising pan then sit the veal on top.
7. Add the brown stock until two-thirds the height of the joint.
8. Cover with a lid and bring almost to the boil on top of the stove.
9. Place into the oven and allow to cook for 1-1½ hours. Frequently baste the joint with the cooking liquor during cooking and skim off any surface fat.
10. Remove the joint when cooked and keep hot.
11. Boil down the cooking liquor until concentrated then add the jus lié.
12. Simmer for 2–3 minutes, then strain into a clean pan.
13. Skim off any fat from the surface of the sauce and check consistency.
14. Remove the string from the joint then cut into neat slices across the grain.
15. Dress the slices in an entrée dish then coat with some of the hot sauce.
16. Serve the remaining sauce in a sauceboat.

#### GARNISHES FOR BRAISED WHITE MEATS:

**Concorde** Garnish the dished meat with 50 g/2 oz each of cooked peas, carrots (glazed if required: page 66) and 100 g/4 oz mashed potatoes.

**Florentine** Arrange the slices of meat on a bed of cooked spinach (page 60) then complete as stated.

**With noodles** Surround the slices of meat with 100 g/4 oz cooked noodles. The noodles may be tossed in margarine or butter, but this increases fat.

## 5.5 WHITE BRAISING OFFAL

### TRADITIONAL PRACTICE

*Increase the quantity of meat to 600 g/1½ lb. Also use 25 g/1 oz lard or dripping in the base recipe instead of oil to sear the meat. This increases fat content.*

### BRAISED SWEETBREADS
**RIS DE VEAU/D'AGNEAU BRAISÉ À BLANC**

4 portions

**BASE INGREDIENTS**

| | | |
|---|---|---|
| 500 g | sweetbreads: lamb or veal | 1¼ lb |
| 50 g | carrot | 2 oz |
| 50 g | onion | 2 oz |
| 25 g | celery | 1 oz |
| 25 g | leek | 1 oz |
| 400 ml | white stock | 16 fl oz |
| 50 ml | cold water | 2 fl oz |
| 10 g | arrowroot | ½ oz |
| | sprig of thyme, ½ bay leaf, 2 parsley stalks | |
| | small pinch salt and white pepper | |

**BASE METHOD**

1 Wash the sweetbreads in cold running water. If the sweetbreads contain excessive blood, soak in cold salted water for 4–6 hours.
2 Place into a saucepan and cover with cold water.
3 Bring to the boil and simmer for 15 minutes approximately.
4 Refresh in cold water.
5 Trim off any membranes and tough tissue.
6 Wash, peel and roughly chop the vegetables.
7 Place the vegetables in a small braising pan or casserole then add the sweetbreads.
8 Barely cover with the stock.
9 Cover with a piece of lightly oiled greaseproof paper and lid.
10 Place into an oven at 175 °C/350 °F and allow to cook. During cooking, skim occasionally and top up with additional stock if required. Cook for 1 hour approximately.
11 When cooked, remove the sweetbreads from the pan and keep hot covered with the cooking paper.
12 Strain the cooking liquor into a clean pan and bring to the boil.
13 Lightly thicken with the arrowroot diluted in the cold water and simmer for 2–3 minutes. If required, top up the cooking liquor to 250 ml/½ pt.
14 Add the sweetbreads and check consistency, temperature and seasoning.
15 Dress in an entrée dish with a little of the thickened cooking liquor.

### TRADITIONAL PRACTICE

*The vegetables are sometimes fried in the fat after colouring the veal at step 5, but this increases fat content.*

### CHEF'S TIP

*The sweetbreads may be kept a little undercooked at this stage, and cooking completed in the strained and thickened cooking liquor.*

## 5.6 BROWN BRAISING

### BRAISED SWEETBREADS
**(RIS DE VEAU/D'AGNEAU BRAISÉ À BRUN)**

For 4 portions, follow the base recipe above but omit the arrowroot, and use brown stock and 250 ml/½ pt jus lié or brown sauce (page 30). Proceed to step 12, then reduce down the cooking liquor until concentrated. Add the jus lié or brown sauce and simmer for 2–3 minutes. Finish for service as stated (steps 14 and 15).

## 5.7 BRAISING OX LIVER *FOIE DE BOEUF BRAISÉ*

> **TRADITIONAL PRACTICE**
>
> *Use 25 g/1 oz lard or dripping in the base recipe instead of oil to fry the liver. Also use traditional brown sauce instead of low-fat sauce. This increases the fat content.*

> **TRADITIONAL PRACTICE**
>
> *When making braised liver with onions, the onions may be fried separately until golden brown then added to the liver before cooking. However, this will increase the fat content in the dish.*

4 portions

### BASE INGREDIENTS

| | | |
|---|---|---|
| 500 g | ox liver | $1\frac{1}{4}$ lb |
| 50 g | onion | 2 oz |
| 50 g | carrot | 2 oz |
| 25 g | leek | 1 oz |
| 25 g | celery | 1 oz |
| 10 ml | oil | $\frac{1}{2}$ fl oz |
| 200 ml | brown stock | 8 fl oz |
| 250 ml | low-fat brown sauce (page 30) | $\frac{1}{2}$ pt |
| $\frac{1}{2}$ | clove garlic (optional) | $\frac{1}{2}$ |
| | sprig of thyme, $\frac{1}{2}$ bay leaf, 2 parsley stalks | |
| | small pinch salt and pepper | |

### BASE METHOD

1. Remove any skin or tubes from the liver then cut into slices.
2. Place the slices of liver into a saucepan and cover with cold water.
3. Bring to the boil, then refresh under cold running water until all the impurities have been removed. Drain well ready for braising.
4. Wash, peel and roughly chop the vegetables.
5. Peel and crush the garlic.
6. Heat the oil in a braising pan or suitable cooking utensil.
7. Add the slices of liver and fry quickly on all sides to develop colour.
8. Add the vegetables and continue cooking for 8–10 minutes.
9. Carefully decant off the excess fat.
10. Add the brown sauce and stock until the liver is barely covered.
11. Bring to the boil and skim off any surface fat.
12. Cover with a lid and place into an oven at 175 °C/350 °F.
13. Allow to cook until tender: $1\frac{1}{2}$–2 hours.
14. When cooked, remove the liver and place into a clean pan.
15. Strain the sauce over the liver.
16. Check consistency, temperature and seasoning. Also skim off any surface fat.
17. Serve the liver in an entrée dish then coat with some of the sauce.
18. Serve the remaining sauce in a sauceboat.

**BRAISED OX LIVER WITH ONIONS** *FOIE DE BOEUF LYONNAISE* Prepare as above, but replace the vegetables and herbs with 250 g/10 oz sliced onion. A bouquet garni may also be included. Do not strain out the onion at step 15. When cooked, dress in the service dish and coat with the onion sauce.

## 5.8 MEAT HOTPOTS

**TRADITIONAL PRACTICE**

*Use 25 g/1 oz lard or dripping in the base recipe in place of oil to fry the meat and kidneys. Also use 500–600 g/1$\frac{1}{4}$–1$\frac{1}{2}$ lb neck cutlets of lamb instead of leg chops. This increases the fat content.*

**CHEF'S TIP**

*Avoid wetting the potatoes used to top the hotpot as this reduces colour development.*

### LANCASHIRE HOTPOT

4 portions

#### BASE INGREDIENTS

| | | |
|---|---|---|
| 10 ml | oil | $\frac{1}{2}$ fl oz |
| 400 g | lean gigot chops | 1 lb |
| 100 g | sliced kidneys | 4 oz |
| 200 g | onion | $\frac{1}{2}$ lb |
| 400 g | potato | 1 lb |
| 750 ml | white stock | 1$\frac{1}{2}$ pt |
| | small pinch salt and pepper | |
| | chopped parsley | |

#### BASE METHOD

1. Peel and slice the onion.
2. Wash, peel and thinly slice the potatoes (2 mm/$\frac{1}{16}$ inch thickness).
3. Heat the oil in a frying pan, then quickly colour the meat and kidneys.
4. Line the base of a small casserole with a layer of the sliced potato and a layer of the onion.
5. Place the seared meat and kidneys on top and lightly season.
6. Add the stock to just below the top of the meat and kidneys.
7. Place the remaining onion on top, then cover with the rest of the potato slices, neatly overlapping in rows.
8. Brush over the potato slices with a little oil.
9. Place into an oven at 175 °C/350 °F and cook slowly for 2 hours approximately. During cooking occasionally press down on the top with a fish slice.
10. Cover with the casserole lid during cooking if developing too much colour.
11. When cooked, clean round the sides of the casserole and sprinkle with chopped parsley.

**BOLTON HOTPOT** Prepare as for the base recipe above, adding 100 g/4 oz washed button mushrooms to the meat and kidneys at step 5. Also add 8–12 oysters to the hotpot when almost cooked: carefully lift back the potato crust and insert the oysters. Complete as stated.

**CHICKEN HOTPOT** Prepare as for the base recipe, substituting a chicken (jointed) for the lamb and kidneys. Additional vegetables may be added to the recipe if desired: e.g. sliced carrot, turnip, celery, root fennel.

## 5.9 CARBONNADES

### TRADITIONAL PRACTICE

*Use 450–570 g/1¼–1½ lb beef. Also replace the oil with 40 g/1½ oz lard or dripping and use plain white flour. Use half the fat to sear the beef and the remaining fat to fry the onions at step 4. Also add 10 g/½ oz sugar to the carbonnade at step 5. This increases the fat content and sweetens the carbonnade.*

### BEEF CARBONNADE *CARBONNADE DE BOEUF*

4 portions

#### BASE INGREDIENTS

| | | |
|---|---|---|
| 400 g | lean topside of beef | 1 lb |
| 40 g | wholemeal flour | 1½ oz |
| 10 ml | oil | ½ fl oz |
| 250 g | onion | 10 oz |
| 250 ml | beer | ½ pt |
| 250 ml | brown stock | ½ pt |
| | pinch salt and pepper | |
| | chopped parsley | |

#### BASE METHOD

1. Trim the meat of all fat, then cut into thin slices.
2. Peel and slice the onion.
3. Pass the meat through the flour.
4. Heat the oil in a frying pan then quickly colour the floured meat.
5. Place the beef and half the onion into a casserole and lightly season.
6. Place the remaining onion over the top, then add the beer and stock until the onion is just covered.
7. Cover with the casserole lid then place into an oven at 190 °C/375 °F approximately.
8. Allow to cook for 2 hours approximately.
9. When cooked, remove all surface fat and clean round the sides of the casserole.
10. Sprinkle with chopped parsley and serve.

### BEEF AND VEGETABLE CARBONNADE

Prepare as for the base recipe above, but use only 200 g/½ lb beef and add vegetables to the carbonnade as follows.

1. Wash, peel and slice 50 g/2 oz each of the following vegetables: carrot, celery, leek, green pepper, red pepper.
2. Soak then cook 50 g/2 oz red kidney beans (page 99).
3. Follow the base method for carbonnades, adding the prepared vegetables and cooked beans to the meat at step 5. Also add a little less stock, as the vegetables will increase the liquid content of the recipe.

**BEEF VEGETABLE AND BEAN CARBONNADE** Prepare as for beef and vegetable carbonnade above, adding 50 g/2 oz cooked red beans to the carbonnade with the vegetables.

## 5.10 ZUCCHINI PEPPERPOT (vegan dish)

2 portions

### BASE INGREDIENTS

| | | |
|---|---|---|
| 10 ml | oil | $\frac{1}{2}$ fl oz |
| 100 g | sliced tofu | 4 oz |
| 100 g | sliced onion | 4 oz |
| $2\frac{1}{2}$ g | crushed garlic | $\frac{1}{4}$ oz |
| 1 | small, sliced, seeded chilli pepper | 1 |
| 1 g | paprika | 1 tsp |
| 150 g | sliced courgette | 6 oz |
| 100 g | sliced red pepper | 4 oz |
| 150 g | cooked red beans with liquor | 6 oz |
| 20 g | tahini | $\frac{1}{4}$ oz |
| 5 ml | Marmite | 1 tsp |
| 150 g | sliced tomatoes | 6 oz |
| 5 g | sesame seeds | $\frac{1}{4}$ oz |

### BASE METHOD

1. Heat the oil in a pan then shallow fry the tofu until lightly coloured.
2. Remove the tofu from the pan and place aside until required for use.
3. Add the onion, garlic and sliced chilli pepper to the pan and cook under cover for 1–2 minutes.
4. Mix in the paprika then add the courgette and red pepper and continue cooking under cover for a short period. Add a little bean cooking liquor and continue cooking until the vegetables just begin to soften.
5. Add the cooked beans, tahini and Marmite and stir through the vegetables.
6. Dress the vegetables in a suitable oven-proof dish.
7. Moisten with a little bean cooking liquor if required.
8. Neatly decorate the top of the bake with the best shaped vegetables; using slices of tomato, courgette, red pepper and the lightly browned tofu.
9. Sprinkle the sesame seeds over the surface then place into a hot oven (230 °C/445 °F).
10. Bake for 20–30 minutes developing a good colour.

### AUBERGINE AND CHICK PEA PEPPERPOT (vegan dish)

Prepare as for the base recipe above, replacing the courgettes with aubergines. Also replace the cooked red beans and liquor, with cooked chick peas and liquor.

## 5.11 BRAISING VEGETABLES

### CHEF'S TIP

*Use a brown vegetable stock and leave out any fat bacon or pork fat to produce a dish suitable for vegetarians.*

### TRADITIONAL PRACTICE

*Cover each blanched vegetable with a slice of fat bacon or pork fat prior to cooking. This is done to protect the surface of the vegetable during cooking. However this practice (which increases fat content) can be omitted when the vegetables are properly covered during cooking.*

4 portions

### BASE INGREDIENTS

| | | |
|---|---|---|
| | main vegetable (see below and opposite) | |
| 50 g | carrot | 2 oz |
| 50 g | *onion | 2 oz |
| 25 g | *celery | 1 oz |
| 25 g | *leek | 1 oz |
| 300 ml | brown stock | 12 fl oz |
| 125 ml | jus lié (page 30) | $\frac{1}{4}$ pt |
| | sprig of thyme, $\frac{1}{2}$ bay leaf, 2 parsley stalks | |
| | small pinch salt and pepper | |

*Not required if braising the same vegetable.

### BASE METHOD

1 Set the oven thermostat to 175 °C/350 °F.
2 Assemble the recipe ingredients and carry out the basic preparation.
3 Arrange the carrot, onion, celery, leek and herbs on the bottom of the cooking pan then place the blanched vegetables on top.
4 Add the brown stock up to two-thirds the height of the blanched vegetables.
5 Cover with a piece of lightly oiled greaseproof paper and a lid.
6 Bring almost to the boil on top of the stove then place into the oven to cook. Cook *cabbage* and *onions* for $1\frac{1}{2}$ hours, *celery* and *fennel* for $2\frac{1}{2}$ hours, *lettuce* for 1 hour, and *leeks* for 45 minutes.
7 When cooked, remove the main vegetable from the pan and keep hot, covered with the cooking paper. If braising celery, fennel, leek or lettuce, portion the vegetables. *Celery*: cut lengthways into four neat portions. *Fennel*: cut lengthways into two neat portions. *Leeks*: press out excess liquid then neatly fold. *Lettuce*: press out excess liquid from each lettuce, cut in half then neatly fold.
8 Boil down the cooking liquor until concentrated then add the jus lié.
9 Simmer for 2–3 minutes, then strain.
10 Dress the vegetable in a vegetable dish then coat with the sauce.
11 Sprinkle with chopped parsley if required.

### BRAISED CABBAGE *CHOU BRAISÉ*

1 Wash a 600 g/$1\frac{1}{2}$ lb cabbage and remove any wilted leaves.
2 Remove the large outer leaves and place aside.
3 Cut the cabbage into 4 wedges, leaving on the centre stalks.
4 Place into boiling salted water along with the outer leaves and cook until the cabbage ribs are limp: 15–20 minutes.
5 Refresh under cold running water, then drain.
6 Remove the centre stalks, then surround each wedge of cabbage with a large outer leaf.
7 Place each portion into a clean cloth then squeeze into a firm ball.
8 Complete as stated in the base recipe above.

## BRAISED CELERY *CÉLERI BRAISÉ*

1 Wash 1 medium head celery (500 g/¼ lb) and trim the root.
2 If necessary, remove any deteriorated leaves.
3 Cut the head to 100 mm/4 inches.
4 Place into boiling salted water and cook for 20 minutes.
5 Drain and complete as stated in the base recipe opposite.

## BRAISED LEEKS *POIREAUX BRAISÉS*

1 Wash 4 medium leeks (500–600 g/1¼–1½ lb). Remove any wilted leaves, then cut off the root ends.
2 Trim the green leaves, then slit each leek lengthways starting just behind the root end.
3 Wash well in cold running water to remove any dirt from the insides.
4 Tie into a bundle.
5 Place into boiling salted water and cook for 5 minutes.
6 Drain then complete as stated in the base recipe opposite.

## BRAISED ONIONS *OIGNONS BRAISÉS*

1 Peel 4 medium onions, leaving a short piece of stem.
2 Place into boiling water and cook for 10 minutes.
3 Drain and complete as stated in the base recipe opposite.

## BRAISED FENNEL *FENOUIL BRAISÉ*

1 Wash 2 heads of fennel and trim the root.
2 Place into boiling water and cook for 10–15 minutes.
3 Drain and complete as stated in the base recipe opposite.

## BRAISED LETTUCE *LAITUE BRAISÉE*

1 Wash 2 large lettuces removing any wilted leaves.
2 Trim the root ends.
3 Place into boiling water and cook for 2 minutes approximately.
4 Refresh under cold running water then drain.
5 Squeeze out excess liquid keeping the outer leaves in place.
6 Complete as stated in the base recipe opposite.

## 5.12 BRAISED CHICORY *ENDIVE BRAISÉE*

### TRADITIONAL PRACTICE

*Use 25 g/1 oz butter instead of the margarine when greasing the pan (step 2). This increases the fat content.*

4 portions

### BASE INGREDIENTS

| | | |
|---|---|---|
| 4 | medium chicory | 4 |
| 5 g | margarine | $\frac{1}{4}$ oz |
| 250 ml | jus lié (page 30) | $\frac{1}{2}$ pt |
| | pinch chopped parsley | |
| | squeeze lemon juice | |
| | small pinch salt | |

### BASE METHOD

1. Wash, trim the root ends, and remove any wilted leaves from the chicory.
2. Lightly grease the base of a casserole with the margarine then place the chicory inside.
3. Squeeze lemon juice over the chicory and season lightly.
4. Cover with a piece of lightly oiled greaseproof paper and a tight fitting lid.
5. Cook in the oven at 175 °C/350 °F for 45 minutes-1 hour.
6. When cooked, remove the chicory from the casserole and keep hot, covered with the cooking paper.
7. Reduce the cooking liquor until concentrated, then add the jus lié and simmer for 1 minute approximately.
8. Skim off any fat.
9. Dress the chicory in a vegetable dish, coat with the sauce and sprinkle with chopped parsley.

## 5.13 BRAISED RED CABBAGE *CHOU FLAMANDE*

### TRADITIONAL PRACTICE

*Use 50 g/2 oz butter instead of margarine and also add 10 g/$\frac{1}{2}$ oz caster sugar prior to cooking: both at step 5. This increases fat and sugar content.*

### CHEF'S TIP

*Cook the cabbage in a porcelain, stainless steel or tin-lined casserole to avoid discolouration. Never use an aluminium or iron pan to cook this dish.*

### CHEF'S TIP

*Add a little stock if the cabbage begins to dry out during cooking.*

4 portions

### BASE INGREDIENTS

| | | |
|---|---|---|
| 500 g | red cabbage | $1\frac{1}{4}$ lb |
| 200 ml | vinegar | 8 fl oz |
| 10 g | margarine | $\frac{1}{2}$ oz |
| 150 g | cooking apple | 6 oz |
| | small pinch salt and pepper | |

### BASE METHOD

1. Wash the cabbage and remove any deteriorated leaves.
2. Cut into wedges and remove the centre stalks.
3. Shred and rewash then place into a casserole and season lightly.
4. Add the margarine and vinegar.
5. Cover with a piece of lightly oiled greaseproof paper and lid and place into the oven at 175 °C/350 °F.
6. Meanwhile, peel and core the apple and cut into 10 mm/$\frac{3}{8}$ inch cubes. Store in lemon water until required.
7. When three-quarters cooked (80–90 minutes), add the diced apple and complete the cooking; a further 30 minutes approximately.
8. Check seasoning then clean the sides of the container prior to service, or serve the cabbage in a vegetable dish.

## 5.14 BRAISING RICE *RIZ PILAFF*

**TRADITIONAL PRACTICE**

*Use 50 g/2 oz butter in the recipe instead of margarine. Shallow-fry the shallot or onion (step 3) in 25 g/1 oz butter, and after cooking add the remaining butter and fork through the rice (step 8). This increases the fat content.*

**TRADITIONAL PRACTICE**

*White rice could be used instead of brown rice in any of these recipes. This reduces the fibre content.*

**CHEF'S TIP**

*When preparing riz pilaffs chefs usually measure the stock and rice by volume. Add 2 measures (usually ladles) of stock to 1 measure of rice.*

**CHEF'S TIP**

*Using vegetable instead of chicken stock will make this a vegetarian dish.*

**HEALTH TIP**

*Pilaff with cheese: use 50 g/2 oz grated cheese in the recipe. This increases the fat content.*

**CHEF'S TIP**

*The type of fish used often names the dish, e.g. haddock kedgeree.*

4 portions

### BASE INGREDIENTS

| | | |
|---|---|---|
| 10 g | margarine | $\frac{1}{2}$ oz |
| 100 g | brown rice | 4 oz |
| 50 g | shallot or onion | 2 oz |
| 180 ml | chicken stock | 7 fl oz |
| | small pinch salt | |
| | pinch mill pepper | |

### BASE METHOD

1 Peel and finely chop the shallots or onion.
2 Melt the margarine in a sauteuse or plat à sauter.
3 Add the shallot or onion and sweat for 2–3 minutes.
4 Add the rice and sweat for 2 minutes approximately, stirring frequently. Avoid burning the rice.
5 Add the stock and seasoning and bring to the boil.
6 Cover with a piece of lightly oiled greaseproof paper and a lid.
7 Place into a hot oven at 220 °C/425 °F and cook allowing all the stock to evaporate: 15 minutes approximately.
8 Lightly loosen the rice grains using a fork.

### PILAFF WITH CHEESE *RIZ PILAFF ITALIENNE*

Fork grated low-fat cheese (50 g/2 oz) through the base recipe after cooking.

### RIZ PILAFF WITH MUSHROOMS *RIZ PILAFF AUX CHAMPIGNONS*

Add 100 g/4 oz sliced mushrooms when sweating the shallot or onion at step 3.

### FISH KEDGEREE *CADGÉRY DE POISSON*

*In addition to the base ingredients for pilaff:*

| | | |
|---|---|---|
| 200 g | fish fillet (white, oily or smoked fish) | 8 oz |
| 1 | hard-boiled egg | 1 |
| 200 ml | curry sauce (pages 31–2) | 8 fl oz |

1 Cook the riz pilaff as stated.
2 Poach the fish.
3 Remove any skin and bone from the fish.
4 Flake into pieces.
5 Cut the hard-boiled egg into dice.
6 Mix the fish and eggs through the riz pilaff using a fork.
7 Check temperature; cover and replace into the oven to thoroughly heat through if required.
8 Dress on a serving dish, e.g. an earthenware dish or silver flat.
9 Serve the curry sauce separately in a sauceboat.

## 5.15 SLICED POTATO DISHES

**TRADITIONAL PRACTICE**

*Shallow-fry the onions in 25 g/1 oz butter before adding to the potatoes. This increases the fat content.*

### SAVOURY POTATOES *POMMES BOULANGÈRE*

4 portions

**BASE INGREDIENTS**

| | | |
|---|---|---|
| 450 g | potato | 1 lb 2 oz |
| 100 g | onion | 4 oz |
| 300 ml | white stock (or vegetable stock) | 12 fl oz |
| 5 g | melted margarine | $\frac{1}{4}$ oz |
| | chopped parsley | |
| | salt and pepper | |

**BASE METHOD**

1. Wash, peel and thinly slice the potatoes: 1 mm/$\frac{1}{16}$ inch approximately.
2. Peel and slice the onion.
3. Lightly oil a shallow earthenware dish.
4. Arrange the sliced potato in layers with the onion and add the seasoning. Leave the best slices of potato aside to finish the top.
5. Add the stock until almost to the top of the potato slices.
6. Neatly arrange the remaining potato slices in overlapping rows across the top.
7. Brush over the surface with the melted margarine.
8. Place in an oven at 200 °C/390 °F and allow to cook for $1\frac{1}{2}$–2 hours approximately. During cooking, occasionally press down the potato slices with a fish slice to produce a firm texture.
9. When cooked, clean round the sides of the dish.
10. Sprinkle with chopped parsley and serve.

## 5.16 CUBED POTATO DISHES

**TRADITIONAL PRACTICE**

*Use whole milk in place of skimmed milk, 20 g/$\frac{3}{4}$ oz butter instead of margarine and white breadcrumbs in place of brown. Cream is also sometimes used in this recipe: replace 50 ml/2 fl oz milk with cream. This increases the fat content.*

### DELMONICO POTATOES *POMMES DELMONICO*

4 portions

**BASE INGREDIENTS**

| | | |
|---|---|---|
| 450 g | potatoes | 1 lb 2 oz |
| 350 ml | skimmed milk | 14 fl oz |
| 20 g | wholemeal breadcrumbs | $\frac{3}{4}$ oz |
| 5 g | melted margarine | $\frac{1}{4}$ oz |
| | salt and pepper | |

**BASE METHOD**

1. Wash, peel and cut the potatoes into cubes: 10 mm/$\frac{1}{2}$ inch approximately.
2. Place the potato cubes into a shallow earthenware dish, lightly season then barely cover with the milk.
3. Cover with a lid then place into an oven at 180 °C/355 °F for 1 hour approximately.
4. When almost cooked, remove the lid and clean the edges of the dish.
5. Sprinkle with the breadcrumbs and melted margarine.
6. Continue cooking until crisp and golden brown.

## 5.17 TURNED POTATO DISHES

**TRADITIONAL PRACTICE**

*Use 30 g/1¼ oz butter instead of margarine. During cooking occasionally brush over the tops of the potatoes with butter and also brush over with butter when serving. This substantially increases the fat content of the dish.*

### FONDANT POTATOES *POMMES FONDANTES*

4 portions

**BASE INGREDIENTS**

| | | |
|---|---|---|
| 600 g | potatoes | 1½ lb |
| 5 g | melted margarine | ¼ oz |
| 300 ml | white stock (or vegetable stock) | 12 fl oz |
| | salt and pepper | |

**BASE METHOD**

1. Wash, peel and turn the potatoes: 50 mm/2 inches in length.
2. Lightly brush the base of a shallow earthenware dish then add the turned potatoes.
3. Add the stock up to half the height of the potatoes.
4. Brush over the tops of the potatoes with the melted margarine.
5. Place into an oven at 220 °C/425 °F for 1–1½ hours.
6. During cooking occasionally baste with the margarine.
7. Continue cooking until the potatoes are golden-brown in colour and the stock has evaporated and been absorbed by the potatoes.
8. Brush over the tops of the potatoes with margarine when serving if required.

**TRADITIONAL PRACTICE**

*Use streaky bacon instead of lean bacon, and fry the lardons and onions in butter. This increases the fat content.*

### BERRICHONNE POTATOES *POMMES BERRICHONNE*

Turn the potatoes a little smaller than for fondant potatoes, i.e. 40 mm/1¾ inches approximately. Prepare following the base recipe, adding 75 g/3 oz diced onion and 50 g/2 oz lardons of lean bacon with the potatoes at step 2.

**TRADITIONAL PRACTICE**

*Use more Parmesan cheese (20 g/¾ oz) when finishing the potatoes. This increases the fat content of the dish.*

**CHAMPIGNOL POTATOES** ***POMMES CHAMPIGNOL*** Turn the potatoes, making them a little smaller than for fondant potatoes, i.e. 40 mm/1¾ inches approximately. Prepare as stated for fondant potatoes. When the potatoes are cooked, sprinkle with a little Parmesan cheese (5 g/¼ oz) then gratinate under a hot salamander.

# Process 6 ROASTING

**DEFINITION** Roasting is a dry heat method of cooking, where prepared food is cooked with the presence of fat in an oven or on a spit.

## REASONS FOR ROASTING FOODS

1 To make foods tender: by breaking down and softening mainly protein, but also starch, cellulose and fibre.
2 To make foods more palatable and digestible.
3 To make foods safer to eat: by destroying bacteria which can cause food poisoning.
4 To produce a particular quality in food, of colour, flavour and texture (e.g. roast venison).

## METHODS OF ROASTING FOODS

1 **Oven roasting.** This is the cooking of food in an oven, mainly by convected heat or forced air convected heat. However, other forms of heat application may also play an important function when roasting: e.g. conducted heat from a roasting tray when roasting potatoes, and radiated heat from the sides of an oven; both of which help to develop colour on the surface of the food. In addition, combination ovens which combine microwave energy or steam with forced air convected heat are also used when roasting.
2 **Spit roasting.** This is the original form of roasting which involves cooking the food by dry heat on a spit which is slowly turned over a heat source such as a charcoal fire, electric elements or gas flames. The main form of heat application is direct radiated heat, but convected heat (hot air) is also present. Conducted heat from metal spit bars may also aid cooking in some instances.

**Pot roasting (*poêler*).** This is included in this chapter although it is not strictly roasting, but a form of casserole cooking. The food is cooked under cover in an oven with butter being used as the traditional cooking fat. An important procedure with this method of cooking is the removal of the lid during cooking to allow the food to develop colour. After cooking, the vegetable base together with the cooking juices provide the basis of the accompanying sauce (see page 130).

**COMMODITIES SUITABLE FOR ROASTING** Good quality joints must be used when roasting meat, poultry and game.

1 **Butcher meats and furred game:** e.g. beef, veal, lamb, mutton, pork and venison.
2 **Poultry and feathered game:** e.g. chicken, turkey, duckling, grouse and pheasant.
3 **Potatoes and parsnips.**

**Pot roasting:** good quality butcher meats, poultry and game (as above) are required for this type of cooking.

## EQUIPMENT USED WHEN ROASTING FOODS

Combination oven

1 Types of ovens: general purpose oven, forced air convection oven, combination ovens (e.g. microwave and convection oven), steam and convection ovens.
2 Spit and rotisserie racks.
3 Small equipment: roasting trays, trivets, temperature probes.

**Pot roasting:** various types of casserole or similar cooking utensils can be used.

## BASIC TECHNIQUES OF ROASTING

**BARDING** This involves covering the surface of the roast with slices of pork or bacon fat. This is to prevent the flesh drying out during cooking; but because it increases fat content, it should only be used where necessary, normally with feathered game (grouse, partridge and pheasant).

**BRUSHING WITH OIL AND BASTING** Both of these processes involve lightly brushing the joint with fat before and during cooking. This is done to prevent the surface of a joint drying out and becoming hard (especially lean joints). Basting is the traditional practice of coating the item with the fat. In order to keep the fat content to a minimum, *brush* with fat rather than baste.

**CARRY-OVER COOKING** This is the further cooking which takes place after the joint has been removed from the oven.

**LARDING** See page 107.

**PLACING IN THE ROASTING TRAY**
**Butcher meats and furred game:** Joints of meat should be placed onto a roasting tray with the fat top upwards. Never place a joint directly onto a roasting tray unless it has bones or vegetables which keep the meat off the tray. Joints should be raised off the roasting tray by being placed onto a trivet or a bed of roots or bones.
**Poultry and feathered game:** Birds should be placed on their sides with the breast downwards then turned during roasting to ensure even cooking (page 128).

**SEARING** This involves starting the cooking of the roast in a hot oven, or shallow-frying the item prior to roasting (see page 126). It is carried out to develop colour and flavour, especially with meat roasts. It is often stated that this procedure *seals* in the juices and therefore retains goodness and reduces weight loss. This is a myth which should be ignored.

**SPEED OF COOKING** The temperature at which an item should be roasted is related to the size of the commodity. The larger the item, the lower the cooking temperature. High temperature roasting should be avoided as it increases shrinkage and weight loss. The temperature range when cooking roasts of average size is usually between 175–200 °C/350–400 °F.

**RESTING, STANDING OR SETTLING A ROAST** This refers to removing a roast from the oven after cooking and leaving it in a warm place for a short period (5–15 minutes depending on size). This is to reduce the risk of being burned when portioning or carving the joint. The food is also easier to carve or portion after resting.

## KEY POINTS

- Remember that roasts are served at a particular degree of cooking, i.e. under-done, medium, well done; and this must be carefully considered when preparing your time plan.
- Always keep your hands well protected and your sleeves long to avoid burns made by spurting hot fat. Take care when removing roasts from the oven. Special care should be taken with large roasts which may move when the tray is lifted.
- Where possible, use lean joints such as rump and good quality topside, and trim off surface fat before serving.

# 6.1 ROASTING BUTCHER MEATS AND FURRED GAME

> **TRADITIONAL PRACTICE**
>
> *Coat the joint with lard or dripping prior to cooking and baste regularly with fat during cooking. This increases the fat content.*

> **CHEF'S TIP**
>
> *Temperatures stated for degrees of cooking are for internal temperatures taken at the thickest part of the joint.*

## BASE METHOD

1 Assemble ingredients and prepare the joint ready for roasting.
*Topside of beef:* Remove excess fat and secure the joint with string. See page 10 for preparation of rib of beef. *Leg of lamb, pork or venison:* Bone out the aitch bone, trim the knuckle and tie with string (page 11).
2 Prepare the bed of root vegetables or bones used to raise the joint off the base of the roasting tray:
a) wash and peel the vegetables, then cut into large pieces
b) trim excess fat from the bones and break them to a suitable size if appropriate
c) place the bed of roots and/or bones into the roasting tray.
3 Place the joint in the roasting tray on top of the vegetables and/or bones.
4 Lightly brush with the oil.
5 Place into a hot oven (225 °C/440 °F) and allow to brown slightly.
6 Season lightly and reduce oven temperature to 150–175 °C/300–350 °F.
7 Allow to cook slowly until the correct degree of cooking is reached:
Underdone: 55–60 °C/130–140 °F
Just done: 66–71 °C/150–160 °F
Well done: 75–77 °C/167–172 °F
*Note:* pork must always reach 80 °C/176 °F.
8 Remove the joint from the oven and store, keeping warm, for a short period.
9 Remove any string then cut into neat slices across the grain of the meat.
10 Arrange on the serving dish then coat with a little hot gravy.
11 Decorate with the watercress and garnish as stated. Serve with gravy and any other appropriate sauces or garnish.

## PREPARATION OF GRAVY

1 Allow the sediment to settle on the bottom of the roasting tray then carefully decant off the fat.
2 Lightly heat the roasting tray until the sediment develops a light brown colour. This is not required if the sediment is already brown.
3 Decant a second time removing any remaining fat.
4 Add the brown stock and simmer for 2–3 minutes.
5 Check seasoning and strain. Skim off surface fat as necessary.

> **TRADITIONAL PRACTICE**
>
> *Use 3 kg/6½ lb rib of beef (depending on bone content) instead of topside. This increases the fat content.*

## ROAST BEEF

10 portions

| | | |
|---|---|---|
| 1¾ kg | lean topside or rump beef | 3 lb |
| 10 ml | oil | ½ fl oz |
| 800 ml | brown stock | 1½ pt |
| | bed of root vegetables or bones | |
| | small pinch salt | |

*Accompaniments:* Gravy, bunch of watercress, Yorkshire pudding (page 230), sauceboat of horseradish sauce.
Cook as stated in the base method above.

*Approximate cooking time:* 1–2 hours (depending on type of joint).

## ROAST LAMB OR MUTTON

10 portions

| | | |
|---|---|---|
| 2 kg | lean leg of lamb | 4 lb |
| 10 ml | oil | $\frac{1}{2}$ fl oz |
| 800 ml | brown stock | $1\frac{1}{2}$ pt |
| | bed of root vegetables or bones | |
| | small pinch salt | |

*Accompaniments*: LAMB: Gravy, watercress, mint sauce (page 35). MUTTON: Gravy, onion sauce (page 34), redcurrant jelly.
Cook as stated in the base method opposite.

*Approximate cooking time:* 2 hours (depending on bone content).

### TRADITIONAL PRACTICE

*Use 3 kg/6$\frac{1}{2}$ lb loin of pork instead of leg of pork. See first tip, page 126 for type of fat used. Also serve the crackling. This increases the fat content.*

### CHEF'S TIP

*To achieve good crisp crackling, rub over the surface of the skin with salt prior to roasting. This increases salt content.*

## ROAST PORK

10 portions

| | | |
|---|---|---|
| 2 kg | lean leg of pork | 5 lb |
| 10 ml | oil | $\frac{1}{2}$ fl oz |
| 800 ml | brown stock | $1\frac{1}{2}$ pt |
| | bed of root vegetables or bones | |
| | small pinch salt | |

*Accompaniments*: Gravy, watercress, sage and onion stuffing (page 37), apple sauce (page 29).
Cook as stated in the base method opposite.

*Approximate cooking time:* 2–3 hours (depending on type of joint).

## ROAST VENISON

10 portions

| | | |
|---|---|---|
| 2 kg | lean leg of venison | 5 lb |
| 10 ml | oil | $\frac{1}{2}$ fl oz |
| 800 ml | brown stock | $1\frac{1}{2}$ pt |
| | bed of root vegetables or bones | |
| | small pinch salt | |

*Accompaniments:* Gravy, watercress, redcurrant jelly.
Cook as stated in the base method opposite.

*Approximate cooking time:* 1–2 hours (depending on type of joint).

# 6.2 ROASTING POULTRY AND FEATHERED GAME

**CHEF'S TIP**

*Although the bed of roots adds flavour to the gravy, it is not essential when roasting poultry and is sometimes not used.*

**TRADITIONAL PRACTICE**

*Coat the bird with melted lard or dripping prior to cooking at step 4. This increases the fat content.*

**CHEF'S TIP**

*Temperatures stated for degrees of cooking are for internal temperatures taken at the thickest part of the bird, i.e. inside thigh.*

**TRADITIONAL PRACTICE**

Serving roast pheasant: *Prepare 3–4 bread croutons and shallow-fry in butter until golden brown. Spread with game farce (page 24) then arrange the pieces of pheasant on top. Also shallow-fry 50 g/2 oz white breadcrumbs until golden brown and serve with the pheasant as an accompaniment. This increases the fat content. Dress pheasant pieces on top of the fried croûtons (spread with farce).*

## BASE METHOD

1 Prepare the bird ready for roasting: pluck, draw and gut, singe and truss as appropriate (page 17).
2 Prepare the bed of root vegetables or bones to raise the bird off the base of the roasting tray:
   a) wash and peel the vegetables, then cut into large pieces
   b) place the bed of roots and/or bones into the roasting tray.
3 Lightly season inside and outside the bird.
4 Place the bird in the roasting tray *on its side.*
5 Lightly brush with oil.
6 Place into the oven at a temperature suitable for the size of bird:
   *Chicken* (1 kg/3 lb): 200 °C/395 °F
   *Duckling* (1 kg/3 lb): 200 °C/395 °F
   *Pheasant* (1 kg/2$\frac{3}{4}$ lb): 200 °C/395 °F
   *Turkey* (3 kg/7 lb): 175 °C/350 °F
7 Allow the bird to cook until lightly coloured then turn onto the other side. The time this takes varies with the type of bird being cooked.
8 Continue cooking until both sides of the bird are light brown.
9 Turn breast up and complete the cooking, allowing a good colour to develop across the surface of the bird. Birds should reach these internal temperatures:
   *Chicken, turkey, duckling* (cooked through): 77 °C/170 °F
   *Duckling, pheasant* (slightly underdone): 62 °C/145 °F
10 Remove from the tray, then sit vent up for a short period to allow steam to escape. Remove the string prior to portioning.
11 Prepare the gravy as stated on page 126.
12 *Chicken, duckling & pheasant:*
   a) Cut into portions.
   b) Dress on the serving dish with the appropriate garnish.
   c) Serve the gravy and appropriate sauces separately.
   *Turkey:*
   a) Carve the bird.
   b) Place the slices of leg meat along the centre of the serving dish.
   c) Neatly arrange the slices of white meat on top then coat with a little hot gravy.
   d) Decorate with the slices of stuffing, chipolata sausages and watercress.
   e) Serve with the gravy, bread sauce and cranberry sauce.

## ROAST CHICKEN

4 portions

| | | |
|---|---|---|
| 1 × 1 kg | chicken | 1 × 3 lb |
| 300 ml | brown chicken stock | 12 fl oz |
| | bed of root vegetables or chicken bones | |

*Accompaniments:* Gravy, watercress, game chips, bread sauce (page 29). Cook as stated in the base method above.

*Approximate cooking time:* 1–1$\frac{1}{2}$ hours.

**CHEF'S TIP**

*It is important that chicken and turkey be cooked through, to reduce the risk of food poisoning.*

## ROAST DUCKLING

4 portions

| | | |
|---|---|---|
| 1 × 2 kg | duckling | 1 × 4 lb |
| 300 ml | brown duck stock | 300 ml |
| | bed of root vegetables or duckling bones | |

*Accompaniments:* Gravy, watercress, game chips, stuffing (page 37) and apple sauce (page 29).

Cook as stated in the base method opposite.

*Approximate cooking time:* 1–1½ hours.

## ROAST PHEASANT

3–4 portions

| | | |
|---|---|---|
| 1 × 1 kg | pheasant | 1 × 2¾ lb |
| 1 | thin slice pork fat for barding (page 125) | 1 |
| 300 ml | brown game stock | 12 fl oz |
| | bed of root vegetables or duckling bones | |

*Accompaniments:* Gravy, watercress, game chips, bread sauce (see traditional practice tip).

Cook as stated in the base method opposite.

*Approximate cooking time:* 45 minutes.

## ROAST TURKEY

10 portions

| | | |
|---|---|---|
| 1 × 3 kg | turkey | 1 × 7 lb |
| 800 ml | brown chicken stock | 1 pt |
| | bed of root vegetables or turkey bones | |

*Accompaniments:* Gravy, watercress, stuffing (page 37), cooked chipolata sausages, bread sauce (page 29), cranberry sauce (page 31).

Cook as stated in the base method opposite.

*Approximate cooking time:* 3 hours.

## 6.3 POT-ROASTING BUTCHER MEATS AND FURRED GAME

### BASE INGREDIENTS

| | meat or game (see below) | |
|---|---|---|
| 50 g | sliced carrot | 2 oz |
| 50 g | sliced onion | 2 oz |
| 25 g | sliced celery | 1 oz |
| 10 g | melted margarine | $\frac{1}{2}$ oz |
| 250 ml | brown veal stock | $\frac{1}{2}$ pt |
| 5 g | arrowroot | $\frac{1}{4}$ oz |
| | small pinch salt and ground pepper | |
| | sprig of thyme, $\frac{1}{2}$ bay leaf, 2–3 parsley stalks | |

### BASE METHOD

1. Prepare the joint for cooking.
2. Quickly shallow-fry the meat in a lightly oiled, pre-heated pan until golden brown.
3. Prepare the vegetables and arrange in a small braising pan or casserole.
4. Place the seared meat on top of the vegetables then lightly season.
5. Coat with the margarine.
6. Cover with a lid and place into a hot oven (220 °C/425 °F).
7. During cooking, remove the lid and baste with the hot fat.
8. Remove the lid when approximately half cooked, and continue cooking until the correct degree of cooking is reached:
   Fillet of beef (underdone): 55–60 °C/130–140 °F
   Cushion of veal (cooked through): 75–77 °C/167–172 °F
9. Remove the joint from the cooking utensil and keep hot.
10. Decant off the fat from the cooking pan then add the brown stock. Allow to simmer for 2–3 minutes.
11. Dilute the arrowroot in a little cold water then stir into the boiling stock and allow to thicken.
12. Simmer for a short period then strain. Skim off fat as necessary.
13. Remove the string from the joint then cut into neat slices across the grain of the meat.
14. Arrange the slices on a serving dish then coat with a little of the thickened cooking liquor and serve immediately.

**TRADITIONAL PRACTICE**

*Coat the joint with 25 g/1 oz butter instead of margarine. This increases the fat content.*

**CHEF'S TIP**

*Temperatures stated for degrees of cooking are for internal temperatures taken at the thickest part of the bird, i.e. the thigh.*

**CHEF'S TIP**

*When serving the joint whole, brush over the surface of the cooked joint with a little meat glaze to enhance its appearance.*

**POT ROASTED FILLET OF BEEF** *FILET DE BOEUF POÊLÉ* For 4 portions, use a 500 g/1 lb piece lean fillet of beef, trimmed and tied with string. Prepare following the base recipe above, cooking for 30–40 minutes.

**POT ROASTED CUSHION OF VEAL** *NOIX DE VEAU POÊLÉ* For 4 portions, use a 500 g/1 lb piece lean cushion of veal, trimmed and tied with string. Prepare following the base recipe above, cooking for 1 hour approximately.

# 6.4 POT ROASTING POULTRY AND FEATHERED GAME

## BASE INGREDIENTS

| | | |
|---|---|---|
| 1 | bird for roasting (see below) | 1 |
| 50 g | sliced carrot | 2 oz |
| 50 g | sliced onion | 2 oz |
| 25 g | sliced celery | 1 oz |
| 250 ml | brown stock | $\frac{1}{2}$ pt |
| 10 g | melted margarine | $\frac{1}{2}$ oz |
| 5 g | arrowroot | $\frac{1}{4}$ oz |
| | pinch salt and ground pepper | |
| | sprig of thyme, $\frac{1}{2}$ bay leaf, 2 stalks parsley | |

## BASE METHOD

1 Prepare the bird ready for roasting: pluck, draw and gut, singe and truss as appropriate (page 17).
2 Prepare the vegetables and arrange in a small braising pan or casserole.
3 Place the bird on top of the vegetables then lightly season.
4 Coat with the margarine.
5 Cover with a lid and place into a hot oven (220 °C/425 °F).
6 During cooking, remove the lid and baste with the hot fat.
7 Remove the lid when approximately two-thirds cooked and continue cooking until cooked through; reaching an internal temperature of 75–77 °C/167–172 °F.
8 Remove the bird from the cooking utensil and keep hot.
9 Decant off the fat from the cooking pan then add the brown stock.
10 Allow to simmer for 2–3 minutes.
11 Dilute the arrowroot in a little cold water then stir into the boiling stock and allow to thicken.
12 Simmer for a short period then strain. Skim off fat as necessary.
13 Remove the string from the bird then cut into portions or leave whole.
14 Neatly arrange the portions in a clean casserole and add a little sauce.
15 Cover with the lid and replace into the oven to correct temperature.
16 Accompany with the cooking sauce when serving.

**TRADITIONAL PRACTICE**

*Coat the bird with 25 g/ 1 oz butter instead of using the smaller quantity of margarine. This increases the fat content.*

**CHEF'S TIP**

*Temperatures stated for degrees of cooking are for internal temperatures taken at the thickest part of the joint. Duckling and pheasant which are to be served slightly undercooked should reach an internal temperature of 62 °C/ 145 °F.*

**HEALTH TIP**

*Serving the bird without the skin will substantially reduce the fat content.*

**POT ROASTED CHICKEN** ***POULET POÊLÉ*** For 4 portions, use one $1\frac{1}{2}$ kg/3 lb chicken, and follow the base recipe above, cooking for 1 hour approximately.

**POT ROASTED GUINEA FOWL** ***PINTADE POÊLÉE*** For 3–4 portions, use one $1\frac{1}{2}$ kg/3 lb guinea fowl, and follow the base recipe above, cooking for 1 hour approximately.

## 6.5 ROASTING POTATOES AND PARSNIPS: traditional

### BASE METHOD

1. Wash and peel the vegetables.
2. Cut the vegetables into even-sized pieces.
3. Drain off any surplus water from the vegetables in a colander.
4. Heat the fat or dripping in a roasting tray.
5. Add the vegetables and shallow-fry for a short period, turning over occasionally with a fish slice.
6. Lightly season then place into a hot oven: 230 °C/445 °F.
7. Turn the vegetables during cooking when the surfaces develop colour. Repeat this procedure several times until the vegetables are cooked crisp and golden brown.
8. Remove from the oven and drain thoroughly.
9. Sprinkle with chopped parsley when serving (optional).

**TRADITIONAL PRACTICE**

*Use lard or dripping instead of oil. This increases the saturated fat content.*

**ROAST POTATOES** *POMMES RÔTIES* For 4 portions, use 500 g/1¼ lb potatoes and 25 ml/1 fl oz oil. Prepare following the base method above, cooking for approximately 1 hour (depending on size).

**TRADITIONAL PRACTICE**

*After removing the potatoes from the oven and draining off the fat, toss in foaming butter (25 g/1 oz). This increases the fat content.*

**OLIVETTE POTATOES** *POMMES OLIVETTES* For 4 portions, use 500 g/1¼ lb potatoes and 25 ml/1 fl oz oil. Cut the potatoes using an olive-shaped parisienne spoon. Alternatively, turn the potatoes into small olives: 20 mm¾ inches approximately in length. Cook as stated in the base method above.

**COCOTTE POTATOES** *POMMES COCOTTES* Prepare as for olivette potatoes above, but turn into large olive shapes: 30 mm/1¼ inches approximately in length.

**NOISETTE POTATOES** *POMMES NOISETTES* For 4 portions, use 750 g–1 kg/1½–2 lb potatoes and 25 ml/1 fl oz oil. Cut the potatoes with a noisette spoon then cook as stated in the base method above.

**PARISIENNE POTATOES** *POMMES PARISIENNE* For 4 portions, use 750 g–1 kg/1½–2 lb potatoes and 25 ml/1 fl oz oil. Cut the potatoes with a parisienne spoon, then cook as stated in the base method above.

**TRADITIONAL PRACTICE**

*After removing the parisienne potatoes from the oven and draining the fat, roll the potatoes in a little meat glaze.*

**PARMENTIER POTATOES** *POMMES PARMENTIER* For 4 portions, use 500 g/1¼ lb potatoes and 25 ml/1 fl oz oil. Cut the potatoes into 10 mm/½ inch cubes, then cook as stated in the base method above.

**PAVÉE POTATOES** *POMMES PAVÉES* Prepare as for parmentier potatoes opposite, but cut into 25 mm/1 inch cubes.

**CHÂTEAU POTATOES** *POMMES CHÂTEAU* For 4 portions, use 500 g/1 lb potatoes and 25 ml/1 fl oz oil. Turn the potatoes into large olive shapes: 60 mm/$2\frac{1}{2}$ inches in length, then cook as stated in the base method opposite.

**ROAST PARSNIPS** *PANAIS RÔTIS* For 4 portions, use 500 g/1 lb parsnips and 25 ml/1 fl oz oil. Prepare following the base method opposite, cooking for approximately 1 hour (depending on size).

## 6.6 ROASTING POTATOES AND PARSNIPS: LOWER FAT

Use the same amount of vegetables as in the traditional method, but replace the fat or dripping with 10 ml/$\frac{1}{2}$ fl oz oil.

### BASE METHOD

1. Wash and peel the vegetables.
2. Cut the vegetables into even-sized pieces.
3. Drain off any surplus water from the vegetables in a colander.
4. Brush the base of a low sided tray with the oil.
5. Place the well drained cut vegetables on the tray.
6. Brush over the surfaces with the remaining oil.
7. Cook in a hot oven (230 °C/445 °F) until crisp and golden brown. Do not turn the vegetables during cooking.
8. Sprinkle with chopped parsley when serving (optional).

# Process 7 GRILLING

**DEFINITION** Grilling is a dry heat method of cooking where prepared food is cooked mainly with radiated heat in the form of infra-red waves.

## REASONS FOR GRILLING FOODS

1 To make foods tender: by breaking down and softening mainly protein, but also starch, cellulose and fibre.
2 To make foods more palatable and digestible.
3 To make foods safer to eat: by destroying bacteria which can cause food poisoning.
4 To produce a particular quality in food, of colour, flavour and texture (e.g. grilled lamb cutlets).

## METHODS OF GRILLING FOODS

1 Grilling foods **over** a heat source which may be fired by charcoal, electricity or gas, e.g. steak grills and barbecue type grills.
2 Grilling foods **under** a heat source fired by gas or electricity, e.g. salamander type grills.
3 Grilling foods **between** electrically heated grill bars.

In methods **1** and **2** above, most of the cooking is done with *radiated heat,* although some cooking occurs by convection from hot air currents and conduction (when the food is touching hot grill bars). In method **3**, most items of equipment cook the food between very hot ridged metal plates with *conduction* being the main method of cooking the food.

## COMMODITIES SUITABLE FOR GRILLING

Good quality cuts must be used when grilling meat, poultry and game.

1 **Butcher meats and furred game:** e.g. various types of steaks, chops, and cutlets.
2 **Offal and bacon:** e.g. sliced liver, kidneys and gammon steaks.
3 **Poultry and feathered game:** various small birds prepared ready for grilling; e.g. spring chicken, grouse and partridge.
4 **Fish and shellfish:** various small whole fish (sole, plaice, trout); cuts of fish (fillets and steaks); and shellfish such as lobster, large prawns and scampi.
5 **Vegetables:** mainly mushrooms and tomatoes.
6 **Made-up items and convenience foods:** e.g. burgers, bitoks, sausages and sliced meat puddings.

## EQUIPMENT USED WHEN GRILLING FOODS

1 Steak grills and barbecue units fired by charcoal, gas, or electricity.
2 Salamanders fired by gas or electricity.
3 Contact grills, infra-red units and toasters.

Simulated charcoal grill

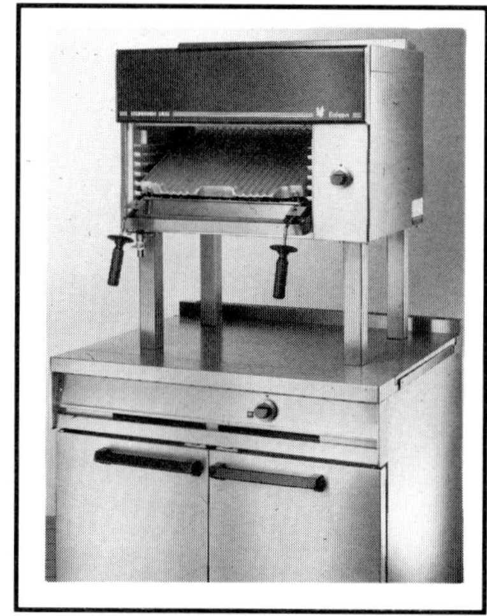

Gas salamander grill

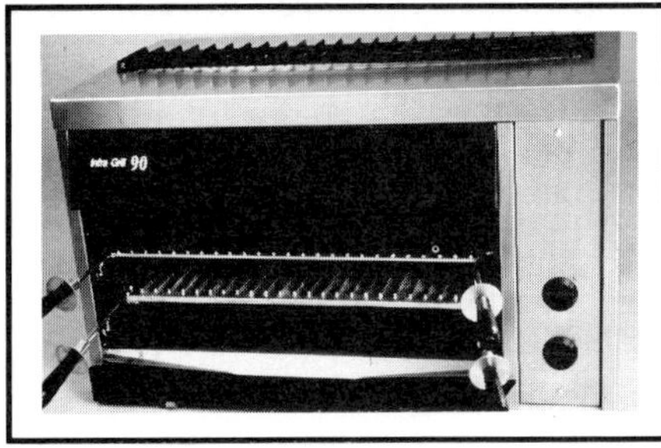

Infra grill

Charcoal-type grill

## BASIC TECHNIQUES OF GRILLING

**BRUSHING WITH OIL** This involves lightly brushing the item with fat before and during cooking. It is done to prevent the surface of the item drying out and becoming hard. Basting with fat (coating the item) should be avoided as this increases fat content.

**FLOURING ITEMS TO BE GRILLED** Coating foods with flour prior to grilling only applies to items which do not develop a good colour when cooking. Whole fish, cuts of fish and liver are usually lightly coated with flour when they are to be cooked under a salamander.

**SEARING** This involves starting the cooking of the item (plain flesh only: not sausages, puddings or breaded items) on a hot part of the grill to develop colour and flavour. It is often stated that this procedure *seals* in the juices and therefore retains goodness and reduces weight loss. This is a myth which should be ignored. See speed of cooking below.

**SPEED OF COOKING** High temperature grilling produces the most suitable infra-red waves to cook food. However, the heat exposure and speed of cooking should cook the food to the correct degree without burning the outer surface. When cooking thick items, such as large steaks and chops, the item may be seared to develop some colour, then the speed of cooking reduced while the item finishes cooking. With thin items such as flattened steaks, small chops and cutlets, the item is usually cooked so that colour and the appropriate degree of cooking are reached at the same time.

**TURNING AN ITEM** Foods being grilled should be turned with tongs or a palette knife: never stab or pierce foods with a fork at any stage of preparation or cooking. This applies to all foods including sausages.

## KEY POINTS

- Remember that grilled foods are served at a particular degree of cooking depending on type of commodity and customer choice, i.e. rare, underdone, medium and well done. The time at which you should begin to cook these items is therefore dictated by the service requirements.
- Ensure that foods which can cause food poisoning (e.g. chicken, pork and made-up items such as sausages) are thoroughly cooked. Knowing when food has reached a specific degree of cooking is an important skill which a cook must learn.
  One way of quickly determining the degree of cooking is to use a temperature probe. The temperature range which indicates the various degrees of cooking is given on pages 126–8.
- Use salt sparingly on grilled foods. This is necessary not only to reduce salt in the diet, but also because adding salt to an item being grilled will retard colour development.
- Where possible, use lean cuts of meat and trim off excess fat before cooking. Also drain the food to remove as much surface fat as possible prior to service.

## 7.1 GRILLING FISH

### TRADITIONAL PRACTICE

*After flouring the fish (step 1) coat with melted butter (25 g/1 oz butter) instead of brushing lightly with oil. Also place 1–2 slices parsley butter (page 32) on top of the fish when serving or serve separately in a sauceboat of ice water.*

### CHEF'S TIP

*When cooking and serving fish it is important to know which side of the fish or fish fillet is the presentation side. This is as follows:* Fish fillets: *This is the underside which was removed from the bone and not the side from which the skin was removed.* Fish steaks: *Either side.* Whole round fish: *Either side.* Whole flat fish: *The white skin side.*

### CHEF'S TIP

*The use of grilling wires is recommended when grilling fish especially when cooking on a barbecue type grill. It is quick and simple and the fish or fish fillets can be turned over easily during cooking.* Procedure: *Preheat and oil the grilling wires. Place the floured and lightly oiled fish onto the wires. Grill one side quickly to develop colour then turn over and complete the cooking.*

### BASE INGREDIENTS

| | | |
|---|---|---|
| | fillets, steaks or whole fish (see below) | |
| | seasoned flour | |
| 10 ml | oil | $\frac{1}{2}$ fl oz |
| | *Garnish:* | |
| 1 | piece of lemon | 1 |
| 1 | branch of parsley | 1 |

### BASE METHOD

1 Lightly coat the fish with the seasoned flour.
2 Place the fish onto a lightly oiled tray with the presentation side downwards.
3 Lightly brush over the surface with oil.
4 Place under a hot salamander and cook until golden brown.
5 Carefully turn over the fish and brush with a little oil.
6 Place back under the salamander and complete the cooking developing a good colour on the presentation side.
7 Arrange the fish on a serving dish and garnish with the lemon and parsley.

**FILLETS: GRILLED FILLETS OF PLAICE** ***FILETS DE PLIE GRILLÉS*** For 1 portion, use two 75 g/3 oz trimmed plaice fillets. Prepare the fillets for cooking (page 19), then cook following the base recipe above.

**WHOLE FLAT FISH: GRILLED LEMON SOLE** For 1 portion, use one 400 g/14 oz lemon sole. Carry out the basic preparation for whole flat fish (pages 19–21), then cook following the base recipe above.

**WHOLE ROUND FISH: GRILLED TROUT** ***TRUITE GRILLÉE*** For 1 portion, use one 200 g/7 oz trout. Carry out the basic preparation for whole round fish (pages 19–21), then cook following the base recipe above.

**FISH STEAKS: GRILLED HALIBUT STEAK** ***TRONÇON DE FLÉTAN GRILLÉ*** For 1 portion, use one 200 g/7 oz halibut steak. Carry out the basic preparation for fish steaks (pages 19–21), then cook following the base recipe above.

**GRILLED HERRING AND MUSTARD SAUCE** Prepare the herring for grilling (pages 19–21) and cook as stated in the base recipe above. Dish with the piece of lemon and branch parsley and serve with a sauceboat of mustard sauce (page 34).

**BARBECUED SARDINES PORTUGUESE STYLE** Prepare six sardines ready for grilling (pages 19–21). Lightly coat with flour, then brush with olive oil mixed with a little lemon juice. Place in a preheated and oiled grilling wire and cook quickly on both sides over a hot barbecue. Serve with lemon wedges and a salad consisting of lettuce, sliced tomatoes, sliced cucumber and shredded onions.

## 7.2 GRILLING BEEF STEAKS, LAMB CHOPS OR CUTLETS

1 portion

### BASE INGREDIENTS

beef steak or lamb chops (see below)
oil
small pinch salt
mill pepper
*Garnish:*
watercress and straw potatoes

### BASE METHOD

1. Season the steak or cutlets, then brush lightly with oil.
2. Place onto the hot, greased grill bars or cooking rack.
3. Turn over the steak when a good colour has been developed and when it is approximately half-cooked.
4. Continue cooking until the correct degree of cooking has been reached.
5. Place the steak on a serving dish and garnish with the watercress and straw potatoes.

**TRADITIONAL PRACTICE**

*Place 1–2 slices parsley butter (page 32) on top of the steak or chop when serving or serve separately in a sauceboat of ice water. This increases the fat content.*

**GRILLED ENTRECOTE STEAK** *ENTRECÔTE GRILLÉE* Prepare a 200 g/8 oz entrecote steak for grilling (page 15) and cook following the base recipe above.

**GRILLED LAMB CUTLETS GREEN MEADOW STYLE** *CÔTELETTES D'AGNEAU GRILLÉES VERT-PRÉ* Prepare 2 lamb cutlets for grilling (page 16) and cook following the base recipe above.

**GRILLED FILLET STEAK GARNI** *FILET DE BOEUF GARNI* Prepare 1 × 150 g/6 oz fillet steak for grilling (page 15) and cook following the base recipe above. Add 1 small grilled tomato, 1–2 grilled mushrooms and a few French-fried onion rings to the basic garnish.

**GRILLED PORK CUTLET HENRY IV** *COTELETTE DE PORC HENRI IV* Prepare 1 × 150 g/6 oz pork chop for grilling (page 16) and cook following the base recipe above. Ensure the pork is thoroughly cooked. Garnish with watercress and pont-neuf potatoes (page 181) instead of straw potatoes.

## 7.3 SPARE RIBS (China)

4 portions (main course)

**BASE INGREDIENTS**

| | | |
|---|---|---|
| 2 kg | spare ribs of pork | 4 lb |
| | *Marinade:* | |
| 200 g | chopped onion | 8 oz |
| 2 | cloves garlic (crushed) | 2 |
| 10 g | peeled root ginger | $\frac{1}{2}$ oz |
| 50 g | honey | 2 oz |
| 100 ml | soy sauce | 4 fl oz |
| 25 ml | oil | 1 fl oz |
| | squeeze lemon juice | |
| | *Garnish:* | |
| 4 | pieces lemon | 4 |

**BASE METHOD**

1 Prepare the ribs ready for cooking:
 a) trim off any fat
 b) divide the ribs into portions: i.e. sections containing 4–6 ribs depending on size
 c) cut between the ribs with a knife but leave attached at the top.
2 Place the ingredients for the marinade into a liquidiser and liquidise until smooth.
3 Pour the marinade into a stainless steel or porcelain bowl.
4 Add the ribs, cover and allow to marinade for 6–8 hours in a cool place turning occasionally.
5 Grill the ribs on each side until cooked, brushing occasionally with the marinade.
6 Serve the ribs garnished with pieces of lemon.

**CHEF'S TIP**

*The ribs are sometimes part-cooked by boiling or steaming prior to marinading and grilling.*

**SPARE RIBS (India)** Prepare as the base recipe above, but coat the ribs with a mixture of lime juice and turmeric. Also use a marinade consisting of: 10 g/$\frac{1}{2}$ oz green chilli flesh; 10 g/$\frac{1}{2}$ oz peeled root ginger; 10 g/$\frac{1}{2}$ oz garlic; 5 g/$\frac{1}{4}$ oz green papaya; 350 ml/14 fl oz plain yoghurt; 10 ml/$\frac{1}{2}$ fl oz oil; chilli powder to taste.

## 7.4 GRILLED LIVER: VEAL OR LAMB
### *FOIE DE VEAU/D'AGNEAU GRILLÉ*

**CHEF'S TIP**

*Coating the liver with flour is necessary to develop colour when cooking under a salamander but may be omitted when cooking on a charcoal type grill.*

1 portion

**BASE INGREDIENTS**

| | | |
|---|---|---|
| 100 g | trimmed sliced liver | 4 oz |
| | seasoned flour | |
| | oil | |
| | *Garnish:* | |
| | watercress and straw potatoes | |

**TRADITIONAL PRACTICE**

*Place 1–2 slices parsley butter (page 32) on top of the liver when serving or serve separately in a sauceboat of ice water. This increases the fat content.*

**BASE METHOD**

1 Prepare the liver ready for grilling (as for fried liver page 154).
2 Pass through the seasoned flour, then brush lightly with oil.
3 Place onto the hot, greased grill bars or cooking rack.
4 Cook quickly and turn over when a good colour has been developed.
5 Continue cooking but remove from the grill while still a little underdone.
6 Place on a serving dish and garnish with watercress and straw potatoes.

## 7.5 GRILLED LAMB'S KIDNEYS *ROGNONS D'AGNEAU GRILLÉS*

**TRADITIONAL PRACTICE**

*As tip above: place the butter in the centre of each kidney.*

For 1 portion, use 2–3 skinned kidneys. Prepare the kidneys: remove the skin, cut lengthways but leave attached and open out. Place on skewer. Season, then brush lightly with oil. Cook following steps 3–6 of Process 7.4 (above), removing any cocktail sticks or skewers before serving.

## 7.6 GRILLING HAMBURGERS

**CHEF'S TIP**

*Serve with French fried onions. This increases the fat content. Also use white breadcrumbs in place of wholemeal ones. This reduces the fibre content.*

4 hamburgers

**BASE INGREDIENTS**

| | | |
|---|---|---|
| 375 g | lean minced beef | 15 oz |
| 25 g | finely chopped onion | 1 oz |
| 15 g | wholemeal breadcrumbs | $\frac{3}{4}$ oz |
| | pinch salt and pepper | |
| | oil | |
| | mill pepper | |
| | *Garnish:* | |
| | watercress | |
| | *Accompanying sauce:* | |
| | barbecue, tomato or piquant sauce | |

**BASE METHOD**

1 Prepare the hamburgers:
   a) thoroughly mix the beef, onion, breadcrumbs and seasoning together
   b) divide into 4 pieces, then shape into burgers
   c) store on an oiled tray until required for use.
2 Brush the hamburgers lightly with oil.
3 Place onto the hot, greased grill bars or cooking rack.
4 Turn over when a good colour has been developed and the burgers are approximately half-cooked.
5 Continue cooking until cooked through.
6 Place on a serving dish and garnish with the watercress.
7 Accompany with the sauce.

**TRADITIONAL PRACTICE**

*Place frozen hamburgers, bitoks and similar made-up items onto the grill in their frozen state.*

**CHEF'S TIP**

*Never pierce sausages with a fork before cooking, as this will make them loose flavour and goodness.*

**GRILLED SAUSAGES** Assemble the sausages ready for grilling then cook as for grilled hamburgers: steps 3–6. *Important:* Frozen sausages may require defrosting (in a hygienic manner) prior to cooking; see instructions on packet.

## 7.7 GRILLING VEGETABLE BURGERS (vegan dish)

> **CHEF'S TIP**
>
> *This dish must not contain any animal produce in order to be suitable for vegans, e.g. use wholemeal bread (breadcrumbs) which does not incorporate animal fat.*

> **CHEF'S TIP**
>
> *The sauce accompanying vegetable burgers must be made with vegetable stock to be suitable for vegetarians (page 36).*

4 burgers

### BASE INGREDIENTS

| | | |
|---|---|---|
| 50 g | chopped onion | 2 oz |
| 1 | clove garlic (crushed) | 1 |
| 25 g | chopped chives | 1 oz |
| 50 g | grated carrot | 2 oz |
| 50 g | chopped celery | 2 oz |
| 50 g | finely diced red pepper | 2 oz |
| 50 g | cooked mung beans | 2 oz |
| 50 g | cooked lentils | 2 oz |
| 50 g | diced courgette | 2 oz |
| 25 g | porridge oats | 1 oz |
| | good pinch chopped parsley | |
| 25 g | wholemeal breadcrumbs | 1 oz |
| 10 g | tomato purée | ½ oz |
| | squeeze lemon juice | |
| 10 ml | soy sauce | ½ fl oz |
| | pinch ground black pepper, chilli pepper, ground coriander and ground cumin | |
| | *Thickening paste:* | |
| 100 ml | water | 4 fl oz |
| 25 g | wholemeal flour | 1 oz |

### BASE METHOD

1 Prepare the thickening paste:
   a) add half the water to the wholemeal flour and whisk to a smooth thick paste
   b) bring the remaining water to the boil then whisk in the flour paste
   c) cook, stirring continuously, until very thick: then quickly cool. Sprinkle the mixture with a little cold water to avoid a skin forming.
2 Place all the ingredients into a bowl – including the cold thickening paste – and thoroughly mix together.
3 Divide into 4 pieces, then shape into burgers using flour to avoid sticking.
4 Place onto a grill tray and brush lightly with the oil.
5 Grill on both sides until cooked and lightly coloured. Avoid over-cooking and drying out.
6 Garnish with watercress and serve with a suitable sauce, e.g. tomato or mustard sauce.

## 7.8 GRILLING CHICKEN

**CHEF'S TIP**

*The split chicken may be part-cooked in an oven prior to grilling. This helps to ensure that the chicken is thoroughly cooked.*

**CHEF'S TIP**

*Carefully remove the small rib bones with a small knife after cooking.*

1 portion

### BASE INGREDIENTS

| | | |
|---|---|---|
| 1 × 350 g | spring chicken | 1 × 14 oz |
| | oil | |
| | mill pepper | |
| | *Garnish:* | |
| | watercress | |

### BASE METHOD

1 Prepare the chicken ready for grilling (page 17).
2 Season with the pepper, then brush lightly with oil.
3 Place onto the hot, greased grill bars or cooking rack: rib cage towards the heat source.
4 Cook steadily, then turn over when a good colour has been developed and the chicken is approximately half-cooked.
5 Continue cooking until golden brown and completely cooked through: the internal temperature at the thickest part should be 80 °C/175 °F.
6 Place on a serving dish and garnish with the watercress.

### GRILLED DEVILLED CHICKEN *POUSSIN GRILLÉ DIABLE*

Prepare as stated in steps 1–4 of the base recipe and then:

5 Continue cooking until golden brown, coating the bird with mustard paste (below) during the final stages of cooking, i.e. the last 3–5 minutes of cooking. The internal temperature when fully cooked should be 80 °C/175 °F at the thickest part.
6 Sprinkle breadcrumbs over the surface of the bird then continue cooking under a salamander until crisp and golden brown.
7 Place on a serving dish and garnish with watercress. Accompany with devil sauce (page 30).

**Mustard paste:**

| | | |
|---|---|---|
| 5 g | English mustard | $\frac{1}{4}$ oz |
| 25 ml | vinegar | 1 fl oz |
| 25 ml | water | 1 fl oz |
| | dash Worcester sauce | |
| | pinch cayenne pepper | |

Mix the ingredients together and use as stated.

## 7.9 SEAFOOD SKEWER *BROCHETTE AUX FRUITS DE MER*

1 portion

### BASE INGREDIENTS

| | | |
|---|---|---|
| 4 | slices monkfish tail | 4 |
| 4 | scampi tails | 4 |
| 8 | cooked mussels | 8 |
| 1 | blanched scallop | 1 |
| 8 | mushrooms | 8 |
| 2 | bay leaves | 2 |
| | *Marinade (50 ml/2 fl oz):* | |
| 25 ml | oil | 1 fl oz |
| 25 g | finely chopped onion | 1 oz |
| $\frac{1}{2}$ | clove garlic (crushed) | $\frac{1}{2}$ |
| | pinch grated lemon zest | |
| | juice from $\frac{1}{4}$ lemon | |
| | ground black pepper (to taste) | |
| | pinch cayenne pepper | |
| | *Accompaniments:* | |
| | piece of lemon | |
| 100–150 g | braised rice (page 121) | 4–6 oz |

### BASE METHOD

1 Mix together the ingredients for the marinade in a suitable bowl.
2 Place the fish, shellfish, mushrooms and bay leaves into the marinade and leave under cover in a cool place for 20–30 minutes.
3 Neatly arrange the items on a skewer.
4 Cook quickly on all sides, occasionally brushing with the marinade.
5 Meanwhile, prepare the braised rice.
6 Serve on a bed of braised rice with the piece of lemon.

**CHEF'S TIP**

*Seafish skewers are often coated with white bread-crumbs prior to grilling.*

## 7.10 MOROCCAN LAMB KEBAB

2 portions

### BASE INGREDIENTS

| | | |
|---|---|---|
| 300 g | boned lean leg of lamb | 12 oz |
| | *Marinade:* | |
| 50 ml | olive oil | 2 fl oz |
| 50 ml | yoghurt | 2 fl oz |
| 25 ml | lemon juice | 1 fl oz |
| 2 | peeled cloves garlic | 2 |
| 20 g | peeled root ginger | $\frac{3}{4}$ oz |
| 1 g | grated lemon zest | $\frac{1}{2}$ tsp |
| $2\frac{1}{2}$ g | ground cinnamon | 1 tsp |
| $2\frac{1}{2}$ g | ground coriander | 1 tsp |
| 1 g | ground cumin | $\frac{1}{2}$ tsp |
| 1 g | chilli pepper | $\frac{1}{2}$ tsp |
| 1 g | ground black pepper | $\frac{1}{2}$ tsp |
| | small pinch salt | |

### BASE METHOD

1 Trim off excess fat from the lamb, then cut into 25 mm/1 inch cubes.
2 Place all the ingredients for the marinade into a liquidiser then liquidise until smooth.
3 Place the lamb into the marinade.
4 Cover and leave in a cool place for 4–6 hours. Turn occasionally while marinading.
5 Thread the pieces of lamb onto the skewers.
6 Brush with marinade and place on hot grill bars or on a tray, under a preheated salamander.
7 Cook gently on all sides, frequently basting with the marinade.
8 Serve with braised rice (page 121).

## 7.11 SPICED VEGETARIAN SKEWER (vegan dish)

1 portion

### BASE INGREDIENTS

| | | |
|---|---|---|
| 4 | pieces peeled onion | 4 |
| 4 | pieces red and green pepper | 4 |
| 4 | medium mushrooms | 4 |
| 4 | slices peeled root ginger | 4 |
| 4 | slices courgette | 4 |
| | *Marinade (40 ml/1 fl oz):* | |
| 25 ml | oil | 1 fl oz |
| $\frac{1}{2}$ | clove garlic (crushed) | $\frac{1}{2}$ |
| | pinch grated lime/lemon zest | |
| | juice from $\frac{1}{4}$ lime/lemon | |
| $\frac{1}{4}$ tsp | garam masala | $\frac{1}{4}$ tsp |
| $\frac{1}{4}$ tsp | turmeric | $\frac{1}{4}$ tsp |
| | hot chilli pepper (to taste) | |
| | ground black pepper (to taste) | |
| | *Accompaniments:* | |
| 50 ml | cucumber raita (page 34) | 2 fl oz |
| 100–150 g | braised rice (page 121) | 4–6 oz |

**CHEF'S TIP**

*The braised rice accompaniment must be made with vegetable stock for this dish to be suitable for vegans.*

### BASE METHOD

1 Mix together the ingredients for the marinade in a suitable bowl.
2 Place the vegetables into the marinade and leave under cover in a cool place for 15 minutes approximately.
3 Neatly arrange on a skewer.
4 Cook on all sides occasionally brushing with the marinade. Avoid over-cooking.
5 Meanwhile prepare the braised rice and raita.
6 Serve the skewer on a bed of braised rice accompanied with the raita.

## 7.12 GRILLED TOMATOES *TOMATES GRILLÉES*

1 portion

### BASE INGREDIENTS

| | | |
|---|---|---|
| 1 × 75 g | tomato | 1 × 3 oz |
| 1 ml | oil | $\frac{1}{4}$ tsp |
| | pinch salt and pepper | |

### BASE METHOD

1. Wash the tomato.
2. Remove the eye with the point of a turning knife.
3. Cut a cross-shaped incision on the top of the tomato.
4. Place on a grilling tray then brush over the top with the oil.
5. Lightly season, then cook gently under the grill. Avoid overcooking.

## 7.13 GRILLED MUSHROOMS *CHAMPIGNONS GRILLÉS*

**CHEF'S TIP**

*When using field mushrooms, peel the mushrooms before cooking. Cultivated mushrooms are left unpeeled. Ensure that all sides of the mushroom are coated with oil. This prevents surfaces becoming hard and dried out.*

1 portion

### BASE INGREDIENTS

| | | |
|---|---|---|
| 60 g | whole mushrooms | $2\frac{1}{2}$ oz |
| $2\frac{1}{2}$ ml | oil | $\frac{1}{2}$ tsp |
| | pinch salt and pepper | |

### BASE METHOD

1. Wash then drain the mushrooms.
2. Wipe off any excess water.
3. Brush over the mushrooms with the oil then season lightly.
4. Place on a grilling tray.
5. Cook quickly under the grill on all sides. Avoid overcooking.

## 7.14 MIXED GRILL

**CHEF'S TIP**

*The choice of ingredients for a mixed grill varies considerably depending on price and type of establishment. When a lower-fat dish is required, use lean commodities (trimmed of as much fat as possible), low fat sausages and lean bacon.*

1 portion

### BASE INGREDIENTS

| | | |
|---|---|---|
| 1 × 75 g | lamb cutlet (page 137) | 1 × 3 oz |
| 1 × 75 g | piece of rump steak (page 137) | 1 × 3 oz |
| 1 × 50 g | sausage (page 139) | 1 × 2 oz |
| 1 | lamb's kidney (page 139) | 1 |
| 1 | bacon rasher | 1 |
| 1 | small tomato (above) | 1 |
| 1–2 | mushrooms (above) | 1–2 |

**TRADITIONAL PRACTICE**

*Serve with straw potatoes and serve 1–2 slices of parsley butter separately in a sauceboat of ice water. This increases the fat content.*

### BASE METHOD

Prepare and grill the individual items as stated in the relevant recipes. Neatly arrange them together on a serving dish accompanied with watercress and the appropriate garnish.

## 7.16 GRILLED SAVOURIES

**TRADITIONAL PRACTICE**

*Use butter in place of margarine. This increases the saturated fat content.*

1 portion

### BASE INGREDIENTS

| | | |
|---|---|---|
| | stuffing (as appropriate) | |
| 3–4 | half-rashers lean or streaky bacon | 3–4 |
| 1 | piece toast | 1 |
| | margarine | |
| | ground pepper and cayenne pepper | |
| | branch of parsley (optional) | |

### BASE METHOD

1. Wrap the bacon rashers around the stuffing.
2. Arrange the parcels on a skewer, and grill gently on each side until cooked.
3. Cut the toast to shape (rectangle, square or circle) and spread it with margarine.
4. Remove the parcels from the skewer and place them onto the toast shape.
5. Lightly season with the pepper, and serve garnished with parsley.

**ANGELS ON HORSEBACK** Use 3–4 shelled oysters as stuffing, and prepare following the base recipe above.

**DEVILS ON HORSEBACK** Carefully remove the stones from 3–4 lightly poached prunes and stuff with 15 g/$\frac{3}{4}$ oz mango chutney. Wrap the bacon rashers around the prunes and complete as stated in the base recipe above.

**CANAPÉ DIANE** Use 4 chicken livers as stuffing, and prepare as above.

### ADDITIONAL SAVOURIES

**CANAPÉ FEDORA** Grill 2 rashers lean or streaky bacon and 2 mushrooms. Warm a stoned olive in the oven or under a grill. Cut 1 piece of toast to shape and spread with margarine. Garnish the toast with the bacon and mushrooms and decorate with the olive.

**CANAPÉ NINA** This is simply a basic toast shape, spread with margarine and garnished with grilled mushrooms.

# Process 8 SHALLOW-FRYING

**DEFINITION** Shallow-frying is a dry heat method of cooking, where prepared food is cooked in a pre-heated pan or metal surface with a small quantity of fat or oil. Shallow-frying is a fast method of cooking because heat is conducted from the hot surface of the cooking pan directly to the food.

## REASONS FOR SHALLOW-FRYING FOODS

1 To make foods tender: by breaking down and softening protein, fat, starch, cellulose and fibre.
2 To make foods more palatable and digestible.
3 To make foods safer to eat: by destroying bacteria which can cause food poisoning.
4 To produce a particular quality in food, of colour, flavour and texture (e.g. sauté potatoes).

## METHODS OF SHALLOW-FRYING FOODS

1 **Meunière:** This is a method of shallow-frying fish and shellfish. The fish is lightly coated with flour before frying and is served with lemon slices and chopped parsley. Nut-brown butter or margarine is poured over the fish when serving: but the quantity used should be kept to a minimum (or not used) to reduce the fat content.
2 **Sauter:** This term has three meanings:
 **a)** As an alternative term for shallow-frying. The term is often used when referring to the shallow-frying of small cuts of butcher meats, poultry or game.
 **b)** To shallow-fry and use a tossing action when turning the food, e.g. when cooking sliced potatoes or mushrooms.
 **c)** To prepare a high quality meat, poultry or game dish served with a sauce. This involves the shallow-frying of a good quality item to a specific degree of cooking. After cooking, the item is removed and the pan swilled with stock, wine or sauce. This procedure (known as *déglacer*) uses the sediment lost from the item being cooked, thereby increasing the flavour and aroma of the sauce (see page 158).
3 **Griddle:** This involves cooking items on a lightly oiled metal plate (griddle plate). A *ridged surface* is used for cooking small cuts of meat, game and poultry to allow the fat to drain from the meat; while a *flat plate* is used for bakery items such as griddle scones (page 172).
4 **Stir-fry:** This is the quick-frying of pieces of fish, meat, poultry and vegetables with fat or oil in a wok.
5 **Sweat:** This involves slow frying items in a little fat, using a lid, and without allowing colour to develop. Sweating is usually a preliminary procedure to certain soups (page 45).

## COMMODITIES SUITABLE FOR SHALLOW-FRYING

Good quality cuts must be used when shallow-frying meat, poultry and game.

1 **Butcher meats and furred game:** e.g. various types of steaks, chops, cutlets, escalopes and medallions.
2 **Offal and bacon:** e.g. sliced liver, kidneys and gammon steaks.
3 **Poultry and feathered game:** cuts for sauter and supremes.
4 **Fish:** various small whole fish (sole, plaice, trout) and cuts of fish (fillets and steaks).
5 **Made-up items and convenience foods:** e.g. burgers, bitoks, sausages and sliced meat puddings.
6 **Eggs:** mainly scrambled eggs and omelettes.
7 **Vegetables:** sliced potatoes, mushrooms, onions, tomatoes and courgettes.
8 **Fruits:** e.g. bananas, peaches, apple and pineapple slices.
9 **Batters and doughs:** e.g. crêpes, scones and pancakes.

## EQUIPMENT USED WHEN SHALLOW-FRYING FOODS

Equipment used includes frying pans, omelette pans, crêpe pans, plat à sauter pans, sauteuse, bratt pans, griddle plates and woks.

Paella/frying pan

Frying pan

Sauteuse

Omelette pan

## BASIC TECHNIQUES OF SHALLOW-FRYING

**SEARING** This involves starting the cooking of the item (plain flesh: not sausages, puddings, breaded items or batters) in a hot pan to develop colour and flavour. It is often stated that this procedure *seals* in the juices and therefore retains goodness and reduces weight loss. This is a myth which should be ignored.

**SPEED OF COOKING** The speed of cooking varies with the item being cooked, but as a general rule, the thicker the item the lower the frying temperature. A common mistake is to fry at too high a temperature resulting in overcooking, fat breakdown and off-flavours.

**TURNING AN ITEM** Foods being shallow-fried should be turned with a palette knife: never stab or pierce foods with a fork at any stage of preparation or cooking. This applies to all foods including sausages.

## KEY POINTS

- Remember that certain shallow-fried foods, e.g. beef dishes, are served at a particular degree of cooking, i.e. rare, underdone, medium and well done. The decision on when to start cooking a particular item must be made in keeping with service requirements.
- Always pre-heat the frying utensil to reduce both fat absorption into the food and the risk of the food sticking to the pan.
- Place the foods with the longest cooking times into the pan first, e.g. chicken *legs* before *wings*.
- Ensure the presentation side of the commodity is fried first so that discolouration or marking with sediment is avoided.
- Keep the frying fat to a minimum, and if possible dry-fry on a non-stick surface.
- Use lean cuts of meat and trim off excessive fat before cooking. Also drain the food to remove as much surface fat as possible prior to service.
- To reduce fat content, cook foods by grilling rather than shallow-frying. This applies to meat, poultry, game and made-up items such as sausages and hamburgers.

## 8.1 SHALLOW-FRYING FISH

**TRADITIONAL PRACTICE**

*Use seasoned flour instead of plain flour. This increases the salt content.*

**CHEF'S TIP**

*The fish should be cooked immediately after coating with the flour.*

**TRADITIONAL PRACTICE**

*Use a mixture of 25 g/1 oz butter and 5 ml/$\frac{1}{4}$ fl oz oil when frying the fish. Also use 75 g/3 oz butter instead of margarine to coat the fish (it then becomes* beurre noisette*). This will increase the saturated fat content.*

**CHEF'S TIP**

*Place fillets of fish into the pan presentation side downwards, i.e. with the underside removed from the bone downwards. This avoids any particles sticking to the surface.*

**TRADITIONAL PRACTICE**

*Sweat the cucumber shapes in 25 g/1 oz butter until cooked. This increases the fat content.*

4 portions

### BASE INGREDIENTS

| | | |
|---|---|---|
| 8 × 75 g | trimmed sole fillets | 8 × 3 oz |
| 10 ml | oil | $\frac{1}{2}$ fl oz |
| 8–12 | thin slices lemon | 8–12 |
| | flour | |
| | chopped parsley | |

### BASE METHOD

1 Heat the oil in a frying pan.
2 Lightly coat the fish fillets with the flour and place into the frying pan.
3 Fry quickly until a good colour is developed, then turn over using a palette knife.
4 Continue frying until cooked.
5 Remove from the pan leaving as little surface fat as possible on the fillets.
6 Neatly arrange on a hot service dish with the presentation side upwards. Garnish with lemon and parsley.

**FISH MEUNIÈRE** Prepare as for the base recipe, but coat the fish with nut-brown margarine when serving:

1 Preheat an iron omelette pan until hot then add 25 g/1 oz margarine.
2 Shake the pan until an even, brown colour is developed.
3 Add a good squeeze of lemon juice and shake through the margarine.
4 Pour over the fish and serve immediately.

**FILLETS OF PLAICE GRENOBLE STYLE** FILETS DE PLIE GRENOBLOISE Prepare as for fish meunière (above), using plaice fillets and wedges of lemon (instead of slices). Also add 50 g/2 oz capers to the nut-brown margarine before coating the fish.

**TROUT DORIA** *TRUITE DORIA* Cook the trout as for meunière (above), but garnish with small, turned pieces of cucumber (100 g/4 oz in total) which have been poached in a little fish stock before coating with margarine.

**SALMON STEAK LOUISIANA STYLE** *DARNE DE SAUMON LOUISIANE* Cook the salmon steaks as stated in the base recipe above. Note that either side of a fish steak may be the presentation side. Garnish the steaks with rondels of banana (1 banana) and a dice of red pepper (1 medium pepper), both lightly fried until cooked. Also add 50 g/2 oz raw tomato concassées to the nut-brown margarine before coating the fish.

## 8.2 SHALLOW-FRYING EGGS

**TRADITIONAL PRACTICE**

*Use 25 g/1 oz butter when frying the eggs instead of the oil. This increases the fat content.*

**SAFETY TIP**

*Serving eggs with a soft yolk may cause food poisoning.*

### BASE INGREDIENTS

| | | |
|---|---|---|
| 1 | egg (size 3) | 1 |
| 10 ml | oil | ½ fl oz |

### BASE METHOD

1 Place the oil into a small frying pan and heat gently. A non-stick frying pan is desirable as the minimum quantity of oil should be used.
2 Break the egg into the pan and fry slowly until cooked.

## 8.3 PAN COOKING: SCRAMBLED EGGS

**HEALTH TIP**

*For a healthier alternative to French style scrambled eggs, see English style scrambled eggs on page 186. French style scrambled eggs are high in fat.*

### FRENCH STYLE SCRAMBLED EGGS *OEUFS BROUILLÉS*

4 portions

### BASE INGREDIENTS

| | | |
|---|---|---|
| 6–8 | eggs (size 3) | 6–8 |
| 50 g | butter | 2 oz |
| | small pinch salt and pepper | |
| 20 ml | cream (optional) | ¾ fl oz |

### BASE METHOD

1 Break the eggs into a bowl and add the seasoning.
2 Whisk together to combine the whites and yolks.
3 Heat half the butter in a saucepan, then add the eggs.
4 Stir the eggs continuously over a moderate heat until a fine mixture is obtained.
5 Remove from the heat and stir through the remaining butter.
6 Stir through the cream and check seasoning.

**SCRAMBLED EGGS ON TOAST** Dress the scrambled eggs on 4 slices of buttered toast. Traditionally the crusts are removed from the bread after toasting.

**SCRAMBLED EGGS WITH HERBS** ***OEUFS BROUILLÉS AUX FINES HERBES*** Add a good pinch of freshly chopped herbs, e.g. parsley, chervil, chives and tarragon to the eggs when cooked (step 5).

**SCRAMBLED EGGS WITH TOMATOES** ***OEUFS BROUILLÉS AUX TOMATES*** Place the scrambled eggs in a serving dish then garnish along the top with 200 g/8 oz hot tomato concassées (page 25).

**SCOTCH WOODCOCK (Savoury)** For 8 portions, dress the scrambled eggs on 8 rectangles of buttered toast. Decorate each toast shape with 2 criss-crossed anchovy fillets and 4 capers. Serve immediately.

## 8.4 FOLDED OMELETTES

**HEALTH TIP**

*Omelettes are high in fat. If possible prepare two-egg omelettes to reduce fat content.*

**TRADITIONAL PRACTICE**

*Use clarified butter in place of margarine or oil. This increases the saturated fat content.*

### PLAIN OMELETTE *OMELETTE NATURE*

1 omelette

**BASE INGREDIENTS**

| | | |
|---|---|---|
| 3 | eggs (size 3) | 3 |
| 5 g | margarine or 5 ml/$\frac{1}{4}$ fl oz oil | $\frac{1}{4}$ oz |
| | small pinch salt and pepper | |

**BASE METHOD**

1. Break the eggs into a small bowl and add the seasoning.
2. Beat well with a fork until the yolks and whites are combined.
3. Heat the omelette pan then add the margarine or oil. Add only enough fat or oil so that it barely covers the base of the pan. When using margarine, do not allow it to colour.
4. Pour off any surplus fat or oil.
5. Pour the eggs into the pan then shake the pan while stirring the eggs.
6. Continue shaking and stirring the eggs until a smooth, very lightly set mixture is obtained.
7. Remove the pan from the heat and loosen the outer edges of the omelette with a fork, i.e. run the fork round between the egg and the pan.
8. Tilt the pan and fold the end of the omelette (handle end of pan) to the centre.
9. Tap the handle or bottom of the pan to move the mixture to the edge of the pan.
10. Fold over the other end to resemble a cigar shape.
11. Turn out of the pan onto a serving dish and neaten the shape if required.

**HAM OMELETTE** *OMELETTE AU JAMBON* Add a small dice of cooked ham (50 g/2 oz) to the beaten egg and proceed as stated in the base recipe.

**CHEESE OMELETTE** *OMELETTE AU FROMAGE* Add 20 g/1 dessertspoon grated Parmesan to the beaten egg and proceed as stated in the base recipe.

**TOMATO OMELETTE** *OMELETTE AUX TOMATES* Prepare the omelette as stated in the base recipe and place on the serving dish. Slit the top of the omelette lengthways and fill with 50 g/2 oz hot tomato concassées (page 25). Sprinkle with chopped parsley and serve.

**JAM OMELETTE** *OMELETTE À LA CONFITURE* Prepare a plain omelette as stated but add a good pinch of caster sugar to the egg instead of salt and pepper. Add a spoonful of warmed raspberry jam to the centre of the egg (step 7) then fold carefully inside. Complete the cooking and place onto a serving dish. Sprinkle the top with caster sugar, then brand a criss-cross pattern on the surface with a hot poker.

## 8.5 FLAT OMELETTES

### SPANISH OMELETTE *OMELETTE ESPAGNOLE*

1 omelette

**BASE INGREDIENTS**

| | | |
|---|---|---|
| 3 | eggs (size 3) | 3 |
| 5 g | margarine (or 5 ml/$\frac{1}{4}$ fl oz oil) | $\frac{1}{4}$ oz |
| | small pinch salt and pepper | |
| | *Garnish:* | |
| 10 g | margarine | $\frac{1}{2}$ oz |
| 50 g | finely sliced onion | 2 oz |
| 25 g | diced pimento | 1 oz |
| 50 g | raw tomato concassées | 2 oz |
| | chopped parsley | |

**BASE METHOD**

1. Lightly fry the onion and pimento in the margarine until tender, then allow to cool.
2. Break the eggs into a small bowl and add the seasoning.
3. Beat well with a fork until the yolks and whites are combined.
4. Add the onion, pimento and chopped parsley and mix through the eggs.
5. Heat the omelette pan then add the margarine or oil. Add only enough fat or oil so that it barely covers the base of the pan. When using margarine, do not allow it to colour.
6. Pour off any surplus fat or oil.
7. Pour the eggs into the pan then shake the pan while stirring the eggs.
8. Continue shaking and stirring the eggs until a smooth, very lightly set mixture is obtained.
9. Remove the pan from the heat and loosen the outer edges of the omelette with a fork, i.e. run the fork round between the egg and the pan.
10. Brush round the edges of the pan down to the omelette with a little melted margarine or oil.
11. Tap the pan and shake with a circular motion until the omelette slides freely.
12. Bring the omelette to the bottom of the pan opposite the handle.
13. Toss over onto the other side and cook lightly.
14. Slide carefully onto the serving dish.

**CHEF'S TIP**

*A simpler method than tossing a flat omelette is to place the omelette pan under a hot salamander to cook the top side of the omelette. After this, simply slide the omelette onto the serving dish.*

**FERMIERE STYLE OMELETTE** ***OMELETTE FERMIÈRE*** Add a garnish of 50 g/2 oz diced cooked ham and a good pinch of chopped parsley to the beaten egg and prepare as stated in the base recipe.

**PAYSANNE STYLE OMELETTE** ***OMELETTE PAYSANNE*** Add the following garnish to the beaten egg and proceed as stated in the base recipe: 25 g/1 oz cooked lean bacon, 25 g/1 oz cooked diced potatoes, 25 g/1 oz cooked sliced onions, 2–3 sorrel leaves sweat in butter and a pinch of chervil.

## 8.6 SHALLOW-FRYING BUTCHER MEATS

**TRADITIONAL PRACTICE**

*Use dripping or lard to fry the meat. This increases the fat content.*

### BASE METHOD

1. Trim off excess fat from the chop then add the seasoning.
2. Place a frying pan on the stove and add only enough oil to produce a thin film on the base of the pan.
3. When the pan is hot add the chop or steak and fry steadily.
4. Turn over when a good colour has developed and the meat is approximately half cooked.
5. Continue cooking until cooked to the desired degree.
6. Remove from the pan and drain well to remove surface fat.

### PORK CHOP CHARCUTIÈRE

1 portion

| | | |
|---|---|---|
| 1 × 200 g | lean pork chop | 1 × $\frac{1}{2}$ lb |
| 100 g | mashed potatoes (optional) | 4 oz |
| 1 | sauceboat sauce charcutière (page 31) | 1 |
| | oil | |
| | small pinch salt and mill pepper | |

Prepare following the base method, ensuring that the chop is thoroughly cooked. To finish, dress the hot mashed potato on a serving dish and place the chop on top. Accompany with the sauce. Alternatively, coat the chop with some of the sauce and serve the remaining sauce separately.

**TRADITIONAL PRACTICE**

*Use a larger steak (e.g. 200 g/8 oz) and double the quantity of French-fried onions. This increases the fat content.*

**CHEF'S TIP**

*If possible use a non-stick frying pan polished with oil when cooking the items.*

### ENTRECÔTE STEAK BOHEMIAN STYLE
*ENTRECÔTE BOHÉMIENNE*

1 portion

| | | |
|---|---|---|
| 1 × 150 g | lean entrecôte steak | 1 × 6 oz |
| 100 g | braised rice (page 121) | 4 oz |
| 50 g | hot tomato concassées | 2 oz |
| 25 g | French-fried onion (page 180) | 1 oz |
| | oil | |
| | small pinch salt and mill pepper | |

Trim any excess fat from the steak, and cook as stated in the base method, keeping the steak underdone unless otherwise requested. To finish, dress the rice on a serving dish and place the steak on top. Decorate the top of the steak with the tomato concassées and surround with French-fried onions.

### LAMB CUTLETS WITH SPICED PEARS AND MINT JELLY

For two portions,trim off excess fat and cook four lamb cutlets as stated in the base method. Garnish with 2 hot pear halves which have been cooked in a spiced syrup (page 82) and filled with mint jelly, and some plain boiled potatoes sprinkled with chopped fresh herbs.

**BEEF HAM ON BREAD** Coat a very thin slice of rump beef with a generous helping of allspice then shallow-fry as stated in the base method. Serve as a sandwich between two slices of buttered batch bread.

## 8.7 SHALLOW-FRYING MADE-UP ITEMS

### BASE METHOD

1 Place a frying pan on the stove and add only enough oil to produce a thin film on the base of the pan.
2 When the pan is hot add the made-up items and fry steadily.
3 Turn over when a good colour has developed and the items are approximately half cooked.
4 Continue cooking until completely cooked through.
5 Remove from the pan and drain well to remove surface fat.
6 Place on a serving dish and coat with the sauce.
7 Serve the remaining sauce separately.

### HAMBURGER WITH PIQUANT SAUCE

4 portions (4 × 100 g/4 oz hamburgers)

| | | |
|---|---|---|
| 375 g | lean minced beef | 15 oz |
| 15 g | finely chopped onion | $\frac{3}{4}$ oz |
| 15 g | wholemeal breadcrumbs | $\frac{3}{4}$ oz |
| 20 ml | egg | $\frac{1}{2}$ |
| | oil | |
| 200 ml | piquant sauce (page 31) | 8 fl oz |
| | small pinch salt and pepper | |

1 Place the minced beef, onion, breadcrumbs, egg and seasoning into a bowl.
2 Mix together thoroughly to form a fine paste.
3 Divide the mixture into 4 pieces.
4 Dust with flour then roll into balls.
5 Flatten into round cakes using a palette knife.
6 Cook as stated in the base method above.

### SAUSAGES

Sausages are cooked following the instructions in the base method above.

### SAUSAGES WITH HAM AND RED CABBAGE

4 portions

| | | |
|---|---|---|
| 8 × 50 g | lower-fat pork sausages | 8 × 2 oz |
| 4 × 50 g | slices of raw, lean ham or gammon | 4 × 2 oz |
| 250 g | braised red cabbage | 10 oz |

Braise the ham with the red cabbage as stated on page 120. When the cabbage is cooked, shallow-fry the sausages as in the base method. Dress the cabbage and ham on a serving dish, then arrange the sausages on top.

**TRADITIONAL PRACTICE**

*Use dripping or lard to fry the meat. This increases the fat content.*

**CHEF'S TIP**

*Hamburgers are often garnished with French-fried onions and served with a suitable sauce or relish, e.g. tomato, devil or Lyonnaise sauce; prepared mustard; piccalilli.*

**TRADITIONAL PRACTICE**

Hamburgers: *use minced beef instead of lean minced beef, and white breadcrumbs. Also cook the onions in 10 g/$\frac{1}{2}$ oz dripping then allow to cool before adding to the hamburger mixture. This increases fat and reduces fibre.* Sausages: *use ordinary sausages in place of lower-fat ones. This increases the fat content.*

**CHEF'S TIP**

*If possible use a non-stick frying pan polished with oil to keep the frying fat to a minimum.*

**CHEF'S TIP**

*Do not prick the sausages, as this will increase flavour and moisture loss. Also fry slowly to avoid bursting the skins and developing too much colour.*

## 8.8 SHALLOW-FRYING OFFAL

**CHEF'S TIP**

*If possible use a non-stick frying pan polished with oil to keep the frying fat to a minimum.*

**TRADITIONAL PRACTICE**

*Use seasoned flour instead of plain flour when coating the liver. This increases the salt content.*

**TRADITIONAL PRACTICE**

*Use dripping or lard to fry the meat. This increases the fat content.*

**TRADITIONAL PRACTICE**

*Use streaky bacon instead of lean bacon to garnish the liver. This increases the fat content.*

### BASE METHOD

1 Place a frying pan on the stove and add only enough oil to produce a thin film on the base of the pan.
2 When the pan is hot, add the main item.
3 Fry quickly and turn them over when a good colour has developed.
4 Continue to fry quickly leaving the liver or kidneys a little underdone.
5 Remove from the pan and drain well to remove surface fat.
6 Place on a serving dish and surround with a ribbon of thickened gravy.
7 Serve the remaining thickened gravy separately.

### FRIED LIVER

4 portions

| | | |
|---|---|---|
| 400 g | piece of liver | 1 lb |
| | flour | |
| | oil | |
| 150 ml | thickened gravy (jus lié: page 30) | 6 fl oz |

Remove the thin outer skin if present and any tubes or gristle. Cut at a slant into thin slices (8–12 slices). Lightly coat with flour. Cook as stated in the base method.

**LIVER AND BACON** Prepare as for fried liver, but garnish the liver with 4 cooked, lean bacon rashers.

**SPICED LIVER** Prepare as for fried liver, but add a good pinch of allspice, ground nutmeg and cayenne pepper to the flour.

**SHALLOW FRIED KIDNEYS** For 4 portions, use 8 lamb's kidneys. Remove the thin outer skin from each kidney, then cut each kidney in half lengthways and trim off any centre fat. Cook as stated in the base method above.

## 8.9 STIR-FRYING MEAT OR POULTRY

**HEALTH TIP**

*Stir-fry dishes are quite high in fat.*

### STIR-FRIED HONEY LEMON CHICKEN WITH WATER CHESTNUTS

4 portions

**BASE INGREDIENTS**

| | | |
|---|---|---|
| 400 g | skinned, boned and sliced chicken | 1 lb |
| 40 ml | oil | $1\frac{3}{4}$ fl oz |
| 1 | clove garlic (crushed) | 1 |
| 5 g | finely chopped root ginger | $\frac{1}{4}$ oz |
| 50 g | sliced onion | 2 oz |
| 125 g | sliced water chestnuts (tinned) | 5 oz |
| $\frac{1}{2}$ | lemon (juice and grated zest) | $\frac{1}{2}$ |
| 25 ml | light soy sauce | 1 fl oz |
| 40 g | honey | 2 tbsp |
| | pinch salt and pepper | |
| | cornflour | |

### BASE METHOD

1 Heat two-thirds of the oil in a wok or frying pan.
2 Add the garlic and root ginger and stir-fry for 10 seconds.
3 Meanwhile, season the chicken and lightly coat with the cornflour.
4 Add the chicken and quickly stir-fry for 3–4 minutes.
5 Remove from the pan and keep hot.
6 Add the remaining oil.
7 Add the onion and water chestnuts and stir-fry for 30 seconds.
8 Replace the chicken into the pan and add the lemon juice and zest, soy sauce and honey.
9 Stir-fry for a further 2 minutes and serve.

## *8.10* STIR-FRYING VEGETABLES

4 small portions

### BASE INGREDIENTS

| | | |
|---|---|---|
| 75 g | strips of carrot | 3 oz |
| 50 g | strips of celery | 2 oz |
| 50 g | small broccoli spears | 2 oz |
| 100 g | strips of green and red peppers | 4 oz |
| 50 g | strips of courgette | 2 oz |
| 100 g | sliced onion | 4 oz |
| 75 g | sliced mushroom | 3 oz |
| 50 g | bean sprouts | 2 oz |
| 50 ml | oil | 2 fl oz |
| 5 g | finely chopped root ginger | $\frac{1}{4}$ oz |
| 1 | clove garlic (crushed) | 1 |
| 50 ml | light soy sauce | 2 fl oz |

### BASE METHOD

1 Heat the oil in a wok or frying pan.
2 Add the garlic and root ginger and stir-fry for 10 seconds.
3 Add the vegetables in order of cooking time. Stir fry the carrot and celery for 1 minute; then add the broccoli and cook for 1 minute; then add the pepper, courgette and onion and cook for a further 1 minute. Lastly add the mushroom and bean sprouts and continue cooking until all the vegetables are lightly cooked.
4 Add the soy sauce, combine with the vegetables and serve.

## 8.11 SHALLOW-FRIED BREADED ITEMS

**TRADITIONAL PRACTICE**

*Use seasoned flour instead of plain flour. This increases the salt content.*

**CHEF'S TIP**

*Cooking at too low a temperature will result in increased fat absorption.*

### BASE METHOD

1 Prepare the main item for cooking. Season lightly and carry out any instructions in the individual recipe.
2 Pass the main item through the flour, eggwash and breadcrumbs (or oats).
3 Place a sauteuse or plat à sauter on the stove and add only enough oil to produce a thin film on the base of the pan.
4 When the pan is hot, add the item and fry steadily, *except* liver which should be fried quickly.
5 Turn over when a good colour has developed and the item is approximately half cooked.
6 Continue frying until cooked and golden brown: ensure pork and chicken are thoroughly cooked. Liver, beef and lamb may be left underdone.
7 Remove from the pan and drain well to remove surface fat.
8 Place onto a serving dish and neatly arrange any lemon slices on top.
9 Place any garnish on the serving dish, e.g. spaghetti napolitaine or Reform garnish.
10 Coat with nut-brown margarine (or butter) or lemon juice if appropriate and serve immediately.
11 Serve any sauce separately.

**HEALTH TIP**

*Shallow-fried breaded items are high in fat.*

### ESCALOPE OF VEAL CORDON-BLEU *ESCALOPE DE VEAU CORDON-BLEU*

1 portion

| | | |
|---|---|---|
| 1 × 150 g | veal escalope (page 15) | 1 × 6 oz |
| 1 × 25 g | slice of Parma ham | 1 × 1 oz |
| 1 × 50 g | slice of gruyère cheese | 1 × 2 oz |
| 1–2 | thin slices lemon | 1–2 |
| 25–50 g | nut-brown margarine (or butter) | 1–2 oz |
| | small pinch salt and pepper | |
| | flour, eggwash and breadcrumbs | |
| | oil | |

Stuff the escalope with the ham and cheese, i.e. place the slice of ham and cheese onto the centre of the escalope and fold inside. Proceed as stated in the base method above.

### ESCALOPE OF PORK NAPLES STYLE *ESCALOPE DE PORC NAPOLITAINE*

1 portion

| | | |
|---|---|---|
| 1 × 150 g | pork escalope (page 14) | 1 × 6 oz |
| 1–2 | thin slices lemon | 1–2 |
| 25–50 g | nut-brown margarine (or butter) | 1–2 oz |
| | small pinch salt and pepper | |
| | flour, eggwash and breadcrumbs | |
| | oil | |
| | *Garnish:* | |
| 75 g | spaghetti Napolitaine (page 56) | 3 oz |

Proceed as stated in the base method above, garnishing the serving dish with the spaghetti.

## CUTLETS REFORM *CÔTELETTES D'AGNEAU REFORM*

1 portion

| | | |
|---|---|---|
| 2 | trimmed lamb cutlets | 2 |
| | small pinch salt and pepper | |
| | flour, eggwash and breadcrumbs mixed with a little chopped ham | |
| | oil | |
| | *Garnish:* | |
| 5 g | margarine | $\frac{1}{4}$ oz |
| 60 g | mixture of cooked ham, tongue, eggwhite, mushrooms, gherkins, beetroot and truffle (optional) – all cut into thin strips | $2\frac{1}{2}$ oz |
| 1 | sauceboat Reform sauce (page 31) | 1 |

Proceed as stated in the base method opposite. Heat the garnish in the margarine, then arrange on the serving dish with the cutlets. Serve with the Reform sauce.

## FRIED LIVER WITH LEMON *FEGATO 'GARBO E DOLCE'*

1 portion

| | | |
|---|---|---|
| 100 g | sliced lamb's liver | 4 oz |
| | small pinch salt and pepper | |
| | flour, eggwash and breadcrumbs | |
| | oil | |
| 1–2 | thin slices lemon | 1–2 |
| | juice from $\frac{1}{4}$ lemon | |
| | pinch sugar | |

Proceed as stated in the base method opposite. Mix together the sugar and lemon juice. Coat the liver with the sweetened lemon juice and serve immediately.

## SIRLOIN STEAK MACFARLANE

1 portion

| | | |
|---|---|---|
| 1 × 175 g | lean entrecôte steak | 1 × 7 oz |
| $\frac{1}{2}$ tsp | prepared mustard | $\frac{1}{2}$ tsp |
| | oil | |
| 1–2 | thin slices lemon | 1–2 |
| 100 ml | tomato sauce (page 33) | 4 fl oz |
| 25 ml | claret | 1 fl oz |
| | chopped parsley | |
| | small pinch salt and pepper | |
| | flour, eggwash and rolled oats | |

Season the steak, spread it lightly with mustard and pass it through the flour, eggwash and oats (used instead of breadcrumbs). Proceed as stated in the base method opposite. Boil together the tomato sauce and claret and reduce to a coating consistency. Surround the steaks with a ribbon of the sauce and serve the remaining sauce separately.

## 8.12 SAUTÉ DISHES USING PREPARED SAUCES

**TRADITIONAL PRACTICE**

*Use seasoned flour instead of plain flour and a mixture of oil and butter when cooking. This increases the salt and fat content.*

**TRADITIONAL PRACTICE**

*Shallow-fry in a mixture of oil and butter. This increases the fat content.*

**TRADITIONAL PRACTICE**

*Enrich the sauces with butter (*monter au beurre*), i.e. add 5 g/¼ oz to the sauce after step 9. Remove the sauce from the heat and blend through the butter. This increases the fat content.*

**CHEF'S TIP**

*Chopped fresh herbs (especially parsley) are sometimes sprinkled over the sauced item after step 13.*

### BASE METHOD

1. Prepare the main item and lightly season with salt, pepper and any spices.
2. Lightly coat any escalopes, medallions or suprêmes with flour. Do not coat beef or kidneys with flour.
3. Place a sauteuse or plat à sauter on the stove and add only enough oil to produce a thin film on the base of the pan.
4. When the pan is hot add the items and shallow-fry steadily, except liver and kidneys which should be fried quickly.
5. Turn over when a good colour has developed and the meat is approximately half cooked.
6. Continue frying until cooked: ensure pork and chicken are thoroughly cooked. Liver, kidneys, beef and lamb may be left underdone.
7. Remove from the pan and drain well to remove surface fat.
8. Keep hot while the sauce is being prepared.
9. Decant off any excess fat from the pan.
10. Add any chopped onion or shallot and cook for 30–60 seconds.
11. Swill the pan with any wine, spirit, lemon juice or mead.
12. Boil quickly until reduced down by two-thirds in volume.
13. Add the sauce or jus lié stated in the recipe.
14. Add any fresh, chopped herbs stated in the recipe.
15. Simmer for 2–3 minutes.
16. Check seasoning and consistency.
17. Dress the hot main item on the serving dish.
18. Coat with the sauce and serve.

### ESCALOPE OF VEAL WITH MARSALA SAUCE *ESCALOPE DE VEAU MARSALA*

1 portion

| | | |
|---|---|---|
| 1 × 150 g | veal escalope (page 15) | 1 × 6 oz |
| 25 ml | Marsala | 1 fl oz |
| 100 ml | jus lié (page 30) | 4 fl oz |
| | flour | |
| | oil | |
| | small pinch salt and pepper | |

Prepare as stated in the base method above.

### MEDALLIONS OF VENISON IN A HONEY MUSTARD SAUCE

1 portion

| | | |
|---|---|---|
| 5 × 30 g | veal medallions (page 15) | 5 × 1¼ oz |
| 5 g | finely chopped onion or shallot | ¼ oz |
| 25 ml | mead | 1 fl oz |
| 100 ml | honey mustard sauce (page 31) | 4 fl oz |
| | flour | |
| | oil | |
| | small pinch salt and pepper | |

Prepare as stated in the base method above.

## OXFORD JOHN

1 portion

| | | |
|---|---|---|
| 150 g | lean leg of lamb cut into medallions (page 15) | 6 oz |
| 25 g | finely chopped onion or shallot | 1 oz |
| 25 g | fried bread croûtons (page 24) | 1 oz |
| 100 ml | jus lié (page 30) | 4 fl oz |
| | good pinch chopped parsley and thyme | |
| | squeeze lemon juice | |
| | flour | |
| | oil | |
| | small pinch salt, mill pepper, ground mace | |

Prepare as stated in the base method opposite.

**CHEF'S TIP**

*To prepare an* Oxford John, *sprinkle hot bread croutons over the meat after coating with sauce. This avoids the croûtons becoming soft and soggy.*

## FILLET STEAK WITH A WHISKY AND HERB SAUCE

1 portion

| | | |
|---|---|---|
| 1 × 175 g | lean fillet steak | 1 × 7 oz |
| 5 g | finely chopped onion or shallot | $\frac{1}{4}$ oz |
| 25 ml | Scotch whisky | 1 fl oz |
| 100 ml | jus lié (page 30) | 4 fl oz |
| | good pinch fresh, chopped thyme, chervil and parsley | |
| | oil | |
| | salt and pepper (to taste) | |

Prepare as stated in the base method opposite. At step 12, coat with the sauce and then sprinkle croûtons over the top.

## SAUTÉD LAMB'S KIDNEYS IN SHERRY SAUCE *ROGNONS D'AGNEAU SAUTÉS AU XÉRÈS*

1 portion

| | | |
|---|---|---|
| 2 | lamb's kidneys (skinned and halved) | 2 |
| 5 g | finely chopped onion or shallot | $\frac{1}{4}$ oz |
| 25 ml | sherry | 1 fl oz |
| 125 ml | jus lié (page 30) | $\frac{1}{4}$ pt |
| | oil | |
| | small pinch salt and pepper | |

Proceed as stated in the base method opposite.

# 8.13 SAUTÉ DISHES COOKED WHITE WITH GARNISHED SAUCES

**TRADITIONAL PRACTICE**

*Shallow-fry in a mixture of oil and butter. This increases the fat content.*

**TRADITIONAL PRACTICE**

*Use traditional velouté sauce in place of the low-fat sauce. Add 25 ml/1 fl oz cream to the Swedish and Hungarian style dishes after step 8, and reduce down by two-thirds. This increases the fat content.*

## BASE METHOD

1. Prepare the main item and lightly season.
2. Lightly coat with the flour.
3. Place a sauteuse or plat à sauter on the stove and add only enough oil to produce a thin film on the base of the pan.
4. When the pan is hot, add the floured item and shallow-fry slowly without developing colour.
5. Turn over when approximately half cooked.
6. Continue frying until cooked.
7. Remove from the pan and drain well to remove fat.
8. Keep hot while the sauce is being prepared.
9. Decant off any excess fat from the pan.
10. Add the chopped onion or shallot and cook for 30–60 seconds without colouring. Also add any paprika at this stage.
11. Add any brandy and flambé.
12. Add any mushrooms and cook for 2–3 minutes without developing colour. Also add any tomato concassées at this stage.
13. Swill the pan with any wine and boil quickly until reduced down by two-thirds in volume.
14. Add the velouté sauce and simmer for 1 minute.
15. Add any lemon juice and check seasoning and consistency.
16. Dress the item on the serving dish, coat with the sauce and serve.

## CHICKEN SUPRÊME SWEDISH STYLE *SUPRÊME DE VOLAILLE SUÉDOISE*

1 portion

| | | |
|---|---|---|
| 1 × 175 g | trimmed chicken suprême (page 18) | 1 × 7 oz |
| 5 g | finely chopped onion or shallot | $\frac{1}{4}$ oz |
| 10 ml | brandy | $\frac{1}{2}$ fl oz |
| 50 g | sliced button mushrooms | 2 oz |
| 100 ml | low-fat chicken velouté (page 34) | 4 fl oz |
| | squeeze lemon juice | |
| | flour | |
| | oil | |
| | small pinch salt and pepper | |

Prepare as stated in the base method above.

## ESCALOPE OF TURKEY HUNGARIAN STYLE *ESCALOPE DE DINDONNEAU HONGROISE*

1 portion

| | | |
|---|---|---|
| 1 × 150 g | turkey escalope (as veal, page 15) | 1 × 6 oz |
| 10 g | finely chopped onion or shallot | $\frac{1}{2}$ oz |
| $\frac{1}{2}$ tsp | paprika | $\frac{1}{2}$ tsp |
| 25 ml | white wine | 1 fl oz |
| 25 g | tomato concasées (page 25) | 1 oz |
| 100 ml | low-fat chicken velouté (page 34) | 4 fl oz |
| | flour | |
| | oil | |
| | small pinch salt and pepper | |

Prepare as stated in the base method above.

## 8.14 SAUTÉ DISHES COOKED BROWN WITH GARNISHED SAUCES

**TRADITIONAL PRACTICE**

*Shallow-fry in a mixture of oil and butter. This increases the fat content.*

**CHEF'S TIP**

*Finish the cooking of chicken joints, e.g. thick pieces of leg and breast, under cover in an oven. Chopped fresh herbs are sometimes sprinkled over the sauced item after step 17.*

### BASE METHOD

1. Prepare the main item and lightly season.
2. Place a sauteuse or plat à sauter on the stove and add only enough oil to produce a thin film on the base of the pan.
3. When the pan is hot add the cuts of meat, poultry or game and shallow-fry steadily, developing colour.
4. Turn over when approximately half cooked.
5. Continue frying until cooked. Ensure pork and chicken are thoroughly cooked. Kidneys, beef, lamb and duckling may be left underdone.
6. Remove from the pan and drain well to remove fat.
7. Keep hot while sauce is being prepared.
8. Decant off any excess fat from the pan.
9. Add the chopped onion, shallot and garlic, and cook for 30–60 seconds.
10. Add any red and green pepper and cook for 1 minute.
11. Add any brandy and flambé.
12. Add any mushrooms and cook for 2–3 minutes.
13. Swill the pan with any wine and boil quickly until reduced down by two-thirds.
14. Add any tomato concassées.
15. Add any jus lié or demi-glace and simmer for 1 minute. Also add any chopped herbs at this stage.
16. Check seasoning and consistency.
17. Dress the main item on the serving dish, coat with the sauce and serve.

### CHICKEN CHASSEUR *POULET SAUTÉ CHASSEUR*

4 portions

| | | |
|---|---|---|
| 1 × $1\frac{1}{2}$ kg | chicken | 1 × $3\frac{1}{4}$ lb |
| 25 g | finely chopped onion or shallot | 1 oz |
| 25 ml | brandy | 1 fl oz |
| 100 g | sliced button mushrooms | 4 oz |
| 50 ml | white wine | 2 fl oz |
| 100 g | tomato concasées (page 25) | 4 oz |
| 350 ml | jus lié (page 30) | 14 fl oz |
| | pinch fresh chopped chervil, tarragon and parsley | |
| | oil | |
| | small pinch salt and mill pepper | |

Cut the chicken into joints (page 18). Prepare as stated in the base method above.

### SIRLOIN STEAK WITH RED AND GREEN PEPPERS

1 portion

| | | |
|---|---|---|
| 1 × 175 g | lean entrecôte steak | 1 × 7 oz |
| 5 g | finely chopped onion | $\frac{1}{4}$ oz |
| 50 g | diced red and green pepper | 2 oz |
| 25 ml | red wine | 1 fl oz |
| 100 ml | jus lié (page 30) | 4 fl oz |
| | oil | |
| | small pinch salt and mill pepper | |

Prepare as stated in the base method above.

## 8.15 SAUTÉ DISHES COOKED WHITE WITH REDUCTION SAUCES

**TRADITIONAL PRACTICE**

*Use seasoned flour instead of plain flour, and shallow-fry in a mixture of oil and butter. Enrich the sauces with butter (*monter au beurre*), i.e. add 5 g/¼ oz to the sauce after step 12. Remove the sauce from the heat and blend through the butter. This increases the fat and salt content.*

### BASE METHOD

1 Prepare the main item and lightly season.
2 Lightly coat the escalopes or suprêmes with flour.
3 Place a sauteuse or plat à sauter on the stove and add only enough oil to produce a thin film on the base of the pan.
4 When the pan is hot add the floured item and shallow-fry slowly, without developing colour.
5 Turn over when approximately half cooked.
6 Continue frying until cooked.
7 Remove from the pan and drain well to remove surface fat.
8 Keep hot while the sauce is being prepared.
9 Decant off any excess fat from the pan.
10 Add the chopped onion or shallot and cook for 30–60 seconds. Do not colour.
11 Swill the pan with any wine and vinegar and boil quickly until reduced down by two-thirds in volume.
12 Add the cream and also boil quickly until reduced to a thin coating consistency. Add any chopped herbs at this stage, e.g. tarragon.
13 Check seasoning.
14 Dress the item on the serving dish, coat with the sauce and serve.

**CHEF'S TIP**

*These dishes are high in fat, especially when using cream in the sauce.*

**HEALTH TIP**

*Half the cream may be replaced by low-fat velouté sauce (page 34). This will reduce the fat content.*

### ESCALOPE OF VEAL WITH CREAM *ESCALOPE DE VEAU À LA CRÈME*

1 portion

| | | |
|---|---|---|
| 1 × 150 g | veal escalope (page 15) | 1 × 6 oz |
| 5 g | finely chopped onion or shallot | ¼ oz |
| 10 ml | sherry | ½ fl oz |
| 100 ml | cream | 4 fl oz |
| | flour | |
| | oil | |
| | salt and pepper (to taste) | |

Prepare as stated in the base method above.

### CHICKEN SUPRÊME WITH WHITE WINE AND TARRAGON SAUCE

1 portion

| | | |
|---|---|---|
| 1 × 175 g | trimmed chicken suprême (page 18) | 1 × 7 oz |
| 5 g | finely chopped onion or shallot | ¼ oz |
| 5 ml | tarragon vinegar | ¼ fl oz |
| 50 ml | dry white wine | 2 fl oz |
| 100 ml | cream | 4 fl oz |
| | good pinch fresh, chopped tarragon | |
| | flour | |
| | oil | |
| | small pinch salt and pepper | |

Prepare as stated in the base method above.

## 8.16 SAUTÉE DISHES COOKED BROWN WITH REDUCTION SAUCES

### TRADITIONAL PRACTICE

*Use seasoned flour instead of plain flour, and shallow-fry in a mixture of oil and butter. Enrich the sauces with butter (*monter au beurre*), i.e. add 5 g/$\frac{1}{4}$ oz to the sauce after step 12. Remove the sauce from the heat and blend through the butter. This increases the fat and salt content.*

### BASE METHOD

1. Prepare the main item and lightly season.
2. Place a sauteuse or plat à sauter on the stove and add only enough oil to produce a thin film on the base of the pan.
3. When the pan is hot, add the cuts of meat, poultry or game and shallow-fry quickly, developing colour.
4. Turn over when approximately half cooked.
5. Continue frying until cooked. Ensure pork and chicken are thoroughly cooked. Kidneys, beef, lamb and duckling may be left underdone.
6. Remove from the pan and drain well to remove fat.
7. Keep hot while the sauce is being prepared.
8. Decant off any excess fat from the pan.
9. Add the chopped onion or shallot and any garlic and cook for 30–60 seconds.
10. Add any brandy and flambé.
11. Swill the pan with any wine and boil quickly until reduced down by two-thirds.
12. Add the cream and also boil quickly until reduced to a thin coating consistency. Also add any chopped herbs at this stage, e.g. tarragon.
13. Add any lemon juice and check seasoning.
14. *Strogonoff:* Mix the meat with the sauce and check temperature. Place into a serving dish. *Steaks:* Dress on a serving dish and coat with the sauce.

### BEEF STROGONOFF

4 portions

| | | |
|---|---|---|
| 400 g | fillet of beef cut into dice or bâtons (page 10) | 1 lb |
| 25 g | finely chopped onion or shallot | 1 oz |
| $\frac{1}{2}$ | clove garlic (crushed) | $\frac{1}{2}$ |
| 25 ml | brandy | 1 fl oz |
| 350 ml | cream | 14 fl oz |
| | pinch fresh, chopped tarragon | |
| | squeeze lemon juice | |
| | oil | |
| | small pinch salt and mill pepper | |

Prepare as stated in the base method above, and accompany with riz pilaff when serving.

### CHEF'S TIP

*These dishes are high in fat, especially when using cream in the sauce.*

### DUCKLING BREAST WITH CHERRY BRANDY AND GREEN PEPPERCORNS

1 portion

| | | |
|---|---|---|
| 1 × 175 g | duckling suprême | 1 × 7 oz |
| 5 g | finely chopped onion or shallot | $\frac{1}{4}$ oz |
| 25 ml | cherry brandy | 1 fl oz |
| 100 ml | cream | 4 fl oz |
| 10 g | green peppercorns | $\frac{1}{2}$ oz |
| | squeeze lemon juice | |
| | oil | |
| | pinch salt and mill pepper | |

Prepare as stated in the base method above, adding the green peppercorns after flaming with the brandy.

### HEALTH TIP

*Half the cream may be replaced by low-fat velouté sauce (page 34). This will reduce the fat content.*

## 8.17 SHALLOW-FRYING VEGETABLES: COOKING BROWN

**CHEF'S TIP**

*If possible, use a non-stick pan and a very small quantity of fat.*

### BASE METHOD

1 Heat the margarine or oil in a frying pan. Use only enough fat to produce a thin film on the base of the pan.
2 Add the prepared vegetables and fry steadily allowing colour to develop.
3 Toss the vegetables during cooking and lightly season.
4 Remove from the pan and serve.

**TRADITIONAL PRACTICE**

*Use 25 g/1 oz butter instead of margarine or oil when cooking the vegetables. This increases the fat content.*

### SHALLOW-FRIED ONIONS *OIGNONS SAUTÉS*

4 portions

| | | |
|---|---|---|
| 600 g | onion | $1\frac{1}{2}$ lb |
| | margarine or oil | |
| | small pinch salt and pepper | |

Peel the onions, then cut into halves from top to bottom. Trim off the root and top ends, and cut lengthways into thin slices. Prepare as stated in the base method above, cooking for 6–8 minutes.

**TRADITIONAL PRACTICE**

*Use 25 g/1 oz butter instead of margarine or oil when cooking the vegetables. This increases the fat content.*

### SHALLOW-FRIED MUSHROOMS *CHAMPIGNONS SAUTÉS*

4 portions

| | | |
|---|---|---|
| 200 g | whole mushrooms | 8 oz |
| | margarine or oil | |
| | small pinch salt and pepper | |

Remove or trim the stalks of the mushrooms and wash to remove any dirt. Prepare as stated in the base method above, cooking for 4–6 minutes depending on size.

## 8.18 SHALLOW-FRYING TOMATOES

**TRADITIONAL PRACTICE**

*Use 25 g/1 oz butter instead of margarine or oil when cooking the vegetables. This increases the fat content.*

4 portions

### BASE INGREDIENTS

| | | |
|---|---|---|
| 4 | medium tomatoes | 4 |
| | margarine or oil | |
| | small pinch salt and pepper | |

### BASE METHOD

1 Wash the tomatoes and remove the eyes, then either leave whole or cut into halves.
2 Heat the margarine or oil in a frying pan. Use only enough fat to produce a thin film on the base of the pan.
3 Add the prepared tomatoes and fry steadily allowing colour to develop.
4 Turn during cooking and lightly season. Cook for 2–4 minutes depending on size.
5 Remove from the pan, sprinkle with a little chopped parsley and serve.

# 8.19 SHALLOW-FRYING VEGETABLES: COOKING WHITE OR SWEATING

**TRADITIONAL PRACTICE**

*Use 40 g/1$\frac{3}{4}$ oz butter instead of the margarine in all of these recipes. This increases the fat content.*

### BASE METHOD

1. Heat the margarine in a sauteuse or small saucepan with a lid. Do not allow the fat to colour.
2. Add the prepared vegetables and cover with a lid.
3. Cook slowly, occasionally tossing or stirring the vegetables (and replacing the lid).
4. When almost cooked, add any cream.
5. When cooked, lightly season and add any herbs.

**TRADITIONAL PRACTICE**

*Aubergines and courgettes: peel the vegetables before cutting into slices. This reduces fibre.*

## SHALLOW-FRIED AUBERGINES

4 portions

| | | |
|---|---|---|
| 2 | small aubergines | 2 |
| 15 g | margarine | $\frac{3}{4}$ oz |
| | small pinch salt and pepper | |

Wash the aubergines and cut them into slices: 5 mm/$\frac{1}{4}$ inch approximately. Cook as stated in the base method above.

## SHALLOW-FRIED CUCUMBER

4 portions

| | | |
|---|---|---|
| 400 g | cucumber | 1 lb |
| 15 g | margarine | $\frac{3}{4}$ oz |
| | small pinch salt and pepper | |

Wash and cut the cucumber into 40 mm/1$\frac{1}{2}$ inch lengths. Cut each length in half, and remove the seeds. Divide the lengths into wedges of a regular size, turning into barrel shapes if required. Cook as stated in the base method above.

**CHEF'S TIP**

*Vegetables finished with cream are high in fat.*

## CUCUMBERS WITH CREAM *CONCOMBRES À LA CRÈME*

Prepare as for shallow-fried cucumber above, adding 50 ml/2 fl oz cream to the cucumbers when almost cooked.

**TRADITIONAL PRACTICE**

*Aubergines and courgettes: peel the vegetables before cutting into slices. This reduces fibre.*

## SHALLOW-FRIED COURGETTES

4 portions

| | | |
|---|---|---|
| 400 g | courgettes | 1 lb |
| 15 g | margarine | $\frac{3}{4}$ oz |
| | small pinch salt and pepper | |

Wash and cut the courgettes into regular-sized pieces, leaving small courgettes whole, if required. Cook as stated in the base method above.

**COURGETTES WITH HERBS *COURGETTES AUX FINES HERBES*** Prepare as for shallow-fried courgettes above, adding a good pinch of fresh, chopped parsley, chives and chervil to the courgettes when cooked.

## 8.20 COOKING A COMBINATION OF VEGETABLES

### BASE METHOD

1 Heat the oil or margarine in a sauteuse or small saucepan with a lid. Do not allow the fat to colour.
2 Add the onion and garlic and cook under cover for 2 minutes approximately.
3 Add any peppers and cook under cover for a further 2–3 minutes.
4 Add the courgette and any aubergine and continue cooking under cover for 6–8 minutes. Toss or stir the vegetables occasionally during cooking.
5 Add the tomato concassées and season lightly.
6 Continue cooking until all the vegetables are tender.
7 Place into a serving dish and sprinkle with chopped parsley if appropriate.

### COURGETTES PROVENCE STYLE
*COURGETTES PROVENÇALE*

**TRADITIONAL PRACTICE**

*Courgettes Provence and ratatouille: increase the olive oil to 50 ml/2 fl oz. This increases the fat content.*

4 portions

| | | |
|---|---|---|
| 10 g | olive oil | $\frac{1}{2}$ oz |
| 50 g | chopped onion | 2 oz |
| 1 | clove garlic (crushed) | 1 |
| 400 g | courgettes | 1 lb |
| 250 g | tomato concassées (page 25) | 10 oz |
| | small pinch salt and mill pepper | |
| | pinch chopped parsley | |

Wash the courgettes and cut them into regular-sized pieces. Cook as stated in the base method above.

### RATATOUILLE

4 portions

| | | |
|---|---|---|
| 25 ml | olive oil | 1 fl oz |
| 100 g | sliced onion | 4 oz |
| 1 | clove garlic (crushed) | 1 |
| 50 g | diced pimento | 2 oz |
| 200 g | courgette | 8 oz |
| 150'g | sliced aubergine | 6 oz |
| 200 g | tomato concassées (page 25) | 8 oz |
| | small pinch salt and mill pepper | |
| | pinch chopped parsley | |

Wash the courgettes and cut into regular-sized pieces. Cook as stated in the base method above.

### PEPERONATA

**TRADITIONAL PRACTICE**

*Increase the oil to 20 ml/$\frac{3}{4}$ fl oz and use 20 g/$\frac{3}{4}$ oz butter in place of the margarine. This increases the fat content.*

4 portions

| | | |
|---|---|---|
| 5 g | margarine | $\frac{1}{4}$ oz |
| 5 ml | olive oil | $\frac{1}{4}$ fl oz |
| 100 g | sliced onion | 4 oz |
| $\frac{1}{2}$ | clove garlic (crushed) | $\frac{1}{2}$ |
| 4 | medium red peppers | 4 |
| 200 g | tomato concassées (page 25) | 8 oz |
| | small pinch salt and mill pepper | |

Wash the red peppers, remove the stalks and seeds and cut into strips. Cook as stated in the base method above.

## 8.21 SHALLOW-FRYING POTATOES

**CHEF'S TIP**

*Sauté potatoes are high in fat.*

### SAUTÉ POTATOES *POMMES SAUTÉES*

4 portions

**BASE INGREDIENTS**

| | | |
|---|---|---|
| 500 g | potatoes (firm-cooking variety) | $1\frac{1}{4}$ lb |
| 30 ml | oil | 1 fl oz |
| | small pinch salt and pepper | |
| | pinch chopped parsley | |

**BASE METHOD**

1. Wash and scrub the potatoes.
2. Boil until just cooked. Do not overcook.
3. Drain and allow to cool.
4. Peel off the skins while still warm.
5. Cut into slices: 3–5 mm/$\frac{1}{8}$–$\frac{3}{16}$ inch in thickness.
6. Heat the oil until quite hot in a frying pan.
7. Add the potatoes and fry quickly.
8. Toss the potatoes occasionally, allowing a good colour to develop on all sides.
9. Lightly season.
10. Place on a serving dish.
11. Sprinkle with chopped parsley and serve.

**TRADITIONAL PRACTICE**

*Use lard or dripping instead of oil when cooking. This increases the fat content.*

### SAUTÉ POTATOES WITH ONIONS *POMMES LYONNAISE*

(4–6 portions) Shallow-fry 200 g/8 oz sliced onion in 20 g/$\frac{3}{4}$ oz margarine until coloured. Meanwhile, prepare the sauté potatoes as stated above. Toss together the potatoes and onion (after step 8) and finish as stated.

**TRADITIONAL PRACTICE**

*Use butter in place of margarine where appropriate.*

### SAUTÉ POTATOES O'BRIEN STYLE *POMMES O'BRIEN*

(4–6 portions) Prepare sauté potatoes as stated above. Add 50 g/2 oz diced, cooked pimento when the potatoes have been fried (after step 8) and toss together.

### SAUTÉ POTATOES PROVENCE STYLE *POMMES PROVENÇALE*

(4–6 portions) Prepare the sauté potatoes as stated above. After browning the potatoes (step 8), add 25 g/1 oz margarine to the pan and allow to foam. Add 1 clove crushed garlic, then toss through the potatoes.

## 8.22 SHALLOW-FRYING FRUITS (except tomatoes)

**CHEF'S TIP**

*If possible, use a non-stick pan and a very small quantity of fat.*

### BASE METHOD

1 Heat the margarine or oil in a frying pan. Use only enough fat to produce a thin film on the base of the pan.
2 Pass the prepared fruit through the flour.
3 Shake off surplus flour.
4 Add the fruit to the pan and fry steadily, allowing colour to develop.
5 Turn during cooking and lightly season.
6 Remove from the pan and use as required.

**TRADITIONAL PRACTICE**

*Use 15 g/½ oz butter instead of margarine or oil when cooking the fruits. This increases the fat content.*

### SHALLOW-FRIED APPLES

1 portion (as a savoury garnish)

| | | |
|---|---|---|
| 1–2 | slices apple | 1–2 |
| | flour | |
| | margarine or oil | |
| | small pinch salt and pepper | |

Wash, peel and core the apple. Cut into rings: 10 mm/⅜ inch approximately. Prepare as stated in the base method above, cooking for 2 minutes approximately.

**TRADITIONAL PRACTICE**

*Use 15 g/½ oz butter instead of margarine or oil when cooking the fruits. This increases the fat content.*

### SHALLOW-FRIED BANANAS

1 portion (as a savoury garnish)

| | | |
|---|---|---|
| ½ | banana | ½ |
| | flour | |
| | margarine or oil | |
| | small pinch salt and pepper | |

Peel and trim the ends of the banana, and remove any strings. Divide into two halves, cutting diagonally across the width. Prepare as stated in the base method above, cooking for 2 minutes approximately.

### SHALLOW-FRIED PINEAPPLE

1 portion (as a savoury garnish)

| | | |
|---|---|---|
| 1–2 | rings fresh pineapple | 1–2 |
| | flour | |
| | margarine or oil | |
| | small pinch salt and pepper | |

Cut off the skin and cut the pineapple into rings: 10 mm/⅜ inch approximately. Cut out the centre stalk from each ring. Prepare as stated in the base method above, cooking for 2 minutes approximately.

## 8.23 SHALLOW-FRIED SAVOURIES

The following savouries may also be prepared using grilled items.

### MUSHROOMS ON TOAST

2 portions

| | | |
|---|---|---|
| 8 | flat mushrooms | 8 |
| 10 g | margarine | $\frac{1}{2}$ oz |
| 1 | slice wholemeal bread | 1 |
| | branch of parsley | |
| | small pinch salt and pepper | |

1 Shallow-fry the mushrooms in 5 g/$\frac{1}{4}$ oz margarine then lightly season.
2 Toast the bread and spread with the remaining margarine.
3 Remove the crusts and cut the bread into two neat rectangles, squares or circle shapes.
4 Neatly dress the hot mushrooms on the toast shapes.
5 Place on a serving dish (usually lined with a dishpaper).
6 Garnish with the parsley, i.e. place it at the side of the savoury, and serve immediately.

**TRADITIONAL PRACTICE**

*For all recipes this page, use 15 g/$\frac{3}{4}$ oz butter instead of margarine. This increases the fat content. Also use white bread in place of wholemeal bread. This reduces the fibre content.*

### CANAPÉ NINA

2 portions

| | | |
|---|---|---|
| 4 | flat, washed and trimmed mushrooms | 4 |
| 4 | slices tomato | 4 |
| 10 g | margarine | $\frac{1}{2}$ oz |
| 1 | slice wholemeal bread | 1 |
| 2 | pickled walnuts | 2 |
| | branch of parsley | |
| | small pinch salt and pepper | |

Prepare as for mushrooms on toast above, adding slices of fried tomato. Top each savoury with a hot pickled walnut.

### CANAPÉ BRISTOL

2 portions

| | | |
|---|---|---|
| 2 | lean bacon rashers | 2 |
| 4 | flat, washed and trimmed mushrooms | 4 |
| 4 | slices beef marrow | 4 |
| 10 g | margarine | $\frac{1}{2}$ oz |
| 1 | slice wholemeal bread | 1 |
| | chopped parsley | |
| | small pinch salt and pepper | |

1 Shallow-fry the bacon rashers and mushrooms in 5 g/$\frac{1}{4}$ oz margarine then lightly season.
2 Poach the beef marrow in a little hot stock.
3 Toast the bread and spread with the remaining margarine.
4 Remove the crusts and cut the bread into two neat rectangles, squares or circle shapes.
5 Neatly dress the bacon, mushrooms and marrow on the toast shapes.
6 Sprinkle with chopped parsley and place on a serving dish (usually lined with a dishpaper).
7 Serve immediately.

**TRADITIONAL PRACTICE**

*Use streaky bacon in place of lean bacon rashers. This increases the fat content.* Note: *poached beef marrow is high in fat.*

## 8.24 COOKING CRÊPES AND PANCAKES

**TRADITIONAL PRACTICE**

*Use whole milk instead of skimmed milk and butter in place of margarine. This increases the fat content.*

**CHEF'S TIP**

*A pinch of ground white pepper may be added to the batter ingredients when preparing savoury pancakes.*

4 portions

### BASE INGREDIENTS

| | | |
|---|---|---|
| 75 g | flour | 3 oz |
| 1 | egg (size 3) | 1 |
| 200 ml | skimmed milk | 8 fl oz |
| 15 g | margarine | $\frac{3}{4}$ oz |
| | small pinch salt | |

### BASE METHOD

1 Sieve together the flour, salt and any pepper.
2 Add the egg and half the quantity of milk.
3 Whisk to a smooth thick paste.
4 Add the remaining milk and whisk to a thin batter (with a consistency similar to single cream).
5 Melt the margarine and whisk into the batter until completely combined.
6 Heat a crêpe pan and add little oil. If available, use a non-stick pan barely polished with oil.
7 When hot, pour off the surplus oil.
8 Add a small quantity of batter, i.e. only enough to form a thin coating on the base of the pan.
9 Tilt the pan to spread the batter evenly across the base of the pan.
10 Cook until golden brown.
11 Turn over and cook the other side.
12 Turn the pancake out of the pan onto a large plate.
13 Cover with a second plate and keep hot.
14 Repeat the cooking procedure until the required number of pancakes is obtained. Place the pancakes one on top of the other and store between the hot plates.

### SAVOURY CRÊPES

### CHICKEN PANCAKES *CRÊPES À LA REINE*

4 portions

| | | |
|---|---|---|
| 12 | pancakes (above) | 12 |
| 300 g | chicken salpicon (page 28) | 12 oz |
| 125 ml | low-fat suprême sauce (page 34) | $\frac{1}{4}$ pt |

1 Place a spoonful of hot chicken salpicon on the centre of each pancake then roll up the pancake.
2 Coat the base of a serving dish with a little suprême sauce then place the pancakes on top.
3 Coat with the remaining sauce and sprinkle with a little chopped parsley.

**TRADITIONAL PRACTICE**

*Use traditional velouté sauce in place of low-fat sauce. This increases the fat content.*

### SEAFOOD PANCAKES *CRÊPES AUX FRUITS DE MER*

4 portions

| | | |
|---|---|---|
| 12 | pancakes (above) | 12 |
| 300 g | seafood salpicon (page 28) | 12 oz |
| 125 ml | low-fat fish velouté (page 34) | $\frac{1}{4}$ pt |

Prepare as for chicken pancakes above, using the seafood salpicon and fish velouté.

**HEALTH TIP**

*Pancakes with cheese are high in fat.*

**TRADITIONAL PRACTICE**

*Use butter in place of margarine. This increases the saturated fat content.*

## PANCAKES WITH RICOTTA CHEESE AND HAM
### *CRÊPES CON RICOTTA E PROSCIUTTO*

4 portions

| | | |
|---|---|---|
| 12 | pancakes (Process 8.24 opposite) | 12 |
| 150 g | ricotta cheese | 6 oz |
| 100 g | chopped ham | 4 oz |
| 1 tbsp | milk | 1 tbsp |
| 10 g | melted margarine | $\frac{1}{2}$ oz |
| 5 g | grated Parmesan cheese | $\frac{1}{4}$ oz |
| | small pinch salt and pepper | |

1 Mix together the ricotta cheese and ham.
2 Season, and add enough milk to produce a soft paste.
3 Place a spoonful of the mixture on the centre of each pancake then roll up each one.
4 Lightly grease the base of a serving dish with a little melted margarine then place the pancakes on top.
5 Coat with the remaining margarine and sprinkle the top with the Parmesan.
6 Bake in a moderate oven until golden brown and thoroughly heated through.

### SWEET PANCAKES

**TRADITIONAL PRACTICE**

*Use double the quantity of caster sugar. This increases the sugar content.*

## PANCAKES WITH LEMON *CRÊPES AU CITRON*

4 portions

| | | |
|---|---|---|
| 12 | pancakes (Process 8.24 opposite) | 12 |
| 4 | wedges lemon | 4 |
| 25 g | caster sugar | 1 oz |
| | squeeze lemon juice | |

1 Sprinkle each pancake with caster sugar then add a squeeze of lemon juice.
2 Fold each pancake in half, then half again.
3 Arrange the pancakes on a serving dish, sprinkle the surface with sugar and garnish with lemon wedges.

## PANCAKES WITH ORANGE
### *CRÊPES À L'ORANGE*

Prepare as for lemon pancakes, using oranges and orange juice.

## PANCAKES WITH JAM *CRÊPES À LA CONFITURE*

4 portions

| | | |
|---|---|---|
| 12 | pancakes (Process 8.24 opposite) | 12 |
| 50 g | warm raspberry jam | 2 oz |
| 25 g | caster sugar | 1 oz |

1 Spread the centre of each pancake with jam then roll up each one.
2 Arrange the pancakes on a serving dish and sprinkle the surface with sugar.

## PANCAKES NORMANDY STYLE *CRÊPES NORMANDE*

4 portions

| | | |
|---|---|---|
| 12 | pancakes (opposite: but note step 1 below) | 12 |
| 25 ml | Calvados | 1 fl oz |
| 400 g | apple pulp (page 29) | 1 lb |
| 25 g | caster sugar | 1 oz |

1 Prepare the pancakes as stated but replace 25 ml/1 fl oz of the milk in the pancake batter with Calvados.
2 Spread the centre of each pancake with hot apple pulp then roll up each one.
3 Arrange the pancakes on a serving dish and sprinkle sugar on top.

## 8.25 GRIDDLE OR GIRDLE SCONES

**TRADITIONAL PRACTICE**

*Use 50 g/2 oz butter instead of margarine and whole milk in place of skimmed milk. This increases the fat content.*

**CHEF'S TIP**

*The scone mixture should be very soft. Keeping the scone mixture soft with as little handling as possible is important in producing high-quality scones.*

### PLAIN GRIDDLE SCONES

10 small scones

**BASE INGREDIENTS**

| | | |
|---|---|---|
| 200 g | plain flour | 8 oz |
| 10 g | baking powder | ½ oz |
| 25 g | margarine | 1 oz |
| 30 g | caster sugar | 1¼ oz |
| ½ | egg (size 3) | ½ |
| 100 ml | skimmed milk | 4 fl oz |

**BASE METHOD**

1. Sieve together the flour and baking powder.
2. Rub in the margarine to achieve a sandy texture.
3. Place the sugar, egg and milk into a bowl and whisk together until combined.
4. Add the flour and mix to a smooth, soft dough. Do not overmix.
5. Roll out the dough using self-raising flour.
6. Cut with a cutter into individual scones.
7. Allow to rest for 20 minutes.
8. Heat the griddle plate or pan and grease lightly.
9. Place the scones onto the griddle or pan and cook until golden brown (3–4 minutes approximately). Ensure the griddle is not too hot.
10. Carefully turn over the scones and finish cooking: a further 3–4 minutes.

**FRUIT SCONES** Prepare as for the base recipe, adding 50 g/2 oz selected fruit, e.g. sultanas, currants or raisins to the flour after sieving.

**WHOLEMEAL SCONES** Prepare as for the base recipe, using wholemeal flour. Also increase the skimmed milk to 125 ml/¼ pt.

**BUTTERMILK SCONES** Prepare the scones as stated in the base recipe but replace the sugar with a pinch of salt, and use buttermilk in place of skimmed milk.

### SWEETCORN PANCAKES

8 pancakes

| | | |
|---|---|---|
| 200 g | cooked or tinned sweetcorn kernels | 8 oz |
| 1 | egg (size 3) | 1 |
| 40 g | self-raising flour | 1¾ oz |
| | small pinch salt and pepper | |

1. Mix the egg through the sweetcorn and season lightly.
2. Add the flour and mix together. Do not overmix.
3. Heat the griddle plate or pan and grease lightly.
4. Drop the mixture onto the griddle or pan using a spoon.
5. Cook until golden brown, ensuring the pan is not too hot.
6. Carefully turn over and finish cooking.

# 8.26 SCOTCH PANCAKES/DROPPED SCONES

**TRADITIONAL PRACTICE**

*All recipes this page: use butter instead of margarine and whole milk in place of skimmed milk. This increases the fat content.*

**CHEF'S TIP**

*Producing good quality Scotch pancakes requires experience. Speed of cooking must be correct and the pancakes should be turned while they still have a damp, visible gloss on the uncooked sides.*

8–10 Scotch pancakes

## BASE INGREDIENTS

| | | |
|---|---|---|
| 200 g | plain flour | 8 oz |
| 10 g | baking powder | $\frac{1}{2}$ oz |
| 25 g | margarine | 1 oz |
| 75 g | caster sugar | 3 oz |
| 1 | egg (size 3) | 1 |
| 130 ml | skimmed milk | $5\frac{1}{4}$ fl oz |

## BASE METHOD

1. Sieve together the flour and baking powder.
2. Rub in the margarine to achieve a sandy texture.
3. Place the sugar, egg and milk into a bowl and whisk together until combined.
4. Add the flour and whisk to a smooth batter.
5. Heat the griddle plate or pan and lightly grease.
6. Drop the mixture onto the griddle or pan using a ladle or piping bag.
7. Cook until golden brown ensuring the griddle is not too hot.
8. Carefully turn over the scones and finish cooking.

## CRUMPETS (made with baking powder)

6 crumpets

| | | |
|---|---|---|
| 200 g | plain flour | 8 oz |
| 10 g | baking powder | $\frac{1}{2}$ oz |
| 50 g | margarine | 2 oz |
| 100 g | caster sugar | 4 oz |
| 1 | egg (size 3) | 1 |
| 250 ml | skimmed milk | $\frac{1}{2}$ pt |

1. Proceed as stated for the base recipe above, but add only half the quantity of milk with the sugar and egg when whisking together at step 3 (this is to avoid forming lumps).
2. When the flour has been added and the ingredients whisked to a smooth thick mixture (step 4) add the remaining milk.
3. Whisk to a smooth thin batter.
4. Cook following steps 5–8 of the base recipe, using a ladle to drop the batter onto the griddle or pan.
5. Turn over the crumpets when all the bubbles have burst on the uncooked side.

**HEALTH TIP**

*Pancakes with maple syrup are high in sugar.*

**PANCAKES WITH MAPLE SYRUP** (4 portions) Prepare 8 Scotch pancakes as stated in the base recipe. Heat 125 ml/$\frac{1}{4}$ pt maple syrup in a saucepan, then add the pancakes and allow to heat through, absorbing the syrup. Place them on a serving dish and spoon over the remaining syrup.

# Process 9 DEEP-FRYING

**DEFINITION** Deep-frying is a dry heat method of cooking, where prepared food is cooked in pre-heated fat or oil. Deep-frying is a fast method of cooking because all the surfaces of the food being fried are cooked at the same time, with temperatures up to 195 °C/383 °F being used.

## REASONS FOR DEEP-FRYING FOODS

1 To make foods tender: by breaking down and softening protein, fat, starch, cellulose and fibre.
2 To make foods more palatable and digestible.
3 To make foods safer to eat: by destroying bacteria which can cause food poisoning.
4 To produce a particular quality in food, of colour, flavour and texture (e.g. apple fritters).

## METHODS OF DEEP-FRYING FOODS

1 **Partial cooking or blanching:** This is the deep-frying of foods until tender, but without developing colour. The reason for blanching foods is that they can be stored on trays until required for service then fried quickly in hot fat until crisp and golden brown. Chips are usually blanched in this manner; fruit fritters and battered vegetables may also be blanched prior to service.
2 **Complete cooking:** This is the deep-frying of foods until fully cooked, where serving takes place immediately, to maintain a crisp, dry product.
3 **Pressure frying:** This is the frying of food under pressure in special fryers. Pressure fryers are usually automated and work on a timed cooking cycle. These fryers are fast at producing high quality fried foods and are safe to use.

## COMMODITIES SUITABLE FOR DEEP-FRYING

1 **White fish:** e.g. some small whole fish (haddock) and fillets of fish.
2 **Chicken or turkey:** portions of poultry.
3 **Made-up items and convenience foods:** e.g. Scotch eggs, savoury cutlets, croquettes and cromesquis.
4 **Vegetables:** Raw – e.g. aubergines, courgettes.
Cooked – e.g. prepared celery, fennel and cauliflower.
5 **Potatoes.**
6 **Fruits:** e.g. bananas, peaches, apple and pineapple slices.
7 **Batters and doughs:** e.g. choux paste (fritters), bun dough and scone dough (doughnuts).

**Important:** Some foods are less suitable for deep-frying because they contain fats or oils which will contaminate the frying medium. Examples of these foods are oily fish, fatty meats and meat products such as bacon, gammon, ham, sausages and meat puddings.

## EQUIPMENT USED WHEN DEEP-FRYING FOODS

Gas deep-fat fryer

1 Fritures (old-fashioned frying vessels – see *key points* opposite).
2 Free-standing fryers (electric or gas) with manual thermostat control.
3 Automatic fryers.
4 Continuous fryers.
5 Pressure fryers.

## BASIC TECHNIQUES OF DEEP-FRYING

**DRAINING FOODS TO BE FRIED** Wet foods should be thoroughly drained and dried as much as possible before being cooked. Placing wet foods into hot fat is very dangerous as the fat reacts violently and rapidly increases in volume.

**COATING FOODS TO BE FRIED** Many fried foods are coated with batter or breadcrumbs prior to frying. This not only produces a crisp, coloured surface but also reduces the juices and fat from the item entering and contaminating the frying medium.

**BATTERED FOODS** Foods which are battered are passed through the batter (usually after coating with flour), and then placed directly into the hot fat. The food should be placed carefully into the fat to avoid splashes of fat which can cause burns. **A basket should never be used when frying battered foods.**

**BREADED FOODS** Foods coated with breadcrumbs are usually fried on trays or in baskets.

**SPEED OF COOKING** (complete cooking) Most foods are usually fried at a temperature which will cook, colour and crisp the food all at the same time. Avoid low temperature frying as this increases fat absorption in the food.

**DRAINING FRIED FOODS AFTER COOKING** Fried foods should be drained thoroughly after cooking to remove surface fat. In addition it is standard practice in many establishments to serve fried food on dishpapers which absorb surface fat.

**HOT STORAGE OF FRIED FOODS** To produce high quality fried food for the customer, the food should be served immediately after frying. Never use a lid to cover fried foods as this produces condensation and softens the crisp coating.

## KEY POINTS

- Always wear sleeves long, to avoid burns to the arms from splashes of fat.
- Always use a well-designed fryer with a thermostat and *never* an old-fashioned friture.
- Never exceed a maximum frying temperature of 195 °C/383 °F.
- Never fry too much food at the one time as this is not only dangerous but will reduce the frying temperature and increase fat absorption.
- Check the accuracy of the thermostat at regular intervals.
- Strain the fat regularly to remove food particles.
- Keep the number of fried foods offered on your menus to a minimum.

## 9.1 DEEP-FRYING BREADED FISH AND SHELLFISH
### *PANER À L'ANGLAISE*

**HEALTH TIP**

*All deep-fried foods are high in fat.*

**CHEF'S TIP**

*Breaded fish may be prepared and stored chilled for short periods prior to cooking.*

**TRADITIONAL PRACTICE**

*Use seasoned flour instead of plain flour. This increases the salt content.*

### BASE INGREDIENTS

fish or shellfish (see below)
flour
eggwash and breadcrumbs
frying oil
*Garnish:*
lemon segments
branch parsley

### BASE METHOD

1 Prepare the fish or shellfish for cooking.
2 Pass the fish through the seasoned flour, eggwash and breadcrumbs.
3 Shake off any loose breadcrumbs then place into the frying basket.
4 Place the basket into the frying oil and cook at 185 °C/365 °F approximately.
5 During frying ensure that the fish are not sticking together.
6 Turn any whole fish or fillets which float, allowing them to cook through and develop an even colour.
7 Remove the basket from the frier and drain well to reduce surface fat.
8 Place on a serving dish lined with a dishpaper.
9 Decorate with the garnish and accompany with an appropriate sauce (e.g. tartare sauce).

**CHEF'S TIP**

*An alternative method of deep-frying is frying French style (*frit à la Francaise*). This style of frying involves passing the fish or shellfish through milk then coating with flour. The fish is then immediately deep-fried using the method of either Process 9.1 or 9.3 (see French fried onions on page 180). This style of frying causes rapid deterioration of the frying oil because flour particles are left in the fat after frying and burn.*

**DEEP FRIED FILLETS OF PLAICE WITH SAUCE TARTARE** ***FILETS DE PLIE FRITS À L'ANGLAISE, SAUCE TARTARE*** For 4 portions, use eight 75 g/3 oz plaice fillets and prepare following the base recipe above, accompanying the fish with tartare sauce.

**SOLE EN GOUJONS** For 4 portions, use 600 g/1 lb 2 oz sole fillets cut into thin strips (page 21) and prepare following the base recipe above.

**DEEP-FRIED SCAMPI** ***SCAMPI FRITS*** For 4 portions, use 400 g/1 lb cooked, shelled scampi tails and prepare following the base recipe above.

## 9.2 DEEP-FRYING FISH AND MEAT IN BATTER

**TRADITIONAL PRACTICE**

*Use seasoned flour instead of plain flour. This increases the salt content.*

**CHEF'S TIP**

*Battered fish must be passed through the flour and batter, then cooked immediately.*

### BASE INGREDIENTS

fish or meat (see below)
flour
frying batter (page 23)
frying oil
*Garnish:*
lemon segments
branch parsley

### BASE METHOD

1 Prepare the fish for cooking.
2 Pass the fish through the seasoned flour.
3 Place into the batter.
4 Remove from the battter, drawing off surplus batter on the sides of the batter bowl.
5 Carefully place into the frying oil and cook at 185 °C/365 °F approximately.
6 During frying ensure that the fish are not sticking together.
7 Turn any whole fish or fillets which float, allowing to cook through and develop an even colour.
8 Remove from the frier and drain well to reduce surface fat.
9 Place on a serving dish lined with a dishpaper.
10 Decorate with the garnish and accompany with an appropriate sauce (e.g. sauce verte).

### DEEP-FRIED FILLETS OF FLOUNDER WITH SAUCE RÉMOULADE *FILETS DE FLET FRITS, SAUCE RÉMOULADE*

For 4 portions, use eight 75 g/3 oz flounder fillets, and prepare following the base recipe above. Serve with sauce rémoulade (page 35).

### FILLETS OF HADDOCK ORLY *FILETS DE AIGLEFIN ORLY*

| 4 portions | | |
|---|---|---|
| 4 × 150 g | haddock fillets | 4 × 6 oz |
| | base ingredients (see above) | |
| 150 ml | tomato sauce (page 33) | 6 fl oz |
| | *Marinade:* | |
| 10 g | finely chopped onion | ½ oz |
| 50 ml | lemon juice | 2 fl oz |
| 50 ml | oil | 2 fl oz |
| | good pinch chopped parsley | |

For 4 portions, use four 150 g/6 oz haddock fillets. Mix together the ingredients for the marinade. Add the fish and allow to marinade for 15 minutes, then remove surplus marinade. Complete by following steps 2–10 of the base recipe above. Garnish with the lemon and parsley and serve with the tomato sauce.

### ESCALOPE OF VEAL/TURKEY ORLY *ESCALOPE DE VEAU/DINDE ORLY*

Prepare as for fish Orly above, using a 100 g/4 oz veal or turkey escalope marinaded for 1 hour. Garnish with the lemon and parsley and serve with tomato sauce.

## 9.3 DEEP-FRYING BREADED POULTRY

### BASE INGREDIENTS

cooked poultry (as appropriate)
flour
eggwash and breadcrumbs

*Garnish:*
lemon wedge
branch parsley

### BASE METHOD

1 Pass the poultry through the seasoned flour, eggwash and breadcrumbs.
2 Shake off any loose breadcrumbs, then place into a frying basket.
3 Place into the frying oil at 175 °C/350 °F approximately.
4 Deep-fry until crisp and golden brown (3–4 minutes). Ensure the poultry is thoroughly reheated, i.e. minimum internal temperature: 85 °C/185 °F.
5 Remove from the frier and drain well to reduce surface fat.
6 Place into a clean basket lined with a napkin or dishpaper.
7 Garnish with the lemon and parsley and serve with a baked or French-fried potato.

**HEALTH TIP**

*All deep-fried foods are high in fat.*

**CHICKEN IN THE BASKET** For 1 portion, use 1 cooked and skinned chicken quarter (wing or leg) and cook following the base recipe above.

**DEEP-FRIED TURKEY ESCALOPE IN THE BASKET** For 1 portion, use 1 raw turkey escalope (75–100 g/3–4 oz) and cook following the base recipe above.

**GUINEA FOWL IN THE BASKET** For 1 portion, use 1 cooked and skinned portion of wing or leg (or a half bird – depending on size) and cook following the base recipe above.

## 9.4 DEEP-FRYING MADE-UP ITEMS

**HEALTH TIP**

*All deep-fried foods are high in fat.*

**CHEF'S TIP**

*When preparing deep-fried pre-prepared frozen items such as fish fingers, breaded fish or croquettes, deep-fry them while still frozen. Deep-fry as stated but place into slightly hotter frying oil (185 °C/365 °F approximately).*

Many items which are deep-fried are ready-made fresh or chilled items. They are simply immersed in the hot fat and fried until crisp and golden brown and thoroughly reheated.

### BASE METHOD

1. Place the made-up item into a frying basket.
2. Immerse into the frying oil at 175 °C/350 °F approximately.
3. Deep-fry until crisp and golden brown (3–4 minutes). Ensure the items are thoroughly reheated, i.e. minimum internal temperature: 85 °C/185 °F.
4. Remove from the frier and drain well to reduce surface fat.
5. Place on a serving dish lined with a dishpaper.
6. Garnish with parsley and accompany with an appropriate sauce.

### CHICKEN CROQUETTES *CROQUETTES DE VOLAILLE*

4 portions

| | | |
|---|---|---|
| 25 g | margarine | 1 oz |
| 25 g | flour | 1 oz |
| 125 ml | chicken stock | $\frac{1}{4}$ pt |
| 200 g | cooked, minced chicken | 8 oz |
| 1 | egg yolk (optional) | 1 |
| | seasoned flour | |
| | eggwash and breadcrumbs | |

*Suitable sauces:*
devil, piquant or tomato

1. Melt the margarine in a saucepan.
2. Add the flour and cook for 2–3 minutes without developing colour.
3. Blend in the hot stock, stirring until smooth with each addition of liquid.
4. Bring to the boil and cook for 1–2 minutes. Stir frequently to avoid burning.
5. Add the minced chicken, then cook for 4–5 minutes stirring frequently to avoid burning.
6. Add the egg yolk and stir through the hot mixture.
7. Cool the mixture quickly.
8. Divide into 4 pieces then shape like corks.
9. Pass the shapes through flour, eggwash and breadcrumbs.
10. Finish as stated in the base recipe above.

## 9.5 DEEP-FRYING RAW VEGETABLES

**CHEF'S TIP**

*Many vegetables are difficult to cook from raw by deep-frying, e.g. carrots, celery, fennel and salsify. However they can be boiled until lightly cooked, cooled quickly and then deep-fried (either breaded: page 176 or battered: page 177).*

**HEALTH TIP**

*All deep-fried foods are high in fat.*

**TRADITIONAL PRACTICE**

*Use seasoned flour in place of plain flour. This increases the salt content.*

### BASE METHOD

1 Place the vegetables into a frying basket and shake off the loose flour.
2 Immerse in the frying oil at 185 °C/365 °F approximately.
3 Deep-fry until crisp and golden brown.
4 Remove from the frier and drain well to reduce surface fat.
5 Place onto a serving dish lined with a dishpaper and serve immediately.

### FRIED AUBERGINES *AUBERGINES FRITES*

4 portions

| 300 g | whole aubergine | 12 oz |
|---|---|---|
| | flour | |

1 Wash, peel (optional) and slice each aubergine into 5 mm/$\frac{1}{4}$ inch slices.
2 Pass the slices through the flour.
3 Complete as stated in the base recipe.

### FRIED COURGETTES *COURGETTES FRITES*

4 portions

| 300 g | whole courgettes | 12 oz |
|---|---|---|
| | flour | |

1 Wash, peel (optional) and slice each courgette into 5 mm/$\frac{1}{4}$ inch slices.
2 Pass the slices through the flour.
3 Complete as stated in the base recipe.

### FRENCH FRIED ONIONS *OIGNONS FRITS À LA FRANÇAISE*

4 portions

| 400 g | whole onions | 1 lb |
|---|---|---|
| | milk | |
| | flour | |

1 Peel, then cut each onion into thin slices: 3 mm/$\frac{1}{5}$ inch thickness approximately.
2 Separate the slices into rings.
3 Place into the milk, then remove and pass through the flour.
4 Complete as stated in the base recipe.

## 9.6 DEEP-FRYING RAW POTATOES: STICK SHAPES

4 portions

### BASE INGREDIENTS

| | | |
|---|---|---|
| 500 g–1 kg | potatoes (depending on potato size and cutting style) | 1–2 lb |

### BASE METHOD

1. Wash and peel the potatoes, then cut into the desired shape (below).
2. Rewash the potatoes under cold running water to remove excess starch.
3. Set the fryer to the correct temperature:
   *thin stick types*: 180–185 °C/355–365 °F
   *thick stick types*: 165–170 °C/330–340 °F
4. Drain the potatoes thoroughly, removing all surface water.
5. Place the potatoes into a frying basket.
6. Deep-fry, occasionally shaking the frying basket to ensure the potatoes are not sticking together.
7. Remove the potatoes when they are tender but still have little or no colour development (blanched).
8. Drain well to remove surface fat.
9. Place on a tray lined with kitchen paper until required for service.
10. When required, place the potatoes into a frying basket.
11. Deep-fry in hot oil (185 °C/365 °F) until crisp and golden brown in colour.
12. Place the potatoes on a serving dish lined with a dishpaper.

**HEALTH TIP**

*All deep-fried foods are high in fat.*

**SAFETY TIP**

*Dry the potatoes thoroughly before deep-frying. It is dangerous to deep-fry wet foods as the hot oil will react violently and rapidly increase in volume.*

**All of the following are prepared using the base method above:**

### MATCHSTICK POTATOES *POMMES ALLUMETTES*

Matchstick shapes: 40 mm × 2 mm × 2 mm/2 inch × $\frac{1}{8}$ inch × $\frac{1}{8}$ inch.

### MIGNONNETTE POTATOES *POMMES MIGNONNETTES*

Stick shapes: 40 × 5 mm × 5 mm/2 inch × $\frac{1}{4}$ inch × $\frac{1}{4}$ inch.

### CHIPPED POTATOES *POMMES FRITES*

Stick shapes: 40 mm × 10 mm × 10 mm/2 inch × $\frac{1}{2}$ inch × $\frac{1}{2}$ inch.

### PONT-NEUF POTATOES *POMMES PONT-NEUF*

Stick shapes: 40 mm × 20 mm × 20 mm/2 inch × 1 inch × 1 inch.

## 9.7 DEEP-FRYING RAW POTATOES: SLICED

**HEALTH TIP**

*All deep-fried foods are high in fat.*

**SAFETY TIP**

*Dry the potatoes thoroughly before deep-frying. It is dangerous to deep-fry wet foods as the hot oil will react violently and rapidly increase in volume.*

**CHEF'S TIP**

*The potato items may be stored in an airtight container for short periods and used when required for service.*

Garnish for 4 main-course portions

### BASE INGREDIENTS

| | | |
|---|---|---|
| 150 g | potatoes | 6 oz |

### BASE METHOD

1. Wash, peel, and cut the potatoes into the required shape (below).
2. Rewash the potatoes under cold running water to remove excess starch.
3. Place the potatoes in a cloth and dry thoroughly.
4. Set the fryer to the correct temperature: 180–185 °C/355–365 °F.
5. Carefully sprinkle the potatoes into the hot fat a few at a time. *Important:* use a metal spider to disperse the potatoes through the fat and allow the steam to escape before adding any more potatoes.
6. Fry the potatoes, occasionally turning with the spider, until crisp and golden brown.
7. Remove from the fryer, draining off as much fat as possible.
8. Place on a tray lined with kitchen paper until required for use.

### CRISPS *POMMES CHIPS*

Thin slices: 1 mm/$\frac{1}{20}$ inch thick approximately.

### STRAW POTATOES *POMMES PAILLES*

Fine strips: 1 mm/$\frac{1}{20}$ inch thick approximately.

### WAFER POTATOES *POMMES GAUFRETTES*

Trellis pattern: 2 mm/$\frac{1}{8}$ inch thick approximately.

Cut the potatoes into olives on a mandolin, using the corrugated blade and giving a half-turn between each slice. This will produce a wafer or trellis pattern. It is important that the blade of the mandolin is set to the correct thickness to cut these potatoes: 2–3 mm/$\frac{1}{16}$–$\frac{1}{8}$ inch.

## 9.8 DEEP-FRYING COOKED OR FROZEN POTATOES

### BASE METHOD

1. Place the potatoes into a frying basket. Do not defrost frozen types: they should be cooked from a frozen state.
2. Immerse into the frying oil at 185 °C/365 °F approximately.
3. Deep-fry until crisp, golden brown and thoroughly reheated.
4. Remove from the frier and drain well to reduce surface fat.
5. Place on a serving dish lined with a dishpaper.

# 9.9 DEEP-FRYING FRUIT FRITTERS

**HEALTH TIP**

*All deep-fried foods are high in fat.*

2 portions

## BASE INGREDIENTS

| | | |
|---|---|---|
| | prepared fruit (see below) | |
| 125 ml | frying batter (page 23) | $\frac{1}{4}$ pt |
| 100 ml | apricot sauce (page 39) | 4 fl oz |
| | flour | |
| | icing or caster sugar | |

## BASE METHOD

1. Pass the prepared fruit through the flour, then place it into the batter.
2. Remove the fruit from the batter, drawing off surplus batter on the sides of the batter bowl.
3. Carefully place the fruit into the frying oil and cook at 180 °C/355 °F approximately.
4. During frying ensure that the fritters are not sticking together.
5. Turn the fritters occasionally, allowing them to cook evenly and develop a crisp, golden-brown surface.
6. Remove from the frier and drain well to reduce surface fat.
7. Place the fritters on a tray and dust over the tops with sugar.
8. Place under a hot salamander until the sugar forms a glaze.
9. Place on a serving dish lined with a doily.
10. Accompany with the apricot sauce.

**APPLE FRITTERS** *BEIGNETS DE POMMES* For 2 portions, use 1 large cooking apple (150 g/6 oz approximately). Wash, peel, core, and slice into rings (5 mm/$\frac{1}{4}$ inch); then complete as stated in the base recipe above.

**APRICOT FRITTERS** *BEIGNETS D'ABRICOTS* For 2 portions, use 4 medium apricots (150 g/6 oz approximately). Wash the apricots, then cut them into halves and remove the stones. Complete as stated in the base recipe above.

**BANANA FRITTERS** *BEIGNETS DE BANANES* For 2 portions, use 2 medium bananas. Peel them and then trim the ends of each banana. Cut each banana once, diagonally across the width. Complete as stated in the base recipe above.

**CHEF'S TIP**

*Tinned pineapple may be used for making pineapple fritters.*

**PINEAPPLE FRITTERS** *BEIGNETS D'ANANAS* For 2 portions, use 2–4 rings fresh pineapple. Remove the skin from the pineapple, then cut the fruit into rings (10 mm/$\frac{1}{2}$ inch thick approximately). Cut out the centre stalks. Complete as stated in the base recipe above.

# *Process 10* MICROWAVE COOKING

**DEFINITION** Microwave cooking is the cooking of food by high-frequency electromagnetic waves. The waves penetrate the food from all directions up to a depth of 20–35 mm/$\frac{3}{4}$–1$\frac{1}{2}$ inch and produce heat. The heat is then transferred through the food by conduction, as it is in conventional cooking.

## REASONS FOR COOKING FOODS USING MICROWAVES

1 To make foods tender: by breaking down and softening protein, fat, starch, cellulose and fibre in a short period of time.
2 To make foods more palatable and digestible.
3 To make foods safer to eat: by destroying bacteria which can cause food poisoning.

## ADVANTAGES OF MICROWAVE COOKING

1 Fast cooking or reheating of food.
2 Rapid defrosting of food.
3 Uses less energy than conventional cookers.
4 Less risk of fire than conventional equipment.
5 May be used in a vending system making food available 24 hours a day.
6 Flavour and nutrient loss may be reduced when foods are cooked with very little or no added liquid.

## DISADVANTAGES OF MICROWAVE COOKING

1 Does not colour the surface of food unless used in conjunction with conventional cooking, i.e. combined microwave and convection oven.
2 Limited cooking capacity.
3 Exact time control required for most foods: foods may be quickly overcooked or toughened in a very short time.
4 Low-power output ovens may present a hygiene risk when reheating chilled foods – see *reheating* (below).

*Note:* Many of the recipes found in a domestic microwave manual, e.g. the cooking of roasts, cakes, yeast goods, etc. have not been included in this chapter. The use of a microwave oven for these applications is not practicable in most commercial situations. This also applies to the use of special browning dishes and browning agents (sauce, liquids) which are coated over foods to produce a brown colour.

## METHODS OF HEATING FOODS USING MICROWAVES

1 **Prime cooking:** This is when food is cooked from raw in the microwave oven. Foods may be cooked in a comparable manner to boiling, poaching, steaming, stewing, braising, and oven cooking without colour. Recipe examples: scrambled eggs and fish Dugléré.
2 **Microwave assisted cooking:** This is when food is cooked by a combination of microwaves and some other form of conventional heat application. This may be shallow-frying or grilling followed by microwave cooking or cooking in a combination oven – see part (2) of *equipment* (opposite). Recipe example: Greek style pork kebabs.
3 **Reheating or regenerating:** Many foods may be cooked conventionally then later reheated in a microwave oven ready for service. The most popular use of this type of equipment in commercial catering is to reheat or regenerate chilled convenience foods. A commercial oven with a power output of 1 kW or over should be used to reheat foods and not a domestic oven (600–700 W output) which may take too long to thoroughly reheat chilled dishes. Insufficient reheating of chilled foods can result in food poisoning, and it is important to follow Government Guidelines when reheating these foods; i.e. foods must reach a minimum internal temperature of 80 °C/176 °F and be held at that temperature for 2 minutes. See also *standing time* (opposite).
4 **Defrosting:** Foods may be taken straight from a deep freeze and rapidly defrosted using a defrost/pulsed power cycle.

## POINTS OF SPECIAL ATTENTION

1 **Types of cooking utensils to be used:** Glass, china, porcelain, polypropylene, high-density polythene or suitable paper containers may be used. Metal containers should not be used as they reflect the microwaves, causing uneven heating; and may damage the oven.

2 **Time control:** Microwave cooking is very fast, therefore very precise time control is essential. Use well-tried and tested recipes and always follow the manufacturer's instructions regarding a particular model. Also use a probe type thermometer to ensure that chilled foods have been thoroughly reheated; do not just follow a suggested reheating time. *Important*: remember that the cooking or reheating time varies with the quantity of food placed in the oven.

3 **Standing time:** Temperatures within food often fluctuate during microwave cooking or reheating. Hot and cold spots may be found within food during heating, therefore it is important to let the food stand for a short period to allow temperatures to even out and complete the cooking or reheating.

## EQUIPMENT USED WHEN MICROWAVE COOKING

1 Microwave ovens with varying power outputs, e.g. 1.1, 1.3 or 2 kW and a defrost cycle. Units may or may not have a turntable and preset controls.

2 Combination ovens, where microwave cooking is combined with convection heating in one oven. Both methods of heat application can be used individually or simultaneously, resulting in an oven which will cook foods quickly and also develop colour. Metal cooking dishes can also be used in this type of oven.

Microwave oven

Combination microwave oven

## BASIC TECHNIQUES OF MICROWAVE COOKING

**ARRANGING FOODS** Microwave energy is usually greater around the edges of a dish than at the centre. Therefore certain foods are arranged in a particular manner to assist even cooking. (See the cooking of broccoli and asparagus on page 192.)

**COVERING** Most foods are covered during cooking to keep the food moist, trap steam, assist in even cooking and shorten the cooking time. Foods are often covered with heat resistant cling film.

**SHIELDING** Thin areas of food (tail-ends of fish, winglets of poultry, etc.) should be covered (shielded) with small strips of tinfoil for part of the cooking or defrosting period. This helps to avoid overcooking.

**STIRRING OR MOVING FOODS** In order to assist even cooking or reheating, many foods are stirred or moved from the outer edge of the dish to the centre.

## KEY POINTS

- Keep the door rim and seal clean to avoid leakage of microwaves.
- Never operate the oven empty, as the oven may be damaged.
- Always follow the manufacturer's instructions.

## 10.1 MICROWAVING EGGS

**TRADITIONAL PRACTICE**

*Use whole milk instead of skimmed milk and add 5 g/$\frac{1}{4}$ oz margarine or butter into the milk and eggs prior to cooking. This increases the fat content.*

### SCRAMBLED EGGS *(ENGLISH STYLE)*

1 portion

| | | |
|---|---|---|
| 1 | egg (size 3) | 1 |
| 50 ml | skimmed milk | 2 fl oz |
| | small pinch salt and pepper | |

1 Break the egg into a suitable heat-resistant bowl (glass or porcelain).
2 Add the milk and seasoning and thoroughly whisk together.
3 Place into the microwave and cook at High for 20 seconds.
4 Stir the eggs from the outside edges of the bowl to the centre.
5 Cook for a further 20 seconds, then allow to stand for 2 minutes.
6 Stir with a fork then serve.

## 10.2 MICROWAVING RICE

**TRADITIONAL PRACTICE**

*Use 50 g/2 oz butter instead of the margarine. This increases the fat content.*

### BRAISED RICE *RIZ PILAFF*

4 small portions

| | | |
|---|---|---|
| 10 g | margarine | $\frac{1}{2}$ oz |
| 50 g | finely chopped onion or shallot | 2 oz |
| 100 g | long grain rice | 4 oz |
| 200 ml | chicken or vegetable stock | 8 fl oz |
| | small pinch salt and mill pepper | |

1 Place the margarine and onion into a suitable heat-resistant dish with lid and cook at High for 45 seconds.
2 Add the rice, stock and seasoning.
3 Cover with the lid and cook at High for 5 minutes.
4 Allow to stand for 4 minutes.
5 Loosen with a fork and serve.

### LEBANESE PILAW

4 portions

| | | |
|---|---|---|
| 200 g | long grain rice | 8 oz |
| 300 g | lean cubes of lamb or mutton | 12 oz |
| 100 g | sliced dried apricots (soaked) | 4 oz |
| 50 g | diced onions | 2 oz |
| 50 g | sultanas | 2 oz |
| 50 g | whole blanched almonds | 2 oz |
| 2 tsp | mixture of ground cumin and coriander | 2 tsp |
| 1 tsp | mixture of ground cinnamon and turmeric | 1 tsp |
| 200 g | chopped tomatoes (fresh or tinned) | 8 oz |
| 300 ml | mutton stock | 12 fl oz |
| | small pinch salt | |

1 Mix all the ingredients together and place into a suitable casserole.
2 Cover with a lid and cook at High for 7 minutes.
3 Cook at Low for 10 minutes.
4 Allow to stand for 10 minutes then check for cooking.
5 Loosen with a fork and serve in the casserole.

# 10.3 MICROWAVING PASTA DISHES

**HEALTH TIP**

*Spaghetti carbonara and garlic macaroni are high in fat.*

## SPAGHETTI ALLA CARBONARA

4 portions

| | | |
|---|---|---|
| 200 g | spaghetti | 8 oz |
| 15 ml | olive oil | $\frac{3}{4}$ fl oz |
| 15 g | butter | $\frac{3}{4}$ oz |
| 50 g | lean bacon cut into dice | 2 oz |
| 50 g | lean ham cut into strips | 2 oz |
| 1 | egg (size 3) | 1 |
| 100 ml | single cream | 4 fl oz |
| 25 g | Parmesan | 1 oz |
| 50 g | grated romano or cheddar cheese | 2 oz |
| | small pinch salt and mill pepper | |

1 Cook and refresh the spaghetti as stated on page 56.
2 Place the oil, butter, bacon and ham into a suitable heat-resistant bowl and cook at High for 30 seconds.
3 Stir then cook for a further 30 seconds. Check to see that the meat is cooked: if not, cook for a few more seconds.
4 Add the egg, cream and cheese and cook at Medium for 1 minute.
5 Thoroughly drain the spaghetti.
6 Place the spaghetti into a suitable dish with a lid: season, then reheat at High for 1 minute. Ensure spaghetti is thoroughly reheated.
7 Mix together the sauce and spaghetti, cover with the lid and heat for a further 25 seconds.

## GARLIC MACARONI *SKORDOMAKÁRONA*

4 portions

| | | |
|---|---|---|
| 200 g | macaroni (thick) | 8 oz |
| 25 ml | olive oil | 1 fl oz |
| | small pinch salt and mill pepper | |
| | *Sauce:* | |
| 25 ml | olive oil | 1 fl oz |
| 4 | medium cloves crushed garlic | 4 |
| 300 g | chopped tomatoes | 12 oz |
| 50 g | kefalotyri or Parmesan | 2 oz |

1 Cook and refresh the macaroni as stated on page 56.
2 Prepare the sauce:
   a) Place the oil, garlic and tomatoes into a suitable heat-resistant bowl and lightly season.
   b) Cook at High for 45 seconds.
   c) Stir, then continue cooking at High until the mixture is the consistency of a thin sauce: a further 45 seconds approximately.
3 Thoroughly drain the macaroni.
4 Place the macaroni into a suitable dish with a lid, season, and mix through the olive oil.
5 Cover and heat at High for 1 minute. Ensure the macaroni is thoroughly reheated.
6 Place into a suitable serving dish (porcelain or china) and pour the sauce over the top.
7 Heat at High for 25 seconds and sprinkle with cheese.

# 10.4 MICROWAVING FISH

**CHEF'S TIP**

*Many different fish dishes can be made using this procedure, e.g. salmon steak with lime and herbs, herring with gooseberries.*

## SPICED TROUT WITH HAZELNUTS

1 portion

| | | |
|---|---|---|
| 1 × 175 g | cleaned and gutted trout | 1 × 7 oz |
| 5 g | margarine or butter | $\frac{1}{4}$ oz |
| 5 g | finely chopped onion | $\frac{1}{4}$ oz |
| 1 tsp | mixture of paprika and ground ginger | 1 tsp |
| | good pinch cayenne pepper | |
| | small pinch salt and pepper | |
| 50 ml | orange juice | 2 fl oz |
| 25 ml | low-fat yoghurt | 1 fl oz |
| 1 | small clove crushed garlic | 1 |
| 10 g | sliced hazelnuts | $\frac{1}{2}$ oz |

1. Season the trout and sprinkle both inside and out with the spices.
2. Cover the head and thin tail piece with tinfoil.
3. Place into a suitable heat-resistant dish.
4. Place the margarine or butter and onion in a small heat-resistant bowl and cook at High for 45 seconds.
5. Add the garlic, orange juice, yoghurt and hazelnuts.
6. Pour over the trout and cover with cling film.
7. Cook at High for $1\frac{3}{4}$ minutes.
8. Remove the tinfoil and check for cooking before serving.

**CHEF'S TIP**

*Many different fish dishes can be made using this procedure, e.g. sole Bercy, fillets of plaice bonne-femme, haddock Mornay.*

## FILLETS OF FISH DUGLÉRÉ STYLE

1 portion

| | | |
|---|---|---|
| 2 × 75 g | fish fillets | 2 × 3 oz |
| 5 g | finely chopped shallot or onion | $\frac{1}{4}$ oz |
| 50 g | tomato concassées (page 25) | 2 oz |
| 25 ml | white wine | 1 fl oz |
| | squeeze lemon juice | |
| 75 ml | low-fat fish velouté (page 34) | 3 fl oz |
| | small pinch salt and pepper | |
| | pinch chopped parsley | |

1. Trim the fish fillets if necessary then fold into three, tucking in the thin areas.
2. Lightly grease a suitable heat-resistant dish and sprinkle the base with the chopped shallot or onion.
3. Place into the microwave oven at High for 45 seconds.
4. Remove from the oven and add the fish fillets.
5. Lightly season, then add the tomato concassées.
6. Sprinkle with parsley, then add the white wine and lemon juice.
7. Cover with a lid or cling film then place into the oven.
8. Cook at High for $1\frac{1}{2}$ minutes.
9. Remove the fillets, place onto a serving dish and keep hot.
10. Replace the dish into the microwave oven and cook at High to reduce down the cooking liquid by two-thirds: $1\frac{1}{2}$ minutes approximately.
11. Mix the cooking liquor and garnish through the fish velouté.
12. Coat the fish with the sauce.
13. Place into the oven at High for 25 seconds.

**TRADITIONAL PRACTICE**

*Use a traditional velouté sauce in place of low-fat sauce, add 25 ml/1 fl oz cream with the lemon juice and white wine. This increases the fat content.*

## 10.5 MICROWAVING MEAT

**CHEF'S TIP**

*Various cuts of meat, e.g. chops, cutlets and steaks can be cooked by microwave-assisted cooking. However, precise timing is essential to achieve the required degree of cooking.*

### GREEK STYLE PORK KEBABS WITH PITTA BREAD
*SOUVLÁKI ME PITA*

1 portion

| | | |
|---|---|---|
| 150 g | lean pork | 6 oz |
| 5 ml | olive oil | 1 tsp |
| 1 | tomato (cut into slices) | 1 |
| $\frac{1}{2}$ | onion (cut into thin rings) | $\frac{1}{2}$ |
| 1 | pitta bread | 1 |
| 25 ml | greek yoghurt | 1 fl oz |
| | pinch chopped parsley | |
| | small pinch salt and pepper | |
| | pinch fresh chopped oregano | |

1. Cut the pork into small cubes (15 mm/$\frac{1}{2}$ inch approximately) and place into a bowl.
2. Lightly season with the salt and pepper.
3. Add the oregano and olive oil and mix together.
4. Arrange the meat on wooden skewers.
5. Quickly fry or grill until golden brown.
6. Place onto a plate and cook at High for 1 minute.
7. Brush over the kebab with a little more oil mixture.
8. Cook at High for a further 1 minute.
9. Check to determine cooking. If the pork is not thoroughly cooked, place back into the oven and continue cooking.
10. When cooked, remove the meat from the skewer.
11. Split the pitta bread; then fill with the meat, sliced tomato and onion rings.
12. Lightly coat with yoghurt, then close the pitta bread.
13. Place in the microwave oven and heat at High for 15 seconds.

## 10.6 HOLLANDAISE SAUCE (Microwave)

**HEALTH TIP**

*Hollandaise sauce is very high in fat.*

### BASE INGREDIENTS

| | | |
|---|---|---|
| 10 ml | vinegar | $\frac{1}{2}$ fl oz |
| 2 | egg yolks (size 3) | 2 |
| 100 g | unsalted butter | 4 oz |
| | squeeze lemon juice | |
| | pinch salt and white pepper | |

### BASE METHOD

1. Place the butter in a suitable bowl and heat at High until soft: 20 seconds approximately.
2. Place the egg yolks into a suitable bowl.
3. Add 20 g/$\frac{3}{4}$ oz of the softened butter to the egg yolks and mix together.
4. Add the vinegar and whisk until combined.
5. Heat at High for 10 seconds then whisk well.
6. Whisk in half the remaining butter.
7. Heat at High for 10 seconds then whisk well.
8. Whisk in the remaining butter.
9. Heat for a further 10 seconds at High then whisk well.
10. Lightly season and mix through the lemon juice.

**BÉARNAISE SAUCE** Prepare as hollandaise sauce above using tarragon vinegar. Also add a little chopped tarragon and chervil to the finished sauce.

## 10.7 MICROWAVING ROOT AND BULBOUS ROOT VEGETABLES

### BASE METHOD: FRESH VEGETABLES

1 Place the vegetable into a suitable heat-resistant dish with lid (glass or porcelain).
2 Add 30 ml/$1\frac{1}{2}$ fl oz water. *Do not add any salt.*
3 Cover with the lid and cook at High.
Whole carrots and small turnips: 4–5 minutes
Sliced carrots, turnips, swedes and parsnips: 4–5 minutes
Whole leeks and onions: 5–6 minutes
Sliced leeks and onions: 5–6 minutes
Cook for half the period of time stated, then stir or turn the vegetables. Also check the water content and top up if necessary.
4 Continue cooking then allow to stand for 2 minutes. *Important:* The exact cooking times of vegetables vary depending on the thickness and maturity of the vegetables used so check during cooking.
5 Drain the vegetable then lightly season if required.

### BASE METHOD: FROZEN VEGETABLES

Proceed as for fresh vegetables but omit the water (step 2) and reduce the cooking time to the following:
Whole carrots and small turnips: 3–4 minutes
Sliced carrots, turnips, swedes and parsnips: 3–4 minutes
Whole leeks and onions: 4–5 minutes
Sliced leeks and onions: 4–5 minutes.
*Important:* Do not defrost the vegetable prior to cooking.

### CARROTS *CAROTTES*

2 portions

| | | |
|---|---|---|
| 250 g | fresh carrots | 10 oz |

1 Wash the carrots.
2 Top and tail the carrots, i.e. cut off the top and bottom ends.
3 Peel with a peeler.
4 Leave small carrots whole. Cut large carrots into even-sized pieces.
5 Cook as stated in the base method above.

### SPRING TURNIPS WITH MIXED HERBS

2 portions

| | | |
|---|---|---|
| 4 | small turnips | 4 |
| | good pinch chopped parsley, chives, chervil | |

1 Wash the turnips.
2 Trim the top and bottom from each turnip.
3 Peel, using a peeler.
4 Cook as stated in the base method above.
5 Sprinkle with the fresh herbs when serving.

## 10.8 MICROWAVING GREEN-LEAF AND FRUIT VEGETABLES

### BASE METHOD: FRESH VEGETABLES

1 Place the vegetables into a suitable heat-resistant dish with lid (glass or porcelain).
2 Add30 ml/$1\frac{1}{2}$ fl oz water to all vegetables except spinach which does not require any water (the water present on the leaves after washing should be sufficient for the cooking process). *Do not add any salt.*
3 Cover with the lid and cook at High.
Peas and spinach: 3–4 minutes
Cabbage, brussels sprouts, French beans and courgettes: 4–5 minutes
Marrow: 5–6 minutes
Cook for half the period of time stated then stir or turn the vegetable. Also check the water content and top up if necessary.
4 Continue cooking, then allow to stand for 2 minutes. *Important:* The exact cooking times of vegetables vary depending on the thickness and maturity of the vegetables used, so check during cooking.
5 Drain the vegetable then lightly season if required.

### BASE METHOD: FROZEN VEGETABLES

Proceed as for fresh vegetables but omit the water. When cooking peas, reduce the cooking time to 3–4 minutes. *Important:* Do not defrost the vegetable prior to cooking.

### CABBAGE *CHOU*

2 portions

| 250 g | fresh cabbage | 10 oz |
|---|---|---|

1 Wash the cabbage, then cut through the bottom stalk.
2 Remove any wilted leaves.
3 Quarter the cabbage and cut out the centre stalk.
4 Remove any large ribs from the leaves.
5 Finely shred the leaves then wash and drain.

Proceed as stated in the base method above.

## 10.9 MICROWAVING CAULIFLOWER (FRESH AND FROZEN)

### CAULIFLOWER *CHOU-FLEUR*

2 portions

| 200 g | fresh cauliflower florets | 8 oz |
|---|---|---|

1 Cut off the stalk at the bottom of the cauliflower just below the flower head.
2 Remove the outer leaves, divide into florets, and wash in salted water.
3 Place the florets into a suitable heat-resistant dish with lid (glass or porcelain).
4 Add 50 ml/2 fl oz water.
5 Cover and cook at High for 5 minutes.
6 Allow to stand for 2 minutes.
7 Drain and lightly season if required.

If cooking frozen cauliflower, omit step 4 (i.e. do not add any water).

## 10.10 MICROWAVING BROCCOLI AND ASPARAGUS

### BASE METHOD

1 Place the broccoli heads or asparagus tips into a suitable heat-resistant dish with lid (glass or porcelain). Arrange with the broccoli heads or asparagus tips to the centre of the dish and the stalks to the outside.
2 Add 50 ml/2 fl oz water, unless cooking frozen vegetables (which do not need extra water).
3 Cover and cook at High: cooking broccoli for 5 minutes and asparagus tips for 3 minutes.
4 Allow to stand for 2 minutes.
5 Drain and lightly season if required.

### BROCCOLI *BROCOLI*

2 portions

| | | |
|---|---|---|
| 200 g | fresh broccoli | 8 oz |

1 Trim the stalks (these should not be excessive) and wash.
2 Split the stalks with a knife if quite thick.
3 Cook as stated in the base method above.

### ASPARAGUS *ASPERGES*

2 portions

| | | |
|---|---|---|
| 2 bundles | fresh asparagus (6–8 medium stalks each) | 2 bundles |

1 Lightly scrape each stem from just under the flower downwards to the root using a peeler or small knife. With large asparagus it may be necessary to remove the tips of the leaves with the back of a small knife.
2 Wash, then cut the bundles evenly across at the root end.
3 Cook as stated in the base method above.

## 10.11 MICROWAVING WHOLE JACKET POTATOES

**CHEF'S TIP**

*A range of filled, baked jacket potatoes can be prepared using a microwave oven, e.g. baked jacket potato with curried vegetables. See page 232 for further examples.*

1 portion

### BASE INGREDIENT

| | | |
|---|---|---|
| 1 × 150 g | potato | 1 × 6 oz |

### BASE METHOD

1 Wash and scrub the potato.
2 Prick all over with a fork.
3 Place on a plate and cook at High for $2\frac{1}{2}$ minutes.
4 Turn over and cook for a further $2\frac{1}{2}$ minutes.
5 Allow to stand for 5 minutes.

# 10.12 MICROWAVING EGG CUSTARD PUDDINGS

> **TRADITIONAL PRACTICE**
>
> *Use 50 g/2 oz sugar and replace the skimmed milk with whole milk. This increases sugar and fat.*

4–6 portions

## BASIC CUSTARD MIXTURE

### BASE INGREDIENTS

| | | |
|---|---|---|
| 2 | eggs (size 3) | 2 |
| 25 g | caster sugar | 1 oz |
| 300 ml | skimmed milk | $\frac{1}{2}$ pt |
| 2–3 | drops vanilla essence | 2–3 |

### BASE METHOD

1 Break the eggs into a bowl.
2 Add the sugar, milk and vanilla essence.
3 Whisk together until thoroughly combined.
4 Cook as stated in the individual recipes below.

## EGG CUSTARD

1 Prepare the basic mixture (above) and pour it into a glass or earthenware pie dish.
2 Sprinkle a little grated nutmeg over the surface.
3 Cook at Low until the custard is set: 4 minutes approximately.
4 If required, lightly colour the surface under a hot grill before serving.

> **TRADITIONAL PRACTICE**
>
> *Use white bread instead of wholemeal bread. This reduces fibre.*

## BREAD AND BUTTER PUDDING

4–6 portions

| | | |
|---|---|---|
| 2 | slices wholemeal bread | 2 |
| 10 g | butter | $\frac{1}{2}$ oz |
| 25 g | sultanas | 1 oz |
| | icing sugar | |
| | basic custard mixture (above) | |

1 Cut the crusts off the bread then spread with the butter.
2 Cut into triangles and arrange in a glass or earthenware pie dish.
3 Add the sultanas.
4 Prepare the basic custard mixture and pour it over the bread.
5 Allow to stand until the bread is soaked with the custard.
6 Cook at Low until the custard is set: 4 minutes approximately.
7 If required, lightly colour the surface under a hot grill.
8 Dust the top with icing sugar.

## CRÈME CARAMEL

4–6 portions

| | | |
|---|---|---|
| 50 ml | water | 2 fl oz |
| 50 g | granulated sugar | 2 oz |
| | basic custard mixture (above) | |

1 Place water and sugar into a 4-portion soufflé case.
2 Cook at High for 3 minutes to dissolve the sugar.
3 Continue cooking at High until the sugar turns to a golden caramel: 6 minutes approximately.
4 Carefully add 15 ml/1 tbsp hot water to the caramel and shake to combine with the caramel. *Important:* Stand well back from the dish and protect the arms with a cloth and long sleeves when adding the water.
5 Allow the caramel to set.
6 Prepare the basic custard mixture and pour it into the dish.
7 Cook at Low until the custard is set: 4 minutes approximately.
8 Allow to become thoroughly cold, then demould onto a serving dish.

# Process 11 COLD PREPARATIONS

**DEFINITION** Cold preparations are cold items which have been prepared and assembled and are either raw, or cooked then cooled.

## REASONS FOR MAKING COLD PREPARATIONS

1 To make foods more palatable and digestible.
2 To produce a particular quality in food, of colour, flavour and texture (e.g. Florida cocktail).
3 To make foods visually attractive (e.g. whole decorated salmon).

## METHODS OF PRODUCING COLD PREPARATIONS

1 Producing and assembling **cold savoury items** which may be accompanied or finished with appropriate sauces or dressings. Categories include:
  **a)** different types of hors d'oeuvre: to include single item, selection (*variés*) and cocktail types
  **b)** different types of salad: to include simple, mixed, fish, meat and poultry salads
  **c)** cold decorative items: e.g. fish, shellfish, meat, poultry and vegetables
  **d)** different types of sandwiches: to include plain, rolled and pinwheel types.
2 Producing and assembling **cold sweet items** which may be garnished and decorated. Categories include:
  **a)** cold mousses, bavarois and charlottes
  **b)** table jellies
  **c)** trifles and condés
  **d)** fresh fruit salads and coupes
  **e)** syllabub.

## COMMODITIES SUITABLE FOR COLD PREPARATIONS

1 **Fresh vegetables** and salad vegetables.
2 **Cold cooked fish, shellfish, meat, poultry and game.**
3 **Convenience and processed foods** e.g. canned, jarred, frozen, smoked and foods in brine.
4 **Fresh fruits.**
5 **Dairy foods** including cream, fromage frais and yoghurt.
6 **Baked goods** such as sponges and finger biscuits.

## EQUIPMENT USED WHEN PRODUCING COLD PREPARATIONS

1 Small equipment, e.g. bowls, whisks, spoons, cutters.
2 Motorised equipment, e.g. mixers, blenders, food processors.
3 Large equipment, e.g. refrigerators, chillers and freezers.

## BASIC TECHNIQUES OF COLD PREPARATIONS

1 **Dividing skills** such as slicing, dicing, shredding, chopping.
2 **Combining skills** such as mixing, binding, dressing, garnishing.
3 **Artistic/creative arrangement of food:** attractive presentation and decoration of different food materials.

## KEY POINTS

- Always use good hygienic practices when handling and storing cold foods and remember the golden rule; keep it clean, keep it cool, keep it covered. See pages 1 and 2.

## 11.1 FRUIT COCKTAILS

**HEALTH TIP**

*Avoid adding sugar to fruit cocktails.*

### BASE METHOD

1 Prepare the fruit:
  a) Prepare any grapefruit and cut into segments.
  b) Prepare any oranges and cut into segments.
  c) Prepare any melon and cut into small balls or cubes.
  d) Prepare any pineapple and cut into cubes.
2 Dress the required fruit in cocktail glasses, with the juice.
3 Top with cherries if required and serve chilled.

### GRAPEFRUIT COCKTAIL

1 portion

| | | |
|---|---|---|
| 1 | small grapefruit | 1 |
| 1 | cherry (optional) | 1 |

Prepare using the base method above.

### ORANGE COCKTAIL

1 portion

| | | |
|---|---|---|
| 1 | large orange | 1 |
| 1 | cherry (optional) | 1 |

Prepare using the base method above.

### MELON COCKTAIL

6–8 portions

| | | |
|---|---|---|
| 1 | melon (honeydew) | 1 |
| 6 | cherries (optional) | 6 |

Prepare using the base method above.

### PINEAPPLE COCKTAIL

6 portions

| | | |
|---|---|---|
| 1 | medium pineapple | 1 |
| 6 | cherries (optional) | 6 |

Prepare using the base method above.

### FLORIDA COCKTAIL

4 portions

| | | |
|---|---|---|
| 2 | small grapefruits | 2 |
| 2 | oranges | 2 |
| 1 | small piece pineapple | 1 |
| 4 | cherries (optional) | 4 |

Prepare using the base method above.

### MIAMI COCKTAIL

4–6 portions

| | | |
|---|---|---|
| 1 | medium grapefruit | 1 |
| 2 | oranges | 2 |
| $\frac{1}{4}$ | pineapple | $\frac{1}{4}$ |
| $\frac{1}{4}$ | melon (honeydew) | $\frac{1}{4}$ |
| 4 | cherries (optional) | 4 |

Prepare using the base method above.

## 11.2 SHELLFISH COCKTAILS

**TRADITIONAL PRACTICE**

*Use traditional Marie-Rose sauce instead of lower-fat sauce. This increases the fat content.*

1 portion

### BASE INGREDIENTS

| | | |
|---|---|---|
| 25–50 g | prepared shellfish (see below) | 1–2 oz |
| 35 ml | lower-fat sauce Marie-Rose (page 35) | $1\frac{1}{2}$ fl oz |
| 1–2 | lettuce leaves | 1–2 |
| 1 | stuffed olive | 1 |

### BASE METHOD

1 Wash the lettuce then drain thoroughly.
2 Finely shred the lettuce then place it into the cocktail glass.
3 Bind the shellfish with a little of the sauce, then place into the cocktail dish on top of the lettuce.
4 Spoon over the remaining sauce and decorate with the olive. Appropriate shellfish may also be used to decorate the cocktail, e.g. whole shrimp or prawn, or a piece of lobster.

### PRAWN/SHRIMP COCKTAIL

Use cooked and peeled prawns or shrimps in the base recipe.

### LOBSTER COCKTAIL

Use cooked, shelled and diced lobster in the base recipe.

### SCAMPI COCKTAIL

Use cooked, shelled and sliced scampi in the base recipe.

### SCALLOP COCKTAIL

Use cooked and diced scallop flesh in the base recipe.

### SEAFOOD COCKTAIL

Use a selection of prepared shellfish in the base recipe.

**HEALTH TIP**

*Potted shrimps are high in fat.*

### POTTED SHRIMPS

4 portions

| | | |
|---|---|---|
| 160 g | cooked and shelled shrimps | 6 oz |
| 75 g | melted butter | 3 oz |
| 1 | piece lemon | 1 |
| 1 | leaf lettuce | 1 |
| 1 | piece tomato | 1 |
| 1–2 | slices cucumber | 1–2 |
| | cress | |
| | pinch pepper | |
| | pinch nutmeg | |

1 Lightly season the shrimps, then add the melted butter.
2 Place into small pots and cool quickly.
3 When cold and set, turn out of the pots onto the lettuce.
4 Garnish with the lemon, tomato, cucumber and cress.

# 11.3 FISH, SHELLFISH AND MEAT SALADS (HORS D'OEUVRE)

## FISH SALAD (traditional)

1 portion

| | | |
|---|---|---|
| 50 g | cooked flaked fish | 2 oz |
| 50 g | piece cucumber | 2 oz |
| 2 | small lettuce leaves | 2 |
| 2 | stoned olives | 2 |
| 2 | anchovy fillets | 2 |
| 6 | capers | 6 |
| | chopped parsley (optional) | |
| | *Dressing:* | |
| 10 ml | lower-fat dressing (page 35) | ½ fl oz |
| | or | |
| 25 ml | lower-fat vinaigrette (page 35) | 1 fl oz |

1 Cut the cucumber into small dice.
2 Add to the flaked fish and mix together with the dressing.
3 Finely shred the lettuce and place onto a serving dish.
4 Arrange the fish mixture on top and decorate with the olives, anchovies, capers and parsley.

**TRADITIONAL PRACTICE**

*Use traditional dressing or vinaigrette in the recipes, add a diced hard-boiled egg at step 2, and peel the cucumber. This increases the fat content and reduces fibre.*

## SCAMPI SALAD *ANTIPASTO DI SCAMPI*

1 portion

| | | |
|---|---|---|
| 25 g | cooked, shelled scampi tails | 1 oz |
| 20 ml | lower-fat dressing (page 35) | ¾ fl oz |
| 10 ml | sour cream | 2 tsp |
| 5 ml | tomato ketchup | 1 tsp |
| 5 ml | brandy | 1 tsp |
| 1 drop | chilli sauce | 1 drop |
| ½ | chicory | ½ |

1 Mix together the dressing, sour cream, ketchup, brandy and chilli sauce.
2 Wash and drain the chicory, then cut into thin slices.
3 Place the sliced chicory on a serving dish.
4 Arrange the scampi tails on top and coat with the sauce.

**TRADITIONAL PRACTICE**

*Use mayonnaise in the recipe. This increases the fat content.*

## MEAT SALAD (traditional)

1 portion

| | | |
|---|---|---|
| 50 g | cooked meat (ham, tongue, beef) | 2 oz |
| 20 g | gherkin | ¾ oz |
| 10 g | onion | ½ oz |
| 20 g | cooked peas | ¾ oz |
| 1 | small tomato | 1 |
| | *Dressing:* | |
| 10 ml | lower-fat dressing (page 35) | ½ fl oz |
| | or | |
| 25 ml | lower-fat vinaigrette (page 35) | 1 fl oz |
| | *Garnish:* | |
| | chopped parsley | |

1 Cut the meat and gherkin into thin strips.
2 Cut the tomato into dice.
3 Mix all the ingredients together and bind with the dressing.
4 Dress on the serving dish and sprinkle with parsley.

**TRADITIONAL PRACTICE**

*Use traditional vinaigrette in the recipe. Also blanch, skin and remove the seeds from the tomato, then dice. This increases the fat content and reduces fibre.*

## 11.4 FRUIT HORS D'OEUVRE

**TRADITIONAL PRACTICE**

*Use traditional vinaigrette instead of the lower-fat variety. This increases the fat content.*

### AVOCADO WITH VINAIGRETTE

2 portions

| | | |
|---|---|---|
| 1 | large avocado | 1 |
| 1 | sauceboat lower-fat vinaigrette (page 35) | 1 |
| 2 | small lettuce leaves | 2 |

1 Cut the pear in half, then remove the stone.
2 Dress each half on a lettuce leaf and serve accompanied with the vinaigrette.

**HEALTH TIP**

*Avoid adding sugar to the grapefruit.*

### CHILLED HALF-GRAPEFRUIT

2 portions

| | | |
|---|---|---|
| 1 | medium grapefruit | 1 |
| 1 | cherry | 1 |

1 Halve the grapefruit.
2 Cut out the centre pith from each half.
3 Cut round the edge and loosen the segments using a grapefruit or turning knife.
4 Decorate the centre of each half with a cherry and serve in coupes.

**CHILLED HALF-GRAPEFRUIT WITH KIRSCH (or other suitable liqueur)** Prepare as for chilled half-grapefruit above, adding a spoonful of liqueur to each prepared half-grapefruit.

**TRADITIONAL PRACTICE**

*Add 5 g/2 tsp each of brown sugar and caster sugar to the grapefruit after the sherry. Also sprinkle with caster sugar prior to heating. This increases the sugar content.*

### GRAPEFRUIT MEXICAINE

2 portions

| | | |
|---|---|---|
| 1 | medium grapefruit | 1 |
| 20 ml | sherry | 2 dsp |
| ½ | red pimento | ½ |

1 Halve the grapefruit and loosen the segments as described above.
2 Place on a grill tray, then sprinkle with the sherry.
3 Allow to macerate for 30 minutes approximately.
4 Cut the pimento into thin strips then neatly arrange on top of the grapefruit.
5 Place under a salamander and allow to heat through and brown. Serve hot.

### CHILLED MELON (honeydew melon)

6 portions

| | | |
|---|---|---|
| 1 | medium melon | 1 |
| 6 | half cherries | 6 |

1 Cut the melon into wedge-shape portions.
2 Decorate each portion with a half cherry and serve chilled.

**MELON VÉNITIENNE** Cut a wedge-shaped portion of melon and decorate like a boat, using a slice of orange impailed like a sail on a cocktail stick. Top with a cherry and serve chilled.

### MELON WITH PARMA HAM

1 portion

| | | |
|---|---|---|
| 1 | portion melon | 1 |
| 1–2 | thin slices parma ham | 1–2 |

1 Cut a wedge-shaped portion of melon.
2 Remove the skin and place the melon on a serving dish or plate.
3 Decorate with the slices of ham.

**OGEN AND CHARENTAIS MELON** For 1 portion, cut a slice off the top of one small, whole melon and remove the seeds. Replace the slice as a lid and serve chilled.

**MELON WITH PORT** Prepare as for Ogen and Charentais Melon (above), but add a measure of port to the interior of the melon and allow to macerate for 20–30 minutes.

## 11.5 VEGETABLE HORS D'OEUVRE

### CRUDITÉ (selection of raw vegetables with dips)

4–6 portions

| | | |
|---|---|---|
| 1 | medium carrot | 1 |
| 2 | stalks celery | 2 |
| ½ | medium green pepper | ½ |
| ½ | medium red pepper | ½ |
| 8–12 | fine French beans | 8–12 |
| 8 | florets cauliflower | 8 |
| 8 | florets broccoli | 8 |
| 50 ml | lower-fat herb dressing/dip (page 35) | 2 fl oz |
| 50 ml | lower-fat avocado dressing/dip (page 34) | 2 fl oz |

1 Wash and prepare the vegetables.
2 Cut the carrots, celery and peppers into sticks: 50 × 4 × 4 mm/2 × $\frac{3}{16}$ × $\frac{3}{16}$ inches approximately.
3 Top and tail the French beans.
4 Place the dips in the centre of a large serving dish.
5 Neatly dress the vegetables in bunches around the dips.

**TRADITIONAL PRACTICE**

*Use traditional dips or dressing. This increases the fat content.*

## 11.6 EGG HORS D'OEUVRE

### EGG MAYONNAISE

1 portion

| | | |
|---|---|---|
| 1 | hard-boiled egg | 1 |
| 1 | leaf lettuce | 1 |
| 40 ml | lower-fat mayonnaise (page 35) | 2 dsp |
| 1 | piece tomato | 1 |
| 2 | slices cucumber | 2 |
| | cress | |

1 Halve the egg and dress it on the lettuce leaf.
2 Coat the two halves of egg with mayonnaise.
3 Garnish with the tomato, cucumber and cress.

**TRADITIONAL PRACTICE**

*Use traditional mayonnaise instead of lower-fat mayonnaise. This increases the fat content.*

## 11.7 FISH AND SHELLFISH HORS D'OEUVRE

**TRADITIONAL PRACTICE**

*Salmon, oysters and caviar: use butter instead of margarine and white bread in place of wholemeal bread. This increases fat and reduces fibre.*

### SMOKED SALMON

1 portion

| | | |
|---|---|---|
| 25–50 g | trimmed smoked salmon | 1–2 oz |
| 1 | piece lemon | 1 |
| | branch parsley | |

1 Cut the salmon at a slant into thin slices.
2 Dress the slices on a serving dish and garnish with lemon and parsley.
3 Serve with wholemeal bread lightly spread with margarine.

### SMOKED TROUT

1 portion

| | | |
|---|---|---|
| 1 | small (or half) smoked trout | 1 |
| 1 | piece lemon | 1 |
| 1 | sauceboat horseradish sauce | 1 |
| | cress | |

1 Remove the skin from both sides of the trout.
2 Place onto a serving dish and garnish with lemon and cress.
3 Serve with the horseradish sauce.

### OYSTERS

1 portion

| | | |
|---|---|---|
| 4–6 | fresh oysters | 4–6 |
| 1 | piece lemon | 1 |

**CHEF'S TIP**

*Do not wash oysters unless they have been badly opened and covered with shell splinters.*

1 Open the oysters:
   a) Hold the oyster in a cloth.
   b) Insert an oyster knife into the hinge, then carefully push and twist to break the hinge.
   c) Draw the oyster knife closely along the top (flat) shell to cut loose the oyster from the top shell. It will still be attached to the bottom shell.
   d) Carefully trim off the beard and remove any small pieces of shell.
   e) Carefully detach the oyster from the remaining shell then turn over. Ensure the oyster juice is not lost but kept in the shell.
   f) Repeat the above procedure to open the remaining oysters.
2 Arrange the oysters in their shells on a bed of crushed ice.
3 Garnish with the lemon and serve with wholemeal bread lightly spread with margarine.

### CAVIAR

1 portion

| | | |
|---|---|---|
| 25 g | caviar | 1 oz |
| 1 | piece lemon | 1 |
| | wholemeal toast and margarine | |

1 Place the opened tin or jar of caviar on crushed ice.
2 Accompany with the lemon and toast spread with margarine.

## 11.8 COMMERCIALLY-PREPARED SMOKED OR COOKED SAUSAGES

**HEALTH TIP**

*Commercially prepared sausages are high in fat.*

### Salami, mortadella, cervelat, garlic sausage

For 1 portion, use 2–3 slices of selected sausage or sausages, and dress them on a serving dish.

# 11.9 LIVER PATÉ

**HEALTH TIP**

*Liver pâté is high in fat.*

**TRADITIONAL PRACTICE**

*Use butter instead of margarine. This increases the saturated fat content.*

## LIVER PÂTÉ *PÂTÉ MAISON*

12–16 portions

### BASE INGREDIENTS

| | | |
|---|---|---|
| 50 g | margarine | 2 oz |
| 100 g | fat bacon | 4 oz |
| 75 g | chopped onion | 3 oz |
| 4 | peeled cloves garlic | 4 |
| 500 g | chicken liver | $1\frac{1}{4}$ lb |
| 50 ml | cream | 2 fl oz |
| | pinch ground pepper | |
| | sprig of thyme, bay leaf | |
| | *Lining fat:* | |
| 500 g | sliced pork fat or bacon | $1\frac{1}{4}$ lb |

### BASE METHOD

1. Melt the margarine then add the fat bacon, onion, garlic and herbs.
2. Cook lightly without developing colour for 4–5 minutes.
3. Add the chicken liver and stiffen in the hot fat.
4. Remove the herbs, then coarsely mince the mixture.
5. Finely mince the mixture, then pass through a sieve if a fine textured pâté is required. Alternatively, liquidise the mixture.
6. Season with pepper then stir in the cream.
7. Lightly flatten the sliced pork fat or bacon with a cutlet bat.
8. Line a porcelain terrine or pâté tin with the pork fat or bacon. Ensure the end of the slices hang over the container.
9. Add the pâté mixture.
10. Draw over the ends of the slices of fat.
11. Neatly cover with further slices of fat.
12. Cover with a lid or greaseproof paper then place into a tray half full of water.
13. Cook at 175 °C/347 °F for $1$–$1\frac{1}{2}$ hours.
14. Allow to cool slightly.
15. Place weights on top of the pâté and cool quickly.
16. When cold: remove the paper, dip the container in tepid water then turn out the pâté.
17. Cut into slices and serve on a bed of lettuce.
18. If required, garnish with tomato, cucumber and cress.
19. Accompany with fingers of hot toast.

**HEALTH TIP**

*Pâté de foie gras is high in fat.*

## PÂTÉ DE FOIE GRAS

1 portion

| | | |
|---|---|---|
| 25–35 g | prepared trimmed pâté | $1$–$1\frac{1}{2}$ oz |
| 1 | slice hot toast or brioche | 1 |
| | curly endive or radicchio | |

1. Remove excess fat and cut into slices 5–10 mm/$\frac{1}{4}$–$\frac{1}{2}$ inch in thickness.
2. Garnish with curly endive and accompany with hot toast or brioche.

## 11.10 VARIETY HORS D'OEUVRE

This consists of an assortment of hors d'oeuvre items which are served in a ravier or hors d'oeuvre dish. Many of the individual hors d'oeuvre in the previous section are suitable for inclusion in a variety hors d'oeuvre.

### POSSIBLE COMPONENTS

a) Fruit cocktail mixtures served in raviers (page 195): orange segments, grapefruit segments, pieces of melon, pineapple and mango.
b) Shellfish cocktail mixtures served in raviers (page 196): prawn, shrimp, lobster or scampi mixtures.
c) Egg mayonnaise (page 199).
d) Pickled fish: Bismark herring, rollmops and soused herring.
e) Smoked fish: thin slices of Gravlax and smoked salmon and pieces of smoked trout (page 200).
f) Thin slices of commercial sausage: mortadella, Polish liver sausage, salami, hunting and garlic sausage.
g) Pieces of liver pâté (page 201).
h) Various simple salads: apple, bean, beetroot, cucumber, potato, rice, and tomato salads (page 203).
i) Various compound salads: coleslaw, japonaise salad, Russian salad and Waldorf salad (page 204).
j) Fish and shellfish salads: fish salad, shellfish salad, and antipasto di scampi (page 197).
k) Meat and poultry salads (page 197).

## 11.11 COCKTAIL HORS D'OEUVRE

This type of hors d'oeuvre is served at cocktail parties or finger buffet receptions and may consist of hot or cold items. Suitable hot items are given in other parts of this book; they could include bouchées (page 222), sausage rolls (page 223), quiche (page 228) and hot savouries (page 145).

### SUITABLE COLD ITEMS

a) Small toast shapes garnished with: slices of tomato, cucumber, smoked salmon, canned sardines, slices of boiled egg, commercial sausage, sliced cooked meats, cheese, anchovies or caviar.
b) Biscuit/pastry shapes: garnished as toast shapes above.
c) Vegetable-based items, such as pieces of celery and cucumber filled with: cottage cheese, fromage frais, cream cheese, piped cheese, pâté, or prawn Marie-Rose.
d) Game chips, cheese straws and various nuts served in small bowls.
e) Cubes of fruit, hard cheese and cooked chipolata sausages.
f) Sandwiches and filled rolls.

## 11.12 SIMPLE OR SINGLE SALADS

**TRADITIONAL PRACTICE**

*Use traditional vinaigrette instead of lower-fat vinaigrette in all these salads. This increases the fat content.*

### BEAN SALAD

4 portions

| | | |
|---|---|---|
| 200 g | cooked beans (butter beans, haricot beans or French beans) | 8 oz |
| 10 g | finely chopped onion | ½ oz |
| 25 ml | lower-fat vinaigrette (page 35) | 1 fl oz |
| | chopped parsley | |

1 Mix together the beans and onion.
2 Bind with the vinaigrette.
3 Dress in a serving dish and sprinkle with chopped parsley.

**TRADITIONAL PRACTICE**

*Peel cucumbers before slicing. This reduces fibre.*

### CUCUMBER SALAD

4 portions

| | | |
|---|---|---|
| 200 g | cucumber | 8 oz |
| 25 ml | lower-fat vinaigrette (page 35) | 1 fl oz |
| | chopped parsley | |

1 Wash the cucumber, then thinly slice.
2 Arrange the slices in a serving dish.
3 Coat with the vinaigrette and sprinkle with parsley.

**CHEF'S TIP**

*Additional vegetables may be added, e.g. cooked peas, sweetcorn, and diced peppers (although this is then more like a compound salad).*

### RICE SALAD

4 portions

| | | |
|---|---|---|
| 100 g | cooked brown or white rice | 4 oz |
| 50 g | tomato concassées (page 25) | 2 oz |
| 25 ml | lower-fat vinaigrette (page 35) | 1 fl oz |
| | chopped parsley | |

1 Mix together the rice and pieces of tomato.
2 Bind with the vinaigrette and place into a serving dish.
3 Sprinkle with chopped parsley.

**TRADITIONAL PRACTICE**

*Blanch and skin tomatoes before slicing. This reduces fibre.*

### TOMATO SALAD

4 portions

| | | |
|---|---|---|
| 4 | medium tomatoes | 4 |
| 10 g | finely chopped onion | ½ oz |
| 15 ml | lower-fat vinaigrette (page 35) | ½ fl oz |
| | chopped parsley | |

1 Wash the tomatoes.
2 Cut the tomatoes into slices and arrange in a serving dish.
3 Sprinkle the onion over the tomato slices.
4 Coat with the vinaigrette and sprinkle with parsley.

**TRADITIONAL PRACTICE**

*Remove the skins from cooked potatoes. This reduces fibre. Also use traditional mayonnaise in place of lower fat mayonnaise. This increases the fat content.*

### POTATO SALAD

4 portions

| | | |
|---|---|---|
| 200 g | cooked potatoes (with skins) | 8 oz |
| 10 g | finely chopped onion | ½ oz |
| 25 ml | lower-fat mayonnaise (page 35) | 1 fl oz |
| | chopped parsley | |

1 Thinly slice or dice the potatoes.
2 Mix through the onion, then bind with the mayonnaise.
3 Place into a serving dish and sprinkle with parsley.

## 11.13 FRUIT-BASED SIMPLE OR SINGLE SALADS

**TRADITIONAL PRACTICE**

*Peel the apples before slicing. This reduces fibre. Also use traditional lemon dressing in place of lower-fat dressing. This increases the fat content.*

### APPLE SALAD
4 portions

| | | |
|---|---|---|
| 3 | medium eating apples | 3 |
| 25 ml | lower-fat lemon dressing (page 34) | 1 fl oz |

1 Wash, core and slice or dice the apples.
2 Bind with the dressing and place into a serving dish.

### GRAPEFRUIT SALAD/ORANGE SALAD
4 portions

| | | |
|---|---|---|
| 2 | large grapefruits | 2 |
| | *or* | |
| 3 | medium oranges | 3 |

1 Cut the grapefruits or oranges into segments.
2 Dress in a serving dish with the juice.

## 11.14 COMPOUND SALADS

**TRADITIONAL PRACTICE**

*Use mayonnaise in place of lower-fat dressing. This increases the fat content.*

### COLESLAW
4 portions

| | | |
|---|---|---|
| 200 g | white cabbage | 8 oz |
| 50 g | carrot | 2 oz |
| 25 g | onion | 1 oz |
| 50 ml | lower-fat dressing (page 35) | 2 fl oz |

1 Wash, peel and finely shred the vegetables.
2 Mix together and bind with the dressing.

Sliced apple, pepper and raisins may also be used in this salad.

**TRADITIONAL PRACTICE**

*Use acidulated cream instead of fromage frais in the mimosa salad. Also use mayonnaise instead of lower-fat dressing in the Waldorf and Russian salads. This increases the fat content.*

### MIMOSA SALAD
4 portions

| | | |
|---|---|---|
| 2 | oranges | 2 |
| 1 | banana | 1 |
| 50 g | grapes | 2 oz |
| 25 ml | fromage frais dressing (page 34) | 1 fl oz |
| 4 | small, washed lettuce leaves | 4 |

1 Cut the oranges into segments.
2 Wash and halve the grapes, then remove the seeds.
3 Peel and slice the banana.
4 Mix the fruit together then bind with the dressing.
5 Dress the mixture on the lettuce leaves.

### WALDORF SALAD
4 portions

| | | |
|---|---|---|
| 2 | eating apples | 2 |
| 1 | stalk celery | 1 |
| 25 g | walnuts | 1 oz |
| 50 ml | lower-fat dressing (page 35) | 2 fl oz |
| 4 | small, washed lettuce leaves | 4 |

1 Wash, core and slice the apples.
2 Wash and slice the celery.
3 Break the walnuts into halves.
4 Mix together the apples, celery and walnuts and bind with the dressing.
5 Dress the mixture on the lettuce leaves.

## RUSSIAN SALAD

4 portions

| | | |
|---|---|---|
| 100 g | carrots | 4 oz |
| 100 g | turnips | 4 oz |
| 50 g | French beans | 2 oz |
| 50 g | peas | 2 oz |
| 50 ml | lower-fat dressing (page 35) | 2 oz |

1 Wash and peel the carrots and turnips then cut into 5 mm/$\frac{1}{4}$ inch cubes.
2 Wash the beans and cut into small diamond shapes.
3 Cook all the vegetables separately in boiling water.
4 Drain well and cool quickly.
5 Mix the vegetables together then bind with the dressing.

**ARABIAN SALAD** Watercress, tomato pieces, diced cucumber and chopped onion mixed together with lemon dressing (page 36).

**SPICED AUBERGINE SALAD** ***BABA GANAOUGE*** Chopped aubergine flesh (cooked in the oven then flesh removed), sliced green peppers, thinly sliced tomatoes and thinly sliced onions mixed together with spiced salad dressing (page 36).

**CAESAR SALAD** Pieces of cos lettuce, diced celery, peppers, peas, crisp-fried croûtons cooked in garlic oil, anchovy fillets, Parmesan cheese, crumbled blue cheese. Mix together with a dressing consisting of lemon juice, garlic oil and mill pepper. Traditionally the dressing includes raw or lightly cooked egg.

**CALIFORNIAN SALAD** Orange segments, sliced pineapple, blanched cauliflower florets and French beans dressed on lettuce leaves and lightly coated with mayonnaise.

**FRENCH SALAD** Lettuce, sliced cucumber, tomato pieces, sliced beetroot and quarters of hard-boiled egg dressed in a serving dish and accompanied with vinaigrette (page 35).

**GREEN SALAD** Green salad vegetables in season, e.g. lettuce leaves, cress, chives, pieces of curly chicory, spring onions and sliced green peppers dressed in a serving dish. Accompany with vinaigrette if required.

**MOROCCAN CARROT SALAD** Strips of raw carrot lightly flavoured with cinnamon and mixed with a dressing of lemon juice and rose water.

**MIXED SALAD** All types of salad vegetables, e.g. lettuce, cucumber, tomatoes, spring onions, cress, radishes, chives, peppers and chicory dressed in a serving dish. Accompany with vinaigrette if required.

**SALAT** Shredded lettuce, sliced cucumber, pieces of tomato, thinly sliced onions and fresh coriander leaves dressed in a serving dish.

**GREEK SALAD** ***SALÁTA HORIÁTIKI*** Pieces of lettuce, tomato, sliced green peppers, sliced cucumber, thinly sliced onions and black olives mixed with a dressing consisting of olive oil, vinegar and chopped oregano. Arranged on a serving dish and garnished with Feta cheese.

## 11.15 COLD FISH, SHELLFISH, MEAT AND POULTRY SALADS

### BASE INGREDIENTS

| | | |
|---|---|---|
| | meat, poultry or fish (as appropriate) | |
| 2–3 | lettuce leaves (or quarters) | 2–3 |
| 1 | piece curly endive | 1 |
| 1–2 | pieces tomato | 1–2 |
| 3–4 | slices cucumber | 3–4 |
| 2 | slices radishes | 2 |
| | cress | |
| 1 | sauceboat lower-fat dressing (page 35) | 1 |

**TRADITIONAL PRACTICE**

*Add 2 wedges of hard-boiled egg to the garnish and use mayonnaise instead of lower-fat dressing. This increases the fat content.*

### COLD SALMON AND SALAD

1 portion

| | | |
|---|---|---|
| 1 × 150 g | piece of poached salmon | 1 × 6 oz |
| | basic salad (above) | |

1 Remove any skin or bone.
2 Dress the fish on the lettuce leaves and garnish with the remaining vegetables.
3 Accompany with the lower-fat dressing.

### COLD TROUT AND SALAD

1 portion

| | | |
|---|---|---|
| 1 × 200 g | poached trout | 1 × 8 oz |
| | basic salad (above) | |

Carefully skin both sides of the fish. Finish as for cold salmon and salad (steps 2 and 3 above).

**BEEF SALAD** For 1 portion, use 2 slices cold roast beef (50–75 g/2–3 oz each) and the salad and dressing (base ingredients above). Dress the beef on the serving dish and garnish with the salad vegetables. Accompany with lower-fat dressing.

### COLD LOBSTER AND SALAD

1 portion

| | | |
|---|---|---|
| ½ | medium, boiled lobster | ½ |
| 6 | capers | 6 |
| 2 | anchovy fillets | 2 |
| 1 | leaf shredded lettuce | 1 |
| | salad and dressing (base ingredients above) | |

1 Prepare the half lobster (page 22).
2 Place the shredded lettuce in the front cavity then sit the shelled claw on top.
3 Dress the lobster on top of the lettuce and decorate the top with the capers and anchovies.
4 Garnish with the salad vegetables.
5 Serve with lower-fat dressing.

## 11.16 COLD MOUSSES AND MOUSSELINES

6–8 portions

### BASE INGREDIENTS

| | | |
|---|---|---|
| | mousse mixture (as appropriate) | |
| 6–8 | small lettuce leaves (or quarters) | 6–8 |
| 6–8 | leaves curly endive | 6–8 |
| 6–8 | pieces tomato | 6–8 |
| 18–24 | slices cucumber | 18–24 |
| 4 | sliced radishes | 4 |
| 6–8 | pieces lemon | 6–8 |
| | fresh dill | |
| | cress | |

### BASE METHOD

1 Line a suitable mould with cling film.
2 Add the mousse when ready and cover with food-quality cling film.
3 Place into a refrigerator and allow to set.
4 Remove the top layer of cling film and turn out onto a serving dish.
5 Remove the remaining cling film.
6 Neatly decorate to taste with the cucumber, radishes and fresh dill.
7 Garnish with the remaining salad vegetables and lemon.

**CHEF'S TIP**

*Alternatively slice the mousse with a sharp stainless steel knife dipped in hot water and serve in portions.*

**SALMON MOUSSE** For 6–8 portions, use the salmon mousse mixture on page 26 and prepare following the base recipe above.

**HAM MOUSSE** For 6–8 portions, use the ham mousse mixture on page 26 and prepare as for the base recipe above. Gherkins and dill cucumber may also be used in the salad.

**COURGETTE AND AVOCADO MOUSSELINES (vegetarian)**
10–12 portions

| | | |
|---|---|---|
| | vegetable mousse mixture (page 26) | |
| 8 | courgettes | 8 |
| 400 ml | avocado dressing | 16 fl oz |
| | fresh mint or tarragon leaves | |

1 Cut the courgettes into thin slices, then blanch in boiling water until tender (do not peel).
2 Refresh in cold water then drain thoroughly.
3 Line suitable individual moulds (small soufflé cases, pudding or dariole moulds) with food-quality cling film.
4 Neatly line the moulds with the strips of courgette – leave the ends of courgette overlapping the moulds.
5 Fill the lined moulds with the vegetable mixture.
6 Fold over the ends of courgette to cover the mixture.
7 Place into a refrigerator and allow to set.
8 Turn out the mousselines onto the serving plates.
9 Surround with the avocado dressing and decorate with the mint or tarragon leaves.

## 11.17 DECORATED SALMON SAUMON NORVÉGIENNE

### TRADITIONAL PRACTICE

*Use mayonnaise instead of lower-fat dressing. This increases the fat content. The traditional sauce served with this dish is sauce Russe. This has not been included due to the high cost of the ingredients involved.*

10–12 small portions

### BASE INGREDIENTS

| | | |
|---|---|---|
| 1 × 4 kg | salmon | 1 × 8 lb |
| 1 | whole cucumber | 1 |
| 3 | medium cooked beetroot | 3 |
| 10–12 | medium whole tomatoes | 10–12 |
| 5–6 | hard-boiled eggs | 5–6 |
| 10–12 | large cooked prawns (in shell) | 10–12 |
| 125 g | cooked shelled prawns | 5 oz |
| 150 g | smoked salmon purée | 6 oz |
| 50 ml | wine vinegar dressing (page 36) | 2 fl oz |
| 50 ml | lower-fat dressing (page 35) | 2 fl oz |
| 500 ml | fish aspic (page 23) | 1 pt |
| 250 ml | sauce Andalouse (page 35) | ½ pt |
| 10–12 | cucumber diamonds | 10–12 |
| | fresh dill leaves | |

### BASE METHOD

1 Prepare the salmon for poaching (page 21).
2 Poach the salmon, sitting on its belly, in vinegar court-bouillon. (Cook as stated on page 75 using enough liquor to cover the fish). Cool quickly.
3 When ready for use, carefully remove from the cold liquor and allow to drain thoroughly.
4 Carefully remove the skin and lightly scrape off any brown flesh.
5 Remove the eyes and replace with a piece of egg white and olive.
6 Carefully place the salmon on a draining tray and coat with the aspic which should be almost setting. Coat with more aspic if required.
7 Cover the base of the serving dish with a layer of aspic and allow to set.
8 Carefully place the salmon onto the serving dish.
9 Prepare the garnish:
   a) Hollow out the cucumber to form cups, reserving lengths of skin for the cucumber diamonds. Cook in boiling water then cool quickly and drain. Store in vinegar dressing until required for use.
   b) Cut the beetroot into quarters then trim into barquette shapes. Store in vinegar dressing until required for use.
   c) Blanch the tomatoes, remove the skin and seeds then reshape in a cloth to resemble small tomatoes. Decorate the tops of the tomatoes with the cucumber diamonds.
   d) Cut the hard-boiled eggs into halves. Decorate with the dill then coat with aspic.
   e) Shell the tails of the whole prawns.
   f) Bind the shelled prawns with the lower-fat dressing.
10 Wipe dry the cucumber barrels and fill with smoked salmon purée, finishing as dome shapes.
11 Wipe dry the beetroot barquettes and fill with prawn mixture.
12 Arrange the whole prawns along the back of the salmon.
13 Neatly garnish round the salmon with the stuffed cucumber cups, beetroot barquettes, eggs and tomatoes.
14 Serve the salmon accompanied with the sauce Andalouse (page 35).

## 11.18 BONED SIRLOIN OF BEEF WITH SALAD

16–20 small portions

### BASE INGREDIENTS

| | | |
|---|---|---|
| 1 × 2 kg | contrefilet of beef (page 10) | 1 × 4 lb |
| 1 | medium curly endive | 1 |
| 1 | radicchio | 1 |
| 1 | bunch watercress | 1 |
| 1 | small bunch chives | 1 |
| 16–20 | gherkins | 16–20 |
| 16–20 | black olives | 16–20 |
| 3 | small tomatoes | 3 |
| 3 | red plums | 3 |
| 3 | dark plums | 3 |
| 2 | nectarines | 2 |
| 1 × 50 g | piece puff pastry | 1 × 2 oz |
| | sprigs of fresh thyme, dill, rosemary, tarragon | |

### BASE METHOD

1. Prepare the beef for roasting (page 10).
2. Roast the beef as described on page 126, keeping it underdone.
3. When cooked, cool quickly.
4. When thoroughly cold, trim the remaining fat from the top of the beef and cut to form a smooth surface.
5. Meanwhile roll out the pastry until thin: $1\frac{1}{2}$ mm/$\frac{1}{8}$ inch approximately.
6. Cut part of the pastry into the shape of a small basket.
7. Cut the remaining pastry into small strips.
8. Eggwash the basket shape, then place the pastry strips on top in overlapping rows to resemble a basket weave.
9. Place on a lightly greased baking tray and brush over the surface with eggwash.
10. Bake until golden brown, then allow to cool.
11. Cut half the beef into thin slices.
12. Place the remaining piece of beef on to a serving dish then sit the puff pastry basket on top.
13. Prepare rose-shaped flowers of different colours from the tomatoes, plums and nectarines.
14. Arrange the fruit flowers over the top of the basket then neatly fill in the spaces with the fresh herbs.
15. Cut the gherkins into fan shapes.
16. Neatly arrange the slices of beef on the serving dish.
17. Decorate with the curly endive, radicchio, watercress, chives, gherkins and olives.
18. Serve accompanied with a suitable cold sauce, e.g. horseradish sauce.

## 11.19 PLAIN SANDWICHES

**TRADITIONAL PRACTICE**

*Use white bread in place of wholemeal and 10 g/½ oz butter in place of margarine. This reduces fibre and increases fat.*

**CHEF'S TIP**

*When preparing large numbers of sandwiches, lay the required number of bread slices in rows along the table. After spreading with margarine, place the filling on alternate rows of bread and then place the remaining slices on top.*

**TRADITIONAL PRACTICE**

*Use plain Cheddar cheese instead of the low-fat type. This increases fat.*

**CHEF'S TIP**

*Do not use the margarine or butter when using a filling which contains fat: e.g. pâté, cream cheese, egg spread.*

1 sandwich (1 round)

### BASE INGREDIENTS

| | | |
|---|---|---|
| 2 | slices wholemeal bread | 2 |
| 5 g | margarine | ¼ oz |
| | appropriate filling (below) | |
| | cress | |

### BASE METHOD

1. Lightly spread the slices of bread with the margarine.
2. Place or spread the filling on one of the bread slices.
3. Place the remaining slice of bread on top of the filling.
4. Trim off the crusts if required.
5. Cut the sandwich diagonally into four, using a serrated knife or bread knife.
6. Place onto a salver or plate lined with a dishpaper.
7. Garnish with cress.

**CHEESE SANDWICH** Prepare as stated in the base recipe above, filling with 1 slice (25 g/1 oz) low-fat Cheddar cheese. Alternatively, use mature Cheddar cheese in half the quantity stated.

**CUCUMBER, TOMATO AND LETTUCE SANDWICH** Prepare as stated in the base recipe above. Fill with 4–6 slices cucumber, 4 slices tomato and 1 lettuce leaf.

**ROAST CHICKEN SANDWICH** Prepare as stated in the base recipe above, filling with 40 g/1½ oz sliced roast chicken (without skin).

**COTTAGE CHEESE AND CHIVE SANDWICH** Prepare as stated in the base recipe above. Fill with 25 g/1 oz cottage cheese, 1 tsp finely chopped chives and a small pinch of white and cayenne pepper.

## 11.20 ROLLED SANDWICHES

**TRADITIONAL PRACTICE**

*Use white bread in place of wholemeal, and increase the cream cheese to 10 g/½ oz. This reduces fibre and increases fat.*

1 sandwich (1 round)

### BASE INGREDIENTS

| | | |
|---|---|---|
| 2 | slices wholemeal bread | 2 |
| 5 g | cream cheese | ¼ oz |
| | appropriate filling (opposite, top) | |
| | cress | |

### BASE METHOD

1 Spread the bread with the cream cheese.
2 Remove the crusts.
3 Place the filling onto one end of the bread and roll up the bread starting from that end.
4 Place onto a salver or plate lined with a dishpaper.
5 Garnish with cress.

### ASPARAGUS ROLLS

Use 4–5 cooked asparagus spears and prepare as in the base recipe.

### SARDINE ROLLS

Use 2–3 sardines (canned) and prepare as in the base recipe.

**SALSIFY ROLLS** Use 2–3 cooked salsify roots and prepare as in the base recipe.

## 11.21 PINWHEEL SANDWICHES

**CHEF'S TIP**

*Do not use the margarine or butter when using a filling which contains fat: e.g. pâté, cream cheese, egg spread.*

**TRADITIONAL PRACTICE**

*Use white bread in place of wholemeal, and butter instead of margarine. This reduces fibre and increases the saturated fat content.*

2 sandwiches (2 rounds)

### BASE INGREDIENTS

| | | |
|---|---|---|
| 1 | long thin slice wholemeal bread | 1 |
| | margarine | |
| | appropriate filling (below) | |

### BASE METHOD

1 Remove the crust from each long side of the loaf of bread, along the top of the loaf, and one end.
2 Cut down the crust at the other end, cutting only down as far as the bottom crust: do not detach. This will act as a stop when slicing the bread.
3 Cut a thin, even slice along the top of the loaf.
4 Lightly spread the surface of the slice with the margarine.
5 Spread over the surface with the filling or fillings (various fillings may be used on the same slice to give a variety of flavours and colours).
6 Tightly roll up the slice, to resemble a Swiss roll.
7 Cut into slices then serve on a salver or plate lined with a dishpaper. Garnish with cress if desired.

**SALMON AND CUCUMBER PINWHEELS** Prepare as for the base recipe. Spread over a layer of cooked and puréed salmon flesh (or canned salmon) then place thin slices of cucumber on top.

### CREAM CHEESE, SPRING ONION AND HAM PINWHEELS

Prepare as for the base recipe. Line the bread with thin slices of ham, then spread over the cream cheese. Sprinkle thinly sliced spring onions over the surface of the cheese then roll up as stated.

# 11.22 COLD MOUSSES (lower-fat recipes)

## VANILLA MOUSSE

8–10 portions

### BASE INGREDIENTS

| | | |
|---|---|---|
| 800 ml | skimmed milk | $1\frac{1}{2}$ pt |
| 50 g | caster sugar | 2 oz |
| 15 g | cornflour | $\frac{3}{4}$ oz |
| 25 g | leaf gelatine | 1 oz |
| 50 ml | whipping cream | 2 fl oz |
| 5–6 drops | vanilla essence | 5–6 drops |

### BASE METHOD

1. Blend the cornflour with a little of the cold milk.
2. Place the remaining milk in a saucepan and bring to the boil.
3. Stir in the diluted cornflour and simmer for 1 minute.
4. Add the sugar.
5. Place the gelatine in a bowl of cold water and allow to soften.
6. Squeeze out the surplus water from the gelatine, add the gelatine to the hot mixture and stir until completely dissolved.
7. Pass through a fine strainer into a clean bowl.
8. Cool quickly, place the bowl on ice and stir until almost set.
9. Meanwhile, lightly whip the cream.
10. Carefully fold the cream through the setting mixture then pour into a suitable mould.
11. Place into a refrigerator and allow to set.
12. When set, dip the mould in tepid water and demould onto a serving dish.
13. Decorate to taste with slices of fresh or poached fruit, cherries, fruit fromage frais etc.

**CHEF'S TIP**

*Avoid using fresh pineapple, as the mousse will not set. Heat the purée before use, to denature the enzyme which prevents the mousse from setting.*

**FRUIT MOUSSES** Prepare as for the base recipe above, but reduce the milk to 400 ml/$\frac{3}{4}$ pt and omit the vanilla essence. Add 400 g/1 lb of cold, unsweetened fruit purée (e.g. pear, peach, raspberry or strawberry) to the mixture at step 8, then complete as stated. Decorate with fruit as appropriate.

**CHOCOLATE MOUSSE** Prepare as for the base recipe, but omit the vanilla essence and add 40 g/$1\frac{3}{4}$ oz cocoa powder. Blend the cocoa powder with a little of the cold milk. Stir into the hot milk until combined, then complete as stated.

**VEGETARIAN MOUSSES** Prepare as for the base recipe above with the following amendments:

1. Use half the quantity of milk, i.e. 400 ml/$\frac{3}{4}$ pt.
2. Add 50 g/2 oz skimmed milk powder to the milk and whisk until combined.
3. Prepare the mixture as stated but *without the gelatine* and cool quickly.
4. Boil 400 ml/$\frac{3}{4}$ pt water and whisk in 5 g/$\frac{1}{4}$ oz sodium alginate. Whisk until dissolved, then allow to cool.
5. Whisk together the two mixtures then quickly fold in the cream.
6. Pour into the mould and complete as stated.

## 11.23 BAVAROIS (traditional)

> **HEALTH TIP**
>
> *Traditional bavarois are high in fat and sugar.*

### VANILLA BAVAROIS

8–10 portions

#### BASE INGREDIENTS

| | | |
|---|---|---|
| 500 ml | skimmed milk | 1 pt |
| 4 | egg yolks (size 3) | 4 |
| 100 g | caster sugar | 4 oz |
| 5–6 drops | vanilla essence | 5–6 drops |
| 20 g | leaf gelatine | $\frac{3}{4}$ oz |
| 250 ml | whipping cream | $\frac{1}{2}$ pt |

#### BASE METHOD

1. Lightly whip the cream and place aside.
2. Place the milk into a saucepan and bring almost to the boil.
3. Whisk together the yolks, sugar and essence in a bowl.
4. Pour the hot milk onto the yolks and sugar and whisk together.
5. Return the mixture to a clean saucepan and place over a low heat.
6. Stir constantly until the mixture thickens, then remove from the heat. Do not boil, as the mixture will curdle.
7. Meanwhile, place the gelatine in a bowl of cold water and allow to soften.
8. Squeeze out the surplus water from the gelatine, add the gelatine to the hot mixture and stir until completely dissolved.
9. Pass through a fine strainer into a clean bowl.
10. Cool quickly, place the bowl on ice and stir until almost set.
11. Carefully fold the cream through the setting mixture then pour into a suitable mould.
12. Place into a refrigerator and allow to set.
13. When set, dip the mould in tepid water and demould onto a serving dish.
14. Decorate to taste, e.g. rosettes of whipped cream, glacé cherries and diamonds of angelica.

> **CHEF'S TIP**
>
> *Folding through the whipped cream when the mixture is almost set produces the light texture.*

**CHOCOLATE BAVAROIS** Prepare as the base recipe above, but omit the vanilla essence and add 40 g/1$\frac{3}{4}$ oz cocoa powder. Blend the cocoa powder with a little of the cold milk. Stir into the hot milk until combined, then complete as stated.

**FRUIT BAVAROIS** Prepare as the base recipe above, but reduce the milk to 300 ml/12 fl oz and omit the vanilla essence. Add 400 g/1 lb of cold, unsweetened fruit purée (e.g. pear, peach, raspberry or strawberry) to the mixture at step 10, then complete as stated. Decorate with fruit as appropriate.

> **CHEF'S TIP**
>
> *Avoid using fresh pineapple, as the mousse will not set. Heat the purée before use, to denature the enzyme which prevents the mousse from setting.*

**VEGETARIAN BAVAROIS** Prepare as for the base recipe above with the following amendments:

1. Use half the quantity of milk, i.e. 250 ml/$\frac{1}{2}$ pt.
2. Add 25 g/1 oz skimmed milk powder to the milk and whisk until combined.
3. Prepare the mixture as stated *without the gelatine* and cool quickly.
4. Boil 250 ml/$\frac{1}{2}$ pt water and whisk in 5 g/$\frac{1}{4}$ oz sodium alginate. Whisk until dissolved then allow to cool.
5. Whisk together the two mixtures then quickly fold in the cream.
6. Pour into the mould and complete as stated.

## 11.24 CHARLOTTES

**TRADITIONAL PRACTICE**

*Use the standard bavarois mixture instead of the lower-fat mousse and decorate to taste with whipped cream. This increases the fat content.*

**CHEF'S TIP**

*To be suitable for vegetarians, use the vegetarian mousse mixture and table jelly on page 215.*

### CHARLOTTE RUSSE

8–10 portions

**BASE INGREDIENTS**

| | | |
|---|---|---|
| 18–20 | finger biscuits (page 245) | 18–20 |
| | lower-fat vanilla mousse (page 212) | |

**BASE METHOD**

1 Trim enough of the finger biscuits into small fan-shapes to line the bottom of a large charlotte mould, and then line the mould. Arrange the points of the biscuits towards the centre and key in neatly together.
2 Line the sides with the remaining biscuits. If required, neatly trim the biscuits so that they fit tightly together.
3 Meanwhile, prepare the mousse or bavarois mixture.
4 Pour in the mixture when ready, then place the mould in a refrigerator and allow to set.
5 Trim the ends off any biscuits which protrude from the mould.
6 Carefully de-mould onto the serving dish.
7 Leave plain or decorate to taste.

**CHARLOTTE MOSCOVITE** Prepare as for the base recipe above, but set a layer of raspberry or strawberry table jelly on the base of the mould in place of the biscuits. When the jelly is set, line the sides of the mould with the biscuits then complete as stated.

**CHARLOTTE MONTREUIL** Prepare as for the base recipe above, using a peach mousse or pieces of peach garnished with bavarois. Decorate with peach slices.

**CHARLOTTE ROYALE** Prepare as for the base recipe above, but line the mould with thin slices of small Swiss roll (page 244) in place of the finger biscuits.

## 11.25 SUMMER PUDDING

6–8 portions

**BASE INGREDIENTS**

| | | |
|---|---|---|
| 1 kg | raspberries (or redcurrants) | 2 lb |
| 10–12 | slices stale white bread | 10–12 |
| | lightly whipped cream | |
| | caster sugar (to taste) | |

**BASE METHOD**

1 Wash and drain the raspberries, and lightly sweeten to taste.
2 Remove the crusts from the bread.
3 Neatly line a deep bowl with the bread. Cut a piece to fit the top of the bowl.
4 Fill the bread-lined bowl with the fruit and cover with the remaining piece of bread.
5 Cover with a plate and weights and store chilled for 12 hours (allowing the bread to become completely saturated with fruit juice).
6 De-mould onto a serving dish and serve with cream.

## 11.26 TABLE JELLIES

### ORANGE JELLY

Yield: 1 litre/2 pt

**BASE INGREDIENTS**

| | | |
|---|---|---|
| 3 | large oranges | 3 |
| 1 | lemon | 1 |
| 850 ml | cold water | $1\frac{3}{4}$ pt |
| 200 g | granulated sugar | 8 oz |
| 2 | egg whites (size 3 eggs) | 2 |
| 4 | coriander seeds | 4 |
| | small bay leaf | |
| $\frac{1}{4}$ | cinnamon stick | $\frac{1}{4}$ |
| 50 g | leaf gelatine | 2 oz |
| 2–3 drops | food colour (optional) | 2–3 drops |

**BASE METHOD**

1. Remove the zest from the oranges and lemon with a peeler and keep.
2. Cut off the white pith and discard.
3. Cut the fruit into slices.
4. Soak the gelatine in a bowl of cold water and allow to soften.
5. Squeeze out the surplus water from the gelatine and place it into a thick-based saucepan.
6. Add the remaining ingredients and whisk thoroughly together.
7. Place onto the stove and slowly bring to the boil. Do not stir once the mixture is hot: over 50 °C/122 °F.
8. Slowly simmer for 20 minutes leaving the crust of the clarification undisturbed.
9. Carefully strain through a muslin or jelly bag into a clean bowl.
10. Check the colour, acidity and sweetness, then test the setting property of the jelly, i.e. drop a small quantity of the mixture onto a chilled plate and allow to set in the refrigerator. If the jelly is too firm, add a little water and retest.
11. Cool the jelly quickly, then pour into a jelly mould and allow to set.
12. When set, dip the mould momentarily into warm water and invert the jelly onto a serving dish.
13. Decorate to taste.

**CHEF'S TIP**

*A little lemon juice and sugar may be added to the jelly at this point if required.*

**LEMON JELLY** Use 3–4 lemons in place of oranges and proceed as stated in the base recipe.

**RASPBERRY/STRAWBERRY JELLY** Use 250 g/10 oz prepared raspberries or strawberries as the fruit and proceed as stated in the base recipe.

**VEGETARIAN TABLE JELLIES** Proceed as stated but *omit the gelatine* and whisk 25 g/1 oz agar into the cold mixture before heating (step 6). Strain the jelly into moulds when hot and cool quickly.

## 11.27 TRIFLES

### TRADITIONAL PRACTICE

*Use sweetened fruit syrup instead of unsweetened fruit juice, and lightly whipped cream in place of fromage frais in the custard. Also increase the cream when decorating. A thick, fresh egg custard sauce may be used in place of a custard powder sauce: i.e. follow the recipe on page 40 but double the quantity of egg yolks. This substantially increases the fat content.*

4 portions

### BASE INGREDIENTS

| | | |
|---|---|---|
| | *Trifle base:* | |
| 16 | sponge biscuits | 16 |
| | *or* | |
| 150 g | génoise sponge | 6 oz |
| | *Trifle mixture:* | |
| 25 g | raspberry jam | 1 oz |
| 100 ml | unsweetened fruit juice | 4 fl oz |
| | *Thick custard sauce:* | |
| 250 ml | milk | $\frac{1}{2}$ pt |
| 15 g | custard powder | $\frac{3}{4}$ oz |
| 25 g | sugar | 1 oz |
| 50 ml | fromage frais | 2 fl oz |
| | *Topping:* | |
| 50 ml | whipping cream | 2 fl oz |
| | blanched almonds, glacé cherries, angelica | |

### BASE METHOD

1 a) *Using sponge biscuits:* Sandwich the biscuits together with jam, then cut into 25 mm/1 inch pieces.
   b) *Using génoise sponge:* Split the sponge through the centre then sandwich together with jam. Cut into dice: 15 mm/$\frac{3}{4}$ inch.
2 Place the sponge or biscuits into a serving dish then lightly moisten with the fruit juice.
3 Prepare the custard sauce (page 39), using the milk, custard powder and sugar.
4 Pour into a bowl, cover with a piece of greaseproof paper then cool quickly.
5 When cold, mix through the fromage frais to produce a smooth, thick consistency.
6 Spread the sauce over the sponge.
7 Whip the cream. *Note:* The cream may be lightly sweetened and flavoured, see Chantilly cream, page 40.
8 Decorate with the cream, almonds, cherries and angelica.

**FRUIT TRIFLE** Prepare as for the base recipe above, adding a dice or small slices of selected ripe or poached fruit (75 g/3 oz peaches, pears, pineapple etc.) to the biscuits or sponge at step 2.

**SHERRY TRIFLE** Prepare as stated in the base recipe above, but add 25 ml/1 fl oz sweet sherry when moistening the biscuits or sponge (step 2).

**SCOTS TRIFLE** Prepare as for the base recipe above, but add 50 g/2 oz small macaroons and 50 g/2 oz ratafia biscuits to the sponge at step 2. Decorate with pistachio nuts and ratafia biscuits.

**JELLY TRIFLE** Prepare as for the base recipe above, but use 200 ml/8 fl oz raspberry table jelly in place of fruit juice. Prepare the jelly, allow to cool then pour over the pieces of biscuit or sponge and allow to set. Finish as stated.

## 11.28 CONDÉS

**TRADITIONAL PRACTICE**

*Use whole milk instead of skimmed milk, and lightly whipped cream in place of fromage frais. Also decorate with rosettes of cream. This increases the fat content.*

**CHEF'S TIP**

*4 poached or canned (unsweetened) pear halves may be used instead of fresh pears. This increases the sugar content. If canned in syrup this is increased still further.*

### PEAR CONDÉ

4 portions

**BASE INGREDIENTS**

| | | |
|---|---|---|
| 50 g | round-grain rice | 2 oz |
| 500 ml | skimmed milk | 1 pt |
| 50 g | sugar | 2 oz |
| 2–3 drops | vanilla essence | 2–3 drops |
| 50 ml | fromage frais | 2 fl oz |
| 2 | ripe pears | 2 |
| 75 ml | apricot glaze (page 38) | 3 fl oz |
| 5 ml | kirsch | 1 tsp |
| 2 | glacé cherries | 2 |
| | angelica diamonds | |

**BASE METHOD**

1 Prepare the rice:
   a) Place the milk in a saucepan and bring to the boil.
   b) Sprinkle in the rice, stirring constantly to avoid lumps.
   c) Slowly simmer until cooked, stirring occasionally to reduce the risk of burning.
   d) When cooked, add the sugar and vanilla essence.
   e) Cool quickly and thoroughly chill.
   f) Fold through the fromage frais.
2 Dress the rice in a serving dish (or 4 individual dishes).
3 Neatly arrange the pears on top.
4 Prepare the apricot glaze and add the kirsch.
5 Coat the fruit with the hot glaze and cool quickly.
6 Decorate with the cherries and angelica.

**APRICOT CONDÉ** Prepare as stated in the base recipe, using poached or canned unsweetened apricot halves.

**PEACH CONDÉ** Prepare as stated in the base recipe, using poached or canned unsweetened peach halves. Fresh ripe peach halves which have been skinned and stoned may also be used.

**PINEAPPLE CONDÉ** Prepare as stated in the base recipe, using canned (unsweetened) or fresh pineapple slices in place of pears.

## 11.29 FRESH FRUIT SALAD

**CHEF'S TIP**

*A whole mixture of fruits in season may be used, e.g. plums, pineapple, raspberries, strawberries, peaches, nectarines etc.*

**TRADITIONAL PRACTICE**

*Use stock syrup instead of unsweetened fruit juice. This increases sugar. Also remove the skin from fruits where appropriate, e.g. apples and pears. This reduces fibre.*

Allow 500 g/1 lb fruit per 4 portions

### BASE INGREDIENTS

| | | |
|---|---|---|
| 1 | medium apple | 1 |
| 1 | medium pear | 1 |
| 1 | medium orange | 1 |
| 25 g | green grapes | 1 oz |
| 25 g | black grapes | 1 oz |
| 25 g | cherries | 1 oz |
| ½ | banana | ½ |
| 75 ml | unsweetened fruit juice | 3 fl oz |
| | large squeeze lemon juice | |

### BASE METHOD

1. Place the fruit juice and lemon juice into a bowl.
2. Wash the apple and pear, then cut into quarters and remove the cores.
3. Cut the quarters into small slices, and place into the fruit juice.
4. Peel the orange, cut into segments and add to the bowl. Also squeeze the juice from the skin and shell of the orange into the bowl.
5. Wash and halve the grapes, then remove the seeds and add to the bowl.
6. Wash and stone the cherries and add to the fruit.
7. When required for service, peel and slice the banana and add to the mixture.
8. Place into a suitable serving dish.

**EXOTIC FRESH FRUIT SALAD** This is a fruit salad which usually contains oriental and Asian fruits such as mangoes, pawpaw, guavas, lychees etc.

## 11.30 DISHES USING FRESH, POACHED OR CANNED FRUITS

**TRADITIONAL PRACTICE**

*Use traditional ice-cream and increase the cream when decorating. This increases the fat content.*

Examples of the various fruits which may be used are peaches, pears, nectarines and bananas. Fresh fruits should be skinned, halved and have stones or seeds removed as appropriate.

**FRUIT CARDINAL** Dress the fruit on lower-fat strawberry ice-cream then coat with Melba sauce (page 40). Decorate with a little whipped cream and toasted sliced almonds.

**FRUIT HÉLÈNE (usually pears)** Dress the fruit on lower-fat vanilla ice-cream and decorate with a little whipped cream. Serve hot chocolate sauce (page 39) separately.

**FRUIT MELBA (usually peaches)** Dress the fruit on lower-fat vanilla ice-cream then coat with Melba sauce (page 40). Decorate with a little whipped cream.

## 11.31 COUPES

**TRADITIONAL PRACTICE**

*Use traditional ice-cream and increase the cream when decorating. This increases the fat content.*

Coupes usually consist of fruit, ice-cream and a sauce or cream served in a coupe dish.

**COUPE ALEXANDRA** Flavour fruit salad (opposite) with kirsch and place into a coupe dish. Add a ball of lower-fat strawberry ice-cream and decorate with a little whipped cream.

**COUPE ANDALOUSE** Place orange segments into a coupe dish then flavour with maraschino liqueur. Add a ball of lemon water-ice and decorate with a little whipped cream.

**COUPE EDNA-MAY** Place a ball of lower-fat vanilla ice-cream in a coupe and cover with ripe stoned cherries (fresh or poached). Coat with Melba sauce (page 40) and decorate with a little whipped cream.

**COUPE JACQUES** Flavour fruit salad (opposite) with kirsch and place into a coupe dish. Add a ball of ice-cream consisting half of lemon water-ice, and half of lower-fat strawberry ice-cream. Decorate with a small rosette of whipped cream and top with a black grape (seeds removed).

**COUPE JAMAIQUE** Place 2–3 small pineapple slices into a coupe dish which have been macerated in rum. Add a ball of lower-fat coffee ice-cream and decorate with a little whipped cream and crystallized violets.

**COUPE VENUS** Pipe a little whipped cream in the base of a coupe dish then place a half peach, flat side up, on top (the cream will prevent the peach from moving). Sit a ball of lower-fat vanilla ice-cream on the peach, top with a large strawberry and surround with whipped cream.

## 11.32 SYLLABUB

**HEALTH TIP**

*Syllabub is high in fat.*

4–6 portions

### BASE INGREDIENTS

| | | |
|---|---|---|
| 250 ml | double cream | ½ pt |
| 25–50 g | caster sugar | 1–2 oz |
| 250 ml | white wine | ½ pt |
| ½ | lemon (zest and juice) | ½ |

### BASE METHOD

1. Place 150 ml/6 fl oz of the wine into chilled glasses.
2. Wash and dry the lemon, then remove the zest using a fine grater. Also squeeze out the juice and reserve.
3. Place the cream in a bowl, add the sugar and whisk to a thick, heavy mixture.
4. Add the remaining wine, lemon zest and juice and blend together.
5. Spoon the syllabub into the glasses with the wine and serve.

# Process 12 BAKING

**DEFINITION** Baking is a dry heat method of cooking where prepared food and food products are cooked by convected heat in a pre-heated oven.

## REASONS FOR BAKING FOODS

1 To make foods tender: by breaking down and softening protein, fat, starch, cellulose and fibre.
2 To make foods more palatable and digestible.
3 To make foods safer to eat: by destroying bacteria which can cause food poisoning.
4 To produce a particular quality in food, of colour, flavour and texture (e.g. Victoria sandwich).

## METHODS OF BAKING FOODS

1 **Baking fruits, vegetables and potatoes:** This is a form of simple oven cooking where the commodities are cooked in an oven until tender (see baked potatoes on page 232).
2 **Baking within a bain-marie (water bath):** This involves placing the item to be baked in a water bath, so that low temperatures may be maintained during cooking. The baking of egg custard mixtures is an example of this type of cooking; where a gentle oven heat is maintained by a bain-marie, reducing the likelihood of the mixture curdling.
3 **Baking flour products:** This is often a more complex form of cooking than methods 1 and 2 above. When baking flour products such as cakes, the dry heat of the oven is usually modified with steam which has developed within the oven from the cake mixture during baking. The oven conditions in this instance should not only provide the correct temperature but also the correct humidity. For example: too dry an oven when baking cakes may result in low-volume cakes, because the crust has formed too quickly.
4 **Cooking eggs:** Cooking shirred eggs (oeufs sur le plat) is also a form of oven cooking which has been included in this chapter.

## COMMODITIES SUITABLE FOR BAKING AND OVEN COOKING

1 **Fruits:** e.g. apples and pears.
2 **Potatoes.**
3 **Milk puddings and egg custard products.**
4 **Flour products:** e.g. cakes, sponges, pastries and yeast goods.
5 **Vegetables** prepared in vegetarian bakes (page 117).
6 **Meat and vegetable hotpots** which are oven cooked.
7 **Eggs** which are oven cooked.

**EQUIPMENT USED WHEN BAKING FOODS** Types of equipment used include general purpose ovens, pastry ovens, forced-air convection ovens, baking ovens with steam injection (for bread) and specialist ovens (e.g. pizza ovens).

**Pizza oven**

Convection oven

Pastry oven

## BASIC TECHNIQUES OF BAKING

**TRAYING UP ITEMS TO BE BAKED** Certain categories of food require the baking tray to be prepared in a particular way. Lightly greasing trays or tins with white fat (and not butter or margarine which may cause the food to stick to the tray) is essential for cakes and sponges. However with some foods it may be advisable to use silicone paper (e.g. brandy snaps) to avoid this problem. Allowance must be made when traying up foods which will expand during baking (e.g. choux paste and yeast goods).

**MARKING FOODS TO BE BAKED** Some products, such as short pastry items (e.g. flans, pies and tarts) have their top edges neatly marked to produce an attractive finish. This is sometimes referred to as *notching* and may be done with the thumb and forefinger or special tweezers.

**GILDING OR COATING WITH EGGWASH** Many items which are to be baked, especially pastry and yeast goods, are lightly brushed with eggwash just prior to baking so that a good colour will develop on the surface of the item.

**SPEED OF COOKING** Most items are baked so that the product rises (if appropriate), develops colour and cooks through at the same time. It is therefore important that the oven is set to the correct temperature and pre-heated before inserting the food.

**PROVING** This is the final fermentation of yeast goods after they have been shaped and placed on the baking tray. It is usually carried out at 28–30 °C/82–86 °F in a moist atmosphere to prevent the surface of the goods developing a skin.

**COOLING** Many baked items are very delicate when hot (e.g. cakes and pastries) and should be cooled or allowed to cool slightly prior to use. This is usually done on a cooling wire designed for the purpose, which allows the air to circulate under the food and prevents condensation and softening of the product.

## KEY POINTS

- When preparing your time plan, remember that many baked goods have long preparation times (yeast goods, large cakes and gateaux) and in addition may have to be served cold.
- Ensure that you allow sufficient time for the oven to reach the correct baking temperature. Do not create a situation where a sponge is ready for the oven but cannot be cooked because the oven is not hot enough.
- Take care to measure and weigh foods accurately. When baking cakes, even small errors can have disastrous consequences; when weighing baking powder ensure the exact amount is used or the cake may be useless.

# 12.1 BOUCHÉES

**HEALTH TIP**

*Puff pastry items are high in fat.*

**CHEF'S TIP**

*Make sure the pastry is allowed to rest as stated, to avoid the items shrinking or becoming misshapen.*

12 cases

## BASE INGREDIENTS

| | | |
|---|---|---|
| 200 g | puff pastry (page 27) | 8 oz |
| | eggwash | |

## BASE METHOD

1 Roll out the pastry until 3–4 mm/$\frac{3}{16}$ inch in thickness.
2 Cut out the shapes using a round, fluted cutter which is 40 mm/1$\frac{1}{2}$ inches in diameter.
3 Place onto a lightly greased baking sheet.
4 Brush over the surfaces with eggwash.
5 Cut deep into the centre of each shape using a lightly greased plain cutter of a smaller diameter (30 mm/1$\frac{3}{16}$ inches) leaving a neat rim around the outer edge of each shape.
6 Allow to rest for 10 minutes then bake at 220 °C/425 °F until fully risen and cooked: 20 minutes approximately.
7 When baked, allow to cool slightly then carefully cut out the centre of each case; this may be used as the lid.
8 Carefully cut out the centre pastry from each shape leaving a neat shell.

## ALTERNATIVE METHOD

1 Roll out the pastry until 2$\frac{1}{2}$ mm/$\frac{1}{10}$ inch in thickness.
2 Cut out the fluted shapes (two per bouchée) with the fluted cutter (40 mm/1$\frac{1}{2}$ inches in diameter).
3 Cut out the centre from half the shapes using a plain, smaller cutter (30 mm/$\frac{3}{16}$ inches diameter) producing neat rims. These smaller circle shapes are the lids.
4 Lightly brush over the larger pastry shapes with water, then neatly place the pastry rims on top.
5 Place the bouchées and lids onto a lightly greased baking tray and brush over the surface with eggwash.
6 Allow to rest for 10 minutes approximately, then bake at 220 °C/425 °F until fully risen and cooked: 20 minutes approximately.

**VOL-AU-VENTS** For 6 vol-au-vents, use 200 g/8 oz puff pastry. Prepare as for bouchées (above) but cut into larger shapes, e.g. use an 80 mm/3 inch fluted cutter and a 60 mm/2$\frac{5}{16}$ inch plain cutter.

## FILLINGS FOR BOUCHÉES AND VOL-AU-VENTS

| | |
|---|---|
| Chicken | (page 28) |
| Chicken and mushroom | (page 28) |
| Game | (page 28) |
| Seafood | (page 28) |
| Vegetarian | (page 28) |

## 12.2 SAUSAGE ROLLS

**HEALTH TIP**

*Puff pastry items are high in fat.*

**CHEF'S TIP**

*Make sure the pastry is allowed to rest as stated, to avoid the items shrinking or becoming misshapen.*

**TRADITIONAL PRACTICE**

*The pastry surface is often stabbed with a fork before cutting the sausage rolls (step 5).*

8 sausage rolls

### BASE INGREDIENTS

| | | |
|---|---|---|
| 200 g | puff pastry (page 27) | 8 oz |
| 250 g | sausage meat | 10 oz |
| | eggwash | |

### BASE METHOD

1. Roll out the pastry into a strip which is $2\frac{1}{2}$ mm/$\frac{1}{10}$ inches in thickness and 80 mm/3 inches wide.
2. Using a little flour, roll the sausage meat into a long rope shape 20 mm/$\frac{3}{4}$ inch in thickness.
3. Place the sausage meat along the centre of the pastry strip.
4. Moisten the edges of the pastry with a little water then fold it over the sausage meat and seal the edges.
5. Brush with eggwash, then cut into 50 mm/2 inch lengths.
6. Place onto a lightly greased baking tray.
7. Allow to rest for 10 minutes approximately, then bake at 220 °C/425 °F until fully risen and cooked: 20 minutes approximately.

## 12.3 CHEESE STRAWS

**HEALTH TIP**

*Puff pastry items are high in fat.*

**CHEF'S TIP**

*Make sure the pastry is allowed to rest as stated, to avoid the items shrinking or becoming misshapen.*

**CHEF'S TIP**

*Check cheese straws regularly during cooking. They cook quickly and also burn quickly.*

20 straws approximately

### BASE INGREDIENTS

| | | |
|---|---|---|
| 100 g | puff pastry (trimmings) | 4 oz |
| 40 g | Parmesan cheese | $1\frac{1}{2}$ oz |
| | pinch paprika | |
| | small pinch cayenne pepper | |
| | eggwash | |

### BASE METHOD

1. Roll out the pastry into a thin sheet – $1\frac{1}{2}$ mm/$\frac{1}{16}$ inch in thickness.
2. Lightly brush over the surface with eggwash.
3. Mix together the cheese, paprika and cayenne pepper, then sprinkle this over the surface of the pastry.
4. Give one single turn (see *puff pastry* – page 27).
5. Roll out to a rectangle $1\frac{1}{2}$ mm/$\frac{1}{16}$ inch thick and 100 mm/4 inches wide.
6. Lightly brush over the surface with eggwash then cut into strips 7 mm/$\frac{1}{4}$ inch wide and 100 mm/4 inches long.
7. Twist each strip to form a spiralled stick shape, and place them onto a lightly greased baking tray.
8. Allow to rest for 15 minutes.
9. Bake at 225 °C/435 °F until crisp and light golden brown in colour: 10 minutes approximately.

## 12.4 PIZZAS

**TRADITIONAL PRACTICE**

*A traditional style pizza can be made by increasing the olive oil to 25 ml/1 fl oz and using strong flour instead of plain flour. Also add the water at 30 °C/86 °F and allow to ferment at 24 °C/76 °F for 40 minutes.*

**CHEF'S TIP**

*Milk may be used in place of milk powder and water.*

**CHEF'S TIP**

*To produce a pizza with a crisp base, a pizza oven or an oven which has a substantial amount of bottom heat is required.*

**TRADITIONAL PRACTICE**

*Increase the oil to 25 ml/1 fl oz. This increases the fat content.*

2 large pizzas

### BASE INGREDIENTS: PLAIN PIZZA DOUGH

| | | |
|---|---|---|
| 200 g | plain flour | 8 oz |
| 5 g | milk powder | $\frac{1}{4}$ oz |
| 15 ml | olive oil | $\frac{1}{2}$ fl oz |
| 10 g | yeast | $\frac{1}{2}$ oz |
| 120 ml | water (room temperature) | $4\frac{1}{2}$ fl oz |
| | small pinch salt | |

### BASE INGREDIENTS: WHOLEMEAL PIZZA DOUGH

| | | |
|---|---|---|
| 200 g | wholemeal flour | 8 oz |
| 5 g | milk powder | $\frac{1}{4}$ oz |
| 15 ml | olive oil | $\frac{1}{2}$ fl oz |
| 10 g | yeast | $\frac{1}{2}$ oz |
| 140 ml | water (room temperature) | $5\frac{3}{4}$ fl oz |
| | small pinch salt | |

### BASE METHOD

1. Thoroughly mix together the flour, salt and milk powder.
2. Break down the yeast in some of the water and add it to the flour.
3. Add the oil and remaining water and mix to a smooth, pliable dough.
4. Cover and allow to ferment at room temperature for 15 minutes.
5. Divide the dough into two pieces and mould them into balls.
6. Roll out into thin rounds. If a thin, crisp pizza is required, roll out to a thickness of 3 mm/$\frac{3}{16}$ inch.
7. Place onto lightly greased pizza tins.
8. Brush over the surface of the pizzas with a little olive oil.
9. Add the topping (see below) leaving a small, clear border round the edge of the pizza.
10. Allow to stand (dry prove) for 30–40 minutes.
11. Bake at 225 °C/435 °F until cooked: 15–20 minutes.

### BASIC TOMATO TOPPING

| | | |
|---|---|---|
| 10 ml | olive oil | $\frac{1}{2}$ fl oz |
| 25 g | chopped onion | 1 oz |
| 1 | medium clove garlic (crushed) | 1 |
| | pinch oregano | |
| 150 g | chopped tomatoes (or canned) | 6 oz |
| 5 g | tomato purée | $\frac{1}{4}$ oz |
| | small pinch salt and pepper | |

1. Sweat the onion and garlic in the oil until soft.
2. Add the oregano and continue cooking for 2 minutes.
3. Add the tomatoes and tomato purée and slowly simmer to a thick sauce consistency.
4. Check seasoning and cool.

## PIZZA NAPOLETANA

| | | |
|---|---|---|
| | basic tomato topping (opposite) | |
| 50 g | sliced Mozzarella cheese | 2 oz |

1 Prepare the pizza base following steps 1–8 of the base method opposite.
2 Prepare the basic tomato topping.
3 Add the topping to the pizza then garnish with the cheese.
4 Finish as stated, i.e. steps 9–11 of the base method.

## PIZZA AI FUNGHI (mushroom pizza)

| | | |
|---|---|---|
| | basic tomato topping (opposite) | |
| 10 ml | olive oil | $\frac{1}{2}$ fl oz |
| 100 g | sliced, washed mushrooms | 4 oz |
| 50 g | sliced mozzarella cheese | 2 oz |

1 Prepare the pizza base following steps 1–8 of the base method opposite.
2 Prepare the basic tomato topping.
3 Lightly cook the mushrooms in the olive oil and cool.
4 Add the topping to the pizza then garnish with the mushrooms and cheese.
5 Finish as stated, i.e. steps 9–11 of the base method.

**TRADITIONAL PRACTICE**

*Use double the quantity of cheese in the recipes. This increases the fat content.*

## PIZZA ALLA CAPRICCIOSA

| | | |
|---|---|---|
| | basic tomato topping (opposite) | |
| 50 g | sliced mozzarella cheese | 2 oz |
| 50 g | sliced cooked ham | 2 oz |
| 50 g | sliced cooked artichoke hearts | 2 oz |
| 50 g | mushrooms fried in olive oil | 2 oz |
| 20 g | sliced olives | $\frac{3}{4}$ oz |

1 Prepare the pizza base following steps 1–8 of the base method opposite.
2 Prepare the basic tomato topping.
3 Add the topping to the pizza then garnish with the cheeses, ham, artichokes, mushrooms and olives.
4 Finish as stated, i.e. steps 9–11 of the base method.

## PIZZA ALLA SICILIANA

| | | |
|---|---|---|
| | basic tomato topping (opposite) | |
| 50 g | sliced mozzarella cheese | 2 oz |
| 100 g | tuna fish (cooked/canned) | 4 oz |
| 50 g | halved olives | 2 oz |

1 Prepare the pizza base following steps 1–8 of the base method opposite.
2 Prepare the basic tomato topping.
3 Add the topping to the pizza then garnish with the cheese, pieces of tuna fish and olives.
4 Finish as stated, i.e. steps 9–11 of the base method.

## 12.5 MEAT AND GAME PIES

**HEALTH TIP**

*Puff pastry items are high in fat.*

**CHEF'S TIP**

*Make sure the pastry is allowed to rest as stated, to avoid the pie crust shrinking or becoming misshapen.*

**CHEF'S TIP**

*Make sure a pie dish of the correct size is used. The filling should almost fill the dish or the pastry will drop into the dish during cooking.*

### STEAK AND KIDNEY PIE

4 portions

**BASE INGREDIENTS**

| | | |
|---|---|---|
| 125 g | puff pastry (page 27) | 5 oz |
| | eggwash | |
| 10 g | oil | ½ oz |
| 300 g | lean diced stewing steak | 12 oz |
| 100 g | sliced ox kidney | 4 oz |
| 100 g | chopped onion | 4 oz |
| 450 ml | brown stock | ¾ pt |
| 10 g | arrowroot | ½ oz |
| 25 ml | cold water | 1 fl oz |
| | good dash Worcester sauce | |
| | good pinch chopped parsley | |
| | small pinch salt and pepper | |

**BASE METHOD**

1. Heat the oil in a saucepan.
2. Add the steak and kidney, developing a light colour.
3. Add the onion and cook for 2–3 minutes.
4. Add the stock and bring to the boil.
5. Simmer slowly until almost cooked.
6. Blend the arrowroot with the cold water.
7. Pour the arrowroot liquid into the meat and stock, stirring continuously until the mixture reboils.
8. Add the Worcester sauce and simmer until cooked.
9. Add the chopped parsley and check the seasoning.
10. Cool quickly and remove any solidified fat.
11. Roll out the pastry until it is 4 mm/$\frac{3}{16}$ inch in thickness.
12. Neatly trim the pastry to the size of the pie dish.
13. Prepare a thin strip of pastry from the remaining pastry to fit the rim of the pie dish.
14. Place the cold meat filling into the pie dish.
15. Lightly dampen the rim of the pie dish with water then line it with the pastry strip.
16. Dampen the pastry strip, then cover with the lid.
17. Press down lightly to seal the pastry.
18. Cut a small hole in the top of the pastry and notch the sides for decoration.
19. Decorate with pastry shapes if required, then brush with eggwash.
20. Allow to rest for 30 minutes approximately.
21. Bake at 200 °C/390 °F until the pastry is cooked and the filling thoroughly reheated: 40 minutes approximately.

### STEAK, KIDNEY AND MUSHROOM PIE

Prepare as for steak and kidney pie above, adding 100 g/4 oz of washed quartered mushrooms after thickening with the arrowroot (step 6).

## VENISON PIE

4 portions

| | *Filling:* | |
|---|---|---|
| 10 g | oil | $\frac{1}{2}$ oz |
| 400 g | lean diced venison | 1 lb |
| 100 g | chopped onion | 4 oz |
| 400 ml | brown game stock | 12 fl oz |
| 50 ml | red wine | 2 fl oz |
| 25 g | redcurrant jelly | 1 oz |
| 50 g | peeled button onions | 2 oz |
| 50 g | washed button mushrooms | 2 oz |
| 10 g | arrowroot | $\frac{1}{2}$ oz |
| 25 ml | cold water | 1 fl oz |
| 125 g | puff pastry (page 27) | 5 oz |
| | eggwash | |
| | small pinch salt and pepper | |

1. Heat the oil or fat in a saucepan.
2. Add the venison and cook until lightly coloured.
3. Add the chopped onion and cook for 2–3 minutes.
4. Add the stock and red wine and bring to the boil.
5. Simmer slowly until almost cooked.
6. Add the whole, button onions and cook for 5 minutes approximately.
7. Blend the arrowroot with the cold water, and pour it into the venison and stock stirring continuously until the mixture reboils.
8. Add the mushrooms and redcurrant jelly and simmer for 1–2 minutes.
9. Cool quickly and remove any solidified fat.
10. Complete following steps 11–20 of the base method opposite.

## CHICKEN PIE

4 portions

| | | |
|---|---|---|
| $1 \times 1\frac{1}{4}$ kg | chicken | $1 \times 2\frac{1}{2}$ lb |
| 8 | small rashers lean bacon | 8 |
| 100 g | peeled button onions | 4 oz |
| 100 g | washed button mushrooms | 4 oz |
| 200 ml | cold white chicken stock | 8 fl oz |
| 125 g | puff pastry (page 27) | 5 oz |
| | chopped parsley | |
| | pinch white pepper | |
| | eggwash | |

1. Joint the chicken, then remove the skin (page 18).
2. Wrap each piece of chicken in a rasher of bacon.
3. Place into the pie dish and add the onions, mushrooms, parsley and pepper.
4. Add only enough stock for the chicken to be barely covered.
5. Finish following steps 11–20 of the base method opposite. *Important:* Test to ensure the chicken is thoroughly cooked before serving.

**TRADITIONAL PRACTICE**

*The skin on the chicken is often left on in this type of pie. This increases the fat content.*

## 12.6 SAVOURY FLANS AND QUICHES

**TRADITIONAL PRACTICE**

*Use the standard quality pastry in place of lower-fat pastry. This increases the fat content.*

**TRADITIONAL PRACTICE**

*Use whole milk instead of skimmed milk and in creme the cheese to 50 g/2 oz. This increases the fat content.*

**CHEF'S TIP**

*To produce flans and quiches with a crisp base, use an oven which has a substantial amount of bottom heat. Also use* cold *milk and eggs, allowing the pastry to cook for the appropriate time before the filling sets.*

### CHEESE AND EGG FLAN

8 portions

#### BASE INGREDIENTS

| | | |
|---|---|---|
| 250 g | lower-fat savoury short pastry (page 27) | 9 oz |
| 2 | eggs (size 3) | 2 |
| 300 ml | skimmed milk | $\frac{1}{2}$ pt |
| 25 g | mature well-flavoured Cheddar | 10 oz |
| | small pinch salt and pepper | |
| | pinch cayenne pepper | |

#### BASE METHOD

1 Line a 200 mm/8 inch flan ring with the pastry (method: page 27).
2 Grate the cheese and add to the flan.
3 Thoroughly whisk together the eggs, milk and seasoning.
4 Add the mixture to the flan. Additional egg mixture may be added to top up the flan when it is in the oven.
5 Carefully place the flan in the oven.
6 Bake at 190 °C/375 °F until cooked: 35–40 minutes.

### VEGETABLE QUICHE

8 portions

| | | |
|---|---|---|
| 250 g | lower-fat savoury short pastry (page 27) | 9 oz |
| 2 | eggs (size 3) | 2 |
| 250 ml | skimmed milk | 8 fl oz |
| 25 g | mature well-flavoured Cheddar | 1 oz |
| 100 g | diced onion | 4 oz |
| $2\frac{1}{2}$ g | crushed clove garlic | 1 |
| 50 g | diced red pepper | 2 oz |
| 50 g | diced green pepper | 2 oz |
| 8 | whole baby sweetcorn | 8 |
| 8 | slices tomato | 8 |
| 25 g | cooked brown rice | 1 oz |
| | small pinch salt and pepper | |
| | pinch cayenne pepper | |

1 Line a 200 mm/8 inch flan ring with the pastry (method: page 27).
2 Place the onion, garlic, peppers and sweetcorn into a saucepan with 50 ml/2 fl oz of the milk, and lightly cook under cover.
3 Allow to cool slightly, then drain and add to the flan.
4 Grate the cheese and add to the flan with the cooked brown rice.
5 Garnish with the sliced tomatoes.
6 Thoroughly whisk together the eggs, milk, cooking liquor from the vegetables and seasoning.
7 Add the mixture to the flan. Additional egg mixture may be added to top up the flan when it is in the oven.
8 Carefully place the flan in the oven.
9 Bake at 190 °/375 °F until cooked: 35–40 minutes.

**TRADITIONAL PRACTICE**

*Sweat the vegetables in 10 g/$\frac{1}{4}$ oz butter or margarine instead of lightly cooking in the milk. This increases the fat content.*

## 12.7 CORNISH PASTIES

**TRADITIONAL PRACTICE**

*Use traditional short pastry in place of lower-fat pastry. This increases the fat content.*

**CHEF'S TIP**

*The mixture of spices used is one of the secrets of a good pasty.*

4 pasties

### BASE INGREDIENTS

| | | |
|---|---|---|
| 300 g | lower-fat savoury short pastry (page 27) | $10\frac{1}{2}$ oz |
| 150 g | lean coarse-minced beef | 6 oz |
| 100 g | finely diced potato | 4 oz |
| 50 g | chopped onion | 2 oz |
| 50 ml | rich brown stock (cold) | 2 fl oz |
| | small pinch salt, pepper and ground mace | |

### BASE METHOD

1. Mix together the minced beef, potato, onion, stock and seasoning.
2. Roll out the pastry until 3–4 mm/$\frac{3}{16}$ inch in thickness.
3. Cut into 4 rounds using a 160 mm/$6\frac{1}{2}$ inch plain cutter.
4. Lightly roll out each round to an oblong shape.
5. Divide the filling into four portions.
6. Place the filling onto the pastry shapes.
7. Lightly dampen around the edges of the pastry with water.
8. Fold the pastry in half bringing the edges upwards over the filling, then seal together.
9. Notch the top of each pasty neatly with the fingers.
10. Place onto a lightly greased and floured baking tray.
11. Brush over the surfaces with eggwash.
12. Bake at 200 °/390 °F until cooked: 40 minutes approximately.

**CHEF'S TIP**

*This dish must not contain any animal products if it is to be suitable for vegans, e.g. the short pastry and wholemeal bread must not contain animal fat.*

### SPICED VEGETABLE PASTIES (VEGAN)

4 pasties

| | | |
|---|---|---|
| 300 g | lower-fat savoury short pastry (page 27) | $10\frac{1}{2}$ oz |
| 5 ml | oil | $\frac{1}{4}$ oz |
| 75 g | chopped onion | 3 oz |
| 1 | clove garlic (crushed) | 1 |
| 1 tsp | ground cumin | 1 tsp |
| $\frac{1}{4}$ tsp | chilli powder | $\frac{1}{4}$ tsp |
| 25 g | wholemeal breadcrumbs | 1 oz |
| 50 g | diced carrot | 2 oz |
| 50 g | diced potato | 2 oz |
| 50 g | tinned tomatoes | 2 oz |
| 50 g | diced red and green peppers | 2 oz |
| 50 g | sweetcorn kernels | 2 oz |
| 50 g | cooked brown rice | 2 oz |

1. Lightly cook the onion and garlic in the oil.
2. Add the spices and cook gently.
3. Add the diced carrot, potato and tinned tomatoes and cook for 4–5 minutes.
4. Allow to cool, then add the remaining ingredients and mix together.
5. Finish as for Cornish pasties above (steps 2–12), using the vegetable filling.

## 12.8 YORKSHIRE PUDDINGS

**CHEF'S TIP**

*Yorkshire puddings can be stuffed with a variety of fillings and served as a snack item. A range of vegetarian snacks can also be made using vegetarian fillings.*

**CHEF'S TIP**

*A thin batter is a key factor in producing a good Yorkshire pudding.*

### TRADITIONAL YORKSHIRE PUDDING

6–8 portions

#### BASE INGREDIENTS

| | | |
|---|---|---|
| 100 g | strong (or plain) flour | 4 oz |
| 1 | egg (size 3) | 1 |
| 250 ml | milk | $\frac{1}{2}$ pt |
| 30 ml | oil | $1\frac{1}{4}$ fl oz |
| | small pinch salt and pepper | |

#### BASE METHOD

1 Place the flour into a mixing bowl.
2 Add the egg and half the milk.
3 Whisk until a smooth thick mixture is formed.
4 Whisk in the remaining milk in stages, until a smooth thin batter is obtained. The batter should be the consistency of thin pouring cream.
5 Allow to rest for 1 hour approximately.
6 Place the Yorkshire pudding tins on a baking tray, then add enough oil to cover the bottom of each tin: 5 mm/1 tsp of oil per tin.
7 Place the tins into an oven at 200 °C/395 °F approximately and allow to become very hot.
8 Fill each tin with batter, then bake until fully risen and set.
9 Turn the puddings upside down to remove the fat from the centres and continue cooking until crisp.

**LOWER-FAT YORKSHIRE PUDDINGS** Prepare as for the base recipe, but replace half the strong flour with wholemeal flour, and use skimmed milk instead of whole milk. Cook in a non-stick Yorkshire pudding tray which has been lightly greased with polyunsaturated white fat and preheated before adding the batter.

**TRADITIONAL PRACTICE**

*Use ordinary sausages and 25 g/1 oz lard or dripping in place of white fat (step 1). This increases the fat content.*

### TOAD-IN-THE-HOLE (lower-fat method)

4 portions

| | | |
|---|---|---|
| 8 | lower-fat sausages | 8 |
| | Yorkshire pudding batter (above) | |
| 250 ml | jus lié (page 30) | $\frac{1}{2}$ pt |

1 Lightly grease a shallow non-stick roasting tray with polyunsaturated white fat.
2 Add the sausages and cook in an oven to develop colour.
3 Arrange the sausages into portions (i.e. groups of 2) then pour in the batter.
4 Bake in an oven at 200 °C/395 °F until cooked: 40 minutes approximately.
5 Serve accompanied with the jus lié.

## 12.9 SHIRRED EGGS *OEUFS SUR LE PLAT*

**TRADITIONAL PRACTICE**

*Use 15 g/$\frac{3}{4}$ oz butter in place of margarine. In addition to using it to grease the dishes (step 1), coat each egg with a little melted butter when serving. This increases the fat content.*

2 portions

### BASE INGREDIENTS

| | | |
|---|---|---|
| 2 | eggs (size 3) | 2 |
| $2\frac{1}{2}$ g | margarine | $\frac{1}{6}$ oz |
| | salt and pepper | |

### BASE METHOD

1 Lightly grease the base of two sur le plat dishes with the margarine.
2 Break an egg into each dish then season lightly.
3 Place the dishes over a gentle heat (usually at the side of a solid top stove) and allow the whites of each egg to set lightly at the base of the dish.
4 Place the dishes in a moderate oven (180 °C/355 °F) and complete the cooking.

## 12.10 STUFFED TOMATOES *TOMATES FARCIES*

4 portions

### BASE INGREDIENTS

| | | |
|---|---|---|
| 4 | medium tomatoes | 4 |
| 100 g | duxelles (page 24) | 4 oz |
| | small pinch salt and pepper | |

### BASE METHOD

1 Wash the tomatoes and neatly remove the eyes using a small knife.
2 Cut off the ends at the opposite side to the eyes.
3 Scoop out the seeds of each tomato leaving a tomato case.
4 Lightly season with salt and pepper.
5 Stuff each tomato with the duxelle then place onto a lightly oiled cooking tray. Cover the stuffed tomatoes with the tomato lids.
6 Place into an oven at 200 °C/390 °F until heated through: 4 minutes approximately.
7 Serve garnished with parsley (optional).

**GRATINATED STUFFED TOMATOES** *TOMATES FARCIES AU GRATIN* Prepare as for the base recipe, but sprinkle over the tops of the tomatoes with breadcrumbs before placing them in the oven for 4 minutes. Take the tomatoes from the oven and gratinate under a hot salamander. Serve garnished with parsley.

# 12.11 BAKING POTATOES

**TRADITIONAL PRACTICE**

*Bake the potatoes on a layer of salt. In addition, a little oil is sometimes brushed over the skin to enhance appearance.*

**CHEF'S TIP**

*Place a piece of butter (5 g/¼ oz approximately) in the cavity of each potato when serving. This increases the fat content.*

4 portions

### BASE INGREDIENTS

| | | |
|---|---|---|
| 4 × 200 g | potatoes | 4 × 8 oz |

### BASE METHOD

1. Wash and scrub the potatoes, then remove any spots of mould or deterioration.
2. Place onto an oven rack and bake at 200 °C/390 °F until cooked: 1–1½ hours approximately.
3. Cut a cross on the top of each potato.
4. Press the sides to open each potato neatly.

## CHEESE AND VEGETABLE POTATOES (vegetarian dish)

4 portions

| | | |
|---|---|---|
| 4 × 250 g | potatoes | 4 × 10 oz |
| 150 ml | low-fat white sauce (page 33) | 6 fl oz |
| ¼ tsp | English mustard | ¼ tsp |
| 50 g | diced onion | 2 oz |
| 50 g | diced red and green pepper | 2 oz |
| 25 g | diced courgette | 1 oz |
| 25 g | sliced mushroom | 1 oz |
| 25 g | sweetcorn kernels | 1 oz |
| 25 g | peas | 1 oz |
| 100 g | low-fat curd cheese | 4 oz |

1. Bake the potatoes as stated above.
2. Blend the mustard with a little cold water and add to the sauce.
3. Add the onion, pepper and courgette to the sauce and cook for 3–4 minutes.
4. Add the mushroom, sweetcorn and peas and cook for a further 2 minutes approximately.
5. Add the cheese and blend it through the mixture.
6. Split the hot baked potatoes and place on a serving dish.
7. Fill with the vegetable garnish.

**HEALTH TIP**

*Butter may be used in place of margarine, but this would increase the saturated fat content.*

## MACAIRE POTATOES

| | | |
|---|---|---|
| 4 × 150 g | potatoes | 4 × 6 oz |
| 20 g | margarine | ¾ oz |
| | small pinch salt and pepper | |

1. Bake the potatoes as stated in the base method.
2. Halve the potatoes and scoop out the pulp.
3. Lightly mash, then add the margarine.
4. Lightly season, then mix to a stiff purée.
5. Transfer the mixture to a floured table and mould it into a roll; then cut into fishcake shapes.
6. Shallow-fry in a lightly oiled pan until golden brown on both sides.

**CHEF'S TIP**

*Cook the finished potatoes in the same manner as a griddle scone, avoiding free surface oil.*

## 12.12 BAKING APPLES

4 portions

### BASE INGREDIENTS

| | | |
|---|---|---|
| 4 | medium cooking apples | 4 |
| 25 g | caster sugar | 1 oz |
| 4 | cloves | 4 |
| 100 ml | water | 4 fl oz |

### BASE METHOD

1. Wash and core the apples.
2. Make an incision around the middle of each apple: cutting through the skin only.
3. Place the apples in an earthenware cooking dish.
4. Place a spoonful of sugar and a clove into the cavity of each apple.
5. Pour the water into the dish.
6. Bake in an oven at 200 °C/390 °F, occasionally basting with the cooking liquor.
7. Cook until tender and lightly coloured: 30 minutes approximately.
8. Serve the apples with their cooking liquor.

**TRADITIONAL PRACTICE**

*Fill the centre of each apple with sugar and top with a small piece of margarine or butter (5 g/¼ oz). This increases both fat and sugar content.*

### BAKED APPLES IN RED WINE *MELE IN VINO ROSSO*

4 portions

| | | |
|---|---|---|
| 4 | medium cooking apples | 4 |
| 25 g | caster sugar | 1 oz |
| 2 | cloves | 2 |
| 100 ml | red wine | 4 fl oz |
| 25 ml | water | 1 fl oz |
| | good pinch grated nutmeg | |
| | small piece cinnamon stick | |

Cook as stated in the base method, adding a little grated nutmeg to each apple at step 4. At step 5, add the cinnamon stick to the dish before pouring in the cooking liquor (the water and red wine). Cook as stated, and serve hot or cold with the cooking liquor.

### BAKED APPLES WITH WALNUTS AND RAISINS *MILA PSITA ME KARYDIA*

4 portions

| | | |
|---|---|---|
| 4 | medium cooking apples | 4 |
| 25 g | caster sugar | 1 oz |
| 50 g | crushed walnuts | 2 oz |
| 50 g | raisins | 2 oz |
| 25 ml | brandy | 1 fl oz |
| 2 tsp | cinnamon | 2 tsp |
| 100 ml | water | 4 fl oz |

Cook as stated in the base method, stuffing the apples with a mixture of the sugar, walnuts, raisins and brandy. Sprinkle each apple with cinnamon, then cook as stated. Serve hot or cold with the cooking liquor.

# 12.13 BAKED EGG CUSTARD

## BASIC EGG CUSTARD MIXTURE

4–6 portions

### BASE INGREDIENTS

| | | |
|---|---|---|
| 2 | eggs (size 3) | 2 |
| 25 g | caster sugar | 1 oz |
| 300 ml | skimmed milk | $\frac{1}{2}$ pt |
| 2–3 drops | vanilla essence | 2–3 drops |

### BASE METHOD

1 Heat the milk in a thick-based pan.
2 Break the eggs into a bowl.
3 Add the sugar and vanilla essence to the eggs, then whisk until combined.
4 Whisk the hot milk through the eggs.
5 Strain into an earthenware pie dish.
6 Clean around the edge of the dish if required, then sprinkle with a little grated nutmeg.
7 Place the pie dish in a tray half-full of water.
8 Cook in a cool oven (160 °C/320 °F) until set: 1–1$\frac{1}{2}$ hours.

**TRADITIONAL PRACTICE**

*Increase the sugar to 50 g/2 oz and use whole milk. The egg content may also be increased by using three small eggs. This increases both fat and sugar content.*

## BREAD AND BUTTER PUDDING

4–6 portions

| | | |
|---|---|---|
| 2 | slices wholemeal bread | 2 |
| 10 g | butter | $\frac{1}{2}$ oz |
| 25 g | sultanas | 1 oz |
| | icing sugar | |
| | basic egg custard mixture (above) | |

1 Cut the crusts off the bread then butter the bread.
2 Cut into triangles and arrange in a pie dish.
3 Add the sultanas.
4 Prepare the basic custard mixture (to step 5) and pour over the bread.
5 Allow to stand until the bread is soaked with the custard.
6 Place the pie dish in a tray half-full of water.
7 Cook in a cool oven (160 °C/320 °F) until set: 1–1$\frac{1}{2}$ hours.
8 Dust the top with icing sugar.

**TRADITIONAL PRACTICE**

*Use white bread instead of wholemeal bread. Also replace 50 ml/2 fl oz of the milk in the egg custard with cream. This increases fat and reduces fibre.*

## CABINET PUDDING

4–6 portions

| | | |
|---|---|---|
| 50 g | diced sponge | 2 oz |
| 25 g | sultanas | 1 oz |
| 25 g | currants | 1 oz |
| 20 g | diced glacé cherries | $\frac{3}{4}$ oz |
| 5 g | diced angelica | $\frac{1}{4}$ oz |
| | basic egg custard mixture (above) | |

1 Lightly grease 6 dariole moulds then add the diced sponge, fruit, cherries and angelica.
2 Add the egg mixture (prepared to step 5) and leave to stand for 2–3 minutes, allowing it to soak into the sponge.
3 Bake following steps 4–5 of crème caramel (opposite).

4 Allow to cool slightly, then remove from the moulds and serve hot.
5 Accompany with a suitable sauce, e.g. custard or jam.

## CRÈME CARAMEL

4–6 portions

| | | |
|---|---|---|
| 50 ml | water | 2 fl oz |
| 100 g | granulated sugar | 4 oz |
| | basic egg custard mixture (opposite) | |

1 Prepare the caramel:
   a) Place the sugar and water into a sugar-boiling pan or small thick-based pan.
   b) Bring to the boil on a low heat stirring occasionally.
   c) Boil for 30 seconds then remove from the boil and check the clarity; the syrup should be clear.
   d) Reboil the syrup and boil quickly: do not stir.
   e) During boiling, occasionally clean round the sides of the pan with a clean brush dipped in water.
   f) Continue boiling until golden brown.
   g) Remove from the heat and place the pan into cold water for 3–4 seconds to stop the boiling action.
   h) Carefully add 30 ml/1 fl oz hot water to the caramel and shake until combined.
2 Pour the hot caramel into 4–6 dariole moulds and allow to cool and set.
3 Prepare the basic custard mixture (to step 5), then pour it into the moulds.
4 Place the moulds in tray half-full of water.
5 Cook in a cool oven (150 °C/300 °F) until set: 1–1½ hours.
6 Remove from the oven and cool: allow to become thoroughly cold.
7 De-mould onto a serving dish.

**CHEF'S TIP**

*Ensure the arms are well protected when carrying out this procedure.*

**CHEF'S TIP**

*Preparing the caramels prior to service and storing in a refrigerator for 4–6 hours ensures they are thoroughly set and results in most of the caramel leaving the mould when they are turned out onto the serving dish.*

## 12.14 BAKED RICE

4 portions

### BASE INGREDIENTS

| | | |
|---|---|---|
| 50 g | round grain rice | 2 oz |
| 40 g | sugar | 1½ oz |
| 2–3 drops | vanilla essence | 2–3 drops |
| 500 ml | skimmed milk | 1 pt |
| | pinch grated nutmeg | |

### BASE METHOD

1 Place the rice and sugar into a pie dish.
2 Add the milk and essence and stir to combine.
3 Sprinkle with nutmeg.
4 Clean round the rim of the dish, then place onto a baking tray.
5 Bake at 180 °C/350 °F until the milk simmers.
6 Reduce the temperature to 150 °C/300 °F and slowly bake until cooked and golden brown: 1½–2 hours.

**TRADITIONAL PRACTICE**

*Use whole milk instead of skimmed milk and add 10 g/½ oz butter to the pudding after sprinkling with the nutmeg at step 3. This increases the fat content.*

## 12.15 SWEET FLANS: SOFT OR TINNED FRUITS

This is suitable for flans incorporating a poached, tinned or ripe soft fruit filling, e.g. apricot, banana, cherry, peach, pear, pineapple.

**TRADITIONAL PRACTICE**

*Use the traditional sweet pastry in place of lower-fat pastry. This increases the fat content.*

**TRADITIONAL PRACTICE**

*Use pears poached in syrup (page 81) and pastry cream (page 39) instead of fromage frais. This increases sugar and fat content.*

### PEAR FLAN

8 portions

#### BASE INGREDIENTS

| | | |
|---|---|---|
| 250 g | lower-fat sweet short pastry (page 27) | 9 oz |
| 400 g | tinned pear halves (unsweetened) | 1 lb |
| 200 ml | pear fromage frais | 8 fl oz |
| 50 ml | apricot glaze (page 38) | 2 fl oz |

#### BASE METHOD

1 Line a 200 mm/8 inch flan ring with the pastry (page 27) and bake blind (page 28).
2 Allow to cool.
3 Drain the pears and leave whole or cut into slices.
4 Spread the fromage frais over the base of the cooked flan.
5 Neatly arrange the pears on top.
6 Meanwhile prepare the glaze, then thinly coat over the pears. Use only a minimum quantity of hot glaze.

**BANANA FLAN** Prepare as the base recipe above, using sliced bananas and banana flavoured fromage frais.

**RASPBERRY FLAN** Prepare as for pear flan above, using raspberries and raspberry flavoured fromage frais. Also use a plain fruit glaze (page 38) in place of apricot glaze.

## 12.16 SWEET FLANS: HARD FRUITS

**TRADITIONAL PRACTICE**

*Use the traditional sweet pastry in place of lower-fat pastry. This increases the fat content.*

### APPLE FLAN

8 portions

#### BASE INGREDIENTS

| | | |
|---|---|---|
| 250 g | lower-fat sweet short pastry (page 27) | 10 oz |
| 1 kg | cooking apples | 2 lb |
| 50 g | caster sugar | 2 oz |
| | pinch ground cloves | |
| 50 ml | apricot glaze (page 38) | 2 fl oz |

**TRADITIONAL PRACTICE**

*Use the traditional sweet pastry in place of lower-fat pastry. This increases the fat content.*

### BASE METHOD

1. Line a 200 mm/8 inch flan ring with the pastry (page 27), and pierce the base with a fork or docker.
2. Place aside 3–4 of the best apples (350 g/14 oz).
3. Peel and core the remaining apples and prepare an apple pulp using three-quarters of the sugar and the ground cloves (page 29).
4. Bake the flan blind (page 28) until half cooked, i.e. until the pastry is set.
5. Take the flan out of the oven and remove the flan ring.
6. Meanwhile, peel and core the selected apples, and cut them into neat, thin slices. Store in lemon water to avoid discolouration.
7. Fill the flan with the apple pulp then decorate the top with overlapping rows of sliced apple.
8. Sprinkle the surface with the remaining sugar.
9. Replace the flan into the oven and bake until cooked: a further 15 minutes approximately.
10. When cooked, thinly coat the surface of the apples with the hot apricot glaze.

## 12.17 FRUIT TARTS

### RHUBARB TART

8 portions

#### BASE INGREDIENTS

| | | |
|---|---|---|
| 300 g | lower-fat sweet short pastry (page 27) | 12 oz |
| 750 g | rhubarb | 1 lb 10 oz |
| 75 g | caster sugar | 3 oz |

#### BASE METHOD

1. Line a 200 mm/8 inch flan ring (page 00) using three-quarters of the pastry, but do not pierce the base.
2. Remove the leaves from the rhubarb, then trim off the heels at the base of the stalks.
3. Wash, then cut into 15 mm/$\frac{1}{2}$ inch lengths.
4. Mix together the rhubarb and sugar and place into the flan case.
5. Roll out the remaining pastry to form a lid.
6. Lightly dampen the top edges of the flan paste then place the lid on top.
7. Press down the edges of the pastry, removing surplus pastry and forming a seal.
8. Cut a small hole in the top of the pie then eggwash if required.
9. Bake at 200 °C/390 °F until cooked: 35–40 minutes.

**APPLE TART** Prepare as for the base recipe above, using apples in place of rhubarb. Reduce the quantity of sugar to 50 g/2 oz (depending on type of cooking apple used).

**BLACKBERRY TART** Prepare as for the base recipe above, using blackberries and reducing the sugar to 50 g/2 oz.

## 12.18 SWEET PIES

### GOOSEBERRY PIE

8 portions

**BASE INGREDIENTS**

| | | |
|---|---|---|
| 800 g | gooseberries | $1\frac{3}{4}$ lb |
| 75 g | caster sugar | 3 oz |
| 200 g | lower-fat sweet short pastry (page 27) | 8 oz |

**BASE METHOD**

1 Top and tail the gooseberries.
2 Lightly scrape over the surfaces, then wash and drain.
3 Place the gooseberries into a pie dish and add the sugar.
4 Roll out the pastry until 3–4 mm/$\frac{3}{16}$ inch thick and large enough to cover the pie dish.
5 Lightly dampen the rim of the dish with water then cover with the pastry.
6 Brush over the surface with eggwash if required.
7 Bake at 200 °C/390 °F until cooked: 35–40 minutes.

**APPLE PIE** Prepare as for the base recipe above, replacing the gooseberries with peeled, cored and sliced apples.

**TRADITIONAL PRACTICE**

*Use the traditional sweet pastry in place of lower-fat pastry. This increases the fat content.*

## 12.19 CREAM BUNS AND PROFITEROLES

### CREAM BUNS

6 buns

**BASE INGREDIENTS**

| | | |
|---|---|---|
| 300 g | choux paste (page 26) | 12 oz |
| 150 g | whipping cream | 6 fl oz |
| 10 g | caster sugar | $\frac{1}{2}$ oz |
| 2–3 drops | vanilla essence | 2–3 drops |
| | icing sugar | |

**BASE METHOD**

1 Place the choux paste into a piping bag with a 15 mm/$\frac{1}{2}$ inch diameter plain tube.
2 Pipe out the paste into small bulbs (15 mm/$\frac{1}{2}$ inch diameter) onto a lightly greased baking tray.
3 Bake at 220 °C/425 °F until fully risen and very crisp: 25 minutes.
4 Allow to cool on a cooling wire.
5 Meanwhile lightly sweeten the cream, flavour with vanilla essence and whip until stiff.
6 Make a small incision in each bun, then fill with the whipped cream.
7 Dust over the surface of each bun with icing sugar.

**PROFITEROLES** Prepare as cream buns above, but pipe the choux paste into small bulbs using a $7\frac{1}{2}$ mm/$\frac{1}{4}$ inch diameter plain piping tube. When filled with cream, dress neatly in a pyramid shape on a service dish or plate then dust over the surface with icing sugar. Accompany with a sauceboat of cold chocolate sauce.

**HEALTH TIP**

*Cream buns, éclairs and profiteroles filled with cream are high in fat.*

**CHEF'S TIP**

*Make sure the items are fully cooked and crisp before removing them from the oven otherwise they may collapse.*

## 12.20 SWEET TURNOVERS

### JAM TURNOVERS

4 turnovers

**BASE INGREDIENTS**

| | | |
|---|---|---|
| 200 g | puff pastry (page 27) | 8 oz |
| 80 g | raspberry jam | 3 oz |
| 1 | egg white | 1 |
| | caster sugar | |

**BASE METHOD**

1 Roll out the pastry into a square with 250 mm/10 inch sides and $2\frac{1}{2}$ mm/$\frac{1}{10}$ inch in thickness.
2 Cut into 4 smaller squares with 125 mm/5 inch sides, then lightly dampen the edges with a little water.
3 Place a spoonful of jam (20 g/$\frac{3}{4}$ oz) onto the centre of each square.
4 Carefully fold over to form a triangle then lightly press down the edges to achieve a good seal.
5 Brush the tops of the turnovers with egg white, then dip into the caster sugar.
6 Place onto a lightly greased baking tray and allow to rest for 20 minutes.
7 Bake at 215 °C/420 °F until cooked: 20–25 minutes.

**HEALTH TIP**

*Puff pastry items are high in fat.*

**CHEF'S TIP**

*When enclosing the filling in a turnover ensure that the filling is not squeezed towards the edges of the pastry. This can prevent a good seal being made and cause the filling to run out when baking.*

**APPLE TURNOVERS** Prepare as for the base recipe, but replace the jam with 100 g/4 oz apple pulp (page 29).

## 12.21 ECCLES CAKES

6 cakes

**BASE INGREDIENTS**

| | | |
|---|---|---|
| 200 g | puff pastry (trimmings) | 8 oz |
| 25 g | margarine | 1 oz |
| 25 g | soft brown sugar | 1 oz |
| 100 g | currants | 4 oz |
| | good pinch mixed spice | |
| | egg white | |
| | caster sugar | |

**BASE METHOD**

1 Roll out the pastry until $1\frac{1}{2}$ mm/$\frac{1}{16}$ inch in thickness.
2 Cut into round shapes with a 100 mm/4 inch round cutter, then lightly dampen the edges of the pastry with water.
3 Mix together the margarine, brown sugar, currants and spice.
4 Place a spoonful of the mixture (25 g/1 oz) in the centre of each shape.
5 Fold the edges of the pastry to the centre to enclose the mixture, then turn over the pastry shape.
6 Roll out into round shapes 75 mm/3 inches in diameter.
7 Brush over the tops with egg white then dip into the caster sugar.
8 Place onto a lightly greased baking tray and allow to rest for 20 minutes.
9 Bake at 215 °C/420 °F until cooked: 20–25 minutes.

**CHEF'S TIP**

*Preparing Eccles or Banbury cakes is an ideal way of using up puff pastry trimmings.*

**CHEF'S TIP**

*Butter may be used in place of margarine, but this would increase the saturated fat content.*

**BANBURY CAKES** Prepare as for Eccles cakes above, but roll out into boat shapes (step 7).

# 12.22 SWEET SOUFFLÉS

### HEALTH TIP

*Butter may be used in place of margarine, but this increases saturated fat. The quantity of fat and eggs used in soufflés makes them quite high in fat.*

## VANILLA SOUFFLÉ

6 portions (3 × 115 mm/4½ inch soufflé cases)

### BASE INGREDIENTS

| | | |
|---|---|---|
| 60 g | caster sugar | 2 oz |
| 60 g | margarine | 2 oz |
| 60 g | plain flour | 2 oz |
| 10 g | cornflour | 1 tsp |
| 250 ml | milk | ½ pt |
| 2–3 drops | vanilla essence | 2–3 drops |
| 5 | eggs (size 3) | 5 |

### BASE METHOD

1 Lightly grease the soufflé cases and coat with caster sugar.
2 Separate the egg yolks from the whites (placing the whites into a clean, grease-free bowl).
3 Cream together the sugar, margarine, flour and cornflour.
4 Bring the milk to the boil.
5 Whisk the creamed mixture into the milk then stir with a spatula until very thick.
6 Add the vanilla essence and continue cooking for 1 minute approximately. Stir constantly to avoid burning.
7 Transfer the mixture to a mixing bowl and allow to cool slightly.
8 Add the egg yolks one at a time and beat through the mixture.
9 Whisk the whites to a stiff snow, then carefully fold through the mixture.
10 Place the mixture into the prepared soufflé cases and lightly smooth down with a palette knife.
11 Clean the rim of each soufflé case.
12 Bake at 200 °C/390 °F until fully risen, cooked and golden brown: 20 minutes approximately.
13 Dredge over the top of each soufflé with icing sugar and serve immediately.

### CHEF'S TIP

*The production of soufflés may be staggered to suit service demands. The basic mixture is made (up to step 8) and then stored until required for use. The soufflés are then finished (within 20–25 minutes of service) as stated (from step 9).*

**CHOCOLATE SOUFFLÉ** Prepare as for the base recipe above, but replace the vanilla essence with 100 g/4 oz grated chocolate: add this to the milk at step 4. *Note:* An extra egg white may be required for this soufflé as the chocolate tends to have a thickening effect on the mixture.

**ORANGE/LEMON SOUFFLÉ** Prepare as for the base recipe above, but omit the vanilla essence and add the following at step 6:
*Lemon soufflé:* The juice and grated zest of 1 lemon.
*Orange soufflé:* The juice and grated zest of 1 orange and the juice of half a lemon.

**LIQUEUR SOUFFLÉ (Cointreau, Grand Marnier, Kirsch etc.)** Prepare as stated in the base recipe above, but omit the vanilla essence and add 30 ml/1¼ fl oz of the relevant liqueur with the egg yolks at step 8.

**PUDDING SOUFFLÉS** Prepare as for sweet soufflés (opposite) with the following amendments:

1 Reduce the eggs in the recipe to 3 eggs.
2 Use 4–6 dariole moulds instead of soufflé cases (buttered and sugared as stated).
3 Cook in a bain-marie (tray half full of water) at the stated temperature for 30–40 minutes.
4 When cooked, carefully turn out the pudding soufflés onto a serving dish and serve immediately. Accompany with a suitable sauce, e.g. custard, orange, lemon, chocolate.

## 12.23 CHEESE SOUFFLÉ

**HEALTH TIP**

*Cheese soufflés are high in fat.*

**HEALTH TIP**

*Butter may be used in place of margarine, but this would increase the saturated fat content.*

**CHEF'S TIP**

*The production of cheese soufflés may be staggered to suit service demands. The basic mixture is made (up to step 10) and then stored until required for use. The soufflés are then finished (within 20–25 minutes of service) as stated (from step 11).*

4 small soufflés (6 × 50 mm/2 inch soufflé dishes)

### BASE INGREDIENTS

| | | |
|---|---|---|
| 25 g | margarine | 1 oz |
| 25 g | flour | 1 oz |
| 200 ml | milk | 8 fl oz |
| 3 | egg yolks | 3 |
| 4 | egg whites | 4 |
| 50 g | grated cheese (Gruyère, Parmesan) | 2 oz |
| | small pinch salt, pepper and cayenne pepper | |
| | grated Parmesan (to coat dishes) | |

### BASE METHOD

1 Lightly grease the soufflé cases, then coat with Parmesan.
2 Heat the milk.
3 Melt the margarine in a saucepan.
4 Add the flour and mix together.
5 Cook for 2–3 minutes without developing colour.
6 Slowly blend in the hot milk, stirring until smooth with each addition of milk.
7 Bring to the boil and cook for 2–3 minutes, stirring constantly to produce a smooth, thick sauce.
8 Remove from the heat and mix in the cheese.
9 Lightly season, then transfer the mixture to a mixing bowl.
10 Add the egg yolks one at a time and beat through the mixture.
11 Whisk the whites to a stiff snow then carefully fold through the mixture.
12 Place the mixture into the prepared soufflé cases then lightly smooth down with a palette knife.
13 Clean the rim of each soufflé case.
14 Bake at 200 °C/390 °F until fully risen, cooked and golden brown: 20 minutes approximately.

## 12.24 PREPARING SMALL CAKES

**HEALTH TIP**

*Cakes are high in fat and sugar.*

**HEALTH TIP**

*Butter may be used in place of margarine, but this would increase the saturated fat content.*

**CHEF'S TIP**

*Never use chilled or cold ingredients as the mixture is likely to curdle when adding the egg.*

**CHEF'S TIP**

*If a mixture begins to curdle before all the egg has been used, add a little of the recipe flour with each further addition of egg to absorb the surface liquid.*

### CUP CAKES

6 cakes

#### BASE INGREDIENTS

| | | |
|---|---|---|
| 50 g | margarine | 2 oz |
| 50 g | caster sugar | 2 oz |
| 1 | large egg | 1 |
| 50 g | plain flour | 2 oz |
| 25 g | self-raising flour | 1 oz |

#### BASE METHOD

1. Ensure the ingredients are at a temperature of 21–22 °C/70–71 °F.
2. Sieve together the plain and self-raising flours.
3. Place the margarine and sugar into a mixing bowl and beat together until light and creamy.
4. Scrape down the bowl to ensure that the mixture is being evenly beaten.
5. Add the egg a little at a time while beating the mixture.
6. Scrape down the bowl as before and continue beating.
7. Add the flour and fold through the creamed mixture.
8. Place the mixture into a piping bag.
9. Pipe into paper cases (or a greased and floured cup-cake tin). Fill to within 15 mm/½ inch of the top of the paper cases.
10. Bake at 205 °C/400 °F until cooked: 20 minutes approximately.

### CHERRY CAKES

Prepare as the base recipe above, adding:

1. 1–2 drops vanilla essence to the margarine and sugar after creaming (step 5).
2. 40 g/1½ oz glacé cherries cut into quarters and added to the cake mixture after folding in the flour (step 7).

**COCONUT CAKES** Prepare as for the base recipe above, and when cold brush over the tops with apricot purée. Coat the tops with white fondant then cover with desiccated coconut.

**HEALTH TIP**

*Butter may be used in place of margarine, but this would increase the saturated fat content.*

### QUEEN CAKES

6 cakes

| | | |
|---|---|---|
| 50 g | margarine | 2 oz |
| 50 g | caster sugar | 2 oz |
| 1 | egg (size 3) | 1 |
| 40 g | plain flour | 1½ oz |
| 10 g | self-raising flour | ½ oz |
| | pieces of glacé cherry, angelica and flaked almonds | |

Prepare as stated in the base recipe above. Decorate the tops of the cakes with the glacé cherry, angelica and flaked almonds before baking.

## 12.25 VICTORIA SANDWICH

**HEALTH TIP**

*Butter may be used in place of margarine, but this would increase the saturated fat content.*

**CHEF'S TIP**

*Never use chilled or cold ingredients as the mixture is likely to curdle when adding the egg.*

**CHEF'S TIP**

*If a mixture begins to curdle before all the egg has been used, add a little of the recipe flour with each further addition of egg to absorb the surface liquid.*

1 × 6 portion cake

### BASE INGREDIENTS

| | | |
|---|---|---|
| 150 g | margarine | 6 oz |
| 150 g | caster sugar | 6 oz |
| 3 | eggs (size 3) | 3 |
| 100 g | plain flour | 4 oz |
| 50 g | self-raising flour | 2 oz |
| 50 g | raspberry jam | 2 oz |

### BASE METHOD

1. Ensure the ingredients are at a temperature of 21–22 °C/70–71 °F.
2. Sieve together the plain and self-raising flours.
3. Place the margarine and sugar into a mixing bowl and beat together until light and creamy.
4. Scrape down the bowl to ensure that the mixture is being evenly beaten.
5. Add the egg a little at a time while beating the mixture.
6. Scrape down the bowl as before and continue beating.
7. Add the flour and fold through the creamed mixture.
8. Divide the mixture into two greased and floured cake tins (175 mm/6¾ inch diameter).
9. Bake at 185 °C/365 °F until cooked: 25 minutes approximately.
10. When cooked, allow to cool slightly then turn out onto a cooling wire. Allow to become cold.
11. Sandwich the two cakes together with the jam.
12. Dredge over the top with icing sugar.

## 12.26 FRUIT CAKE

**HEALTH TIP**

*Cakes are high in fat and sugar.*

**HEALTH TIP**

*Butter may be used in place of margarine, but this would increase the saturated fat content.*

1 × 6 portion cake

### BASE INGREDIENTS

| | | |
|---|---|---|
| 100 g | margarine | 4 oz |
| 100 g | caster sugar | 4 oz |
| 3 | eggs (size 3) | 3 |
| 100 g | plain flour | 4 oz |
| 50 g | self-raising flour | 2 oz |
| 150 g | clean, dry sultanas | 6 oz |

### BASE METHOD

1. Ensure the ingredients are at a temperature of 21–22 °C/70–71 °F.
2. Sieve together the plain and self-raising flours.
3. Place the margarine and sugar into a mixing bowl and beat together until light and creamy.
4. Scrape down the bowl to ensure that the mixture is being evenly beaten.
5. Add the egg a little at a time while beating the mixture.
6. Scrape down the bowl as before and continue beating.
7. Add the flour and fold through the creamed mixture.
8. Carefully blend through the fruit.
9. Line a suitable size cake tin with paper.
10. Place the mixture into the tin, then lightly smooth down the top.
11. Bake at 180 °C/355 °F until cooked: 1 hour approximately.
12. Allow to cool slightly then turn out onto a cooling wire and allow to become cold.

# 12.27 SWISS ROLL

### CHEF'S TIP

*Avoid overcooking. Even short periods of overcooking can result in a Swiss roll which breaks when rolling up.*

### HEALTH TIP

*Swiss rolls are high in sugar and quite high in fat.*

### CHEF'S TIP

*Replacing a small quantity of the plain flour with self-raising flour helps to counteract the loss of aeration caused by handling. Use 65 g ($2\frac{1}{2}$ oz) plain flour and 10 g ($\frac{1}{2}$ oz) self-raising flour both thoroughly mixed together.*

## BASE METHOD

1. Prepare the basic sponge:
   a) Sieve the flour, together with any cocoa powder.
   b) Place the eggs and sugar into a mixing bowl.
   c) Warm the eggs and sugar over hot water.
   d) Whisk the eggs and sugar until very light and fluffy (ribbon stage).
   e) Add any colour and lightly stir through the mixture.
   f) Carefully fold through the flour.
2. Line a baking tray (300 × 200 mm/12 × 8 inches) with lightly greased greaseproof paper.
3. Spread the sponge mixture onto the baking tray.
4. Bake at 235 °C/455 °F until cooked: 4–5 minutes.
5. Invert onto a clean tea towel, or greaseproof paper sprinkled with caster sugar.
6. Remove the lining paper.
7. *Jam Swiss roll:* Spread with the jam, then carefully roll up, using the cloth or paper. Allow to cool then remove the cloth or paper.
   *Chocolate Swiss roll:* Place a sheet of greaseproof paper on top of the sponge. Roll up, with the paper inside the sponge, and allow to cool (inside the cloth or paper). Meanwhile, whip the cream, sugar and vanilla essence. Unroll the sponge, remove the paper then spread with the whipped cream. Re-roll the sponge and use as required.

## PLAIN SWISS ROLL

4–6 portions

| | | |
|---|---|---|
| 3 | eggs (size 3) | 3 |
| 75 g | caster sugar | 3 oz |
| 75 g | plain flour | 3 oz |
| 75 g | warmed raspberry jam | 3 oz |

Prepare using the base method above.

## CHOCOLATE SWISS ROLL

4–6 portions

| | | |
|---|---|---|
| 3 | eggs (size 3) | 3 |
| 75 g | caster sugar | 3 oz |
| 50 g | plain flour | 2 oz |
| 15 g | cocoa powder | $\frac{1}{2}$ oz |
| | chocolate colour | |
| | *Filling:* | |
| 200 ml | whipping cream | 8 fl oz |
| 15 g | caster sugar | $\frac{1}{2}$ oz |
| 2–3 drops | vanilla essence | 2–3 drops |

Prepare using the base method above.

## 12.28 SPONGE BISCUITS

**HEALTH TIP**

*Sponge biscuits are high in sugar and quite high in fat.*

**CHEF'S TIP**

*Replacing a small quantity of the plain flour with self-raising flour helps to counteract the loss of aeration caused by handling. Use 115 g($4\frac{1}{2}$ oz) plain flour and 10 g($\frac{1}{2}$ oz) self-raising flour both thoroughly mixed together with the strong flour.*

20 biscuits approximately

### BASE INGREDIENTS

| | | |
|---|---|---|
| 3 | eggs (size 3) | 3 |
| 150 g | caster sugar | 6 oz |
| 125 g | plain flour | 5 oz |
| 25 g | strong flour | 1 oz |

### BASE METHOD

1. Prepare the basic sponge:
   a) Sieve together the plain and strong flours.
   b) Place the eggs and sugar into a mixing bowl, and warm over hot water.
   c) Whisk the eggs and sugar until very light and fluffy (ribbon stage).
   d) Carefully fold through the flour.
2. Place the mixture into a piping bag fitted with a plain tube: 12 mm/$\frac{1}{2}$ inch in diameter.
3. Pipe out into round/finger biscuits onto a sheet of greaseproof paper.
4. Invert the biscuits onto a layer of caster sugar then press lightly with the fingers.
5. Carefully lift off the sugar and place onto a baking tray.
6. Bake at 235 °C/455 °F until cooked: 4 minutes approximately.
7. Dampen the back of the paper to remove the biscuits.

## 12.29 GÉNOISE SPONGE

**HEALTH TIP**

*Use the low-fat sponge on page 246 as an alternative to this traditional recipe.*

**HEALTH TIP**

*Butter may be used in place of margarine, but this would increase the saturated fat content.*

10–12 portions

### BASE INGREDIENTS

| | | |
|---|---|---|
| 5 | eggs (size 3) | 5 |
| 150 g | caster sugar | 6 oz |
| 150 g | plain flour | 6 oz |
| 60 g | melted margarine | $2\frac{1}{2}$ oz |

### BASE METHOD

1. Prepare the basic sponge:
   a) Sieve together the flour and any cocoa powder.
   b) Place the eggs and sugar into a mixing bowl, and warm over hot water.
   c) Whisk until very light and fluffy (ribbon stage).
   d) Stir through any flavouring, e.g. coffee essence.
   e) Carefully fold through the flour.
2. Carefully blend through the melted butter.
3. Place the mixture into a greased and floured cake tin: 250 mm/10 inches in diameter.
4. Bake at 200 °C/390 °F until cooked: 25–30 minutes.
5. Allow to cool slightly then turn out onto a cooling wire.

**CHOCOLATE GÉNOISE** Prepare as for génoise sponge above, but replace 25 g/1 oz of the flour with cocoa powder.

## 12.30 LOW-FAT SPONGE

This can be used in place of the traditional génoise for gâteaux. The sponge is also suitable for preparing steamed sponge puddings (page 90).

14–16 portions

### BASE INGREDIENTS

| | | |
|---|---|---|
| 280 g | caster sugar | $9\frac{1}{2}$ oz |
| 380 g | high-ratio cake flour | $13\frac{1}{2}$ oz |
| 250 ml | skimmed milk | 9 fl oz |
| 15 g | glycerine | $\frac{1}{2}$ oz |
| | egg colour (optional) | |
| 3 | eggs (size 3) | 3 |
| 20 g | baking powder | $\frac{3}{4}$ oz |

### BASE METHOD

1 Prepare the batter:
   a) Sieve 130 g/$4\frac{1}{2}$ oz caster sugar and 250 g/9 oz cake flour into a mixing bowl.
   b) Blend in the milk and glycerine and whisk to a smooth batter.
   c) Mix through any egg colour.
2 Place the eggs and remaining sugar into a mixing bowl, then warm over hot water.
3 Whisk the eggs and sugar until very light and fluffy (ribbon stage).
4 Carefully blend the batter through the whisked eggs.
5 Meanwhile sieve together the remaining flour, baking powder and any cocoa powder.
6 Carefully fold the flour through the egg and batter mixture.
7 Place the mixture into a greased and floured cake tin: 250 mm/10 inches in diameter.
8 Bake at 190 °C/375 °F until cooked: 25–30 minutes.
9 Allow to cool slightly then turn out onto a cooling wire and allow to become cold.

**CHEF'S TIP**

*Using glycerine will reduce staling, especially with a sponge which is low in fat.*

**CHOCOLATE SPONGE** Prepare as for the base recipe above, but replace 50 g/$1\frac{1}{2}$ oz of the flour with cocoa powder at step 5.

**COFFEE SPONGE** Prepare as for the base recipe above, but thoroughly dissolve 30 g/1 oz coffee extract or flavouring in the milk before use.

**ALMOND SPONGE** Prepare as for the base recipe above but replace 50 g/ $1\frac{1}{2}$ oz of the flour with ground almonds at step 5.

**TRADITIONAL PRACTICE**

*Use the traditional génoise sponge on page 245 instead of the low-fat sponge. This increases the fat content.*

## 12.31 CHOCOLATE GÂTEAU (low-fat)

**TRADITIONAL PRACTICE**

*Use the traditional sponge (page 245) in place of the lower-fat sponge. Also use stock syrup in place of the fruit juice, 400 g/14 oz of chocolate buttercream (page 38) in place of the whipped cream and decorate with 50–100 g/2–4 oz chocolate pieces. This substantially increases fat and sugar content.*

16 portions

### BASE INGREDIENTS

| | | |
|---|---|---|
| | low-fat chocolate génoise (opposite) | |
| 250 ml | whipping cream | 9 fl oz |
| 15 g | caster sugar | ½ oz |
| 2–3 drops | vanilla essence | 2–3 drops |
| 60 g | chocolate vermicelli | 2 oz |
| 30 g | grated chocolate | 1 oz |
| 120 ml | unsweetened fruit juice | 4 fl oz |

### BASE METHOD

1. Split the sponge through the centre then dampen with fruit juice.
2. Whip the cream with the sugar and vanilla essence.
3. Use two-thirds of the cream to sandwich together the two halves of sponge, and then apply a thin coat of cream around the sides.
4. Cover the sides with the vermicelli.
5. Spread the remaining cream on top of the gâteau then neatly mark with a serrated scraper.
6. Sprinkle the grated chocolate over the top.

**TRADITIONAL PRACTICE**

*Use the traditional sponge (page 245) in place of the lower-fat sponge. Also use stock syrup in place of the fruit juice, 400 g/14 oz of coffee buttercream (page 38) in place of the whipped cream and increase the toasted almonds to 100 g/4 oz. This substantially increases fat and sugar content.*

## COFFEE GÂTEAU (low-fat)

16 portions

| | | |
|---|---|---|
| | low-fat coffee génoise (opposite) | |
| 250 ml | whipping cream | 9 fl oz |
| 15 g | caster sugar | ½ oz |
| 2–3 drops | vanilla essence | 2–3 drops |
| 90 g | nibbed almonds | 3 oz |
| 60 g | toasted, flaked almonds | 2 oz |
| 120 ml | unsweetened fruit juice | 4 fl oz |

1. Proceed as for chocolate gâteau above (steps 1–3) using coffee génoise.
2. Cover the sides with nibbed almonds.
3. Spread the remaining cream on top of the gâteau, then neatly mark with a serrated scraper.
4. Decorate the top with the toasted, flaked almonds.

## APRICOT GÂTEAU (low-fat)

16 portions

| | | |
|---|---|---|
| | low-fat génoise (opposite) | |
| 24 | dried apricots | 24 |
| 600 g | apricot fromage frais | 1 lb 5 oz |

1. Poach 16 of the apricots (page 82) and allow to cool.
2. Finely dice the remaining apricots.
3. Prepare the sponge following the base method above, and carefully add the diced apricots after folding in the flour at step 6.
4. When cold, split the sponge into two or three layers, then dampen with the apricot poaching liquor. A little apricot liqueur may also be added to the liquor.
5. Sandwich together the sponge layers with half the fromage frais.
6. Decorate the sides and top of the gâteau with the remaining fromage frais and poached apricots.

## 12.32 OVEN SCONES

10 scones

### BASE INGREDIENTS

**PLAIN SCONES**

| | | |
|---|---|---|
| 200 g | plain flour | 8 oz |
| 10 g | baking powder | $\frac{1}{2}$ oz |
| 25 ml | oil | 1 fl oz |
| 30 g | caster sugar | $1\frac{1}{4}$ oz |
| 1 | egg (size 3) | 1 |
| 100 ml | skimmed milk | 4 fl oz |

**WHOLEMEAL SCONES**

| | | |
|---|---|---|
| 200 g | wholemeal flour | 8 oz |
| 10 g | baking powder | $\frac{1}{2}$ oz |
| 25 ml | oil | 1 fl oz |
| 30 g | caster sugar | $1\frac{1}{4}$ oz |
| 1 | egg (size 3) | 1 |
| 125 ml | skimmed milk | 5 fl oz |

### BASE METHOD

1. Thoroughly mix together the flour and baking powder.
2. Place the oil, sugar, egg and milk into a mixing bowl and whisk until combined.
3. Add the flour and lightly mix to form a soft, sticky dough.
4. Scrape out onto a board dusted with self-raising flour.
5. Dust over the top with flour, then roll out to 25 mm/1 inch thickness. Avoid absorbing additional flour into the dough when rolling out.
6. Cut out the scones with a plain cutter and place onto a lightly greased baking tray.
7. Leave plain or brush over the tops with eggwash.
8. Lightly stab with a fork and allow to rest for 15 minutes approximately.
9. Bake at 240 °C/465 °F until cooked: 12–15 minutes.

**FRUIT SCONES (sultana, raisin, currant scones)** Prepare as for plain scones above, adding 50 g/2 oz selected clean fruit with the flour at step 3.

**TRADITIONAL PRACTICE**

*Use 50 g/2 oz butter instead of oil and rub into the flour after step 1. Also increase the sugar to 50 g/2 oz and use 75 ml/3 fl oz whole milk instead of skimmed milk. This increases both fat and sugar content.*

**CHEF'S TIP**

*The scone mixture should be very soft. Keeping the scone mixture soft, with as little handling as possible, is important in producing high quality scones.*

## 12.33 MERINGUE

**HEALTH TIP**

*Meringue is very high in sugar.*

**CHEF'S TIP**

*Ensure all equipment is scrupulously clean and free from grease. The most common reason for a poor meringue mixture is the presence of grease. Even traces of grease on equipment will prevent a good meringue being made.*

**HEALTH TIP**

*All of these dishes are high in fat and sugar.*

4–6 portions

### BASE INGREDIENTS

| | | |
|---|---|---|
| 4 | egg whites (size 3) | 4 |
| 200 g | caster sugar | 8 oz |
| | small pinch salt | |

### BASE METHOD

1. Thoroughly clean the scale pan, whisk, bowl and any spoons.
2. Scald the utensils in very hot water then dry with a clean grease-free cloth.
3. Place the egg whites into the whisking bowl and add the pinch of salt.
4. Add a small quantity of recipe sugar: 25 g/1 oz approximately.
5. Whisk the whites adding two-thirds of the sugar in small quantities until a firm meringue is produced. Add the sugar at intervals of 20 seconds approximately.
6. Add the remaining sugar and gently fold through the meringue.

### MERINGUE SHELLS

1. Prepare the meringue as stated in the base recipe above.
2. Line a baking tray with greaseproof paper.
3. Place the meringue in a piping bag fitted with a plain tube.
4. Pipe out the meringue into oval or round shapes onto the lined tray and dredge over the tops with caster sugar.
5. Bake in a cool oven (120 °C/248 °F approximately) until dry and crisp without developing colour.

### MERINGUES WITH ICE-CREAM

4 portions

| | | |
|---|---|---|
| 8 | meringue shells (above) | 8 |
| 4 | scoops vanilla ice-cream | 4 |
| 8 | wafer biscuits | 8 |
| | whipped cream | |

1. Place each scoop of ice-cream between two shells.
2. Dress in coupes and decorate with rosettes of cream.
3. Accompany with the wafer biscuits.

**SMALL VACHERIN SHELLS** Prepare as for meringue shells above but pipe out into oval or round cases.

### FRUIT VACHERINS

4 portions

| | | |
|---|---|---|
| 4 | vacherin shells (above) | 4 |
| 100 g | drained fruit salad | 4 oz |
| | whipped cream | |
| | fruit glaze (optional) | |

1. Pipe a little whipped cream into each vacherin case.
2. Decorate with the fruit salad.
3. Coat with a little fruit glaze (page 38) if required.

# 12.34 BREAD ROLLS

**CHEF'S TIP**

*To produce good quality rolls, it is important to observe the time/temperature guidelines.*

**TEMPERATURE FORMULA**

*To obtain a required dough temperature the following formula is used to determine the temperature of the water to be added (example as in recipe):*

*a) Measure the flour temperature: e.g. 18 °C/66 °F.*

*b) Multiply required dough temperature by 2: i.e. 24 °C × 2 = 48 °C/ 76 °F × 2 = 152 °F.*

*c) Subtract the flour temperature (a) from total (b): to obtain water temperature: 48 − 18 °C = 30 °C/ 152 − 66 °F = 86 °F.*

15 rolls

## BASE INGREDIENTS

**PLAIN BREAD ROLLS**

| | | |
|---|---|---|
| 500 g | strong white flour | $1\frac{1}{4}$ lb |
| 10 g | salt | $\frac{1}{2}$ oz |
| 10 g | margarine | $\frac{1}{2}$ oz |
| 15 g | yeast | $\frac{1}{2}$ oz |
| 280 ml | water | 11 fl oz |

**WHOLEMEAL BREAD ROLLS**

| | | |
|---|---|---|
| 500 g | strong wholemeal flour | $1\frac{1}{4}$ lb |
| 10 g | salt | $\frac{1}{2}$ oz |
| 10 g | margarine | $\frac{1}{2}$ oz |
| 20 g | yeast | $\frac{3}{4}$ oz |
| 300 ml | water | 12 fl oz |

## BASE METHOD

1 Thoroughly mix together the dry ingredients, i.e. flour, salt and any milk powder.
2 Add the fat and rub into the flour.
3 Measure the water and warm to the correct temperature: 30 °C/86 °F (assuming flour is room temperature – see *temperature formula*).
4 Break down the yeast in some of the water and add to the flour.
5 Add almost all the remaining water, keeping back a small quantity to correct the consistency if required.
6 Mix the dough thoroughly to produce a smooth, pliable, elastic-like texture. The dough should leave the fingers cleanly without any wet stickiness.
7 Cover the dough and allow to ferment at 24 °C/76 °F.
*Plain rolls:*
a) Allow to ferment for 45 minutes then *knock back* (fold and press down firmly with the knuckles three or four times).
b) Re-cover and allow to ferment for a further 15 minutes.
Total time: 1 hour.
*Wholemeal rolls:*
a) Allow to ferment for 30 minutes then *knock back* (see (a) above).
b) Re-cover and allow to ferment for a further 15 minutes.
Total time: 45 minutes.
8 Divide the dough into 50 g/2 oz pieces then mould into ball shapes.
9 Place onto a lightly greased tray and allow to prove in a little steam until doubled in size: 30–40 minutes at 28 °C/83 °F approximately.
10 Bake at 235 °C/455 °F until crisp and golden brown: 12–15 minutes.
11 When baked, remove from the oven and place onto a cooling wire.

# 12.35 YEAST BUNS

### HEALTH TIP

*Buns are quite high in fat and sugar.*

### CHEF'S TIP

*To produce good quality rolls, it is important to observe the time/temperature guidelines.*

### TEMPERATURE FORMULA

*To obtain a required dough temperature the following formula is used to determine the temperature of the water to be added (example as in recipe):*

*a) Measure the flour temperature: e.g. 18 °C/66 °F.*

*b) Multiply required dough temperature by 2: i.e. 27 °C x 2 = 54 °C/ 81 °F x 2 = 162 °F.*

*c) Subtract the flour temperature (a) from total (b): to obtain water temperature: 54 − 18 °C = 36 °C/ 162 − 66 °F = 96 °F.*

## PLAIN BUNS

16 buns

### BASE INGREDIENTS

| | | |
|---|---|---|
| 500 g | strong white flour | $1\frac{1}{4}$ lb |
| 5 g | salt | $\frac{1}{4}$ oz |
| 75 g | caster sugar | 3 oz |
| 75 g | margarine | 3 oz |
| 25 g | yeast | 1 oz |
| 250 ml | water | $\frac{1}{2}$ pt |

### BASE METHOD: PREPARING THE DOUGH

1. Thoroughly mix together the dry ingredients, i.e. flour, salt, sugar and any milk powder.
2. Add the fat and rub into the flour.
3. Measure the water and warm to the correct temperature, i.e. 36 °C/96 °F (assuming flour is room temperature – see *temperature formula*).
4. Break down the yeast in some of the water and add to the flour.
5. Add almost all the remaining water, keeping back a small quantity to correct the consistency if required.
6. Mix the dough thoroughly to produce a smooth, pliable, elastic-like texture. The dough should leave the fingers cleanly without any wet stickiness.
7. Cover the dough and allow to ferment at 27 °C/81 °F for 45 minutes.
8. Knock back (fold and press down firmly with the knuckles three or four times).
9. Recover and allow to ferment for a further 15 minutes. Total time: 1 hour.

### BASE METHOD: COOKING THE YEAST BUNS

10. Divide the dough into 50 g/2 oz pieces then mould into ball shapes.
11. Place onto a lightly greased tray and allow to prove in a little steam until doubled in size: 30–40 minutes at 28 °C/83 °F approximately.
12. Bake at 235 °C/455 °F until crisp and golden brown: 12–15 minutes.
13. When baked, place onto a cooling wire.

**CURRANT BUNS** Prepare as for the base recipe above, adding 75 g/3 oz clean, dry currants to the dough after step 6. Brush over with **bun wash** (1 egg, 40 g/$1\frac{3}{4}$ oz sugar and 150 ml/6 fl oz milk whisked together) when removing from the oven.

**DEVON SPLITS** Prepare as for plain buns above. When cold, cut through the top of each bun to form a split, and pipe in a little raspberry jam. Fill with whipped cream, then dust over the tops with icing sugar.

**SWISS BUNS** Prepare as for plain buns above, but divide into 40 g/$1\frac{3}{4}$ oz pieces (step 10). Mould into ball shapes, then roll into finger shapes. When cold, coat the buns with lemon-flavoured fondant.

**HEALTH TIP**

*Buns are quite high in fat and sugar.*

**HEALTH TIP**

*Butter may be used in place of margarine, but this would increase the saturated fat content.*

## CHELSEA BUNS

16 buns

| | | |
|---|---|---|
| | plain bun dough (page 251) | |
| 25 g | melted margarine | 1 oz |
| | *Filling:* | |
| 50 g | currants | 2 oz |
| 50 g | sultanas | 2 oz |
| 10 g | mixed peel | $\frac{1}{2}$ oz |
| 25 g | caster sugar | 1 oz |
| | good pinch mixed spice | |

1 Prepare the basic bun dough, and divide it into two pieces.
2 Roll out each piece into a square: 10 mm/$\frac{1}{2}$ inch in thickness.
3 Brush the surface of the dough with melted margarine.
4 Mix together the ingredients for the filling, then sprinkle evenly over the surface of the dough.
5 Roll up each piece of dough like a Swiss roll, then brush over the surfaces with melted margarine.
6 Cut into 25 mm/1 inch thick slices.
7 Place close together on a lightly greased baking tray.
8 Prove and bake as stated for plain buns.
9 When removing from the oven, lightly brush with melted margarine and sprinkle with caster sugar.

**HEALTH TIP**

*Buns are quite high in fat and sugar.*

## HOT CROSS BUNS

16 buns

| | | |
|---|---|---|
| 500 g | strong white flour | $1\frac{1}{4}$ lb |
| $2\frac{1}{2}$ g | salt | $\frac{1}{2}$ tsp |
| 60 g | caster sugar | $2\frac{1}{2}$ oz |
| 20 g | milk powder | $\frac{3}{4}$ oz |
| 60 g | margarine | $2\frac{1}{2}$ oz |
| $\frac{1}{2}$ | egg (size 3) | $\frac{1}{2}$ |
| 25 g | yeast | 1 oz |
| 250 ml | water | $\frac{1}{2}$ pt |
| 50 g | currants | 2 oz |
| 50 g | sultanas | 2 oz |
| 15 g | mixed peel | $\frac{3}{4}$ oz |
| | good pinch mixed spice | |
| | *Crossing mixture:* | |
| 100 g | plain flour | 4 oz |
| 25 g | white fat | 1 oz |
| 90 ml | water | $3\frac{3}{4}$ fl oz |
| | pinch baking powder | |

1 Prepare the basic bun dough as for Process 12.35 (page 251), but:
   a) add the mixed spice to the dry ingredients (step 1)
   b) add the egg the same time as the water (step 5)
   c) add the fruit and peel to the dough after step 6.
2 Prepare the crossing mixture: cream together the flour, fat and baking powder then add the water while beating to produce a thin paste. Place the mixture into a piping bag.
3 When the buns are fully proved, pipe a cross on each bun.
4 Bake as stated then brush over with bun wash (see currant buns: page 251) when removing from the oven.

## BATH BUNS

24 buns approximately

| | | |
|---|---|---|
| | plain bun dough (page 251) | |
| 200 g | sultanas | 8 oz |
| 100 g | mixed peel | 4 oz |
| 100 g | sugar nibs | 4 oz |

1 Prepare as for plain buns (Process 12.35: page 251) and add the sultanas, peel and sugar nibs to the dough after step 6.
2 Divide the dough into 24 rough-shaped pieces and place onto the lightly greased baking tray.
3 Sprinkle a few sugar nibs over each bun after proving.
4 Glaze with bun wash when removing from the oven (see currant buns: page 251).

## 12.36 CROISSANTS

**HEALTH TIP**

*Croissants are high in fat, especially saturated fat.*

**HEALTH TIP**

*Butter may be used in place of margarine, but this would increase the saturated fat content.*

24 croissants

### BASE INGREDIENTS

| | | |
|---|---|---|
| 500 g | strong white flour | $1\frac{1}{4}$ lb |
| 5 g | salt | $\frac{1}{4}$ oz |
| 10 g | caster sugar | $\frac{1}{2}$ oz |
| 20 g | milk powder | $\frac{3}{4}$ oz |
| 50 g | margarine | 2 oz |
| 25 g | yeast | 1 oz |
| 250 ml | cold water | $\frac{1}{2}$ pt |
| 1 | egg | 1 |
| 200 g | butter or pastry margarine | 8 oz |

### BASE METHOD

1 Thoroughly mix together the dry ingredients, i.e. flour, salt, sugar and milk powder.
2 Add the margarine and rub into the flour.
3 Break down the yeast in some of the water and add to the flour.
4 Add the egg and almost all the remaining water, keeping back a small quantity to correct the consistency if required.
5 Mix the dough thoroughly to produce a smooth, pliable, elastic-like texture. The dough should leave the fingers cleanly without any wet stickiness.
6 Cover and allow the dough to rest for 20 minutes.
7 Finish the dough as for traditional puff pastry (page 27) using the additional butter or pastry margarine and giving three half turns. Allow 15 minutes between each turn.
8 When the dough is ready, roll out into a rectangle: 5 mm/$\frac{1}{4}$ inch in thickness.
9 Cut into two strips 125 mm/6 inches wide.
10 Cut each strip into triangles with the base of each triangle measuring 125 mm/6 inches approximately.
11 Roll up each triangle starting at the base, then bend to form a crescent.
12 Place onto a lightly greased baking tray then brush with eggwash.
13 Allow to prove (not too warm: 25 °C/77 °F) until doubled in size.
14 Bake at 240 °C/464 °F until crisp and golden brown: 10–15 minutes.

# 12.37 PREPARING BABAS AND SAVARINS

**HEALTH TIP**

*Savarins and babas are high in fat and sugar.*

**TRADITIONAL PRACTICE**

*Use butter in place of margarine. This increases the saturated fat content.*

## BASIC DOUGH FOR BABAS AND SAVARINS

8 portions

### BASE INGREDIENTS

| | | |
|---|---|---|
| 1 | egg (size 3) | 1 |
| 2 | egg yolks | 2 |
| 25 g | caster sugar | 1 oz |
| 100 g | strong flour | 4 oz |
| 50 g | softened margarine | 2 oz |
| | *Ferment:* | |
| 100 g | strong flour | 4 oz |
| 5 g | milk powder | $\frac{1}{4}$ oz |
| 10 g | yeast | $\frac{1}{2}$ oz |
| 125 ml | water | $\frac{1}{4}$ pt |

### BASE METHOD

1 Prepare the ferment:
   a) Mix together the flour and milk powder.
   b) Warm the water to 40 °C/104 °F.
   c) Break down the yeast in some of the water.
   d) Add to the flour and whisk to a smooth batter.
   e) Ferment in a warm place for 30 minutes approximately.
2 Add the egg, egg yolks and sugar and mix together.
3 Add the flour and thoroughly mix together.
4 Add the softened margarine in three parts, beating thoroughly between each addition.

## RUM BABAS

8 babas

| | | |
|---|---|---|
| | basic dough (above) | |
| 50 g | currants | 2 oz |
| 300 ml | soaking syrup (opposite) | 12 fl oz |
| 50 g | apricot glaze (page 38) | 2 oz |
| 200 ml | whipped cream | 8 fl oz |
| | glacé cherries, pieces of angelica | |

**CHEF'S TIP**

*Babas and savarins which have been baked and stored for 12–24 hours absorb the syrup better than when freshly baked.*

1 Prepare the dough as stated in the base recipe, then mix through the currants (after step 4).
2 Grease 8 dariole moulds, then pipe in the mixture so each mould is only half full.
3 Fully prove until doubled in volume.
4 Bake at 235 °C/455 °F until cooked: 20 minutes approximately.
5 Remove from the moulds and allow to cool.
6 Prepare the syrup and flavour with rum.
7 Soak the babas in the syrup until moist through to the centre.
8 Brush over each baba with the hot apricot glaze.
9 Decorate with the cream, glacé cherries and angelica. A little syrup may also be added to the plate or serving dish.

## SAVARIN

8 portions

| | | |
|---|---|---|
| | basic dough (opposite) | |
| 300 ml | soaking syrup (below) | 12 fl oz |
| 50 g | apricot glaze (page 38) | 2 oz |
| 200 ml | whipped cream | 8 fl oz |
| | glacé cherries, pieces of angelica | |

1 Prepare the dough as stated in the base recipe opposite.
2 Grease a savarin mould, then pipe in the mixture, only half filling the mould.
3 Fully prove until doubled in volume.
4 Bake at 235 °C/455 °F until cooked: 20–25 minutes.
5 Remove from the mould and allow to cool.
6 Prepare the syrup.
7 Soak the savarins in the syrup until moist through to the centre.
8 Brush over the surface with hot apricot glaze.
9 Decorate with the cream, glacé cherries and angelica. A little syrup may also be added to the plate or serving dish.

**CHEF'S TIP**

*Babas and savarins which have been baked and stored for 12–24 hours absorb the syrup better than when freshly baked.*

**FRUIT SAVARIN** Fill the savarin with fruit salad and decorate to taste. A suitable liqueur (orange, cherry, blackcurrant) may also be added to the syrup.

## SOAKING SYRUP

Yield: 300 ml/12 fl oz approximately

| | | |
|---|---|---|
| 250 ml | water | ½ pt |
| 100 g | sugar | 4 oz |
| ½ | lemon | ½ |
| ½ | orange | ½ |
| ½ | bay leaf | ½ |
| ¼ | cinnamon stick | ¼ |
| 2–3 | coriander seeds | 2–3 |
| 2 | cloves | 2 |

1 Remove and keep the zest from the lemon and orange.
2 Place the water, sugar, zest, bay leaf, cinnamon stick, coriander seeds and cloves into a saucepan.
3 Bring to the boil and simmer for 2–3 minutes.
4 Allow to cool, then strain.
5 Squeeze the juice from the lemon and orange and add to the syrup.
6 Add the liqueur, e.g. rum, kirsch, cassis.

**CHEF'S TIP**

*The syrup may be prepared hot, i.e. add the fruit juice to the boiling syrup, strain, and allow to cool slightly before adding the liqueur.*

# GLOSSARY

| | |
|---|---|
| **à la broche** | spit-roasted. |
| **abattis de volaille** | offal from poultry – giblets, e.g. heart, liver, neck. |
| **abats** | offal – liver, kidneys, heart. |
| **agar-agar** | a setting agent prepared from seaweed. |
| **al dente** | a term used to describe lightly cooked pasta, and vegetables, which have a firm texture. |
| **appareil** | a prepared mixture of food. |
| **aromates** | aromatic herbs, spices and vegetables. |
| **aspic** | savoury jelly. |
| **au four** | baked in an oven. |
| **bain-marie** | 1. a piece of equipment containing a water bath: used to keep foods hot without burning.<br>2. a container used for the hot storage of sauces, soups, etc.<br>3. a shallow container of water used for cooking food slowly and without burning. |
| **bard (barder)** | to cover the surface of meat, poultry or game with slices of pork or bacon fat to prevent the flesh drying out when cooking (especially roasting). Increases the fat content of the item. |
| **baron** | a large joint of meat – *beef*: double sirloin of beef, *lamb*: saddle and two legs. |
| **barquette** | a small boat-shaped pastry tartlet. |
| **baste (arroser)** | to coat a joint or bird etc. with the roasting fat during cooking. Increases the fat content of the roast. |
| **bat out (battre)** | to flatten out pieces of flesh with a cutlet bat usually between polythene. |
| **bavarois** | a light-textured cold sweet traditionally set with gelatine. |
| **beard (ébarber)** | to remove the outer fringe or trail from shellfish, especially oysters. |
| **besan flour** | chick pea flour: high in fibre (7%), does not contain gluten and can be substituted for wheat flour in many soups, sauces and stews. |
| **beurre fondu** | melted butter. |
| **beurre manié** | a mixture of butter and flour which is used to thicken sauces, soups, stews and French-style peas. |
| **beurre noisette** | butter cooked until nut-brown and flavoured with lemon juice. |
| **bitoks** | a mixture of minced meat moulded into small hamburger shapes and grilled or shallow-fried. |
| **blanch (blanchir)** | 1. the first cooking of French-fried potatoes.<br>2. to immerse in boiling water, to either:<br>i) enable the removal of skin from tomatoes,<br>ii) enable the removal of tough tissue and membrane from sweetbreads prior to cooking, or<br>iii) make vegetables limp prior to braising.<br>3. to remove the initial scum when preparing stocks, cooking liquors or soups.<br>4. to help retain the colour of vegetables by plunging into boiling water and cooking for a short time.<br>5. to whiten bones or flesh. |
| **bombe** | a mixture of ice-creams frozen in a bombe mould. |
| **bouchée** | a small case made with puff pastry. |
| **bouillon** | unclarified stock. |
| **bouquet garni** | a faggot or bundle of herbs consisting of bay leaves, parsley stalks and thyme. |
| **brine** | a mixture of water, salt and saltpetre (and sometimes sugar and aromates) used for pickling beef, tongue, etc. |
| **brunoise** | small cubes, i.e. 1 mm/$\frac{1}{16}$ inch approximately. |
| **carbonnade** | a meat stew (usually beef) made with onions and beer. |
| **canapé** | a hot or cold savoury consisting of pieces of food served on a base of bread, toast or biscuit. |
| **cellulose** | a type of indigestible carbohydrate found in plant cell walls; contributes to the fibre content of food. |
| **cereals** | cultivated grasses; a rich source of dietary fibre, e.g. wheat, rice, rye and oats. |
| **chapelure** | browned breadcrumbs. |
| **charlotte** | a sweet mixture (usually bavarois) set in a charlotte mould. |
| **chauffant** | a basket in a saucepan of very hot, salted water; used mainly for reheating vegetables. |
| **chemiser** | to coat an item of food or line a mould with jelly. |
| **chiffonnade** | finely cut strips of food, e.g. lettuce or sorrel. |
| **chinois** | a conical strainer. |
| **clarification** | a mixture containing egg whites, used to clarify stocks or jellies. |
| **clarify** | to make clear, e.g. consommés, jellies. |
| **clouté** | studded, e.g. a studded onion (an onion encircled by a bay leaf and pierced with a clove). |
| **coat or mask (napper)** | to cover or coat with sauce. |
| **cocotte** | an oven-proof dish with a lid. |
| **compote** | poached fruit served in a bowl. |
| **concassé** | roughly chopped, e.g. tomatoes, parsley. |
| **consommé** | clear soup. |
| **contrefilet** | a piece of beef from a boned sirloin (situated across from the fillet). |
| **cook out** | the cooking of a roux before adding liquid. |
| **cordon** | a ribbon or thread of sauce circling a dish. |
| **côte** | rib or chop, e.g. côte de boeuf – rib of beef. |
| **coupe** | an individual glass serving bowl or a type of dessert served in individual glass bowls. |
| **court-bouillon** | a liquor for cooking fish. |
| **crêpe** | a pancake. |
| **cromesquis** | a mixture of cooked food, e.g. beef, chicken or game shaped into cylinders, wrapped in bacon, passed through batter and deep-fried. |
| **croquette** | a mixture of cooked food, e.g. beef, chicken or duchesse potato shaped into cylinders, passed through egg and breadcrumbs and deep-fried. |
| **croûtons** | a dice of crisp fried bread served with soup. |
| **crudités** | small, even-sized pieces of raw vegetables often served with a dip. |

**cullis (coulis)** a sauce made from a purée of fruit or vegetables.
**dariole** a small, cork-shaped mould.
**darne** a fish steak cut from a round fish, e.g. salmon or cod.
**daube** a type of stew consisting of large pieces of meat cooked under cover in an oven with wine, bacon, herbs, vegetables and orange peel.
**deglaze (deglacer)** to swill out a cooking utensil in which food has been cooked, using stock, wine or sauce etc. This is to retain the flavour of the sediment or soluble extracts.
**demi-glace** a refined brown sauce made by reducing down an equal quantity of rich brown stock and espagnole.
**dietary fibre** a combination of complex carbohydrates that pass through the digestive system largely unchanged.
**dishpaper** a lining paper *without* perforations, for service dishes.
**docker** a piece of equipment with several spikes used for stabbing pastry prior to baking.
**doily** a fancy lining paper for service dishes (usually *with* perforations).
**duxelle** very finely chopped mushrooms cooked with shallots in a little oil or butter.
**eggwash** eggs whisked with a little water. Often brushed over foods prior to baking (to develop a good brown colour) or used when coating foods with breadcrumbs (paner).
**enrich with butter (monter au beurre)** to add butter to sauces, soups or stews so as to add flavour and richness in taste. This significantly increases fat content.
**entrecôte** a steak cut from the contrefilet of beef (boned sirloin).
**escalope** a thin and flattened slice of meat, poultry or game.
**espagnole** basic brown sauce.
**estouffade** a rich brown beef stock or brown beef stew.
**farce** forcemeat or stuffing.
**fécule** starch flour, e.g. arrowroot, cornflour, potato flour or rice flour.
**ferment** to allow a yeast batter or dough to rest for a certain time at a specific temperature in order for the yeast to develop and multiply.
**fines herbes** mixed herbs, e.g. parsley, chives, chervil.
**flake** to break cooked fish into pieces.
**flame (flamber)** to set on fire a spirit (brandy, whisky or liqueur) within a cooking process.
**fleurons** puff pastry crescents.
**flûtes** slices cut from a thin French loaf, used as a garnish for soup.
**foie gras** large goose liver.
**frappé** chilled or iced, e.g. melon frappé.
**friandises** a name for petits fours.
**fricassée** a white stew made with fish, meat, poultry or vegetables cooked in sauce.
**friture** a frying-kettle.
**fromage blanc** a soft French cheese which varies from 1–8% in fat content.
**fromage frais** See *fromage blanc* above.
**froth** to coat a roast with flour just before cooking is completed, to achieve a good colour.
**fructose** sugar found in ripe fruit and honey.
**fumé** smoked, e.g. saumon fumé.
**garam masala** mixture of spices used in Indian dishes: coriander, cinnamon, cumin, cardamon, ginger, black pepper.
**gelatine** gum obtained from animal flesh used for setting jellies and bavarois. Not suitable for vegetarian dishes.
**ghee** clarified butter (Indian).
**gibier** game.
**gild (dorer)**
1. to allow a brown colour to develop.
2. to coat with eggwash prior to cooking in order to develop a brown colour.

**glace** ice or ice-cream.
**glaze (glacer)**
1. to brown a dish under a grill.
2. to coat a flan or tart with glaze.
3. to cook glazed vegetables.
4. to cover with fondant.
5. to sprinkle with sugar then caramelise under a grill or in a hot oven.

**glucose** a simple sugar found in plants, honey and blood.
**gluten** a vegetable protein found in wheat, rye, oats and barley.
**gnocchi** small savoury dumplings made with potato, choux paste or semolina.
**grate (râper)** to pass food through a grater.
**gratinate (gratiner)** to sprinkle with breadcrumbs or cheese and brown under a grill or in an oven.
**green** a term used for unsmoked bacon.
**griddle** to cook on a solid surface or plate, e.g. griddle scones.
**hors d'oeuvre** first course of a meal consisting of an individual dish or a selection of small items designed to stimulate the appetite.
**haché** chopped or minced.
**incise (ciseler)** to cut small incisions across the back of fish prior to grilling or shallow-frying.
**joint (découper)** to cut poultry or feathered game into suitable pieces for sautés, stews or pies.
**jardinière** vegetables cut into stick or baton shapes, e.g. 2 × 2 × 15 mm/$\frac{1}{8} \times \frac{1}{8} \times \frac{3}{4}$ inch approximately.
**julienne** thin strips, e.g. 1 mm/$\frac{1}{16}$ inch thick.
**jus lié** a light sauce, made from stock (usually veal) thickened with arrowroot. Often called 'thickened gravy'.
**lacto-ovo-vegetarian** a person who only eats plant foods and egg and milk products.
**lacto-vegetarian** a person who only eats plant foods and milk foods.
**lactose** the sugar in milk.
**lard (larder)** to insert strips of pork or bacon fat into raw flesh with special needles. Increases the fat content of the item.
**lardons** bâtons or dice of bacon used as a garnish.

| | |
|---|---|
| **lemon water** | a mixture of lemon juice and water used for storing peeled fruits and certain vegetables; to avoid discolouration. |
| **liaison** | a mixture of cream and egg yolks, used to thicken sauces, soups or stews. |
| **macédoine** | cube shapes, e.g. 5 mm/$\frac{1}{4}$ inch approximately. |
| **macerate (macérer)** | to soak food in wine or liqueur, often applied to fruits. |
| **maltose** | a sugar formed from starch. |
| **mandoline** | a machine used for slicing potatoes or vegetables. |
| **marinade** | a liquor used to increase tenderness and add flavour to meat, game or poultry. |
| **mignardises** | a name for petits fours. |
| **mirepoix** | a basic vegetable preparation consisting of roughly-chopped onion, carrot, celery, leek, thyme, bay leaf and parsley stalks. Used in many sauces, soups, stews and braised dishes. |
| **mise en place** | preparation prior to cooking or serving. |
| **noisette** | a cut of meat from a boned loin of lamb, mutton or venison. |
| **paysanne** | root vegetables cut into triangle, square or circle shapes approximately 10 mm/$\frac{1}{2}$ inch in size. |
| **plat à sauter** | a shallow pan with straight sides used for frying. |
| **pluches** | leaves or shreds of herbs, e.g. chervil, thyme. |
| **prove** | the final fermentation of yeast goods after shaping but prior to baking. |
| **pulses** | the dried seeds from pods of vegetables, e.g. beans. A rich source of dietary fibre. |
| **purée** | to make food into a fine mass or puree by passing it through a sieve or liquidiser. |
| **quark** | a skimmed-milk, soft cheese of German origin which is low in fat (1%). |
| **quenelles** | food moulded into egg-shapes, e.g. a mixture of finely diced or minced chicken, meat or vegetables. |
| **ragout** | a stew usually consisting of beef, venison or rabbit. |
| **ramekin** | a small tartlet usually containing cheese. |
| **ravier** | oblong hors d'oeuvre dish. |
| **réchauffer** | to reheat. |
| **reduce (réduire)** | to boil down a liquid or sauce, reducing its volume. |
| **refresh (rafraîchir)** | to cool food under cold running water. |
| **ribbon stage** | to whisk eggs and sugar until they are very light and fluffy. When held on the whisk the mixture shows fairly stiff peaks which drop slowly when held upright. |
| **rissoler** | to shallow-fry and develop colour on the surface of food; to brown. |
| **rocher** | a scoop of ice-cream. |
| **roux** | a mixture of fat and flour used to thicken sauces, soups and stews; high in fat. See *thickening paste.* |
| **sabayon** | a mixture of egg yolks and liquid (water, wine or vinegar) whisked over heat until very light and creamy – see *ribbon stage.* |
| **salamander** | a grill where food is placed *under* the heat source. |
| **salmis** | a stew of feathered game. |
| **salpicon** | small pieces of food, e.g. fish, shellfish, meat, poultry, game or vegetables, bound with a sauce. |
| **sauteuse** | a shallow pan with sloping sides used for frying and preparing sabayons etc. |
| **score** | to mark or cut the outer surface of a joint lightly, prior to roasting or pot-roasting. |
| **seal** | to expose the surface of flesh to high temperature cooking for a short period. This is done to develop flavour and colour but does not retain juices as is often stated. See *sear* below. |
| **sear** | to shallow-fry or oven-cook the surface of food until brown, to develop colour and flavour. This is a more accurate term than *seal,* as it does not imply that juices are being retained. |
| **season (assaisonner)** | to add salt or salt and pepper to food. |
| **sec, sèche** | dry. |
| **set** | to shallow-fry the outer surface of food so as to remove the raw appearance or to develop colour. |
| **sieve (passer)** | to pass food through a sieve. |
| **singe** | to brown; usually applied to foods prepared with a roux. |
| **sippets** | small pieces of dried bread served with soup. |
| **skim (dégraisser/dépouiller)** | to remove impurities (fat and scum) from the surface of a liquid. |
| **sodium alginate** | a setting agent obtained from seaweed. |
| **soubise** | a white onion sauce or purée. |
| **soufflé** | a very light sweet or savoury dish served either hot or cold. |
| **soy sauce** | a seasoning sauce made from fermented soya beans. |
| **spatula** | a flat wooden spoon. |
| **sucrose** | common sugar; sugar obtained from sugar cane and sugar beet. |
| **sweat (suer)** | to shallow-fry food; usually using a lid and avoiding colour development. |
| **tamis** | a fine cloth used for straining sauces and soups. |
| **tenderloin** | alternative name for a fillet of beef. |
| **terrine** | an earthenware casserole with a lid or a dish of meat or fish cooked in this type of dish. |
| **thickening paste** | a mixture of flour and liquid (stock, milk or wine) whisked to a paste: used to thicken sauces, soups and stews. A non-fat method for thickening liquids. |
| **timbale** | a deep, round dish. |
| **tranche** | a slice or rasher. |
| **tronçon** | a fish steak cut from a flat fish, e.g. turbot. |
| **truss (brider)** | to tie poultry and feathered game using a trussing needle and string, prior to cooking. |
| **turn (tourner)** | 1. to cut vegetables into barrel or olive shapes.<br>2. to cut a spiral design on mushrooms. |
| **vegan** | a person who does not eat any foods of animal origin, e.g. milk, cheese, eggs, honey, etc. |
| **vegetarian** | a person who does not eat animals of any kind nor any products derived from an animal carcase or flesh (e.g. gelatine, caviar, cheese containing animal rennet). |
| **zest (zeste)** | the rind of citrus fruits, e.g. lemon, orange, lime and grapefruit. |

# INDEX


Almond sauce 39
Anchovy sauce 34
Andalouse sauce 35
Angels on horseback 145
Antipasto di scampi 197
Apple
baked 233
baked with walnuts and raisins 233
baked in red wine 233
flan 236
fritters 183
pie 238
pulp/sauce 29
shallow-fried 168
stewed 105
tart 237
turnovers 239
Apricot
condé 217
dried – poached 82
fritters 183
gâteau (low-fat and traditional) 247
sauce 39
Arabian salad 205
Asparagus
boiling of 62
microwave cooked 192
rolled sandwiches 211
soup 48–9
Aspic jellies 23
Aubergine
and chick pea pepperpot 117
deep-fried 180
shallow-fried 165
Aurore sauce 34
Avocado
dressing 34
with vinaigrette 198

Baba Ganaouge 205
Bacon
carcase diagram 14
important points 14–15
Baked potatoes 232
Baked rice 235
Baking
apples 233
egg custard 234
information, key points 220–1
potatoes 232
powder 40
Banana
flan 236
fritters 183
shallow-fried 168
Banbury cakes 239
Bath buns 253
Batter
crêpe 170
frying 23
Bavarois
chocolate 213
fruit 213
vanilla 213
vegetarian types 213
Bean salad 203
Beef
and vegetable carbonnade 116
and vegetable and bean carbonnade 116
aspic 23
boiled French style 59
boiled with dumplings 58
braised 108–9
braised in red wine sauce 108–9
braised steaks 108–9
carbonnade 116
carcase diagram 9
chilli con carne 99
classification of 4, 9, 10
cold decorated sirloin with salad 209
common cuts from 15
consommé 51
curry (European) 97
entrecôte Bohemian style 152
fillet steak with whisky and herbs 159
goulash 96
grilled entrecôte steak 137
grilled fillet steak garni 137
ham on bread 152
hamburgers 153
important points 10
olives 108–9
pot-roasted fillet of beef 130
roast 126
salad (main course) 206
sirloin steak MacFarlane 157
sirloin steak with red and green peppers 161
steak and kidney pie 226
steak, kidney and mushroom pie 226
steak, kidney and mushroom pudding 86
steak and kidney pudding 86
stew 95
stock 36
strogonoff 163
Beetroot
boiling of 65
steamed (high-pressure) 91
steamed (low-pressure) 85
Berrichonne potatoes 123
Best end of lamb, preparation of 12
Beurre manié 37
Biscuits, sponge 245
Blackberry, tart 237
Blanquettes, lower-fat and trad. 102
Boiled beef
and dumplings 58
French style 59
Boiled fowl with onion sauce 59
Boiled gammon, cabbage and parsley 58
Boiling
eggs 52
flower, stem and fruit vegetables 62
fresh meats or poultry 59
glazed vegetables 66
green leaf and leguminous vegetables 60
information, key points 42–3
pulse vegetables 67
rice 53
root vegetables 64
Bolonaise sauce
low-fat 29
traditional 29
Bolton hotpot 115
Bouchées
chicken, game, seafood 222
vegetarian 222
Bouquet garni 24
Braising
cabbage 118
celery 118–19
chicory 120
fennel 118–19
information, key points 106–7
leeks 118–19
lettuce 118–19
onions 118–19
ox liver with onions 114
pickled meats and offal 110
potatoes 122–3
poultry and feathered game 111
red cabbage 120
red meats and venison 108–9
rice 121
rice (microwaved) 186
sweetbreads (white and brown) 113
white meats 112
Brandy
cream 40
sauce 40
Bread and butter pudding 214
microwaved 193
Bread rolls 250
Bread sauce 29
Broad beans, boiling of 60–1
Broccoli, boiling of 62
microwaved 192
Broths, various 44
Brown sauce
lower-fat 30
traditional 30
Brussels sprouts
boiling of 60
steamed 92
Mornay 61
Brown stock 36
Buns (choux) cream 238
Buns (yeast)
Bath 253
Chelsea, hot cross 252
Devon splits, Swiss 251
plain, currant 251
Butter beans, boiling of 67
Buttercreams, various 38
Buttered vegetables 61, 63, 65

Cabbage
boiling of 60
braised (red) 120
braised (white) 118
English style 61
microwave cooked 191
steamed 92

Cabinet pudding 234
Caesar salad 205
Cakes
Banbury 239
cherry 242
coconut 242
cup 242
Eccles 239
fruit 243
queen 242
Swiss roll 244
Victoria sandwich 243
Californian salad 205
Canapé
Bristol 169
Diane 145
Fedora 145
Nina (grilled) 145
Nina (shallow-fried) 169
Caper sauce 34
Carbonnades of beef 116
Carrot
boiling of 64
glazed 66
microwave cooked 190
Cauliflower
boiling of 62
microwave cooked 191
soup 48–9
Caviar 200
Celery
braised 118–19
soup 48–9
Cereals, fibre content of 6
Champignol potatoes 123
Chantilly cream 40
Charlotte
Montreuil 214
Moscovite 214
royale 214
russe 214
Cheese
and egg flan 228
and vegetable potatoes 232
fat content of 5
omelette 150
sandwiches 210
sauce 34
soufflé 241
straws 223
Chelsea buns 252
Cherry cakes 242
Chestnut stuffing 37
Chicken
and feathered game, trussing 18
aspic 23
bouchées 222
broth 44
chasseur 161
consommé 51
crêpes 170
curry (Indian) 98
cutting for sauté 18
deep-fried croquettes 179
deep-fried in basket 178
fricassée à l'ancienne 101
fricassée (lower-fat and trad.) 101
grilled 141
grilled, devilled 141
grilling of 141
hotpot 115
mousse/mousseline 25
pie 227
poached, English style 80
poached suprême with mushrooms 79
poached with braised rice 80
pot-roasted 131
roast 128
salpicon 28
sandwiches 210
stir-fried honey lemon 154
stock 36
suprêmes, preparation of 18
suprême Swedish style 160
suprême Tsarina 79
suprême with melon and prawns 79
suprême with white wine and tarragon 162
various sizes 16
vol-au-vents 222
Chicory, braised 120
Chilli con carne 99
Chipped potatoes 181
Chocolate
bavarois 213
buttercream 38
gâteau (low-fat and trad.) 247
mousse 212
sauces 39
soufflé 240
Choux paste gnocchi 73
Choux pastry 26
Christmas pudding (trad. and vegetarian) 89
Coconut cakes 242
Cod steak, poached (Jerusalem artichoke and lime) 74
Coffee buttercream 38
Coffee gâteau (low-fat and trad.) 247
Cold preparations, information and key points 194
Coleslaw 204
Commercially prepared sausages 200
Condé
apricot 217
peach 217
pineapple 217
Consommé, various 51
Contrefilet, preparation of 10
Corn on the cob
boiling of 62
with butter 63
Cornish pasties 229
Cottage cheese and chive sandwiches 210
Coupe
Alexandra 219
Andalouse 219
Edna-may 219
Jacques 219
Jamaique 219
Venus 219
Courgette
and avocado mousselines 207
deep-fried 180
Provence style 166
shallow-fried 165
with herbs 165
Cream cheese, onion and ham pinwheel sandwiches 211
Cranberries, stewed 105
Cranberry sauce 31
Cream buns (choux) 238
Cream
fat content of 6
sauce 34
Creamed potatoes 68
Crécy soup 47
Crème caramel 235
microwaved 193
Crêpe batter 170
Crêpes
chicken 170
normande 171
savoury 170
seafood 170
sweet 171
with jam 171
with lemon 171
with orange 171
with ricotta cheese and ham 171
Crisps 182
Croissants 253
Croquette potatoes 69
Croquettes, chicken, deep-fried 179
Croûtons 24
Crudité 199
Crumpets 173
Cucumber
salad 203
shallow-fried 165
tomato and lettuce sandwiches 210
with cream 165
Cup cakes 242
Currant buns 251
Curried eggs 52
Curry
beef (European) 97
chicken (Indian) 98
sauce (Anglo/Indian) 31
sauce (vegetarian) 32
Custard sauce 39
Cutting techniques 7

Dairy foods, fat content of 5
Dauphine potatoes 69
Decorated salmon norvégienne 208
Decorated sirloin with salad 209
Deep-frying
aubergines 180
breaded fish and shellfish 176
breaded poultry 178
chicken in basket 178
chipped potatoes 181
cooked potatoes 182
courgettes 180
crisps 182
escalope, Orly style 177
fish in batter 177
fruits (fritters) 183
guinea fowl in basket 178
information, key points 174–5
made-up items 179
matchstick potatoes 181
mignonnette potatoes 181
onions (French style) 180

plaice, sauce tartare 176
Pont-Neuf potatoes 181
potatoes 181
raw vegetables 180
scampi 176
sole, en goujons 176
straw potatoes 182
turkey escalope in basket 178
wafer potatoes 182
Delmonico potatoes 122
Devils on horseback 145
Devon splits 251
Dressings
fromage frais (avocado) 34
garlic 36
lemon salad dressing 36
mustard and dill 36
spiced salad dressing 36
wine vinegar 36
Dropped scones/Scotch pancakes 173
Duchesse potatoes 69
Duck and duckling, important points 17
Duckling
braised 111
breast with cherry brandy and green peppercorns 163
roast 128–9
Duxelles 24

Eccles cakes 239
Egg mayonnaise 199
Egg custard puddings (microwaved) 193
Egg sauce 34
Eggs
bénédictine 72
boiled 52
Bombay 72
curried 52
florentine 72
microwaving of 186
Mornay 72
poaching of 72
Scotch 52
scrambled 149
scrambled on toast 149
scrambled (microwaved) 186
scrambled with herbs 149
scrambled with tomatoes 149
shallow-frying of 149
shirred (sur le plat) 231
steamed 84
tripe eggs 52
English stuffing 37
Entrecôte
Bohemian style 152
grilled 137
Escalopes
pork, Naples style 156
preparation of 14–15
turkey, Hungarian style 160
veal, cordon-bleu 156
veal, with cream 162

Farce à gratin 24
Fats and oils 6
Fat
content in basic commodities 4
how to reduce 3
Fennel, braised 118–19
Fibre, how to increase 4
Figs (dried), poached 82
Fillet steak in whisky and herb sauce 159
Fish
basic preparation of 19–21
cuts of 21
deep-fried in batter 177
Dugléré (microwaved) 188
fat content of 5
important points 19
kedgeree 121
meunière 148
mousse, mousseline 25
salad (hors d'oeuvre) 197
shallow-frying of 148
steamed 84
steamed with lemon and artichokes 84
stock 36
storage of 19
Flageolet beans, boiling of 67
Flans
apple 236
banana 236
cheese and egg 228
pear 236
raspberry 236
Florida cocktail 195
Flounder, deep-fried with rémoulade sauce 177
Fondant potatoes 123
Fore rib, preparation of 10
Fowl, boiled with onion sauce 59
French beans
boiling of 60–1
steamed 92
French salad 205
French-fried onions 180
Fresh egg custard sauce 40
Fricassées (lower-fat and trad.) 101
Fritters, fruit various 183
Fromage frais dressing 34
Fruit
basic preparation of 7
bavarois 213
cakes 243
cardinal 218
cocktails, various 195
dried, poached 82
fibre content of 6
Hélène 218
Melba 218
mousses (low-fat) 212
poached 81–2
salad (exotic) 218
salad (fresh) 218
savarin 255
scones 248
tart 237
trifle 216
vacherins 249
Frying batter 23–4

Game
aspic 23
basic preparation (feathered) 16–18
bouchées 222
consommé 51
farce 25
fat content of (feathered) 5
salpicon 28
stock 36
vol-au-vents 222
Gammon, boiled, with parsley sauce 58
Garlic
butter 32
dressing 36
Garnishes, for braised meats 108
Gâteaux
apricot (low-fat and trad.) 247
chocolate (low-fat and trad.) 247
coffee (low-fat and trad.) 247
Glazed vegetables 66
Glazes
apricot, plain fruit 38
fish, meat, poultry 25
Gnocchi
italienne 73
parisienne 73
Gooseberry
pie 238
sauce 31
stewed 105
Goulash of beef 96
Grapefruit
cocktail 195
half, chilled 198
half with kirsch 198
mexicaine 198
salad 204
Gravy, preparation of 126
Greek salad (salata Horiatiki) 205
Green salad 205
Griddle scones 172
Grilled entrecôte steak 137
Grilling
beef steaks, lamb chops or cutlets 137
fillet steak garni 137
fish 136
hamburgers 139
information, key points 134–5
kidneys 139
lamb cutlets green meadow 137
liver 138
mixed grill 144
mushrooms 144
pork chop Henri IV 137
sausages 139
savouries 145
tomatoes 144
vegetable burgers 140
Guinea fowl
deep-fried in basket 178
pot-roasted 131

Haddock
deep-fried, Orly style 177
poached with parsley sauce 75
Halibut
(suprême), Cubat 77
(steaks), grilled 136
(steak), poached 74
Ham
braised 110

important points 14–15
mousse/mousseline mixture 26
mousse and mousselines 207
omelette 150
stock 36
Hamburgers
grilled 139
with piquant sauce 153
Haricot beans
boiling of 67
soup 46
Herb sauce/dressing 35
Herring, grilled with mustard sauce 136
Hollandaise sauce 32
microwaved 189
Hors d'oeuvre 195–202
Hot cross buns 252
Hot water pastry 26
Hotpots 115
Hungarian sauce 34
Hygiene, basic points 2

Irish stew 103
with fennel and butter beans 103

Jam
omelette 150
sauce (cold) 40
sauce (hot) 39
turnovers 239
Jelly
fruit 215
lemon 215
orange 215
trifle 216
vegetarian 215
Jerusalem artichokes, boiling of 65
Jus lié 30

Kebabs (Greek) microwave assisted 189
Kedgeree 121
Kidneys
in sherry sauce 159
shallow-frying of 154
Knives, handling of 7

Lamb, mutton
best end, preparation of 12
carcase diagram 11
common cuts from 16
cutlets Reform 157
cutlets with spiced pears and mint jelly 152
grilled cutlets green meadow style 137
important points 11
kidneys, grilled 139
leg, preparation of 11
liver, grilled 138
mutton, Bolton hotpot 115
mutton, brown stew 95
mutton, Irish stew 103
mutton, Lancashire hotpot 115
mutton, roast 126–7
Oxford John 159
saddle, preparation of 12
Lancashire hotpot 115
Lardons 25
Lasagne verdi al forno 55
Lebanese pilaw (microwaved) 186
Leeks, braised 118–19
Leg of lamb, preparation of 11
Leg of pork, preparation of 14
Leg of veal, preparation of 13
Lemon
jelly 215
salad dressing 36
sauce 39
soufflé 240
Lentil
purée 67
soup 46
Lettuce, braised 118–19
Liaison 38
Liqueur soufflé 240
Liver
and bacon 154
fried with lemon 157
pâté 201
shallow frying of 154
spiced 154
Lobster
cocktail 196
(cooked), cutting of 22
salad (main course) 206

Macaroni
and meat pie 57
garlic (microwaved) 187
Marie-Rose sauce 35
Marinade
instant 25
plain 25
Marquise potatoes 69
Marrowfat peas, boiling of 67
Mashed potatoes 68
with cheese 68
Mashed turnips 65
Matchstick potatoes 181
Mayonnaise (lower-fat and trad.) 35
Meat
hotpots 115
microwave assisted cooking 189
products, fat content of 5
salad (hors d'oeuvre) 197
Medallions of veal in honey mustard sauce 158
Melba sauce 40
Melon
chilled 198
cocktail 195
vénitienne 198
with Parma ham 198
with port 199
Meringue 249
shells 249
vacherins 249
with ice-cream 249
Miami cocktail 195
Microwave, important points 184–5
Microwave-cooked
fish 188
potatoes 192
puddings 193
rice 186
vegetables 190–92
Microwave-finished pasta dishes 187
Mignonnette potatoes 181
Milk, fat content of 6
Mimosa salad 204
Minestrone 45
Mint sauce 35
Minted peas 61
Mirepoix 24
white 24
Mixed
grill 144
salad 205
vegetables (macedoine) 65
Mornay sauce 34
Moroccan
carrot salad 205
lamb kebabs 142
Mousse
chocolate 212
fruit 212
sweet (lower-fat) 212
vanilla 212
vegetarian 212
Mousse/mousselines
chicken 26
courgette and avocado 207
fish 26
ham 207
ham, basic mixture 26
salmon 207
vegetables 26
Mushroom
grilled 144
on toast 169
shallow-fried 164
soup 48–49
Mustard
and dill dressing 36
sauce 34
Mutton stock 36

Noodles, Italian style 55
Nutrition, points on 3

Ogen and charentais melon 199
Oignon clouté 24
Omelettes
cheese 150
fermière 151
flat 151
folded 150
ham 150
jam 150
paysanne 151
plain 150
Spanish 151
tomato 150
Onion
braised 118–19
French-fried 180
sauce 34
shallow-fried 164
Orange
cocktail 195
jelly 215
salad 204
sauce 39
soufflé 240
Ox liver, braised with onions 114
Oxford John 159
Oxtails, stewed 95
Oysters 200

Pancakes
  Scotch/dropped scones 173
  *see* crêpes 170
  sweetcorn 172
  with maple syrup 173
Parsley
  butter 32
  potatoes 68
  sauce 34
Parsnips
  boiling of 64
  glazed 66
  roasting of (traditional) 132
  roasting of (lower-fat) 133
Pasta
  boiling of 54–6
  dishes, (microwave finished) 187
  dried — boiling of 56
  green 54
  plain 54
  reheating of 54–6
  wholemeal 54
Pasties, Cornish, spiced vegetable 229
Pastitsio 57
Pastry
  choux 26
  hot water 27
  puff 27
  short (savoury and sweet) 27
  short, wholemeal 28
  cream 39
Pâté
  de foie gras 201
  liver 201
Pea purée 67
Peach Condé 217
Peach/pear Hélène 218
Peach/pear Melba 218
Pear
  flan 236
  poached 81
Peas
  boiling of 60
  French style 66
  minted 61
Pease pudding 67
Peperonata 166
Pepperpots
  aubergine and chick pea 117
  zucchini 117
Pheasant
  important points 17
  roast 128–9
Pies
  apple and gooseberry 238
  chicken 227
  steak and kidney 226
  steak, kidney and mushroom 226
  venison 227
Pilaff
  with cheese 121
  with mushrooms 121
Pineapple
  cocktail 195
  Condé 217
  fritters 183
  shallow-fried 168
Pizzas
  al funghi 225
  alla capricciosa 225
  alla siciliana 225
  basic tomato topping 224
  napoletana 225
  plain 224
  wholemeal 224
Plaice (fillets)
  deep-fried, sauce tartare 176
  Grenoble style 148
  grilled 136
  Mornay 77
Plain omelette 150
Poaching
  cod steak with Jerusalem artichokes and lime 74
  cuts of fish 74
  egg, bénédictine 72
  egg, Bombay 72
  egg, florentine 72
  egg, Mornay 72
  fresh fruits 81
  haddock with parsley sauce 75
  halibut steak 74
  information, key points 70–1
  poultry (portions) 79
  poultry (whole) 80
  salmon steak hollandaise 74
  shellfish 76
  soft fruits 81
  trout, court-bouillon style 75
  whole fish 75
Pont-Neuf potatoes 181
Pork
  carcase diagram 13
  chop charcutière 152
  common cuts from 16
  cuts, preparation of 14
  escalopes Naples style 156
  escalopes, preparation of 14–15
  grilled pork cutlet Henri IV 137
  important points 13
  kebabs (Greek) microwave assisted 189
  leg, preparation of 14
  roast 126–7
  spare ribs (Chinese and Indian) 138
Pot-roasting
  butcher meats and furred game 130
  chicken 131
  cushion of veal 130
  fillet of beef 131
  guinea fowl 131
  poultry and feathered game 131
Potage paysanne 45
Potatoes
  baked 232
  berrichonne 123
  boiling of 68
  champignol 123
  cocotte 132
  creamed 68
  croquettes 69
  dauphine 69
  deep-fried 181–2
  deep-fried chipped 181
  deep-fried crisps 182
  deep-fried matchstick 181
  deep-fried mignonnette 181
  deep-fried Pont-Neuf 181
  deep-fried straw 182
  deep-fried wafer 182
  Delmonico 122
  duchesse 69
  fondant 123
  gnocchi 73
  Macaire 232
  marquise 69
  mashed 68
  mashed with cheese 68
  microwaved 192
  noisettes, parisienne 132
  olivette 132
  panées, château 133
  Parmentier 132
  parsley 68
  roast 132
  roasting of (traditional) 132
  roasting of (lower-fat) 133
  salad 203
  sautées 167
  sautées, lyonnaise 167
  sautées, O'Brien 167
  sautées, provençal 167
  savoury 122
  soup 47
  steamed (low-pressure) 85
  steamed (high-pressure) 91
Potted shrimps 196
Poultry
  basic preparation of 16–18
  deep-fried, breaded 178
  fat content of 5
  important points 16–17
Prawn/shrimp cocktail 196
Prawns, poached 76
Profiteroles 238
Prunes, poached 82
Pudding
  baked egg custard 234
  bread and butter 234
  cabinet 234
  chocolate sponge 90
  crème caramel 235
  soufflés 241
  steamed sultana 90
  summer 214
  vanilla sponge pudding 90
Puff pastry 26
Pulse purées 67

Queen cakes 242
Quiche, vegetable 228

Raita, cucumber 34
Raspberry
  flan 236
  jelly 215
  poached 81
Ratatouille
  shallow-frying 166
  stewing 104
Red beans
  boiling of 67
  soup 46
Rémoulade sauce 35

Rhubarb
poached 82
stewed 105
tart 237
Rice
and crisp vegetables 53
baked 235
boiled 53
braised (microwave cooked) 186
braising of 121
salad 203
Roasting
beef 126
butcher meats, furred game 126–7
chicken 128
duckling 128–9
information, key points 124–5
lamb and mutton 126–7
parsnips (lower-fat) 133
parsnips (traditional) 132
pheasant 128–9
pork 126–7
potatoes 132
poultry, feathered game 128–9
turkey 128–9
venison 126–7
Rum babas 254
Russian salad 205

Saddle of lamb, preparation of 12
Sage and onion stuffing 37
Salads
apple 204
Arabian 205
bean 203
beef (main course) 206
Caesar 205
Californian 205
compound 204–5
cucumber 203
fish (hors d'oeuvre) 197
French 205
Greek (salata Horiatiki) 205
green 205
lobster (main course) 206
meat (hors d'oeuvre) 197
Mimosa 204
mixed 205
Moroccan carrot 205
orange 204
potato 203
rice 203
Russian 205
salat (Indian) 205
salmon (main course) 206
scampi (hors d'oeuvre) 197
simple 202
single, fruit 204
spiced aubergine 205
tomato 203
trout (main course) 206
Waldorf 204
Salat (Indian) 205
Salata Horiatiki (Greek salad) 205
Salmon
cold decorated norvégienne 208
Louisiana style 148
mousse, mousselines 207
salad (main course) 206
smoked 200
steak, poached hollandaise 74
Salmon and cucumber pinwheel sandwiches 211
Salpicon
chicken 28
game 28
seafood 28
vegetables 29
Salt, how to reduce 3
Sandwiches
asparagus rolls 211
cheese 210
cheese, spring onion and ham pinwheels 211
chicken 210
cottage cheese and chive 210
Cucumber, tomato and lettuce 210
pinwheel 211
plain 210
rolled 210
salmon and cucumber pinwheels 211
sardine rolls 211
Sardines
barbecued, portugaise 136
rolled sandwiches 211
Sauces
almond 39
anchovy 34
Andalouse 35
apple 29
apricot 39
aurore 34
béarnaise 33
bolonaise (low-fat) 29
bolonaise (traditional) 29
bordelaise 30
brandy cream (cold) 40
brandy 40
bread 29
brown (lower-fat) 30
brown (traditional) 30
caper 34
Chantilly cream 40
charcutière 31
cheese 34
chocolate 39–40
cranberry 31
cream 34
curry (vegetarian) 32
curry (Anglo/Indian) 31
custard 39
devil 31
egg 34
fresh egg custard 40
gooseberry 31
hard butter types 32
herb 35
hollandaise 32
hollandaise (microwaved) 189
honey mustard 31
Hungarian 34
Italian 31
jam (hot) 39
jam (cold) 40
jus lié 30
lemon 39
lyonnaise 31
Madeira 31
Marie-Rose 35
mayonnaise (lower-fat) 34
mayonnaise (traditional) 35
Melba 40
mint 35
Mornay 34
mousseline 33
mustard 34
onion 34
orange 39
paloise 33
parsley 34
piquante 31
raita (cucumber) 34
Reform 31
rémoulade 35
suprême 34
syrup 39
tartare 35
tomato (lower-fat) 33
tomato (traditional) 33
velouté 34
vinaigrette (lower-fat) 35
vinaigrette (traditional) 35
white (lower-fat) 33
white (traditional) 33
Sausage rolls 223
Sausages
grilled 139
shallow-frying of 153
smoked, commercial 200
with ham and red cabbage 153
Sauté dishes
brown with garnished sauces 161
brown with reduction sauces 163
using prepared sauces 158
white with garnished sauces 160
white with reduction sauces 162
Sauté potatoes 167
lyonnaise 167
O'Brien 167
provençal 167
Savarin 254–5
Savouries (*see also* canapés)
grilled 145
Scotch woodcock 149
Savoury potatoes 122
Scallops
cocktail 196
poached 76
preparation of 22
Scampi
cocktail 196
deep-fried 176
poached 76
salad (hors d'oeuvre) 197
Scones
buttermilk 172
dropped/Scotch pancakes 173
fruit 248
griddle 172
oven 248
wholemeal 172
Scotch
broth 44
eggs 52
woodcock 149

Scots trifle 216
Scrambled eggs
French style 149
microwaved 186
on toast 149
with herbs 149
with tomatoes 149
Seafood
bouchées/vol-au-vents 222
cocktail 196
crêpes 170
salpicon 28
skewers 142
Self-raising flour 40
Shallow-frying
apples 168
aubergines 165
bananas 168
breaded items 156
butcher meats 152
combination of vegetables 166
courgettes 165
crêpes, pancakes 170
crumpets 173
cucumber 165
eggs 149
fish 148
fruits 168
griddle scones 172
hamburgers 153
information, key points 146–7
kidneys 154
liver 154
made-up items 153
mushrooms 164
offal 154
onions 164
pineapple 168
potatoes 167
sausages 153
savouries 169
vegetables (brown) 164
vegetables (sweating) 165
Shallow-poaching
fish (fillets) 77
fish (whole) 78
Shellfish
cocktails 196
important points 21
poaching of 76
preparation of 22
storage of 21
Sherry trifle 216
Short pastry (savoury and sweet) 27
Shrimps
poached 76
potted 196
Sirloin
preparation of 10
steak with red and green peppers 161
Skewers
Moroccan lamb kebabs 142
seafood 142
spiced vegetarian 143
Skordomakárona (microwaved) 187
Smoked
salmon 200
trout 200
Sole
Dover, bonne-femme 78
en goujons 176
fillets (florentine) 77
lemon, Bercy 78
lemon, grilled 136
Soufflés
cheese 241
chocolate, orange/lemon 240
liqueur and vanilla 240
pudding 241
Soups
asparagus 48–9
broths 44
cauliflower 48–9
celery 48–9
consommés 51
Crécy 47
haricot bean soup 46
lentil 46
minestrone 45
mushroom 48–9
potage paysanne 45
potato 47
red bean soup 46
split pea 46
summer vegetable 47
tomato 50
yellow split pea 46
Spaghetti
alla carbonara (microwave finished) 187
bolonaise 57
italienne 56
milanaise 56
napolitaine 56
Spanish omelette 151
Spare ribs (Chinese and Indian style) 138
Spiced salad dressing 36
Spiced vegetable pasties 229
Spinach
boiling of 60
purée 61
Split pea soup 46
Sponge
biscuits 245
génoise (plain, chocolate) 245
low-fat types 246
Steak and kidney pie 226
Steak, kidney and mushroom pie 226
Steaming
cherry roll 88
cherry pudding 87
currant roll 87
currant pudding 87
date pudding 87
date roll 88
eggs 84
fish 84
fruit roll 88
green vegetables 92
information, key points 83
meat puddings 86
raisin pudding 87
raisin roll 88
root vegetables (high pressure) 91
sponge puddings 90
suet rolls 88
sultana pudding 87
sultana roll 88
sweet suet puddings 87
vegetables (low pressure) 85
Stewing
fruits 105
information, key points 93–4
Stews
brown beef 95
brown lamb and mutton 95
brown veal 95
Irish stew 103
oxtail 95
vegetable (Indian) 104
vegetable, ratatouille 104
Stir-frying
honey lemon chicken 154
meat or poultry 154
vegetables 155
Stock syrup 41
Stocks, various 36
Straw potatoes 182
Strawberries, poached 81
Studded onion 24
Stuffed tomatoes 231
Stuffed and gratinated tomatoes 231
Stuffings, various 37
Sugar, how to reduce 3
Summer pudding 214
Summer vegetable soup 47
Suprême sauce 34
Suprêmes of chicken, preparation of 18
Swedes, boiling of 64
Sweet potatoes, boiling of 68
Sweetbreads, braised (white, brown) 113
Sweetcorn pancakes 172
Swiss buns 251
Swiss roll, plain and chocolate 244
Syllabub 219
Syrup for babas/savarins 255
Syrup sauce 39
Syrups, stock 41

Table jellies 215
Tartare sauce 35
Tarts
apple 237
blackberry 237
fruit 237
rhubarb 237
Thickenings
liaison 38
lower-fat 38
Time plan, preparation of 1
Toad-in-the-hole 230
Tomato
concassées 25
grilled 144
omelette 150
salad 203
sauce (lower-fat) 33
sauce (traditional) 33
soup 50
stuffed 231
stuffed, gratinated 231
Tongue, braised 110
Trifle
fruit 216

jelly 216
Scots 216
sherry 216
Trout
Doria 148
grilled 136
Montrose 78
poached 75
poached, court-bouillon style 75
salad (main course) 206
smoked 200
spiced (microwaved) 188
Turkey
escalope Hungarian style 160
escalope in basket 178
escalope, Orly style 177
important points 17
roast 128–9
Turnips
and swedes, glazed 66
boiling of 64
mashed 65
spring (microwaved) 190
steamed (high pressure) 91
steamed (low pressure) 85
Turnovers, apple and jam 239

Vacherins 249
Vanilla
bavarois 213
buttercream 38
mousse 212
soufflé 240
Veal
blanquette (lower-fat and trad.) 102
braised cushion 112
brown stew 95
carcase diagram 12
common cuts from 15
escalopes cordon-bleu 156
escalope, Orly style 177
escalope with cream 162
escalope with Marsala sauce 158
important points 13
leg, preparation of 13
pot-roasted cushion 130
stock 36
Vegetable
broth 44
burgers, grilled 140
quiche 228
mousse/mousseline 26
stock 37
stuffing 109
stew (Indian) 104
Vegetables
basic cuts of 8–9
basic preparation of 7
braising of 118–20
buttered 61, 63, 65
deep-fried 180
fibre content of 6
hollandaise 63
microwaved 190–2
milanaise 63
mixed (macedoine) 65
Mornay 63
stir-frying of 155
with cream 63
with fresh herbs 63
Vegetarian
bavarois 213
bouchées/vol-au-vents 222
mousse 212
salpicon 29
skewers (spiced) 143
table jellies 215
Velouté sauces 33
Venison
braised 108–9
braised in red wine sauce 108–9
medallions 158
pie 227
roast 126–7
Victoria sandwich 243
Vinaigrette (lower-fat and trad.) 35
Vol-au-vents
chicken 222
game 222
seafood 222
vegetarian 222

Wafer potatoes 182
Waldorf salad 204
White sauce
lower-fat 34
traditional 33
White stock 36
Wholemeal pastry 28
Wine vinegar dressing 36
Wing rib, preparation of 10
Work organisation 1

Yeast goods
bread rolls 250
buns 251–3
croissants 253
pizzas 224–5
rum babas 254
savarins 254–5
Yellow split pea soup 46
Yorkshire pudding (low-fat and trad.) 230

Zucchini pepperpot 117